Holocaust and Genocide D

This book provides a detailed analysis of one of the most prominent and widespread international phenomena to which criminal justice systems have been applied: the expression of revisionist views relating to mass atrocities and the outright denial of their existence. Denial poses challenges to more than one academic discipline. To historians, the gradual disappearance of the generation of eyewitnesses raises the question of how to keep alive the memory of the events, and the fact that nega-tionism is often offered in the guise of historical 'revisionist scholarship' also means that there is need for the identification of parameters that can be applied to the office of the 'genuine' historian. Legal academics and practitioners, as well as political scientists, are faced with the difficulty of evaluating methods to deal with denial and must in this regard identify the limits of freedom of speech, but also the need to preserve the rights of victims. Beyond that, the question arises whether the law can ever be an effective option for dealing with revisionist state-ments and the revisionist movement. In this regard, *Holocaust and Genocide Denial: A Contextual Perspective* breaks new ground, exploring the background of revisionism, the specific methods devised by individual States to counter this phenomenon, and the rationale for their strategies. Bringing together authors whose expertise relates to the history of the Holocaust, genocide studies, international criminal law and social anthropology, the book offers insights into the history of revision-ism and its varying contexts, but also provides a thought-provoking engagement with the challenging questions attached to its treatment in law and politics.

Dr Paul Behrens is a Reader (Associate Professor) in Law at the University of Edinburgh.

Dr Nicholas Terry is a Lecturer (Assistant Professor) in the Department of History at the University of Exeter.

Dr Olaf Jensen is an Honorary Associate Member of the Stanley Burton Centre of Holocaust and Genocide Studies at the University of Leicester.

Holocaust and Genocide Denial

A Contextual Perspective

Edited by
Paul Behrens, Nicholas Terry
and Olaf Jensen

Routledge
Taylor & Francis Group
LONDON AND NEW YORK

First published 2017
by Routledge
2 Park Square, Milton Park, Abingdon, Oxfordshire OX14 4RN
711 Third Avenue, New York, NY 10017

a Glasshouse book

Routledge is an imprint of the Taylor & Francis Group, an informa business

First issued in paperback 2018

British Library Cataloguing in Publication Data
A catalogue record for this book is available from the British Library

Library of Congress Cataloging-in-Publication Data
Names: Behrens, Paul, editor. | Terry, Nicholas, editor. | Jensen, Olaf, editor.
Title: Holocaust and genocide denial : a contextual perspective / edited by Paul Behrens, Nicholas Terry, and Olaf Jensen.
Description: First edition. | Abingdon, Oxon [UK] ; New York : Routledge, 2017. | Includes bibliographical references and index.
Identifiers: LCCN 2016054659 | ISBN 9781138672734 (hbk) |
ISBN 9781315562377 (ebk)
Subjects: LCSH: Genocide. | Holocaust denial–Law and legislation. | Nuremberg Trial of Major German War Criminals, Nuremberg, Germany, 1945–1946.
Classification: LCC KZ7180 .H63 2017 | DDC 345/.0256–dc23
LC record available at https://lccn.loc.gov/2016054659

ISBN: 978-1-138-67273-4 (hbk)
ISBN: 978-0-367-02425-3 (pbk)

Typeset in Baskerville
by Taylor & Francis Books

Contents

Contributors

Elisabeth Anstett, PhD, is a social anthropologist and researcher at the Centre National de la Recherche Scientifique (CNRS) working at the IRIS (Institut de recherche interdisciplinaire sur les enjeux sociaux) in Paris. Her area of expertise covers Russia and Byelorussia, on which she has published extensively. Her recent works deal with the social impact of mass exhumations, and more broadly with the legacy of genocide and mass violence in Europe. With historian Jean-Marc Dreyfus, she is directing the 'Human Remains and Violence' book series at Manchester University Press, and is also one of three General Editors of *Human Remains and Violence: An Interdisciplinary Journal*.

Niamh Barry, BL, BCL, LLM, is a practising barrister in Ireland. She has extensive practical experience in the international criminal tribunals, having worked as an intern for both the International Criminal Tribunal for the former Yugoslavia (where she was part of the Defence Advisory Team of Radovan Karadžić) and the International Criminal Tribunal for Rwanda (where she worked for Trial Chamber III). Prior to her call to the Bar in Ireland, Ms Barry worked as a researcher with the Irish Supreme Court. She has also worked as a researcher with the Irish Department of Justice and Equality, specialising in immigration and asylum law, and as an Advisor for the Permanent Irish Mission to the United Nations in New York.

Paul Behrens, PhD, LLM, is a Reader (Associate Professor) in Law at the University of Edinburgh. He has taught in the past at the University of Leicester, is a member of the Surrey International Law Centre, Associate of the Stanley Burton Centre for Holocaust and Genocide Studies and member of the Scottish Centre for International Law. He has been Visiting Lecturer/Visiting Researcher at Uppsala (Sweden), Stockholm (Sweden), Kiel (Germany) and other universities. Dr Behrens is co-author of *Elements of Genocide* (Routledge 2012) and *The Criminal Law of Genocide* (Ashgate 2007), and has written articles and papers on various aspects of international criminal law. His recent publications include 'Between Abstract Event and Individualised Crime: Genocidal Intent in the Case of Croatia', 28:4 *Leiden Journal of International Law* (2015) 923. He has also published in the field of diplomatic law, including the monograph *Diplomatic Interference and the Law* (Hart Publishing 2016). Dr Behrens also contributes regularly to newspapers (including *The Guardian, The Scotsman, Süddeutsche Zeitung*) on issues of international law and constitutional law, and has given media interviews on these topics.

Björn Elberling, Dr. jur., is Attorney (Rechtsanwalt) in Kiel and a former Research Fellow at the Walther Schücking Institute for International Law, University of Kiel. He works primarily in criminal and media law. Together with Alexander Hoffmann, he has been actively involved in campaigns organising protests and blockades against the annual neo-Nazi marches in Wunsiedel commemorating Rudolf Hess, and in Dresden on the anniversary of the city's bombardment on 13/14 February 1945. He currently represents a victim in the trial against accused members and supporters of the 'National Socialist Underground'. Dr Elberling's recent publications include a German-language commentary on Article 5 of the European Convention of Human Rights (in: Ulrich Karpenstein/Franz Mayer (eds), *Kommentar zur Europäischen Menschenrechtskonvention* (C.H. Beck 2012, 2nd edn 2015), and *The Defendant in International Criminal Proceedings: Between Law and Historiography* (Hart Publishing 2012).

Caroline Fournet, PhD, LLM, is Associate Professor and Rosalind Franklin Fellow at the Department of Criminal Law and Criminology at the University of Groningen, where she holds a Chair in Comparative Criminal Law. Her research focuses on the crime of genocide as well as on the use of forensic evidence in international criminal justice. She is currently Editor-in-Chief of the *International Criminal Law Review* (Brill) and one of the co-editors of the academic journal *Human Remains and Violence: An Interdisciplinary Journal* (Manchester University Press). Her publications include *International Crimes – Theories, Practice and Evolution* (Cameron May 2006); *The Crime of Destruction and the Law of Genocide: Their Impact on Collective Memory* (Ashgate 2007); and *Genocide and Crimes Against Humanity – Misconceptions and Confusion in French Law and Practice* (Hart 2013).

Nariné Ghazaryan, PhD, is an Assistant Professor in Law at the University of Nottingham. She was previously Lecturer at Brunel University, London. Dr Ghazaryan is an expert on the political and legal relations of Armenia. Her most recent article on this subject (on the ability of the European Union (EU) to influence the relations between Turkey and Armenia) was published in the *Armenian Yearbook of International and Comparative Law* (2013). She has also translated into Russian the Opinion of Geoffrey Robertson QC on the issue of Armenian Genocide. Her research interests lie primarily in the area of EU External Relations Law. She has authored a number of publications on the EU's relations with its neighbouring countries, including *The European Neighbourhood Policy and the Democratic Values of the EU* (Hart Publishing 2014).

Mark Hobbs, PhD, MA, is a Lecturer in the Humanities at the University of East Anglia. Dr Hobbs specialised in genocide and 'ethnic cleansing' in the

Balkans during the late 1980s and 1990s. He is currently conducting research into the history of Holocaust denial from a British perspective. In this context, he explores the chronological developments of denial in the UK from 1942 to the present day, and investigates the methods of Holocaust deniers and their resonance (or lack thereof) in British society and in extreme right circles. His research also analyses attempts that have been made by institutions, individuals and campaign groups to combat Holocaust denial and the methods they employ. In the past Dr Hobbs has written on Holocaust denial in Europe.

Alexander Hoffmann is Attorney (Rechtsanwalt) in Kiel and a former Research Fellow at the Universities of Kiel and Regensburg. He works primarily in criminal, media and immigration law. Together with Björn Elberling, he has been actively involved in campaigns organising protests and blockades against the annual neo-Nazi marches in Wunsiedel commemorating Rudolf Hess, and in Dresden on the anniversary of the city's bombardment on 13/14 February 1945. He represents a victim in the trial against accused members and supporters of the 'National Socialist Underground'. Together with Björn Elberling, he publishes a blog with regular reports on developments in the trial, in the German, English and Turkish languages, available at www. nsu-nebenklage.de.

Olaf Jensen, PhD, is an Honorary Associate Member of the Stanley Burton Centre for Holocaust and Genocide Studies at the University of Leicester, of which he was Director for several years. His research focuses particularly on National Socialism and the Holocaust, and intersects Oral History with Social Psychology.

His past publications include writings on the Holocaust in history and memory and genocidal intent. He is co-author of *Britain and the Holocaust – Remembering and Representing War and Genocide* (Palgrave Macmillan 2013), and *Ordinary People as Mass Murderers – Perpetrators in Comparative Perspectives* (Palgrave Macmillan 2008). In his book *Geschichte machen. Strukturmerkmale des intergenerationellen Sprechens über die NS-Vergangenheit in deutschen Familien* (Tübingen 2004), he discusses the effects of National Socialism, the Second World War and the Holocaust on the intergenerational autobiographical memory in German families. Dr Jensen is joint founder (together with Claus-Christian W. Szejnmann) of the book series The Holocaust and its Contexts, published by Palgrave Macmillan.

Freda Kabatsi, LLM, LLB, Dip. LP., is currently a Lecturer at the Catholic University of Eastern Africa, Nairobi, Kenya. She is also an Advocate and member of the East African Law Society. She is a frequent commentator on issues relating to genocide and is currently researching media freedom vis-à-vis genocide (for her PhD). Ms Kabatsi was formerly a Senior State Attorney in Uganda. She was one of Uganda's delegates at the Review Conference of the Rome Statute of the International Criminal Court in Kampala, Uganda, in

2010. She was also country delegate at the 46th Session and the 47th session of the Asian-African Legal Consultative Organization (AALCO) (in 2007 and 2008). Ms Kabatsi's publications include 'Defining or Diverting Genocide: Changing the Comportment of Genocide', 5:3 *International Criminal Law Review Journal* (2005).

Paolo Lobba, PhD, LLM, is a Legal Officer in the Supreme Court Chamber of the *Extraordinary Chambers in the Courts of Cambodia*. In this capacity he is currently assisting the judges with the appeals in the cases against former leaders of the Khmer Rouge. Dr Lobba obtained a double PhD in criminal law and procedure (Bologna and Berlin, *summa cum laude*), has worked as postdoctoral researcher in academia, and has published various articles in peer-reviewed journals. His research focuses particularly on the crime of denialism, the EU policies and legislation combating racism and xenophobia, judicial dialogue on human rights and the role of victims in international criminal trials. He co-edited vol. 84 of the *Nordic Journal of International Law*, entitled 'The Cross-fertilisation Rhetoric in Question: Use and Abuse of the European Court's Jurisprudence by International Criminal Tribunals'. Other recent publications include 'Holocaust Denial Before the European Court of Human Rights: Evolution of an Exceptional Regime', 26 *European Journal of International Law* (2015) 237–253; and 'Lubanga Judgment on Victims' Reparation: Handing Off the Hot Potato?', in T. Marinello (ed.), *The International Criminal Court in Search of its Purpose and Identity* (Routledge 2014), 108–129.

Christian Mentel, MA, is an Associated Researcher at the Zentrum für Zeithistorische Forschung Potsdam, Germany (ZZF), and a member of *Zeitgeschichte-Online*'s editorial staff. His research focuses mainly on post-1945 German history, discourse and debates, and historical revisionism. Together with Niels Weise, he recently published *Die zentralen deutschen Behörden und der Nationalsozialismus. Stand und Perspektiven der Forschung* (Munich/Potsdam 2016) on the history of German authorities in respect to Nazism. Also, together with Martin Sabrow, he edited *Das Auswärtige Amt und seine umstrittene Vergangenheit. Eine deutsche Debatte* (Frankfurt am Main 2014). Among Mr Mentel's numerous publications dealing with negationism and the Nazi past are 43 partly co-authored comprehensive articles in *Handbuch des Antisemitismus*, 8 vols, ed. Wolfgang Benz, Berlin et al. 2008–15.

Sejal Parmar, PhD, LLB, is Assistant Professor at the Department of Legal Studies and a core faculty member of the Centre for Media, Data and Society at the Central European University (CEU). Her main field of expertise and research is international and European human rights law, particularly on freedom of expression. Before coming to CEU, Parmar worked as Senior Legal Officer at ARTICLE 19. She is currently researching and writing a monograph entitled *Freedom of Expression Under Pressure*. She is an Associate Editor of the *International Journal of Human Rights* and represents CEU's

Department of Legal Studies at the Association of Human Rights Institutes (AHRI). Alongside her academic work, she regularly acts as an expert for intergovernmental organisations, including the Council of Europe and the Organization for Security and Co-operation in Europe (OSCE), and has been appointed to the Academic Advisory Board of the Community of Democracies. She is also a member of the Advisory Committee of Universal Rights Group, the Geneva-based human rights think tank, and acts as a consultant for various non-governmental organisations. She was awarded her LLB in Law (honours) from the London School of Economics and Political Science, her PhD in Law from the European University Institute in Florence, and has been called to the Bar of England and Wales.

Clotilde Pégorier, PhD, LLM, DESS, is a Lecturer in the School of Law at the University of Essex. She has previously held teaching and research positions at the Universities of Zurich, Lucerne and Exeter, and completed her PhD at the latter institution in 2011. Her primary research interests lie in the fields of international criminal law, international humanitarian law, refugee law, and European and comparative law. Dr Pégorier's recent works include *Ethnic Cleansing: A Legal Qualification* (Routledge 2013). She has also written articles and book chapters on various topics, including genocide denial, crimes of persecution and transitional justice issues.

Martin Petrov, LLM, is a former Chief of the Office of the Registrar at the International Criminal Tribunal for the former Yugoslavia (ICTY), where he oversaw external communication and outreach, among other things, and maintained extensive contacts with the countries of the former Yugoslavia. He has previously served as Head of the ICTY's Office of Legal Aid and Detention and has worked in that capacity with persons accused before the ICTY and their defence lawyers. Petrov has extensive experience in several international courts and tribunals and has most recently led a major reorganisation project at the Registry of the International Criminal Court, assessing the performance of all judicial support functions (court management, legal aid, detention, witness support, language services, etc.), as well as all administrative services (human resources, budget and finance, security, IT, etc.), with a view to recommending structural and operational changes. Prior to that, he was in charge of the planning team for the establishment of an EU-funded special tribunal for Kosovo and proposed a legal and institutional framework for the holding of extraterritorial trials. Petrov holds an LLM from the University of Montreal (Canada) and an LLM from the University of Sofia (Bulgaria).

Dejana Radisavljević, LLM, is a PhD candidate at the University of Sheffield, where her research is concerned with international criminal sentences. She has several years' experience with the United Nations Mechanism for International Criminal Tribunals, working as a Legal Assistant in its branches in Tanzania and the Netherlands. Ms Radisavljević is an expert contributor to the

International Criminal Court commentary of the Case Matrix Network (Dr Mark Klamberg, ed.). She completed her Master's studies in Public International Law in 2012 at the University of Leicester, with a particular focus on the two ad hoc international criminal tribunals and the International Criminal Court.

Michael Salter, PhD, LLB, is Professor at the University of Central Lancashire (since 2000). He has published over 40 refereed articles and four books, the most recent on the Holocaust and the Nuremberg Trials (Nijhoff 2009, 2 vols). Professor Salter obtained his LLB from the University of Southampton in 1978 and his PhD from the University of Sheffield in 1986. He held lecturing posts at the Universities of Sheffield, Birmingham, Ulster, Lancaster, and Central Lancashire. His published works include *Nazi War Crimes, US Intelligence and Selective Prosecution at Nuremberg: Controversies Regarding the Role of the Office of Strategic Services* (Routledge 2007); *US Intelligence, the Holocaust and the Nuremberg Trials* (Brill/Nijhoff 2009, 2 vols); 'Negotiating Nolle Prosequi at Nuremberg: The Case of Captain Zimmer', 3 *Journal of International Criminal Justice* (2005), 649–665 (with Maggi Eastwood); and 'Ribbentrop and the Ciano Diaries at the Nuremberg Trials', *International Journal of Criminal Justice* (2006), 1–25 (with Lorie Charlesworth).

Nicholas Terry, PhD, is a Lecturer in Modern European History in the Department of History at the University of Exeter. While completing his PhD, he was a Charles F. Revson Foundation Fellow at the United States Holocaust Memorial Museum. He has also held teaching positions at Queen Mary University of London and the University of Bristol. In 2010, he was an Historical Consultant for the Metropolitan Police War Crimes Unit. Dr Terry's recent publications include 'How Soviet was Russian Society Under Nazi Occupation?', in Chris Szjenmann (ed.), *Rethinking History, Dictatorships and War. Essays in Honour of Richard Overy* (Continuum 2009); and '"Do not burden one's own army and its hinterland with unneeded mouths!" The Fate of the Soviet Civilian Population Behind the "Panther Line" in Eastern Belorussia, October 1943–June 1944', 30 *Beiträge zur Geschichte des Nationalsozialismus* (2015). His first monograph, *Auschwitz: The Practice of Extinction*, will be published by Bloomsbury in 2017.

Introduction

Paul Behrens, Nicholas Terry and Olaf Jensen

The facts of the Holocaust are clear; the suffering of its millions of victims is beyond reasonable dispute. It is evidenced by the words and writings of those who escaped the machinery of death, and indeed of those who devised it and kept it in running order. The documentary and architectural proof is overwhelming. Films demonstrate the conditions of the concentration camps; there are witness statements of those who liberated Bergen-Belsen, Auschwitz and the other places in which the human capacity for evil had been given a new definition.

As if that were not enough, the events have been subjected to judicial examination – ranging from the trial of the International Military Tribunal at Nuremberg to trials in the 21st century; proceedings in which the killings, torture and mistreatment received meticulous examination and had to withstand scrutiny under adversarial systems.

That is not only true of the Holocaust: other instances of mass violence, in particular the killing of an estimated 800,000 Tutsis in Rwanda in 1994 and the massacre of some 7,000 Bosnian Muslims at Srebrenica in 1995, are equally well documented, and they, too, were subjected to examination in courtroom settings, where exacting standards for the evaluation of evidence were applied by international criminal tribunals.

In light of this, it is legitimate to ask why Holocaust and genocide denial would merit a study in its own right. The claims of deniers, after all, carry a degree of absurdity which puts them well within the ranks of those who maintain that the landing on the Moon was a hoax and that the Earth is flat. And there is the risk that even the mention of such claims gives them a prominence that they do not deserve. Ignoring them seems the safer option and in due time, so the thinking goes, they will wither away.

In that regard, however, the denial of mass violence is a rather different matter. There is nothing trivial about it. To the survivors of the events and their families, denial causes renewed suffering. It targets one of the few things that they salvaged from the horrors of the time: their right to the memory of the events, which is an integral part of their personalities. It typically attacks their dignity, for the denial of mass violence carries the implied message that the reports of these events had been an invention.

Nor is such denial the pastime of a few eccentric individuals. Holocaust denial in particular has become an industry. The denialist movement has held conferences,[1] publishes journals[2] and has established organisations such as the 'Institute for Historical Review' and the 'Committee for Open Debate on the Holocaust'. Its followers are keen to occupy the spotlight in print media[3] and on the internet.[4]

For the denialist movement, that is not the limit of its impact. For a considerable while now, the message sent out by its leaders has occupied a political platform too, underlining the gravity of the conduct and the danger of its consequences. Jean-Marie Le Pen, the former leader of the French Front National, was quoted as saying that the Nazi death camps were a 'footnote of history',[5] Nick Griffin, the leader of the British National Party, called the Holocaust a 'holohoax'.[6]

Holocaust denial that thus enters the political arena, carries the potential of triggering responses from politicians of the 'established' parties and of receiving a platform in the mainstream media.[7] It is a dangerous development: it shows that the treatment of deniers as outsiders with a message that is considerably removed from serious political discourse can no longer be guaranteed. Once they are included in debates with political figures from mainstream parties, they may well appear, to an average viewer, to have equal standing in such discourse and their message as worthy of consideration.

Even that is not the limit of the consequences of denial. Not all situations of political denial are alike, and not all denial on the political stage is promoted by parties that are somewhat on the fringes of the political spectrum in their own countries. In 2006, it was a head of State who welcomed some of the world's most prominent deniers to a government-run conference under the title 'Review of the Holocaust: Global Vision': Iranian President Ahmadinejad,[8] who, even

1 Cf US Newswire, 'Arab League Holocaust denial symposium is no surprise, AJ Congress says, as it calls on European Community to denounce conference', 29 August 2002; Xinhua General News Service, 'Right-wing antisemitism in Europe on rise', 27 November 1993.

2 Notable examples include the *Journal of Historical Review* (1980–2002), *Vierteljahreshefte für freie Geschichtsforschung* (1997–2006) and *Inconvenient History* (2009–present).

3 Cf the reference in P. Grosswiler, 'Sunlight on Holocaust Denial', *Bangor Daily News* (Maine), 27 January 2000. Grosswiler highlights the numerous newspaper advertisements taken out by deniers in the 1990s.

4 For an early report on the use of the internet by Holocaust deniers, see Anti-Defamation League, 'High Tech Hate: Extremist Use of the Internet', *US Newswire*, 21 October 1997.

5 Geoffrey Varley, 'France Repents Holocaust, but Le Pen Prospers', *Agence France Presse*, 1 October 1997.

6 Robert Mendick, 'Loophole Lets BNP on to Council', *The Independent*, 16 April 2000.

7 See e.g. for a critical evaluation of Nick Griffin's 2009 appearance on the BBC programme 'Question Time': Robert Winnett and Rosa Prince, 'BNP on Question Time: Nick Griffin Uses BBC Appearance to Attack Muslims and Gays', *The Telegraph*, 22 October 2009.

8 US Fed News, 'Top Academics, Political Leaders Seek "Incitement to Genocide" Charges Against Iran, President Ahmadinejad', 12 December 2006.

before that event, had been quoted as saying that the killing of the Jews in Europe was a 'myth'[9] and who, on the second day of the meeting, asserted that the 'Zionist regime will be wiped out soon the same [as] the Soviet Union was'.[10] In circumstances of this kind, it is not easy to dismiss the view that denial is capable of preparing the commission of new crimes – against the same victim group that had been targeted when the violence first reared its head.

It is not the purpose of this book to engage in a debate with deniers, and it does not aim to elevate their statements to the level of academic discussion. Its objectives, and the questions it seeks to answer, are quite different. They can, broadly, be understood under four principal categories.

There are, first of all, questions that attach to the denialist movement itself. They relate to the individuals who engage in conduct of that kind and highlight the need for an investigation into the purposes that are at the root of their activities. Do all deniers act from the same motivations, and is there room for differentiations according to their position within the movement, their presence in journals and internet fora and other platforms? What are the historical origins of denialism, and have its techniques changed over time? An examination of that kind also raises questions about the character of the movement. How far is it possible to speak of a coherent organisation? Have splits within the movement emerged? And how prevalent is the danger of denial today?

Second, how does the law deal with denial? Criminalisation certainly occupies an increasingly important position in the battle to protect the dignity of victims and survivors of the atrocities and to preserve the memory of the relevant events. Yet the legal option has also invited criticism – not least with regard to the impact that criminalisation may have on specific human rights. Recent cases – including that of *Perinçek* before the European Court of Human Rights (ECtHR)[11] – have also invited the question whether laws against denial can rely on a justifiable basis in all situations in which mass violence had been committed, or whether the temporal and spatial relationship between the events and its negation must play a role in the decision to resort to this option. The efficiency of sanctions under the criminal justice system is a further point of consideration in this context. But questions also arise from the position of courts even outside the application of laws criminalising denial: do courts dealing with the adjudication of genocide and crimes against humanity have an obligation to work towards the preservation of memory and the defeat of denialism as well?

Third: if the law courts controversy, the question of alternative options to address denialism must be explored. Are methods outside criminalisation –

---

9 Ibid., Gregory Gordon, 'From Incitement to Indictment? Prosecuting Iran's President for Advocating Israel's Destruction and Piecing Together Incitement Law's Emerging Analytical Framework', 98 *Journal of Criminal Law and Criminology* (2008), 868.
10 Ibid.
11 ECtHR Grand Chamber, *Perinçek v Switzerland* (Application no. 27510/08), (2016) 63 *EHRR* 6, Judgment, 15 October 2015.

educational initiatives and even direct confrontation with the deniers – viable, and do they carry a legitimate expectation of efficiency? Are there dangers that attach to their adoption? Similar points arise where responses by the international community are concerned. What tools are at its disposal to combat denialism, and would it even be possible to establish common ground among independent States for the adoption of a homogenous position on conduct of this kind?

A fourth point concerns the role of historians in situations marked by denialism. What is the position in which they find themselves when faced with statements that negate or seek to minimise the relevant international crimes? Given, in particular, the fact that denialism in certain contexts might have been advanced not only by private individuals, but might have been adopted as State policy, questions unavoidably attach to the range of options available to historians and other scholars of social sciences to address denialism and to present an accurate factual account to their peers as well as the public at large. Has the capacity of academics to do their work, at least in some countries, come under threat?

A study of that kind can, inevitably, not stay within the domain of one particular academic subject area. Denialism crosses disciplinary boundaries. As long as criminalisation remains a popular tool for combatting denial, practising lawyers and legal academics are directly concerned by the underlying phenomenon; and it is the legal profession that has to evaluate the suitability of this option in light of its potential impact on human rights law.

For historians and scholars of the social sciences, the impact of denialism is even more direct. It is, after all, a typical feature of the denialist movement that some of its prominent members strive for the veneer of scholarly writings and claim that their texts have to be taken seriously in the discourse of the relevant discipline.[12] That poses a direct challenge to professional historians and social scientists, and highlights the need for the high standards of quality that the discipline expects of those who are its acknowledged members. Genocide scholars are not unique among academics in contending with pseudoscholarship, due to the proliferation of conspiracy theories,[13] pseudosciences,[14] pseudohistory,[15]

---

12   In this regard, genocide denialists follow a playbook used by science deniers and other 'merchants of doubt'; cf Naomi Oreskes and Erik M. Conway, *Merchants of Doubt: How a Handful of Scientists Obscured the Truth on Issues from Tobacco Smoke to Global Warming* (New York: Bloomsbury, 2010).
13   The academic literature on conspiracy theories is now vast; the best introduction is Jovan Byford, *Conspiracy Theories: A Critical Introduction* (Basingstoke: Palgrave Macmillan, 2011).
14   For a good summary of the extensive literature on pseudoscience, see the contributions in Massimo Pigliucci and Maarten Boudry (eds), *Philosophy of Pseudoscience: Reconsidering the Demarcation Problem* (Chicago: The University of Chicago Press, 2013).
15   Unlike the phenomena of pseudoscience and conspiracy theories, relatively little research has been conducted on pseudohistory. But see Ronald H. Fritze, *Invented Knowledge: False History, Fake Science and Pseudo-religions* (London: Reaktion Books, 2009).

pseudoarchaeology[16] and pseudolegal theories[17] in the late 20th and early 21st centuries. Genocide denialism profits from this wider climate of misinformation and distrust of academic consensus, and seeks to establish itself as the 'other side' of a debate that does not in fact exist.

For the purposes of the current study, it was therefore essential to offer a view of Holocaust and genocide denial that was not restricted to one academic area, but to take a contextual view of the underlying phenomenon. It is for that reason that the work was conceived, from the outset, as a collaborative effort. What emerged was a volume to which 18 authors from the fields of history, law and anthropology contributed, dealing with topics which range from denial in relation to the Nuremberg trials to denial as addressed by the European Union Framework Decision of 2008, and from denial of the massacre of the Armenians in 1915 to denial in the age of the internet.

The chapters of the substantive part of the book have been grouped into three main parts. Part I is dedicated to a scholarly investigation of the history of Holocaust denial as one of the principal emanations of denialism even in the 21st century. It thus traces the development of the phenomenon from the very days of the Second World War to the age of Web 2.0 and offers reflections on the evolution of the movement, but also on trends and methodologies that may have been apparent even in its early stages but which carry significance even to this day.

Part II opens up the debate to the denial of genocide and crimes of mass violence in various parts of the world. That includes the negation of the Holocaust in Germany, denial in the former Soviet Union, but also denialist activities in Rwanda, Bosnia and Herzegovina, Turkey and in Iran under Ahmadinejad. In so doing, it reflects not only on the factual phenomenon of denial and the driving forces behind activities of this kind, but also offers an investigation of criminalisation and other methods employed by States and institutions that are faced with denial and negationism.

Part III takes up the thread and critically analyses options at the disposal of individual States and the international community to address the relevant conduct. It thus explores key features of national and supranational strategies, but it also reflects on other, especially educational, initiatives and examines the efficiency of the relevant alternatives. A conclusion offers reflections on some of the key findings that were introduced in the substantial part of the study.

The phenomenon that emerges from these examinations is disturbing. It is capable of exerting a grave impact on survivors of the events and their families, but its consequences reach beyond that: they challenge societies and the international community as a whole and can disrupt relations between independent

16 Garret G. Fagan (ed.), *Archaeological Fantasies: How Pseudoarchaeology Misrepresents the Past and Misleads the Public* (London: Routledge, 2006).
17 Pseudolegal theories have been advanced in recent years by the 'sovereign citizen' and 'freeman on the land' movements; cf Donald J. Netolitzky, 'The History of the Organized Pseudolegal Commercial Argument Phenomenon in Canada', 53:3 *Alberta Law Review* (2016), 609–642.

States. Holocaust and genocide denial are activities that academia can ill afford to ignore.

For the context of this study (and unless otherwise indicated in the individual chapters), the terms 'denialism' and 'negationism' are employed to refer both to the outright denial of the Holocaust or a situation of genocide, and to revisionism. They thus encompass any deliberate attempt to falsify information or to misinform an audience about the factual events underlying the Holocaust or the relevant genocide. The terms 'denial' and 'negation' are used to refer to the negation of the facts of the Holocaust or a situation of genocide; the term 'revisionism' is used to refer to a modification of the account of the Holocaust or a situation of genocide that had been established by reputable scholars – frequently in the form of a trivialisation or attempted justification of the relevant events.

Opinions expressed by the individual authors are their own; they are not necessarily indicative of the opinions of the institutions of which they may be members, or of other contributors of this work. The cut-off point for the consideration of literature, law and factual developments was 31 October 2016.

Part I

Development and concept of genocide denial

Chapter 1

Alexander Ratcliffe

British Holocaust denial in embryo

Mark Hobbs

Exploring the roots of Holocaust denial is a valuable endeavour because it reveals a great deal about the development of 'historical revisionism' by far right groups and individuals. This chapter will examine the antecedents of British Holocaust negationism in the United Kingdom during the Second World War from an historical perspective. As a 'bystander' nation, Britain, with its close proximity to occupied Europe, proves to be a useful case study because individuals were denying Nazi crimes committed against European Jews whilst genocide was taking place. However, it was not in Britain that the first deniers were to be found; clearly the first to deny the atrocities against the Jews of Europe were the Nazis themselves. As Heinrich Himmler stated in a secret Posen speech in October 1943, the final solution was to be a 'never to be written' page of glory in Germany's great history.[1] His words were matched with action, and evidenced by the destruction of records, dismantling of killing facilities and excavations of mass graves as the Soviet Army marched into Eastern Europe.[2]

This chapter centres on the British Second World War publications of Alexander Ratcliffe, a supporter of fascism, anti-Catholicism, anti-Semitism and leader of the neo-fascist Protestant Defence League. Other individuals, most notably the anti-Nazi anti-Semite journalist Douglas Reed, who was also proclaiming that the Jews were not being exterminated and arguing against the reports in the British media and House of Commons, will be examined for purposes of comparison. Ratcliffe was obstinate in his denial and attracted the attention of the British government on several occasions.[3] Ratcliffe represents the beginning of a genealogy of Holocaust negationism in the United Kingdom; he had overt links with the far right individuals who would follow him – most notably Arnold Leese, leader of the Imperial Fascist League. Leese would tutor and finance Colin Jordan and

1 Cited in L. Dawidowicz, *The War Against the Jews* (1975, Penguin Books), 191–2.
2 See: H.R. Huttenbach, 'Mandating State Security: Keeping the Holocaust Hidden', *Journal of Genocide Research* (2003, Vol. 5, No. 2), 309–11.
3 *Hansard* HC Deb 4 February 1943, vol. 386, cols 1045–6; *Hansard* HC Deb 25 February 1943, vol. 387, cols 314–5W; *Hansard* HC Deb 4 November 1943, vol. 393, cols 852; *Hansard* HC Deb 29 March 1945, vol. 409, cols 1518–9; and Home Office Registered Papers, H/O 45/25398.

other leading members of the National Front and British far right.[4] Indeed,
Ratcliffe, along with Reed and Leese, would become part of the history of
Holocaust negationism. They would become the men who formulated news of the
final solution in the rubric of existing anti-Semitic conspiracy theory.

Defining genocide denial is an important part of understanding differences in
interdisciplinary approaches. For the historian, defining genocide denial, or in this
instance Holocaust denial, is a multi-layered endeavour and different from legal
definitions which did not exist within the context under study. For the historian,
understanding the circumstances from which denial emerged is a prerequisite of
the discipline; however, defining how it resembles denial today without anachro-
nistically applying the label 'denial' based on modern conceptions of the term is a
challenge. This is why it is useful to see denial like that of Ratcliffe and Reed as
denial in 'embryo'. It is clear that these forms of denial were attacking the validity
of the genocidal events taking place in continental occupied Europe. These
denials were also locked in a context in which knowledge about the final solution
was fragmentary, incomplete and conceptualised within a framework in which
anti-Semitism was an intrinsic part of the public and governmental discourses
regarding Jews in the United Kingdom.[5] Establishing legal definitions or social
scientific classifications and then imposing them on a given individual or form of
denial literature in their specific historical context is a complex endeavour. The
law is situated in the practice of justice and prosecution, verdicts of guilty or not,
whereas for the historian the classification of denial is positioned in the scholastic
endeavour of explaining and contextualising. Understanding the law in relation to
Holocaust denial in a given country is extremely valuable for the historian, as it
not only delineates the legal framework in which denial is understood and judged,
but it also reveals a great deal about a country's approach to denial in its definition
(or lack of such) within that legal system.

When thinking about individuals like Ratcliffe and Reed it is necessary to begin
by posing four questions: first, what do we understand as 'Holocaust denial' in the
material being examined? Second, in what context is Holocaust denial being

4 See: M. Walker, *The National Front* (1977, Collins), 15–25; and S. Taylor, *The National
Front in English Politics* (1982, Macmillan Press), 3–18.
5 For information on anti-Semitism in British society, see: T. Kushner, *The Persistence of
Prejudice: Antisemitism in British Society during the Second World War* (1989, Manchester
University Press); T. Kushner, 'Different Worlds: British Perceptions of the Final
Solution During the Second World War' in D. Cesarani (ed.), *The Final Solution: Ori-
gins and Implementation* (1994, Routledge). For detailed study of the British govern-
ment's response to the plight of Europe's Jews, see: L. London, 'British Responses to
the Plight of the Jews in Europe 1933–45' in M. Berenbaum & A.J. Peck (eds), *The
Holocaust and History: The Known, the Unknown, the Disputed and the Examined* (2002, Indiana University Press); L. London, *Whitehall and the Jews, 1933–1948: British Immigration
Policy, Jewish Refugees and the Holocaust* (2000, Cambridge University Press); and G.L.
Weinberg, 'The Allies and the Holocaust' in M. Berenbaum & A.J. Peck (eds), *The
Holocaust and History: The Known, the Unknown, the Disputed and the Examined* (2000, Indi-
ana University Press), 481–510.

placed? Third, what form is the denial taking, how were the arguments presented and what link does it have to contemporary denial? Fourth, what can we learn from this type of prototype denial? In what follows I explore these questions and think about the value of using historical methods to understand the context in which denial was formed and also how these early forms of denial help us better understand its relationship with contemporary Holocaust denial.

It is clear that 'Holocaust denial' is a misnomer and anachronistic, as the term 'holocaust' had not yet been mobilised into the cohesive and monolithic concept of the 'Holocaust' we understand today. It is therefore important not to be tele-ological, and to understand that what is being denied are the reports of massacres against Jews, persecution of the Jews and the idea that a mass extermination of the Jews of Europe was taking place.[6] This early denial focused on the murder of Jews specifically rather than other victimised groups. It is significant that individuals like Reed and Ratcliffe were giving Nazi crimes and persecutions a distinctly Jewish dimension before the British government, legal professionals and historians had fully understood the nature of Nazi anti-Semitism and the forces driving the final solution. As Andrew Sharf explains, this lack of understanding about the nature of the crimes committed against the Jews of Europe, not just in Germany, and the suffering inflicted upon them, was in part due to an 'inability to grasp the meaning of suffering wholly outside one's immediate experience and for which there was little historical precedent'. Additionally, as Sharf also notes, such attitudes were also shaped by the 'widespread dislike of Jews in England'.[7]

During the Second World War the British government adopted a policy of playing down the distinct Jewish dimension of Nazi crimes. As Tony Kushner emphasises, the British government maintained a strong desire not to 'blend its universalist principles – of winning the war first and refusing to discriminate in favour of the persecuted Jews'.[8] In essence, as Kushner demonstrates, the reason for this thinking was born out of a fear of public unrest if unassimilated Jews were rescued and brought to Britain.[9] Kushner also explains how Britain objected to 'stressing the Jewish aspects of the impact of the Nazi crimes, and the implications this had for rescue' by the War Refugee Board.[10] It is also salient to highlight the Ministry of Information's explicit decree in 1941 which talked of the presentation of Nazi brutality and stated 'horror stuff [...] must be used very sparingly and must always deal with treatment of indisputably innocent people. Not with violent political opponents. And not with Jews'.[11] Ratcliffe therefore represented the fears of the British government in relation to the perceived potential of anti-Semitic

6 D. Reed, *Less We Regret* (1943, J. Cape), 251–6.
7 A. Sharf, *The British Press and the Jews under Nazi Rule* (1964, Oxford University Press), 194, 209.
8 T. Kushner, *The Holocaust and the Liberal Imagination: A Cultural and Social History* (1994, Blackwell), 200.
9 London, 'British Responses to the Plight of the Jews in Europe 1933–45', 511–5.
10 Kushner, *The Holocaust and the Liberal Imagination*, 199.
11 Quoted in Kushner 'Different Worlds', 251.

outbursts. While the British government's fears about anti-Semitism are evident from the material that Ratcliffe was publishing, it is clear that his denial of Jewish suffering was another matter.

Ratcliffe focused specifically on Jewish atrocity stories, and was at odds with the British government's stance of relative silence or promotion of a narrative of universal suffering.[12] Thus in order to assess the material from Ratcliffe it must be understood that current understanding of the Holocaust cannot be brought to bear, and instead the material should be viewed in the context of wartime Britain, the context of the time, and within the culture of anti-Semitism, paralysis regarding questions of rescue, a lack of specific and corroborative detail, and a lack of understanding of the unprecedented nature of the crimes that were taking place.

Context and historicisation help understand the shape and form of negation during, and in the immediate aftermath of, the Second World War. Denial was not being published in literature devoted entirely to Nazi crimes against the Jews. Denial did not take the form with which we are familiar in contemporary society (for example, Arthur Butz's *The Hoax of the Twentieth Century: The Case Against the Presumed Extermination of European Jewry*, or Richard Verrall's *Did Six Million Really Die?*[13]). Indeed, it seems today as if Holocaust denial is the main aspect of the far right 'history' and conspiracy theory, and that other conspiracy theories about Jews stem from this idea rather than the other way around. These early examples of denial are texts that predominantly promoted pre-existing, pre-war, nineteenth-century anti-Semitic conspiracy theories.[14] Denial of Nazi atrocities became absorbed into the remit of the conspiratorial anti-Semitic publications. For Ratcliffe, denial was the first line of argument and was attributable to his belief that the Jews were engaged in a programme of conspiracy and control of society.[15] Ratcliffe's primary aim was not solely directed at questioning the validity of the 'atrocity stories'; instead, he highlighted the supposed Jewish control of Britain and the world. Ratcliffe explained at length his theory of how Jews control all major business and banks.[16] With this mindset it is clear how denial of the final solution was absorbed into his mental landscape.

That Jews were placed at the centre of Ratcliffe's denial of atrocity stories is not surprising and reveals a lot about the way in which anti-Semitic conspiracy

12 The British government was not alone in favouring a narrative of universal suffering. The Church of England also used a similar principle. See: T. Lawson, *The Church of England and the Holocaust, Christianity, Memory and Nazism* (2006, Boydell Press), 172–9.
13 A. Butz, *The Hoax of the Twentieth Century: The Case Against the Presumed Extermination of European Jewry* (1976, Historical Review Press); R.E. Harwood, *Did Six Million Really Die? The Truth at Last* (1974, Historical Review Press).
14 For discussion on these forms of denial see: C. Holmes, *Anti-Semitism in British Society: 1876–1939* (1979, Edward Arnold Press), especially chapters three, four and five.
15 Arnold Leese would deny the Holocaust but approved of a theoretical Holocaust. See A. Leese, *Gothic Ripples* (14 January 1953).
16 A. Ratcliffe, *The Truth about the Jews* (1943, self-published), 5–6.

theorist and far right figures viewed the world. Individuals like Ratcliffe believe the world is controlled by Jews, a world view which sees life through a *Protocols of Zion* prism. Ratcliffe demonstrates this in a pamphlet he released in 1946 entitled *Twelve Falsehoods about the Jews: A Vindication*, in which he presented ironic answers to questions he posed.[17] The arguments and sources used by Ratcliffe would also be adopted by the deniers who succeeded him, and indicate why such individuals believed that the Jews would 'benefit' from the Holocaust and understood the creation of the State of Israel from this conspiratorial epistemology.

The arguments presented and the form or presentation were dependent on the author, but in the case of Ratcliffe it is clear that denial was a very simplistic argument. The presence of negationism alongside conspiratorial notions regarding the Jews justifies his claims that 'atrocity' stories were 'mere invention'. Ratcliffe also sought to place the 'atrocity stories' alongside other examples of 'atrocity stories' from the Jews, stating '[f]or when was there a war in which Jews were not "persecuted"? It not being generally known, of course, that most wars of Europe have their origin in Jew propaganda one way or another'.[18] Ratcliffe later stated that 'only an idiot (there is no other word for it) would place any confidence in the ridiculous stories of the "atrocities" committed under Hitler towards the Jews. Some of the stories and especially the "photographs" (probably faked in Jewish cinema studios) are enough to make a cat laugh'.[19] Ratcliffe then supported these claims by resting his arguments on the book *Falsehoods in War Time* by Arthur Ponsonby.[20] Ratcliffe used the book to explain how atrocity stories used in the First World War had been a form of propaganda, these stories had been created in 'lie photograph factories in the hands of Jews'. Ratcliffe prophesied that 'when the war is over we will have another "Falsehood in War Time" with the press condemning the very lying photographs which they themselves published in regard to Hitler's "atrocities" against the Jews'. After this statement, Ratcliffe reached the conclusion 'let all sane folk realise that all this talk about the perse-cution of the Jews in Germany is mostly of Jewish invention. If Hitler is out to "massacre" the Jews, then why has he not begun in Germany? There is not a single authentic account on record of a single Jew having been massacred or unlawfully put to death under the Hitler regime'.[21]

There are several important aspects to Ratcliffe's denial. First, it is clear that his arguments are crude; there was little attempt to formulate a theory supported by sources, other than one mention of the work by Ponsonby. This is likely due to the lack of a detailed historiography and the specific detail of the murder of Europe's Jews which would emerge on the liberation of the concentration and death camps of Nazi-occupied Europe and Germany or from the evidence at the

17 A. Ratcliffe, *Twelve Falsehoods about the Jews: A Vindication* (1946, self-published), 3.
18 A. Ratcliffe, *The Truth about the Jews*, 1.
19 Ibid., 15–6.
20 A. Ponsonby, *Falsehood in War-Time: Containing an Assortment of Lies Circulated Throughout the Nations During the Great War* (1928, George Allen & Unwin).
21 A. Ratcliffe, *The Truth about the Jews*, 15–6.

Nuremburg Tribunals. Ratcliffe could not have put forward the arguments that individuals like Arthur Butz, David Irving, Richard Verrall, Ernst Zündel, Fred Leuchter or Carlo Mattogno advanced. His denials were limited by the information available, and while it is important to stress that newspaper accounts existed, that there were survivors who had escaped camps while the genocide was still in operation, and limited announcements from the government had been made, neither the information nor the level of understanding of the Holocaust was as detailed as that which we possess now. Nor did the Holocaust occupy the same position it occupies in British collective memory today.[22]

Ratcliffe's arguments were rudimentary and demonstrate the seedbed on which later deniers' arguments would be based. For example, Richard Verrall used Ponsonby's book in his 1974 work, *Did Six Million Really Die?* The book was produced under the pseudonym Richard E. Harwood, and Verrall directed his readers to the publication for more information on 'the forgery of wartime atrocity photographs'.[23] David Irving would also attempt to suggest that Jews were only arrested because of the 'crimes of the Jews concerned'. Irving claimed that the Jews in Germany were being arrested and sentenced for offences under criminal law. In 1996 he wrote in *Goebbels: Mastermind of the Third Reich*, that Goebbels would highlight, '[e]very malfeasance of the criminal demi-monde and identify it as Jewish [...] In 1932 no fewer than thirty-one cases of fraud, mainly insurance swindles would be committed by Jews'.[24] While the statements of Ratcliffe and Irving differ in detail, both Irving and Ratcliffe sought to justify Jewish persecution and claimed that any persecution of Jews was based on legal means.

It is clear that Ratcliffe's reporting was based on the information he had at the time and the way he interpreted and filtered the information through his conspiratorial world view. As stated above, Ratcliffe did have more information at his disposal than he chose to include; he did not include specific information about the crimes he sought to deny, instead choosing to amalgamate all information under the umbrella of 'atrocity stories'. The British press had reported accounts of the murder of Jews by gas in specially 'erected extermination camps' and recounted mass shootings of Jews in Eastern Europe.[25] Whatever his reason for excluding specific reports, the net result was to combine all available information under one monolithic label of 'atrocity stories'. This technique is also evident in

22 For discussion on the development of British collective of the Holocaust see: O. Jensen & C. Shaples, *Britain and the Holocaust: Remembering and Representing War and Genocide* (2013, Palgrave); and A. Pearce, *Holocaust Consciousness in Contemporary Britain* (2014, Routledge).
23 R.E. Harwood, *Did Six Million Really Die?*, 24.
24 D. Irving, *Goebbels: Mastermind of the Third Reich* (1996, Focal Point), 95–6.
25 For a selection of examples of British newspaper coverage before the publication of *The Truth About Jews*, see: 'Massacre of Jews' *The Times* (30 June 1942), 2; 'Extermination' *The Manchester Guardian* (27 October 1942), 4; 'The Abyss' *The Observer* (13 December 1942); 'Barbarity to Jews Retribution by Allies, Commons Endorse a Pledge' *The Times* (18 December 1942), 4; and 'Hitler's Slaughter of the Jews: Inter Allied Report' *The Manchester Guardian* (21 December 1942), 6.

more contemporary forms of denial which seek to play on a presumed public understanding of the Holocaust in which deniers focus on undermining the historical accounts of sites of extermination that are prevalent in the public discourse, for example Auschwitz. The main reason for this is to capture a wider audience by focusing on elements of the history of the Holocaust that are most familiar to the wider public rather than the complexities debated in academic literature.[26]

Ratcliffe was not the only individual active in refuting the Holocaust during and in the immediate aftermath of the war, Douglas Reed also sought to refute the murder and suffering of the Jews of Europe. Like Ratcliffe, Reed singles out and identifies Jewish suffering under Nazism as the main focus of his denial. In doing so Reed demonstrates the precision with which anti-Semites seek out Jews for attack at a moment in which the British government was seeking to stress the universality of suffering in Nazi Europe. Reed should not be considered on the far right of the political spectrum, as Richard Thurlow explains: 'some right wing exponents of the conspiracy theory of history may be opposed to fascism and Nazism.'[27] Reed was such a man who was critical of Hitler and Nazism (as well as Fascism and Bolshevism) but was anti-Semitic in his outlook. As a news reporter in Germany during the 1930s he based his views and 'evidence' on his own experiences. Reed did not believe in Hitler's anti-Semitic policies and felt that they were a sham and 'was blind to the fact that antisemitism was the driving force behind Hitler's policies'.[28] For Reed, Hitler could not be a real anti-Semite because he believed the actions of, as he saw it, 'organised Jewry' were as repugnant as those of Hitler, and as such 'two such evil forces could not be opposed to each other'.[29] Reed, like Ratcliffe, saw and divided the world along Manichean lines. Later Reed would claim that Hitler had aided Zionism and communism through his actions.[30]

Reed therefore could not accept the reality of the Nazis' genocide of the Jews of Europe. Reed chose several methods to deny that the Nazis were murdering the Jews of Europe. Reed was more detailed in his dismissal of the Nazi genocide than Ratcliffe. In *Lest We Regret*, Reed quoted from several reports regarding the extermination of European Jews and sought to deconstruct them and disprove them.[31] Reed claimed that the Jews were using 'extermination stories' to aid them in creating a Jewish state in Palestine and linked the atrocities to the right-wing belief that the war was being fought for Jewish interests. When Anthony Eden, on 17 December 1942, confirmed reports about atrocities against the Jews in Europe and read a declaration of the Allied governments to the

---

26 For more discussion of this technique, see: M. Hobbs, 'Writing "History" for Hitler: Holocaust Denial since 1945' in C. Carmichael & R. Maguire, *The Routledge History of Genocide* (2015, Routledge), 201–4.

27 R. Thurlow, 'Anti-Nazi Antisemite: The Case of Douglas Reed', *Patterns of Prejudice* (1984, Vol. 18, No. 1), 18.

28 Ibid., 30.

29 Ibid., 30.

30 D. Reed, *From Smoke to Smother* (1948, J. Cape), 282.

31 D. Reed, *Lest We Regret*, 251–4.

House of Commons in which he condemned 'in the strongest possible terms' the policy of extermination,[32] Reed replied to the statement as follows:

> We have made no graver mistake. We formally tell the Germans, from our House of Commons, that anything they may endure at our hands will be solely on behalf of the Jews! [...] We have lent our name to the threat of Jewish vengeance![33]

This tactic was expanded by later Holocaust deniers in order to present the suffering of other groups, especially the Germans, above those of Jews.

The idea that the war was fought for Jewish vengeance, interests or as a 'Jewish war' became a staple in the lexicon of Holocaust denial during the war, in its immediate aftermath, and in contemporary negationism and revisionism.[34] This notion proposed that the war was created and brought about by Jews to stop Hitler because of his persecution of the Jews in Germany, and as an epic clash between two races: the Aryan race and the Jewish race.[35] This idea became a stock trope of Holocaust deniers.[36] Reed also presented his theories about 'extermination stories' in a different way, choosing to focus on the word 'extermination' often used in British newspapers. Reed argued that the word was used 'habitually and without flinching' by the media and politicians, and that in 'a few years' time with the facts and figures, [we] will possess proof of the greatest example of mass-misinformation in history'.[37] This projection of what the future course of far right 'history' would entail, provided the template and mission for future deniers. Furthermore, Reed's objection to the use of the term 'extermination' was a semantic argument, focusing on the word rather than the actual events being described.[38] This method of focusing on definitions (for example, genocide) and semantics rather than the actual crimes themselves would become a stock tool of deniers.[39] While it is possible to argue Reed misinterpreted the dimensions of Nazi persecution, it is clear that when his other anti-Semitic utterances are combined with his specific attacks on the reports in British newspapers and in the House of Commons, Reed was actively denying what was taking place

---

32 *Hansard* HC Deb 17 December 1942, vol. 385 c 2083.
33 D. Reed, *Lest We Regret*, 258–9.
34 D. Lipstadt, 'Holocaust Denial' in P. Hayes & J.K. Roth, *The Oxford Handbook of Holocaust Studies* (2012, Oxford University Press), 560–74.
35 See M. Hobbs, 'Writing "History" for Hitler: Holocaust Denial since 1945', 199–200.
36 Pre-war fascist and post-war neo-Nazi Arnold Leese wrote a book called *The Jewish War of Survival* in which he states that the war had been created by Jews and fought for Jewish interests. In fact Leese was so confident in his claims he sent the book to Hermann Göring's defence team at Nuremburg. See: A. Leese, *The Jewish War of Survival* (1945, self-published).
37 D. Reed, *Lest We Regret*, 250.
38 Ibid., 252.
39 This idea of 'piggybacking' on academic debate has been explored by Robert Eaglestone. See R. Eaglestone, *Postmodernism and Holocaust Denial* (2001, London, Icon Books), 18.

in order to support his own anti-Semitic world view. For Reed the reports were the product of a Jewish conspiracy which appeared 'at the very moment victory loomed' in order to secure a Jewish state and 'to open Palestine for many more [Jews] in breach of our pledge to the Arabs'.[40] This notion that the formation of the State of Israel was based on the Holocaust would become a standard trope of the Holocaust denier.

Douglas Reed's denial of 'extermination' reports, and Ratcliffe's rejection of 'atrocity stories', are linked by their shared attempts to undermine Jewish suffering and discredit the accounts that were emerging from occupied Europe and to perpetuate a Jewish world conspiracy which absorbed the new information into its remit. What is clear from examining these two individuals is that a lot is revealed about not only the antecedents of Holocaust denial but how we understand these roots and the link they share to the future course of Holocaust denial. One key belief shared by the two men was that once the war was over, these 'stories' would be disproved. This assumption could be viewed as an invitation to anti-Semites and the far right after the war to continue the fight against the 'stories', but also contains an unacknowledged realisation of the magnitude of what the Nazis were being accused of, and that such information was not going to be ignored after the war. This is something that has not been explored enough in the literature on Holocaust denial.

Reed and Ratcliffe presented and couched their arguments differently. Reed chose to approach the claims with a more detailed, analytical criticism of the reports appearing in the newspapers and sought to cast doubt on the reliability of the witnesses and language used.[41] Ratcliffe attacked the validity of the information emerging by dismissing it out of hand, as a Jewish fake, and was absorbed into the traditional anti-Semitic arguments espoused in his pamphlets and newspaper. The mechanisms used to attack the details at hand bear an overt symmetry to recent trends in Holocaust denial. Ratcliffe's attack on the photographs that were appearing would be used time and time again by deniers.[42] Ratcliffe's and Reed's attempts to downplay the number of individuals murdered has become a stock trope of the denial movement. Reed also attempted to negate the suffering of the Jews in favour of other groups. This mirrors the later tactics of deniers like David Irving and Richard Verrall to favour the suffering of Germans in Allied bombing raids, or Colin Jordan who equated the murder of British soldiers in Palestine in 1947 with the crimes of Adolf Eichmann.[43]

40 D. Reed, *Lest We Regret*, 251, 257.
41 Ibid., 258–9.
42 For example, R.E. Harwood, *Did Six Million Really Die? The Truth at Last* (1974, Historical Review Press), 24; J.C. Ball, *Air Photo Evidence: Auschwitz, Treblinka, Majdanek, Sobibour, Bergen Belsen, Balzec, Babi Yar, Katyn Forest* (1992, J.C. Ball); see Irving v. Lipstadt and Penguin books Trial Transcript: *Irving v. Lipstadt*, Day 10 Wednesday 26 January 2000. www.hdot.org/en/trial/transcripts/.
43 C. Jordan, 'The Eichmann Trial: What about Jewish Atrocities?' *Combat* supplement, *Combat Magazine* (No. 10 Jan.–Feb., 1961).

The publications of Reed and Ratcliffe demonstrate how the initial arguments and tools to discredit the crimes of the Nazis against the Jews were used and expanded upon by the individuals who succeeded them. The link between Reed and far right individuals was looser than that of Ratcliffe.[44] Ratcliffe had overt links with Arnold Leese, the leader of the pre-war Imperial Fascist League and post-war editor of *Gothic Ripples*, a publication in which Leese would perpetuate the notion of a Jewish world conspiracy. Leese, considered the 'English Hitler', would tutor Colin Jordan and leave him his house to continue his legacy – 74 Princedale Road, which would become the headquarters of many of the neo-Nazi and fascist parties and movements throughout the late 1950s, 1960s and early 1970s.[45] Ratcliffe would publish many of Leese's anti-Semitic cartoons and Leese would publish an article announcing Ratcliffe's death in Ratcliffe's newspaper *The Vanguard* in 1947.[46] Thus Ratcliffe's links with the future course of Holocaust denial and the far right demonstrate the likelihood that his arguments inspired a new generation of deniers, who responded to new information and sources as they emerged in the following decades.

It is clear that the arguments used by contemporary Holocaust deniers are present in the literature of Reed and Ratcliffe.[47] What is striking about the literature from the period under study is its overt link with anti-Semitism, or more specifically with the idea of a 'world Jewish conspiracy'. Both Reed and Ratcliffe attempted to suggest they were not anti-Semites, but rather seeking 'truth'.[48] However, as demonstrated above, their anti-Semitism was overt and omnipresent in their publications. This was to be expected given the flexibility of such conspiracy theories; it was this elasticity which easily incorporated new information into pre-existing anti-Semitic thinking. This is particularly important when such literature is compared to the pseudo-academic apparatus that is employed by Holocaust deniers who camouflage this overt anti-Semitism behind the 'academic' façade of Holocaust denial. This is not the case of all Holocaust deniers: individuals like Colin Jordan, Lady Jane Birdwood and groups like Column 88 and Combat 18 all publish material where Holocaust denial is still placed along an anti-Semitic diatribe unrelated to the Holocaust.[49] What these initial responses to the crimes against the Jews from Nazi-occupied Europe demonstrate, is the ease

44 R. Thurlow, 'Anti-Nazi Antisemite', 33.
45 R. Thurlow, *Fascism in Britain: From Oswald Mosley's Black Shirts to the National Front* (1998, London, I.B Tauris), 47. For information on 74 Princedale Road, see: M. Walker, *The National Front*, 28, 33, 37, 40, 45 & 47.
46 Leese advertised in *The Vanguard* between September 1945 and November 1946. The article by Leese can be found in *The Vanguard* (No. 351, 1947, February).
47 For a list of the contemporary arguments made by Holocaust deniers, see: D.E. Lipstadt, 'Denial', 560–1. For detailed examination of the methods of Holocaust deniers, see: M. Shermer & A. Gorbman, *Denying History: Who Says the Holocaust Never Happened and Why Do they Say It?* (2009, University of California Press), 99–173.
48 A. Ratcliffe, *The Truth about the Jews*, 1, 15–6; and D. Reed, *Lest We Regret*, 251–4.
49 For details of the actions of these individuals and organisations, see: M. Whine, 'Holocaust Denial in the United Kingdom' in J.H Brinks, S. Rock & E. Timms (eds),

with which they are absorbed into traditional anti-Semitic rhetoric. While the arguments of deniers may have become more sophisticated as they engaged with the mounting academic studies on the Holocaust, they emerged as the product of anti-Semitic rhetoric that existed before the Holocaust. However, the growing awareness of the Holocaust certainly propagated more aggressive responses from the far right and Holocaust deniers who saw the Nazi genocide as a barrier in the public imagination to support of the ideologies they promulgated.

Today Holocaust denial has been established as a 'discipline' in its own right amongst the far right and followers of conspiracy theories. This sea change is perhaps explicable in response to the growing changes in far right parties to be considered legitimate and viable alternatives to mainstream political parties.[50] Holocaust denial therefore provides a different mantle. It has been used, of course, to expunge the crimes of the Nazis and to present fascism and Nazism as legitimate alternatives to democratic institutions, as argued by Lipstadt.[51] Today it is used as a flag to attract like-minded individuals and followers to its cause. Holocaust revisionism and negationism almost stand as an expression of anti-Semitic hatred which carefully camouflages overt anti-Semitic rhetoric, allowing its proponents to present a public face with the label of 'legitimate historical revisionism' while keeping the more ugly side of their anti-Semitic views behind closed doors and away from a public audience. Yet such an explanation is not always enough to explain why denial is lodged in the character of post-war far right thinking. It is also necessary to understand that denial and anti-Semitic conspiracy theories are part of the epistemological basis on which Nazi, neo-Nazi and far right positions understand the world.

In comparing these early forms of denial to more recent examples, similarities and differences emerge. As we have seen, the principal arguments for attack remain largely unchanged. The arguments may have become more sophisticated and incorporate more detailed attacks on specific sites of mass murder like Auschwitz, but the main trajectory of attack remains constant: that the numbers of Jews killed are grossly exaggerated; the evidence that pertains to the Holocaust has been falsified; what murders did take place do not represent a systemic extermination policy; and any killing of the Jews took 'place because of the crimes of the Jews concerned' (e.g. they were partisans or criminals). What has changed since these early inceptions is the way in which denial is 'packaged', and this has largely been due to changes that have taken place in the far right as a result of changes in society. This has forced such groups to reinvent their particular brand of neo-fascism and extreme right ideologies in line with an electorate that has little appetite for racist and bigoted ideologies.

Nationalist Myths and Modern Media: Contested Identities in the Age of Globalisation (2006, Tauris), 69–82.

50 M.J. Goodwin, *New British Fascism: Rise of the British National Party* (2011, Routledge), chapter 3.

51 D. Lipstadt, *Denying the Holocaust: The Growing Assault on Truth and Memory* (1992, Plume), 216–19.

Studying individuals like Ratcliffe and their prototypal denial is a valuable pursuit for the public and academic understanding of Holocaust denial, but also for those who study anti-Semitism and racial hatred in Britain as well as the changing shape of the far right. The study of this early denial demonstrates how our knowledge of the Holocaust has developed and how far right publications have responded to the growing scholastic research on the Holocaust. Furthermore, such material demonstrates how denial was predestined to be a product of individuals with extreme anti-Semitic views, and used as a measure of political expedience to explain away Nazi crimes that tarnished their ideologies.

The study of these individuals and their publications is also of value in other contexts. Ratcliffe was subject to investigation by the British government and questions in the House of Commons. Studying these reactions and responses can reveal much about processes and legal debate over the way in which the British government dealt with such publications and would provide interesting comparisons with other European countries which have Holocaust denial enshrined in specific laws. The denial espoused by Ratcliffe provides a rich vein of material that explains the context in which denial was forged, the basic arguments it presented, and provides the historian with an insight into its origins. It also serves the interests of legal professionals and academics as to the development of legal recourse against such material, and provides other social science disciplines with insights into the psychological and sociological foundations of Holocaust denial. While individuals like Ratcliffe and Reed may not represent the more complex and entangled arguments of more contemporary deniers, they provide an important foundation in the development of Holocaust denial which has been overlooked in the literature of Holocaust denial historiography.

Chapter 2

Countering Holocaust denial in relation to the Nuremberg trials

Michael Salter

Whoever denies the genocide destroys the memory of the victims and prepares the repetition of collective deaths.[1]

I Introduction

By 'genocide denial' I understand expressions of ideas, beliefs and theories aiming to deny, grossly minimise, or otherwise trivialise acts of genocide in ways that are reasonably perceived as insulting to the memory of the victims of such gross international criminality.[2] As was stated in the appeal hearing of the *Irving v Penguin Books* defamation case:

Holocaust denial means not necessarily a blank refusal to acknowledge a Nazi policy of mass murder of Jews and other minorities but a systematic endeavour, by marginalising and excusing what happened, to accuse those who insist upon it of being Zionist propagandists.[3]

States as well as groups, organisations and individuals can be perpetrators.[4] Here, the underlying political motivation behind such expressions is often similar to that

1 Yves Ternon, Du Négationnisme: mémoire et tabou (Paris: Desclée de Brouwer, 1999), 14.
2 For an extended helpful discussion, see Pascale Bloch, 'Response to Professor Fronza's The Punishment of Negationism', 30(627) *Vtl L. Rev.* (2006). For a survey of the extent, see Rafael Medoff and Alex Grobman, 'Holocaust Denial: A Global Survey', 2006, Wyman Institute for Holocaust Studies, available at www.wymaninstitute.org/articles/HolocaustDenial2006.pdf.
3 [2001] EWCA Civ 1197, [95] – quoting from Sedley LJ's earlier refusal of leave of 18 December 2000. See also the definition of Prof. Evans in his expert report for the earlier High Court hearing summarised at 2000 WL 362478 para. 8.4.
4 Turkey still denies the Armenian genocide and criminalises its affirmation as an 'insult to Turkishness' under article 301 of its Penal Code. For a critique, see www.amnesty.org/en/library/info/EUR44/035/2005. Only in 1995 did France publicly admit responsibility for deporting almost 70,000 Jews to Nazi death camps – only

which first motivated previous acts of genocide. In my area of World War II war crimes trials research, genocide denial mainly consists of Holocaust denial.[5]

Such denial includes specific claims that, notwithstanding well-established historical facts to the contrary,[6] the Nazis did not murder c.6 million Jews, that the notion of murderous gas chambers is a myth, and that any deaths of Jews occurring under the Nazis took place only because of wartime privations.[7] Such denial persists despite the fact that this genocide is one of the best-documented instances, with a broad range of mutually corroborating and compelling evidence reaffirming its various elements.[8]

This chapter is written from the perspective and experience of a legal researcher conducting empirical archival research primarily into the Nuremberg process.[9] This decade-long programme has included my obtaining, analysing and integrating original US intelligence documentation in relation to Nazi war crimes in general,[10] and the Holocaust in particular.[11] The latter has culminated in my two-volume study of the contributions US intelligence officials made to the Holocaust-related aspects of the Nuremberg trials process, including the mass organised theft of Jewish-owned works of art.[12] In particular, and over the last decade, I have focused upon analysing previously secret, classified documentation

2,800 of whom returned. See Gail Russell Chaddock, 'Cleric's Comments Ignite the Fury of French Media', *Christian Sci Monitor*, 25 July 1996, 5.

5 Berel Lang, 'Six Questions on (or about) Holocaust Denial', 49 *History and Theory* (May 2010), 157–68, at 162.

6 For a website containing an impressive array of evidence reaffirming the reality of the Holocaust including original Nazi documentation, courts records and academic articles, see www.holocaust-history.org.

7 For a fuller summary, see Deborah Lipstadt, *Denying the Holocaust: The Growing Assault on Truth and Memory* (New York: Free Press/Macmillan, 1993); and her useful summary 'Denying the Holocaust' on the BBC history website, www.bbc.co.uk/history/worldwars/genocide/deniers_01.shtml.

8 Ibid. See also Richard Evans, *Lying About Hitler* (New York Basic Books, 2001); Deborah E. Lipstadt, *History on Trial: My Day in Court with David Irving* (New York: Harper Collins, 2005); Robert Jan van Pelt, *The Case for Auschwitz: Evidence from the Irving Trial* (Indiana: Indiana University Press, 2002); Jean-Claude Pressac; *Auschwitz: Technique and Operation of the Gas Chambers* (The Hague: Beate Klarsfeld Foundation, 1989); Laurence Rees, *Auschwitz: The Nazis and the 'Final Solution'* (London: BBC Books, 2005); Michael Shermer and Alex Grobman, *Denying History: Who Says the Holocaust Never Happened and Why Do they Say it?* (Calgari: University of California Press, 2000).

9 For a sample, see M. Salter, 'War Crimes Prosecutors and Intelligence Agencies: The Case for Assessing Their Collaboration', 16(3) *Intelligence and National Security* (2001) (co-author Ian Bryan), 93–120; 'The Prosecution of Nazi War Criminals and the OSS: The Need for a New Research Agenda', 2(1) *Jnl of Intelligence History* (2002), 77–117.

10 M. Salter, *Nazi War Crimes, US Intelligence and Selective Prosecution at Nuremberg: Controversies Regarding the Role of the Office of Strategic Services* (Abingdon: Routledge, 2007).

11 'The Visibility of the Holocaust: Franz Neumann and the Nuremberg Trials', in Robert Fine and Charles Turner (eds), *Social Theory After the Holocaust* (Liverpool: Liverpool University Press, 2000), 197–218.

12 M. Salter, *US Intelligence, The Holocaust and the Nuremberg Trials* (The Hague: Brill/Nijhoff, 2009, 2 vols); 'A Critical Assessment of US Intelligence's Investigation of Nazi Art Looting', 13(2) *Journal of International Criminal Justice* (2015), 257–80.

that the Central Intelligence Agency (CIA) has recently declassified, which reveals the substantial contribution of Anglo-American intelligence officials to key aspects of the Nuremberg process, together with selective subversion of aspects of these trials by means of unofficial immunity deals.[13]

My overall interdisciplinary project, sometimes developed in conjunction with other researchers from various disciplines including law and military history,[14] has involved publishing a series of studies and case studies on the interaction between intelligence officials and Nazi war crimes prosecutors confronting evidence of genocide.[15] The newly available evidence of Nazi-led genocidal activity uncovered and, in part, transmitted into the Nuremberg process by US intelligence officials, has proven so overwhelming that not even my two-volume, 800-page monograph, published in 2009, has been able fully to do it justice. A close and critical empirical analysis of such intelligence documentation, much of it generated for ulterior strategic wartime purposes, gave me no reason to debate the brute factual existence of the Holocaust, and thus to consider its denial as a position meriting scholarly consideration. Indeed, with every new document I uncovered and analysed the opposite proved to be the case.

Whilst debates over legal doctrine in relation to any specific genocide can be accused of presupposing the existence of that genocide without first establishing it from compelling sources, this objection cannot apply to my own or similar projects. That is, legally informed empirical studies analysing the implications of the original documentary trail left by perpetrators, victims, criminal investigators, witnesses and prosecutors. However, the unwelcome presence of expressions of denial manifests itself not in this documentary trail itself but rather in misleading materials made available to school and university students over the internet: the topic of my next section.

---

13 Michael Salter, 'Uncovering the Hidden Geo-Political Dimensions of Prosecuting Nazi War Crimes: The Covert Support Given by Military and Intelligence Officials for General Karl Wolff in his 1948–49 Trials', 2(1) *The Covert Policing, Terrorism & Intelligence Law Review* (2014), 1–32; 'Negotiating Nolle Prosequi at Nuremberg: The Case of Captain Zimmer', 3 *Journal of International Criminal Justice* (2005), 649–65 (with Maggi Eastwood).

14 Michael Salter, 'Contrasting Strategies within the War Crimes Trials of Kesselring and Wolff' (with military historian Dr Von Lingen), 26 *Liverpool Law Review* (2005), 225–66.

15 Specific case studies include: 'Ensuring the After-Life of the Ciano Diaries: Allen Dulles' Provision of Nuremberg Trial Evidence', 21(4) *Intelligence and National Security* (2006), 568–603 (co-written with Charlesworth); 'The Nazis' Persecution of Religion as a War Crime: The OSS's Response within the Nuremberg War Crimes Process' (Claire Hulme, LLS), 3(1) *Rutgers Journal of Law and Religion*; 'Intelligence Agencies and War Crimes Prosecution: Allen Dulles' Involvement in Witness Testimony at Nuremberg', 2 *Journal of International Criminal Justice* (2004), 826–54; 'War Crimes and Legal Immunities: The Complicities of Waffen-SS General Karl Wolff in Nazi Medical Experiments', 4 *Rutgers Journal of Law and Religion* (2003) (co-authored with Suzanne Ost). See also the contributions contained in our interdisciplinary collection: '60 Years On: New Research on the Office of Strategic Services' (Introduction to the special issue of the *Journal of Intelligence History*, which I edited in Summer 2002).

2 Legal teaching and research

I teach both foundational and third-year undergraduate LLB modules entitled 'war crimes trials', as well as international criminal law in the UK and more recently China. In this work, I regularly have to mark student essays, projects and dissertations where questions relating to evidence of the Holocaust and other genocides, including the admissibility of atrocity film evidence, take centre stage.[16] Some of the students' works have fallen into the well-prepared trap of basing their factual claims and arguments about the Nuremberg trials upon statements contained in documents self-published on dubious websites – whose names ought not to be dignified with a scholarly citation.[17]

This is far from a unique context or confined to university-level students.[18] As Kay Andrews, from the UK Holocaust Educational Trust, stated to the BBC, Holocaust denial sites questioning the basic fact of a genocide can effectively mislead school pupils and other students:

> With the internet, you've got to be fairly well-educated to see through what revisionist websites are trying to do. I think as soon as you look at them closely you can work it out, but part of the problem that we find is teachers will send pupils off to do internet research and not guide them to specific sites. So as a result kids put the Holocaust into a search engine, which comes up with all of this stuff, and at 14-years-old they are not mature enough to make that distinction between a denialist site and a more legitimate site.[19]

Some of these denial websites make little effort to disguise their underlying fascist or extreme nationalist political agendas, even in their chosen web addresses. However, many others are far more strategic, using apparently mainstream designations, such as Campaign for Real History, 'British Journal for …', 'Journal of Historical Review' etc.,[20] in which are published heavily footnoted pseudo-

---

16 On atrocity film court evidence, see Susan Twist, 'Evidence of Atrocity of Atrocious Evidence: The Controversial Use of Atrocity Film at Nuremberg', 26(3), *Liverpool Law Review* (2005), 267–302; Lawrence Douglas, 'Film as Witness: Screening Nazi Concentration Camps before the Nuremberg Tribunal', 105(449) *Yale L.J.* (1995); Leonidas E. Hill, 'The Trial of Ernst Zundel and the Law in Canada', 6 *Simon Wiesenthal Center Ann.* 165, 184 (1989); Salter, *Nazi War Crimes*, 255–76.

17 More generally, see Carlos C. Juerta and Dafna Shiffman-Huerta, 'Holocaust Denial Literature: Its Place in Teaching the Holocaust', in Rochelle L. Millen, *New Perspectives on the Holocaust: A Guide for Teachers and Scholars* (New York: NYU Press, 1996).

18 Hence, educationalists have produced counter-denial factsheets aimed at school students: www.holocaustdenialontrial.org/en/learning. More generally, see Geri J. Yonover, 'Anti-Semitism and Holocaust Denial in the Academy: A Tort Remedy', 101 *Dick. L. Rev.* (1996), 71, 83 n 75.

19 Raffi Berg, 'The Fight against Holocaust Denial', BBC News: news.bbc.co.uk/1/hi/world/europe/4436275.stm.

20 Jürgen Matthäus, *Contemporary Responses to the Holocaust* (New York: Praeger/Greenwood 2004), 141.

academic studies. There seems to be a concerted strategy to misrepresent Holocaust denial as mundane and academic 'revision' of always contingent interpretations about the historical record.[21]

As I have found out to my cost when searching the internet for discussions of the role of US intelligence in the Nuremberg trials, one can be directed to specific webpages that have all the appearance of a serious historical forum, with scans of original archival documentation and so forth. During one such search, I came across an editorial statement on 'Focal Point Publications' that there exists original documentation suggesting that US intelligence officials among the American prosecution staff at Nuremberg had fabricated or tampered with film evidence the prosecutors later presented to the court. Given that I was writing a book chapter on how such atrocity film evidence had been sourced, organised and edited, and its impact upon the trials, I immediately fired back a response to this forum. I politely but firmly asked the anonymous writer for some substantiation for this claim, as – if true – it could obviously alter my argumentation in relation to such evidence. The reply to my question came from none other than Irving himself, who, it turns out, was the moving force behind this publisher's website. This stated that the details were contained in his monograph on the trials – a reject version of which, with some pages missing – he sent to me. I later received two further communications but replied to neither.[22]

The lesson I have learned, which I reinforce every year to my war crimes students, is that genuine-sounding historical websites can be operating as fronts for genocide denying or relativising activists, and that such deniers have a political agenda of masquerading as real historians faithful to the meaning of primary documentation, whilst actually distorting the historical record to reaffirm their preconceived ideological agenda(s).

When I independently secured the original documentation from the US National Archives, the charge of 'tampering with evidence' turned out to amount to little more than a completely normal and expected editing of film evidence to optimally support the overall prosecution case. Given the adversarial nature of the Nuremberg trials, one would expect no less from either prosecutors or – for that matter – defence lawyers. Irving's deception, apparently supported by carefully selected extracts of original documents, lies in reinterpreting legitimate film editing as if this constituted 'tampering'.

The subtext, I suggest, is that Irving – and others with a similar negationist agenda – are regularly frustrated by the stock response that the details of the Nazi genocide have already been proven in considerable detail by the Nuremberg

---

21 Gavriel D. Rosenfeld, 'The Politics of Uniqueness: Reflections on the Recent Polemical Turn in Holocaust and Genocide Scholarship', in David Cesarani and Sarah Kavanaugh, *Holocaust: Critical Concepts in Historical Studies* (Abingdon: Routledge, 2004), 376; Lydia Morris, *Rights: Sociological Perspectives* (Abingdon: Routledge, 2006), 238 n.1.

22 Correspondence on file with the author.

trials evidence, most of which stemmed from the record keeping of the Nazis themselves.[23] Whilst attempting to minimise their clients' personal responsibility and legal accountability, defence lawyers at these and follow-up Holocaust trials freely acknowledged the facts of this programme of mass killing and accepted prosecution documentation substantiating it.[24] Furthermore, many pioneering studies on the Holocaust, including that of Raul Hilberg, draw heavily upon the treasure trove of information gathered for these trials.[25] In addition, the prosecution of deniers, such as Ernst Zündel, relied strongly upon evidence, including Office of Strategic Services (OSS) atrocity film evidence entitled 'Nazi Concentration Camps', that had previously been deployed to dramatic effect at Nuremberg.[26] It is indeed arguable that both war crimes trials and other legal hearings in which genocide denial claims have featured centrally, possess an impressive capacity to provide *educationally instructive* and well-substantiated accounts of atrocities. These have enhanced credibility insofar as prosecution evidence survives rigorous scrutiny of their meaning, scope and implications by defence lawyers, and is finally accepted by judges as reliable and compelling evidence sufficient to prove a case beyond reasonable doubt.[27]

Attempts at genocide denial are clearly flying in the face of proven historical evidence consisting of hundreds of original documents and witness testimony. The latter's authenticity was vindicated by a trial process in which defence lawyers found it nearly impossible to challenge, let alone discredit, their authenticity, other than in two or three irrelevant instances.

Outside these 'common sense' reactions to instances of denial, virtually every serious scholarly study of the Nuremberg evidence and its implications is able to provide a mass of reasons discrediting Holocaust denial. This is true even in less obviously relevant areas, such as the origins and organisation of so-called 'mercy killings' of sick and mentally disabled German civilians,[28] the organisation and

---

23 Lawrence Baron, 'The Holocaust and American Public Memory, 1945–1960', 17(1) *Holocaust and Genocide Studies* (2003), 62–88.

24 Laurence Douglas, *The Memory of Judgement, Making Law and History in the Trials of the Holocaust* (New Haven: Yale University Press, 2001), ch. 8.

25 Raul Hilberg, *The Destruction of the European Jews* (3rd revised edition, New Haven: Yale University Press, 2003; first edition 1961).

26 Douglas, *The Memory of Judgement*, 222 n.23.

27 Ibid., as well as Laurence Douglas, 'The Didactic Trial: Filtering History and Memory in the Courtroom', 14(4) *European Review* (2006), 513–22; 'History and Memory in the Courtroom: Reflections on Perpetrator Trials', in *The Nuremberg Trials International Criminal Law Since 1945/Die Nürnberger Prozesse Völkerstrafrecht seit 1945*, Herbert Reginbogin and Christoph Safferling (eds) (K.G. Sauer Verlag, 2006); see also Nathan Stoltzfus and Henry Friedlander (eds), *Nazi Crimes and the Law* (New York: Cambridge University Press, 2008).

28 See, for example, the Nazi's use of physical extermination on sick and disabled German citizens detailed in Paul Weindling, *Nazi Medicine and the Nuremberg Trials: From Medical War Crimes to Informed Consent* (London: Palgrave Macmillan, 2006); Aly Gotz et al., *Cleansing the Fatherland: Nazi Medicine and Racial Hygiene* (New York: Johns Hopkins University Press, 1994).

operation of labour/concentration camps that were not set up or designated as death camps, the mass killing of Russian prisoners of war (POWs), and the systematic mistreatment of Slavic populations generally in Eastern Europe.[29] In other words, virtually every serious historical study of Nuremberg evidence, including those that do not focus specifically on the genocide of Jews and Gypsies, provides additional background of extreme brutality, which is consistent with a genocidal orientation, and which lends support to the more directly relevant Nuremberg evidence relating to these genocides. Taken as a whole, the Nuremberg evidence paints a convincing picture of a regime determined to physically annihilate all those it defined as its 'racial enemies'. Hence, the idea that somehow European Jews, the most vilified of all these enemies, would be the one group that was exempted from mass killing would strike anyone familiar with this general trial evidence as absurd, even if they were unfamiliar with the specific trial evidence concerning the Holocaust.

From the perverse perspective of genocide deniers, attempting to discredit the Nuremberg trial evidence by any means possible, including by reference to the involvement of US intelligence officials, makes sense. It makes sense but only as an instrumental means to a pre-given end, even where the latter is concealed behind the rhetoric of conducting 'real history'. Yet, it is this twisting of evidence to fit a preconceived prejudice formulated in defiance of any evidence whatsoever, which is itself arguably associated with an effort to recuperate fascism, and which renders such illusory interpretations the opposite of 'real history'.

3 Countering denial without affording undeserved recognition

How then can fellow legal historians of the Nuremberg trials best respond to instances of denial within our field? Scholars' responses to genocide denial include refusals to engage Holocaust deniers or their arguments out of a concern that doing so is already to concede too much and to lend them unwarranted legitimacy.[30] Others, following the lead of American historian Deborah Lipstadt, have focused on the methods and motivations of Holocaust denial without legitimising the deniers themselves by taking them as legitimate partners within a genuine academic debate. Lipstadt, for instance, states: 'We need not waste time or effort answering the deniers' contentions. It would be never-ending … Their commitment is to an ideology and their "findings" are shaped to support it.'[31]

29 This formed a major part of the Nuremberg evidence against defendant Hans Frank, former governor of Poland: law2.umkc.edu/faculty/projects/ftrials/nuremberg/franktest.html.

30 Wilhelm Heitmeyer and John Hagan, *International Handbook of Violence Research* (Berlin: Springer, 2003).

31 Deborah Lipstadt, 'Foreword' to *From the Protocols of the Elders of Zion to Holocaust Denial Trials: Challenging the Media, the Law, and the Academy*, Debra Kaufman et al. (eds) (New York: Vallentine Mitchell & Co. Ltd, 2007), vi.

At the other extreme of this spectrum, exemplified by Ken McKay's Nizkor Project, is found the claim that it is better expressly to confront such deniers openly. One should not hesitate in pointing out inaccuracies, gaps, contradictions and errors in their use of historical 'evidence' and claims supposedly based on such claims. This careful and well-evidenced type of rebuttal, which resembles a criminal prosecutor's careful dissection of a defendant's alibi, is a more effective response than efforts at censorship or criminalisation of such offensive expressions.

Nevertheless, it would, I suggest, prove counterproductive to engage in an open and public debate with David Irving *et al.* To do so would risk suggesting that established academic historians are recognising his work as the embodiment of genuine scholarship with which one is having merely an academic disagreement for purely scholarly reasons. This is already an excessive and unwarranted concession, which bears little relationship to reality. Attempts by genocide deniers to attract attention to their absurd and politically motivated claims by either involving or provoking public debates with established academics, thus need to be resisted. They must be rejected out of a concern that the very attempt at engagement contains an implicit endorsement that such claims somehow demand scholarly reactions, analysis. It presumes that they are at least potentially legitimate contributions to academic historical debate, which they are clearly not. The idea of my own work directing readers to take seriously Irving's claims as a debating partner is repugnant at every imaginable level: cognitive, political and ethical.

On the other hand, there are dangers in simply passing over in silence the claims of negationists when one has already secured full copies of original documentation that refutes them. This is particularly true where the latter's implications are, when read in context, almost the opposite of that which Irving ascribes to them – for example in relation to the 'tampering with evidence' claim. In my view, there is a lot to be said for Lipstadt's response in her 1993 book *Denying the Holocaust.* This focuses not on debating the truth-quality of the claims, as if these were legitimate contributions to academic debate. Instead, it concentrates on uncovering the questionable pseudo-analytical methods Irving and other Holocaust deniers deploy to falsify the historical record. At least as an instructive act of immunisation, there remains merit in highlighting the methods and techniques through which such polemical works deliberately misrepresent empirical archival evidence. That is, to expose the interpretive recipe being deployed to cook up claims misrepresented as 'factual'. It is useful to show how these methods and techniques aim to give a spurious appearance of 'justification' to pseudo-'conclusions' that were formulated well in advance of any acts of empirical investigation, and in that sense are deeply prejudicial in an emphatic sense of that term.

The libel trials of 1996, which Irving initiated against both Lipstadt and Penguin Books, saw various expert witnesses, including historians Christopher Browning and Richard Evans, present fulsome expert witness essays for the court. These summarised the massively detailed evidence concerning the reality of the Holocaust, and under cross-examination these academics effectively demolished Irving's main arguments to the contrary. The court later fully upheld their critiques in resounding and memorable terms.

My own response to the dilemmas of engagement is set out in a book devoted to the Nuremberg trials. I have presented what I take to be the implications of such evidence, noting in passing – and then only in footnote – the absurdity of efforts to interpret archival documentation as substantiation of the genocide denial agenda. There, I refused to provide any specific source for the latter or to identify its author's name. The last thing I wanted to do there was to give publicity to either these claims or their author's wider projects, or to suggest that readers take them seriously as contributions to academic debate. My overall response has been a negation of a denial in a manner that, through deliberate non-recognition, discredits the latter in passing, and does so in a manner that treats such denial with the contempt the historical evidence itself suggests it deserves.[32]

My second response has been to devote a two-volume study to evidence of the Holocaust gathered, sometimes as a by-product of other activity, by US intelligence agents and intelligence sources (including communication intercepts).[33] This study is grounded in a massive amount of primary documents recently declassified by the CIA, which I extensively quote. The overall implication of both the primary archival material and my account of it is clear. Namely, that nearly all the sources who provided and then analysed evidence of the ongoing Holocaust from 1941 through to the spring of 1945 were unaware of a systematic pre-planned genocidal campaign directed against European Jews. This included leftist German-Jewish research analysts for US intelligence, such as Franz Neumann, Herbert Marcuse and Otto Kirchheimer. Nevertheless, massive evidence of the particular details of phases of precisely such an overarching genocidal campaign clearly informs thousands of pages of original documentation, which my book organises, summarises and presents. These relate to the plunder of works of art and other valuables, and evidence of the operation of death camps. OSS research analysts and others later reworked this material into prosecution briefs.

Although not written expressly as a rebuttal to genocide denial for reasons I have already discussed, any fair reading would conclude that the overall effect is precisely and overwhelmingly that. My book shows how there was undoubtedly an intensifying campaign of persecution culminating in acts of mass murder, the details of which are covered in thousands of different intelligence reports stemming from a multitude of sources. None of the latter possessed any specific interest in even searching out such evidence, let alone in fabricating it. On the contrary, the reality of the unfolding Holocaust thrust itself upon these sources in hundreds of episodic reports generally devoted to quite other topics of more immediate military-strategic interest. These intelligence sources had no concept or word for genocide. Not even OSS German-Jewish research analysts whose

---

32 Salter, *Nazi War Crimes*, 262–3.
33 Salter, *US Intelligence*.

families were among the victims of Nazi genocide were able to comprehend the overall picture as it was unfolding event by event across Europe.

In my book, I discuss the criticism that intelligence analysts were unreasonably slow in piecing together the growing mass of evidence that episodic and localised acts of mass slaughter were indeed part of a single unfolding campaign centrally directed by Eichmann and overseen by Himmler. However, the question of whether these acts actually happened as a matter of historical fact is shown to be so self-evident that their denial can only be considered to be bizarre and perverse. In short, within this specific scholarly field located at the intersection of intelligence history and legal history, my strategy has been to counter genocide denial through the means deniers clearly detest: hundreds of pages of well-sourced descriptions of the details of an unfolding genocidal campaign.

4 Legal and constitutional issues in denying denial

There is little doubt concerning either the social harms committed by acts of denial, or the problems that can stem from inappropriate or counterproductive forms of criminalisation or other forms of legal accountability. Anyone involved in legally grounded research into genocide cannot avoid becoming aware of a range of human rights, constitutional, comparative and international law issues and dilemmas arising from attempts to criminalise expressions of genocide denial, many of which concern the nature, scope and limits of protections for 'freedom of expression'.[34]

We can ask whether legal/constitutional protection of the non-fictional status of historic genocides in effect transforms *public acceptance* of these facts into a mandatory requirement of citizenship, a legally coerced remembrance.[35] If so,

---

34 Yakaré-Oulé (Nani) Jansen, 'Denying Genocide or Denying Free Speech? A Case Study of the Application of Rwanda's Genocide Denial Laws', 12(2) *Journal of International Human Rights* (2014), 191–213; Lawrence R. Douglas, 'Policing the Past: Holocaust Denial and the Law', in *Censorship and Silencing: Practices of Cultural Regulation*, Robert C. Post (ed.) (New York: Getty Research Institute Press, 1998); and also his 'The Memory of Judgment: The Law, the Holocaust, and Denial', 7(2) *History and Memory* (1996), 132; John C. Knechtle, 'When to Regulate Hate Speech', 110(3) *Penn St. L. Rev.* (2006), 539, 552; Viktor Mayer-Schönberger and Teree E. Foster, 'A Regulatory Web: Free Speech and the Global Information Infrastructure', 3 *Mich. Telecomm. Tech. L. Rev.* (1997), 45, available at www.mttlr.org/wp-content/journal/volthree/foster.pdf; Emanuela Fronza, 'The Punishment of Negationism: The Difficult Dialogue Between Law and Memory', 30(609) *Vt. L. Rev.* (2006), 621–2; Russell L. Weaver et al., 'Holocaust Denial and Governmentally Declared "Truth": French and American Perspectives', 41 *Tex. Tech L. Rev.* (2009), 495, 499. The current writer is currently writing a summary of these issues together with proposals for a UK-wide genocide denial law.

35 *Lehideux* judgment, para. 47 (see n 37 below). This argument insists that such prohibitions not only endorse official representations of the past but also impede the reconsideration of explanations based on a review of the past, which is the necessary scholarly activity of all historians.

then – from a human rights perspective – is it the role of the State, supported by legal sanctions, to instruct citizens to accept (or at least not openly dissent from) specific historical beliefs? Should the State promote a mandatory core of basic truths about historical genocides in ways that are analogous to the social values defended by other laws against blasphemy, sedition, treason and defamation?[36] If we accept the policy of granting such historical facts a privileged status of this kind, if only as the lesser evil, this would still provoke familiar human rights objections based on liberal objections to any form of 'censorship'.

In response, it is arguable that our participation in the public discourse of a liberal democratic State presupposes a minimal commitment to regulating truth-telling, good faith and respect for empirical evidence. In turn, such a democratic value commitment requires at least a symbolic form of legal enforcement, particularly in the extreme case represented by expressions of genocide denial oriented towards a fascistic politics.

The fact that some of these issues have been judicially tested with negative outcomes for deniers seeking to abuse the right to 'freedom of expression', including by the European Court of Human Rights, has also generated understandable interest. Arguably, it has been shown that criminalisation can be effected without undue and unwarranted restrictions on other rights.[37] It is difficult to see how the type of research involved in my research programme, whose methodology is archival and empirical, can ever hope to provide categoric answers to the dilemmas involved in criminalisation of denial. Yet this is not necessarily a fatal objection to my own form of socio-legal research, and it certainly does not render it irrelevant to these issues. It is simply that the implications of its findings operate at a different level. Perhaps the best antidote to expressions of denial that falsely

36 One has to be careful with this issue as certain criminal measures against genocide denial clearly are not directed against the mere holding of a negationist opinion as such, and therefore cannot be attacked as 'thought crimes'. For example, the French prohibition requires expression in public places or public meetings by speech, writings, drawings, paintings, emblems, pictures, or transferred by audiovisual means.

37 Paul Lobba, 'Holocaust Denial before the European Court of Human Rights: Evolution of an Exceptional Regime', 26(1) *European Journal of International Law* (February 2015), 237–25 *R Krymowski* [2005] 1 S.C.R. 101; *R Zundel* [1992] 2 S.C.R. 731; *Lehideux v France* (case no. 55/1997/839/1045, application no. 24662/94, Publication 1998-VII, no. 92); *Garaudy v France*, 2003-IX Eur. Ct. H.R. 333, 339–41; *X Federal Republic of Germany*, European Commission of Human Rights 16 (July 1982); *Faurisson v France*, 2 BHRC UN Doc. CCPR/C/58/D/550/1993, 1 (United Nations Human Rights Committee, 1996); *Chauvy v France* (2005) 41 E.H.R.R. 29; *Witzsch v Germany* (App. No.41448/98, April 20, 1999). Cf. S. Gorton, 'The Uncertain Future of Genocide Denial Laws in the European Union', 47(2) *George Washington International Law Review* (May 2015), 421–45. For analysis of how expressions of denial fall outside Art. 10 protections, see Hannes Canni, Dirk Voorhoof, 'The Abuse Clause and Freedom of Expression in the European Human Rights Convention: An Added Value for Democracy and Human Rights Protection', 29 *Neth. Q. Hum. Rts.* (2011), 54; Cooper and Marshall-Williams, 'Hate Speech, Holocaust Denial and International Human Rights', [1999] *E.H.R.L.R.* 693.

claim to be rooted firmly in historical fact is well-researched empirical/archival studies, which are clearly detached from any Zionist political agenda. The overall effect of such studies upon their readership is surely to place the issues raised by deniers into the same category of those of the flat Earth society.

At the level of transnational criminal law policy, personally I believe that, with the possible exception of 'public and direct incitement to genocide' provisions under article 3 of the 1948 Genocide Convention, these constitutional and human rights issues and dilemmas cannot, in any event, be answered 'in principle'. At least, not in a manner that can rightly claim to hold good for every actual or conceivable context of application. The idea that any proposed common approach to transnational legal regulations can be devised that is equally applicable to, and appropriate for, the ultra-liberalism of the US context, a nation whose own history involved mass crimes against indigenous peoples, and – at the other end of the spectrum – Rwanda, the former States of Yugoslavia and Israel, strikes me as fanciful in the extreme.[38] On the other hand, a common European Union position – based on the 2008 Framework Decision – is not at all unrealistic.[39]

It may be comforting to believe that there is a universal human interest in repressing genocide that demands an equally universalistic international criminal law response. However, the facts of even twentieth-century history (even following the creation of the League of Nations and later the United Nations), suggest that more political will and other resources generally tend to be devoted to carrying out genocidal programmes than is allocated to actively resisting them by, say, military or other means, or even prosecuting the perpetrators.[40] It is difficult to imagine another area where the normative/ethical imperatives are so out of kilter with State policies. Yet, there is always the possibility of challenging and defeating false historical claims about historical genocides on their own ground, of showing that the methods and formulae deployed to support such claims do not bear careful scrutiny. Indeed, this is the central message and claim that the present short study has sought to convey and substantiate.

38 Zachary Pall, 'Light Shining Darkly: Comparing Post-Conflict Constitutional Structures Concerning Speech and Association in Germany and Rwanda', 42(1) *Colum. Hum. Rts. L. Rev.* (2010–11), 5. On the dangers of contextually inappropriate over-generalisation and legal transplantation within transnational and comparative legal analysis, see Bogusia Puchalska and Michael Salter, 'Comparing Legal Cultures of Eastern Europe: The Need for a Dialectical Analysis', 16(2) *Legal Studies* (1996), 157–84.
39 Yanis A. Yakiş, 'European Union Framework Decision On the Offence of Denying a Crime', 23 *Review of Armenian Studies* (September 2011), 63–92; A. Kučs, 'Denial of Genocide and Crimes against Humanity in the Jurisprudence of Human Rights Monitoring Bodies', 40(2) *Journal of Ethnic & Migration Studies* (February 2014), 301–19. For a critical view, see Stuart Gorton, 'The Uncertain Future of Genocide Denial Laws in the European Union', 47(2) *George Washington International Law Review* (May 2015), 421–45.
40 Ben Kiernan, *Blood and Soil: A World History of Genocide and Extermination from Sparta to Darfur* (New Haven: Yale University Press, 2009); Robert Gellately, *The Specter of Genocide: Mass Murder in Historical Perspective* (Cambridge: Cambridge University Press, 2003).

5 Conclusion

In my own experience as a legal historian, I have had to confront some of the challenges and dilemmas of responding to genocide denial, and I have sought to articulate and share these experiences in this study, while also discussing the pros and cons of alternative responses. Laws criminalising genocide denial can be supported not as mere qualifications or exceptions to human rights but as reaffirmations of the right to life and the rejection of the abuse of rights that any system of legal rights inevitably presupposes. The insight that all legal research is interpretive and selective, while acts of interpretation necessarily rely on beliefs, assumptions and indeed prejudices that are not fully acknowledged, is not a fatal objection to my arguments. It does not merit responding to my critical remarks as a self-contradictory 'prejudice against prejudice' – as if all prejudices are on a par, and none are more socially dangerous than others. It is simply false to equate the blanket denial of the very existence of a genocidal campaign with a selective interpretation of evidence and the inevitable open-ended revision of the historical record that stems from these contingencies. As a result, while it would make good sense for me to reply constructively to alternative arguments made in response to the present chapter, such that readers could hear a wider range of positions in relation to the challenges raised by denial, it would make no sense to invite a denier to participate in this debate. The selective interpretations and reinterpretations of the former are on a different level from those of the latter.

Chapter 3

Holocaust denial in the age of web 2.0

Negationist discourse since the Irving-Lipstadt trial

Nicholas Terry

Twenty-four years ago, Deborah Lipstadt labelled Holocaust denial a 'growing assault on truth and memory'.[1] How has the phenomenon of Holocaust denial developed in recent years? At first glance, denial appears to be everywhere on the internet. Tap the words into Google, and the curious internet surfer will be rewarded with more than 3.4 million hits to web pages within the English-speaking world alone. Yet raw search engine results tell us little about the true size of actually existing Holocaust denial, or about the vitality of so-called 'Holocaust Revisionism' in the present day. Closer scrutiny of Holocaust denial on the internet suggests that despite a spate of highly publicised news stories, far from growing in recent years, the 'Revisionist' movement is arguably in relative decline.

This chapter therefore offers a brief outline of the recent history of the Holocaust denial movement since the Irving-Lipstadt libel trial at the turn of the millennium in 2000. This date is far from arbitrary, but reflects a genuine turning-point in the history of 'Revisionism', as well as the start of a new phase in the evolution of this movement since the end of the Second World War, stimulated *but also* stymied by the development of internet technology and the arrival of 'web 2.0'. Far from exploiting the new opportunities opened up by the world wide web, 'Revisionists' have found it difficult to compete for attention in a crowded marketplace for fringe ideas, and have been eclipsed by a number of new internet-based conspiracy theories.[2] Moreover, despite the return of conspiracist anti-Semitism after 9/11[3]

---

1 Deborah E. Lipstadt, *Denying the Holocaust. The Growing Assault on Truth and Memory* (New York: The Free Press, 1993).
2 The rise of conspiracy theories and pseudoscientific beliefs in the era of web 2.0 has been the subject of considerable commentary from journalists; see among other accounts David Aaronovitch, *Voodoo Histories. The Role of the Conspiracy Theory in Shaping Modern History* (London: Jonathan Cape, 2009); and Jonathan Kay, *Among the Truthers. A Journey Through America's Growing Conspiracist Underground* (New York: Harper Collins, 2011).
3 See Pierre-André Taguieff, *Precheurs de haine. Traversee de la judeophobie planetaire* (Paris: Mille et une nuits, 2004); Tobias Jaecker, *Antisemitische Verschwörungstheorien nach dem 11. September. Neue Varianten eines alten Deutungsmusters* (Münster: LIT Verlag, 2004).

and a rise in anti-Zionism since the start of the Second Intifada in September 2000,[4] Holocaust denial has been unable to profit from these trends and has failed to attract intellectuals or activists in significant numbers in Western societies. Thus, while Holocaust denial continues to have great brand recognition, it now has surprisingly few customers.[5]

I Three phases in the history of Holocaust denial

Among the many reasons for the stagnation of Holocaust denial is the simple fact that this is no longer a new phenomenon and no longer carries with it the shock of the new or the frisson of an unfamiliar idea. The history of the 'Revisionist' movement can be divided straightforwardly into three phases: an era of gestation and codification from the 1940s through to 1978; a heyday starting with the Faurisson Affair of 1978 through to 2002; and the current era of relative decline from 2002 to the present. Central to the codification of 'Revisionism' as the outright *denial* of the Holocaust was the French author Paul Rassinier, whose writings took on an implacably negationist stance from the end of the 1950s.[6] Although Rassinier was originally on the left, and briefly served as a deputy for the French Socialist Party, negationism circulated almost exclusively within extreme right circles in France,[7] Germany[8] and the United States.[9] In the first era of denial, negationist ideas attracted little mainstream publicity until the so-called 'Auschwitz Lie' offensive mounted by neo-Nazi circles in 1970s West Germany.[10]

The Faurisson Affair of 1978 marked the moment when 'Revisionism' properly entered the public sphere and attracted significant commentary from intellectuals,

4 Robert Wistrich, *A Lethal Obsession. Anti-Semitism from Antiquity to the Global Jihad* (New York: Random House, 2010); Anthony Julius, *Trials of the Diaspora: A History of Anti-Semitism in England* (Oxford: Oxford University Press, 2010); David Hirsh, *Anti-Zionism and Antisemitism: Cosmopolitan Reflections* (New Haven, CT: Yale Initiative for the Interdisciplinary Study of Antisemitism Occasional Papers, 2007), research.gold.ac.uk/2061/. All web links cited were accessed 15 September 2016.

5 As the present author stated to the *Jewish Chronicle* in 2010: 'Holocaust Denial in Decline, Says Historian', *The Jewish Chronicle*, 7 October 2010, www.thejc.com/news/uk-news/39171/holocaust-denial-decline-says-historian

6 Florent Brayard, *Comment l'idee vint a M. Rassinier. Naissance du revisionnisme* (Paris: Fayard, 1996); Nadine Fresco, *Fabrication d'un anti-Semite* (Paris: Seuil, 1999).

7 Valérie Igounet, *Histoire du négationnisme en France* (Paris: Seuil, 2000).

8 Elke Mayer, *Verfälschte Vergangenheit. Zur Entstehung der Holocaust-Leugnung in der Bundesrepublik Deutschland unter besonderer Berücksichtigung rechtsextremer Publizistik von 1945 bis 1970* (Frankfurt am Main: Peter Lang, 2003).

9 Lipstadt, *Denying the Holocaust*.

10 There is currently no scholarly work systematically examining the negationist offensive in Germany during the 1970s. For shorter essays, see Hermann Langbein, 'Überblick über neonazistisches Literatur', *Zeitgeschichte* 2:9–10 (1975), 236–42; as well as Hermann Graml, 'Alte und neue Apologeten Hitlers' in Wolfgang Benz (ed.), *Rechtsextremismus in Deutschland. Voraussetzungen, Zusammenhänge, Wirkungen* (Frankfurt am Main: Fischer, 1984), 30–66.

journalists and academics.[11] Although several first-phase negationist authors had also been university professors,[12] the arguments of Robert Faurisson, professor of literature at the University of Lyons-III, not only grabbed media attention but also prompted refutation and reflection in an intellectual climate shaped on the one hand by postmodernism and on the other by the globalisation of the collective memory of the Holocaust.[13] Inspired by Faurisson's success in attracting attention, Willis Carto, the shadowy director of the American extreme right organisation Liberty Lobby, established the Institute for Historical Review (IHR) in 1979 as a pseudoscholarly clearing-house for a now fully internationalised Holocaust denial movement. From 1979 to 2002, the IHR organised a series of 'Revisionist' conferences to bring together Holocaust deniers from around the world while also publishing a quarterly, later bimonthly, *Journal of Historical Review*.[14] A series of public scandals in France together with two widely publicised trials of Canadian neo-Nazi activist Ernst Zündel in 1985 and 1988[15] convinced 'Revisionists' that they now had momentum, a belief bolstered by the conversion of the right-wing popular historian David Irving to the 'Revisionist' cause and by a new-found emphasis on physical evidence.

This 'forensic turn' in negationism, exemplified by the infamous Leuchter report and its tests of cyanide traces in the ruins of the gas chambers of Birkenau,[16] marked a shift from the pseudohistory of Rassinier and Faurisson towards

11 The Faurisson Affair has generated an extremely substantial literature. See in particular Nadine Fresco, 'The Deniers of the Dead', *Dissent* (Fall 1981, original: 1980); Pierre Vidal-Naquet, 'Un Eichmann du papier', *Esprit* (1980), reprinted and translated into English in *Assassins of Memory* (New York: Columbia University Press, 1992); Alain Finkielkraut, *The Future of a Negation. Reflections on the Question of Genocide* (Lincoln: University of Nebraska Press, 1998, original: 1982). The most comprehensive study is Igounet, *Histoire du négationnisme*, 199–405; and most recently, Igounet, *Robert Faurisson. Portrait d'un négationniste* (Paris: Éditions Denoël, 2012).
12 Among others, Austin App, David Hoggan, Harry Elmer Barnes and Arthur Butz; cf Lipstadt, *Denying the Holocaust*.
13 Daniel Levy and Natan Sznajder, *The Holocaust and Memory in the Global Age* (Philadelphia: Temple University Press, 2006).
14 Frank P. Mintz, *The Liberty Lobby and the American Right. Race, Conspiracy, and Culture* (Westport, CT: Praeger, 1985); George Michael, *Willis Carto and the American Far Right* (Gainesville: University Press of Florida, 2008). Carto and the IHR are also given substantial coverage in Leonard Zeskind, *Blood and Politics: The History of White Nationalism from the Margins to the Mainstream* (London: Macmillan, 2009).
15 As with the Faurisson Affair, the literature on the Zündel trials is now substantial. See among other works Gabriel Weimann and Conrad Winn, 'The Misperception of Public Opinion: The Canadian Nazi Trials and their Implications', *PS* 19:3 (1986), 641–5; Alan Davies, 'A Tale of Two Trials: Antisemitism in Canada 1985', *Holocaust and Genocide Studies* 4:1 (1989), 77–88; Lawrence Douglas, *The Memory of Judgement. Making Law and History in the Trials of the Holocaust* (New Haven: Yale University Press, 2001), 212–56; Marouf J. Hasian, *Rhetorical Vectors of Memory in National and International Holocaust Trials* (East Lansing: Michigan State University Press, 2006), 109–31.
16 Shelley Shapiro (ed.), *Truth Prevails. Demolishing Holocaust Denial. The End of the Leuchter Report* (New York: Beate Klarsfeld Foundation, 1990); Robert Jan Van Pelt, *The Case*

pseudoscientific argumentation. After the errors of the Leuchter report were swiftly exposed, German negationists tried to improve on the gambit with a new forensic report by a young German doctoral student of chemistry, Germar Rudolf, whose 'Rudolf Report' helped sustain a prolonged propaganda offensive in reunified Germany during the first half of the 1990s.[17] Simultaneously, American revisionists were scoring their greatest successes in garnering media attention, including TV appearances, achievements which went some way to justifying the contemporary alarmism expressed in Deborah Lipstadt's description of denial as a *growing* assault on truth and memory.

With hindsight, however, the seeds of the eventual disintegration of the 'IHR coalition' became visible around this same time. In 1993, control of the IHR was wrested from Willis Carto by disgruntled employees in a dispute over the disbursement of a substantial inheritance and over ideological disagreements.[18] Throughout the second era of 'Revisionism', advocacy of Holocaust denial in Europe remained almost entirely confined to the extreme right, despite the high-profile support given to Faurisson by a small number of far left activists.[19] The instrumentalisation of denial as political propaganda by far right parties in France, Germany and the UK[20] reflected the greater chances of electoral success for such parties in Europe. By contrast, while a number of white nationalist groupuscules in the United States and Canada advocated and espoused denial, the IHR always sought to propagate the idea more widely, especially within traditionalist or fundamentalist Christian denominations and the Libertarian movement. The attempted 'mainstreaming' of 'Revisionism' also brought in many aficionados who were less than comfortable with the naked Hitler-worship displayed by many within Carto's inner circle.[21] Deprived of the financial support of the Liberty Lobby, the IHR turned to the internet in the mid-1990s,[22] at the

for Auschwitz. Evidence from the Irving Trial (Bloomington: Indiana University Press, 2002), 354–98.

17 This phase is well covered in Anthony Long, 'Forgetting the Führer: The Recent History of the Holocaust Denial Movement in Germany', *Australian Journal of Politics and History*, 48:1 (2002), 72–84.

18 The split, resulting from an internecine squabble over an inheritance from a member of the Edison family, is comprehensively covered in Michael, *Willis Carto and the American Far Right*, 195–208.

19 The phenomenon of left-wing negationism is a central topic of the literature on the Faurisson Affair; on this see also chapter one of Elhanan Yakira, *Post-Zionism, Post-Holocaust. Three Essays on Denial, Forgetting, and the Delegitimation of Israel* (Cambridge: Cambridge University Press, 2010).

20 Michael Whine, 'Holocaust Denial in the United Kingdom' in Jan Hermann Brinks, Stella Rock and Edward Rimms (eds), *Nationalist Myths and Modern Media. Contested Identities in the Age of Globalisation* (London: I.B. Tauris, 2005), 69–81.

21 Michael Shemer and Alex Grobman, *Denying History. Who Says the Holocaust Never Happened and Why Do They Say It?* (Berkeley: University of California Press, 2000), 101–2.

22 Mark Weber, 'Internet Web Site Offers Instant Worldwide Access to Revisionism', *Journal of Historical Review* (hereafter JHR), 16:1 (1996), 40.

same time as other prominent deniers established their first websites, with the Zündelsite as well as the website of the Committee for the Open Debate on the Holocaust (CODOH) emerging as front runners in the era of 'web 1.0'.

While 'Revisionists' hailed the internet as the ideal medium to promote their 'counterhegemonic discourse'[23] and wage guerrilla warfare against mainstream consensus, from the outset, denier ideas on the internet were contested. Early efforts to channel propaganda via the Usenet discussion list alt.revisionism were challenged by amateur 'anti-revisionists', initially organised around the Canadian-based website Nizkor, later by the Holocaust History Project, members of which offered crucial support in the climax to the second era of negationism, the libel case against Deborah Lipstadt brought by the British Holocaust denier David Irving in early 2000.

The ensuing defeat in the Irving-Lipstadt trial exposed the internal contradictions within 'Revisionism' and destroyed the credibility of a series of denier arguments, especially regarding the death camp of Auschwitz-Birkenau.[24] Irving's tactical decision to concede other extermination sites to concentrate on Auschwitz was viewed as a strategic error by his fellow 'Revisionists', who decried his refusal to submit an expert report by Germar Rudolf in his appeal, and who rapidly distanced themselves from the former public face of the movement.[25] In the wake of Irving's defeat, the chickens also came home to roost from the 1993 split between Liberty Lobby and IHR.[26] The trial had led to renewed media scrutiny of the 'Revisionist' project, and the IHR helpfully staged two final conferences in 2000 and 2001 to allow magazines and newspapers to get an inside look at the rump of the scene.[27] After limping on for two more years, the *Journal for Historical Review* suspended publication in early 2003, having completed the delayed run of six issues for 2002. From around 6,000 subscribers at the time of the split with Carto, the journal now had fewer than 300.[28] One of the IHR's prominent critics, Germar Rudolf, was himself forced to admit two years later that the number

23 Barney Warf and John Grimes, 'Counterhegemonic Discourses and the Internet', *Geographical Review* 87:2 (1997), 259–74.
24 The trial is now the subject of a substantial literature; see D.D. Guttenplan, *The Holocaust on Trial. History, Justice and the David Irving Libel Case* (London: Granta, 2001); Richard Evans, *Telling Lies about Hitler. The Holocaust, History and the David Irving Trial* (London: Verso, 2002); Van Pelt, *The Case for Auschwitz*; Deborah E. Lipstadt, *History on Trial. My Day in Court with a Holocaust Denier* (New York: Harper Perennial, 2005).
25 E.g. Costas Zaverdinos, 'Suppressing Debate about Auschwitz: The Rudolf Case, Irving's Libel Suit and the Future of Revisionism', *JHR* 19:4 (2000), 26ff.
26 Yale Edeiken, 'The IHR at the Crossroads', 2002, www.holocaust-history.org/ihr/
27 John Sack, 'Inside the Bunker', *Esquire* 135 (February 2001), 98–105, 138, 140; Mark Weber, 'John Sack's Defective Esquire Article', *JHR* 19:6 (2001), 26ff; Robert H. Countess, 'Esquire Magazine berichtet über Revisionismus. Hintergrund zu John Sacks Kontakten zum Revisionismus', *Vierteljahreshefte für freie Geschichtsforschung* (VffG), 5:1 (2001), 81–4.
28 Germar Rudolf, 'IHR: Is the Ship Sinking? Background and Effects of a Nine-Year Crisis' and Ted O'Keefe, 'Exit the Whistleblower: My Fall from Grace at IHR', both VHO, 2002, www.vho.org/GB/c/GR/IHRCrisis.html

of subscribers to his own journal, the *Vierteljahreshefte für freie Geschichtsforschung*, had fallen below 600, and the journal was no longer covering its costs.[29]

The reasons for the commercial decline of 'Revisionism' in print form were multiple. First, the audience for 'Revisionism' had been steadily ageing since the 1980s, and was not significantly rejuvenating itself.[30] A number of once-prominent 'Revisionist' authors passed away in the years after 2002, including the Belgian researcher Jean-Marie Boisdefeu, the German negationist Wilhelm Stäglich and the French writer Roger Garaudy. Second, the internet strategy had backfired on the negationists by removing any incentive for all but the most committed supporters to pay for the journals or books. While negationist literature was duplicated all across the internet, no money made its way back to the publishers unless readers felt like digging deep into their pockets to subsidise the endeavours. Finally, the impact of the Irving trial defeat cannot be underestimated; after several decades of trying, 'Revisionism' had manifestly failed to deliver on the repeated promises to destroy the 'hoax' of the Holocaust. The attempt to go mainstream, identified by Michael Shermer and Alex Grobman in 2000, ironically foundered within two years of the libel trial defeat.[31]

The demise of the IHR caused a number of sometime stalwarts to cease contributing to the remaining journals or website outlets. Samuel Crowell, the most prominent author of the web 1.0 generation, submitted no new articles after 2002, only resurfacing briefly in 2011 to publish a slightly revised edition of his earlier work, before vanishing again.[32] Others, such as Enrique Aynat, had already ceased activity at the end of the 1990s.[33] In 2003, Germar Rudolf reported that 'Dr. Robert H. Countess … recently felt that revisionism in the English world is "imploding", and Prof. Arthur R. Butz called the current activities in this field "comatose"'.[34]

Other 'Revisionist' leaders, meanwhile, openly declared their apostasy from the cause. After spending a year in Austrian jail in 2006 on charges dating back to the 1990s, David Irving significantly distanced himself from 'Revisionism' in an interview in *The Guardian* in the autumn of 2007, accepting the facticity of extermination in the so-called Operation Reinhard camps of Belzec, Sobibor and

29 Germar Rudolf, 'Übergabe', *VffG*, 8:4 (2004), 370. Rudolf also claimed to have incurred debts of €20,000 to his printers and $20,000 to his attorney fighting his asylum appeal.

30 See on this Aryeh Tuchman, 'Generational Changes in the Holocaust Denial Movement in the United States' in Alvin H. Rosenfeld (ed.), *Deciphering the New Antisemitism* (Bloomington: Indiana University Press, 2015), 350–72.

31 Michael Shermer and Alex Grobman, *Denying History: Who Says the Holocaust Never Happened and Why do they Say it?* (Berkeley, CA: University of California Press, 2000), 101–2.

32 Samuel Crowell, *The Gas Chamber of Sherlock Holmes and Other Writings on the Holocaust, Revisionism, and Historical Understanding* (Charleston, WV: Nine-Banded Books, 2011).

33 Robert Faurisson, 'Sombre bilan du révisionnisme historique. Nouvelle perspective', AAARGH, 2 (2004).

34 Germar Rudolf, 'The Dawning of a New Era', *The Revisionst* 1:1 (2003), 2.

Treblinka while continuing to equivocate over Auschwitz.[35] This stance provoked outrage from the remaining diehards, who rewrote the history of their movement and denied that Irving had ever really been 'one of them' all along.[36] In January 2009, the director of the IHR, Mark Weber, since reduced to maintaining a news-orientated website and appearing on far right talk radio shows in the United States, announced to the horror of his onetime comrades that Holocaust revisionism was no longer relevant to the cause of anti-Zionism.[37] In responding to Weber's intervention, one of the more reflective negationists came close to admitting the intellectual bankruptcy of the enterprise. 'Is revisionism dead?' asked Serge Thion. 'As an open quest, an intellectual commitment, it has probably reached its limits.'[38] A few years later, the Danish 'Revisionist' Christian Lindtner openly declared his opposition to denial, provoking further outrage from the true believers.[39]

2 Gurus

Nonetheless, the third phase of 'Revisionism' after 2000–02 saw the denier movement regroup and retrench in certain respects. Above all, the demise of the IHR forced a reconsideration of *where* and *how* 'Revisionist' ideas were to be published. The mere existence of an 'institute' camouflaged several grave weaknesses in second-phase 'Revisionism', namely its lack of scholarly prowess. None of the erstwhile directors of the IHR possessed doctorates, while the *Journal of Historical Review* devoted significant space to non-Holocaust topics as well as puff pieces.[40] From 1997 to 2005, therefore, the German negationist Germar Rudolf attempted to rectify the credibility gap by publishing a more heavyweight journal alongside a series of 'Holocaust Handbooks' designed to showcase 'Revisionist' research achievements.[41] Thus, paradoxically, the period *after* 2000 represented the high-water mark of 'Revisionist' pseudoscholarship, both in terms of output as well as quality. Under Rudolf's aegis, a firm distinction emerged between 'guru' researchers and 'cheerleader' authors capable only of writing puff pieces or regurgitating other people's ideas. Erstwhile gurus such as Faurisson, meanwhile,

35 Matthew Taylor, 'Discredited Irving Plans Comeback Tour', *The Guardian*, 29 September 2007.
36 Jürgen Graf, 'David Irving and the "Aktion Reinhardt Camps"', *Inconvenient History*, 1:2 (2009).
37 Mark Weber, 'How Relevant is Holocaust Revisionism', IHR website, 7 January 2009, www.ihr.org/weber_revisionism_jan09.html
38 Serge Thion, 'On Mark Weber's Gloomy Mood', January 2009, vho.org/aaargh/fran/livres9/OnMarkWeber.pdf
39 Jürgen Graf, 'The Moral and Intellectual Bankruptcy of a Scholar: Dr. Christian Lindtner and Holocaust Revisionism', *National Journal*, 22 July 2011, globalfire.tv/nj/11en/history/Graf_on_Lindtner_01.htm
40 Shemer/Grobman, *Denying History*, 77–80.
41 Thirty-three volumes have been published or reprinted in this series. See holocausthandbooks.com

were relegated to cheerleader status after it became clear they were incapable of contributing semi-serious research articles and no longer attempted to use primary sources.[42]

Since 2000, the most prominent negationist researchers have been the Italian negationist Carlo Mattogno, active since 1985, the Swiss anti-Semite Jürgen Graf, active since the early 1990s, and the Swedish writer Thomas Kues (a pseudonym), the sole author of any note to emerge in third-phase 'Revisionism'. Mattogno in particular stands out for his hyperproductivity, having authored or co-authored close to 50 books and pamphlets in 30 years. Unlike the overwhelming majority of 'Revisionist' authors, Mattogno, Graf and Kues (MGK) cite primary sources and have conducted archival research, yet none of them is in fact a properly trained historian, nor does any of them possess more than a Master's degree in any other discipline. Thus, while MGK have undoubtedly raised the quality of negationist research to a new level, this has come at the expense of an increasing isolation and inability to communicate their ideas to other 'Revisionists', much less mainstream academics.

Mattogno's output after 2000 began by trying to shut the Auschwitz stable door after the horse had bolted during the Irving-Lipstadt trial: the overwhelming majority of his publications still focus on Auschwitz. Yet the increased sophistication masks a deeper inability to summarise negationist arguments succinctly and coherently, leading other once-prominent 'Revisionists' such as Arthur Butz and Robert Faurisson to criticise Mattogno in particular for his longwinded and overly technical approach.[43] As Faurisson noted in 2011, 'for a very long time he appeared to me as a man suffering a terrible complex because he was not a scholar. This already is not a sign of intelligence'.[44] Mattogno's response to this criticism[45] betrays the fundamentally pseudoscholarly nature of negationism, because it is quite clear that no one is peer reviewing or making constructive criticisms of his work. This deficiency is replicated in Mattogno's work with Graf and Kues on the Operation Reinhard camps of Belzec, Sobibor and Treblinka, where the reader can easily find significant contradictions between the three authors.[46]

In style and approach, third-phase 'Revisionism' differs relatively little from its second-phase predecessor; only marginal changes can be noted at the level of

42 Just four unpublished documents are cited across the 1 million words of Faurisson's collected writings to 1998; cf Robert Faurisson, *Écrits revisionnistes* (Paris, 1998); on this bluff see also Ignounet, *Histoire du négationnisme*, 255–9.

43 Arthur R. Butz, 'Two Cutting-Edge Works of Revisionism', 4 October 2011, revblog. codoh.com/2011/09/two-cutting-edge-works-of-holocaust-revisionism/#more-1607

44 Email from Robert Faurisson to Arthur Butz, 3 October 2011, reproduced on groups. yahoo.com/group/ReportersNotebook/message/7445

45 Carlo Mattogno, 'Arthur Butz and "Auschwitz The Case for Sanity": An Insufficiently Dispassionate Review', 2 January 2012, revblog.codoh.com/2012/01/arthur-butz-and-auschwitz-the-case-for-sanity-an-insufficiently-dispassionate-review/#more-1693

46 Published between 2002 and 2010. See note 41.

content. No new studies of Holocaust demographics have been attempted by negationists since the 1980s, despite the importance of the 'numbers game' to earlier authors such as Rassinier;[47] denial remains fixated on gas chambers, cremation and killing sites. However, negationists have been totally unable to repeat the forensic coups of Leuchter and Rudolf, with little effort being made to carry out pseudoscientific experiments 'in the field'. The last such attempt, a claimed ground penetration radar survey of Treblinka by the Australian engineer Richard Krege associated with the Adelaide Institute, has like its predecessors fallen flat, because more than a decade on, the alleged study remains entirely unpublished[48] and has been refuted by the results of professional archaeological investigations. These studies – undertaken at Belzec, Sobibor, Treblinka and Chelmno over the past 15 years[49] – now form the object of obsessive and ghoulish commentaries by Mattogno as well as lesser luminaries. While the gurus have examined all major extermination camps associated with the Holocaust, there is still no comprehensive negationist study of the 'Holocaust by bullets' in Poland and the occupied Soviet Union. Although MGK announced their intention to embark on such a study in 2011,[50] both Graf and Kues subsequently dropped out of the project due to other commitments, leaving Mattogno to finish it on his own.[51]

Pseudoscholarly 'Revisionism' bears all the hallmarks of a 'degenerating research programme', to use the terminology of the philosopher of science Imre Lakatos. In this regard, negationism mirrors a common tendency among conspiracy theory pseudoscholarship more generally.[52] Not only are there simply fewer 'Revisionist' researchers, but their books have lengthened as the gurus are forced to confront a larger body of evidence for the Holocaust. Moreover, denier research remains resolutely negationist, with significantly more effort expended attacking eyewitnesses, documents and forensic evidence generally thought to

47 Alfred Kokh and Pavel Polian (eds), *Denial of the Denial, Or: The Battle of Auschwitz: The Demography and Geopolitics of the Holocaust: The View from the Twenty-First Century* (Boston: Academic Studies Press, 2012; Russian original: 2008).

48 'Treblinka Ground Penetration Radar Examination Finds No Trace of Mass Graves', *JHR* 19:3 (2000), 20.

49 Andrzej Kola, *Bełżec: The Nazi Camp for Jews in Light of Archaeological Sources: Excavations 1997–1999* (Warsaw and Washington: The Council for the Protection of Memory of Combat and Martyrdom and the United States Holocaust Memorial Museum, 2000); Andrzej Kola, 'Badania archeologiczne terenu byłego obozu zagłady Żydów w Sobiborze', *Przeszłość i Pamięć. Biuletyn Rady Ochroni Pamięci Walk i Męczeństwa* 4 (2001); Isaac Gilead, Yoram Haimi and Wojciech Mazurek, 'Excavating Nazi Extermination Centres', *Present Pasts* 1:1 (2009), 10–39; Łucja Pawlicka-Nowak, 'Archaeological Research in the Grounds of the Chełmno-on-Ner Former Extermination Center', in Łucja Pawlicka-Nowak (ed.), *Chełmno Witnesses Speak* (Łódź, 2004), 42–67; Caroline Sturdy Colls, 'Holocaust Archaeology: Archaeological Approaches to Landscapes of Nazi Genocide and Persecution', *Journal of Conflict Archaeology* 7:2 (2012), 7–104.

50 Thomas Kues, 'Facing a New Decade', *Smith's Report* 179 (February 2011), 7.

51 Now scheduled for December 2017: holocausthandbooks.com/index.php?page_id=39

52 Steve Clarke, 'Conspiracy Theories and Conspiracy Theorizing', *Philosophy of the Social Sciences* 32:2 (2002), 131–50.

prove mass murder than in locating any evidence that might support 'Revisionist' conspiracy claims about Allied and Soviet manipulation, or which might prove an alternative explanation of the fate of the Jews in Nazi and Axis hands.

All of the remaining negationist gurus combine a deep and abiding ignorance of the overwhelming majority of recent Holocaust research with *ad hominem* attacks on historians and an obsessive 'refutational' style aimed at real or hallucinated debate partners,[53] something which also marks out other 'revisionist' schools of history writing.[54] Yet these arguments are largely howled into the void, since the response to MGK's work has been a deafening silence from academics. This in turn has led MGK to believe they are really onto something, in a classic illustration of the topsy-turvy circular logic of fringe pseudoscholars, since the lack of response from academics must mean that historians *cannot* refute the negationist gurus.[55] What emerges, above all else, from surveying the work of 'serious' revisionism is, moreover, its striking irrelevance to the concerns of contemporary Holocaust research.[56]

3 Cheerleaders

The degeneration of the 'Revisionist' research programme is most visible in the activities and antics of the somewhat larger pool of 'cheerleader' deniers. This category includes both dedicated propagandists and prominent advocates for the 'Revisionist' cause who are better known for other beliefs. What both groups share in common is that neither contributes in any meaningful way to the

53 In 2011, a 'history workshop' of amateur and trained historians, including the present author, produced a lengthy refutation of MGK's work; see 'Holocaust Controversies, Belzec Sobibor Treblinka. Holocaust Denial and Operation Reinhard. A Critique of the Falsehoods of Mattogno, Graf and Kues' (December 2011), archive.org/details/ BelzecSobiborTreblinka.HolocaustDenialAndOperationReinhard.ACritique. A 1396-page response appeared in the autumn of 2013, bloated to more than twice the length of the refutation by 'fisking' it paragraph by paragraph, rendering the response largely unreadable. Carlo Mattogno, Jürgen Graf, Thomas Kues, *The 'Extermination Camps' of 'Aktion Reinhardt' – An Analysis and Refutation of Factitious 'Evidence', Deceptions and Flawed Argumentation of the 'Holocaust Controversies' Bloggers* (Uckfield: Castle Hill, 2013).

54 See the comments by Michael Witzel on Indian nationalist pseudohistoriography in 'Rama's Realm: Indocentric Rewritings of Early South Asian Archaeology and History' in Garret G. Fagan (ed.), *Archaeological Fantasies: How Pseudoarchaeology Misrepresents the Past and Misleads the Public* (London: Routledge, 2006), 206–7.

55 It is striking that the majority of responses to or refutations of negationism since the Faurisson affair have been produced by non-specialists; only in rare cases have historians of the Holocaust become involved in this pseudocontroversy, usually in the course of trials such as the Zündel or Irving-Lipstadt cases. On the dilemma of responding to fringe claims and stimulating the impression of a debate between two 'sides', see in particular Michael D. Gordin, *The Pseudoscience Wars: Immanuel Velikovsky and the Birth of the Modern Fringe* (Chicago: University of Chicago Press, 2012).

56 This irrelevance answers one of the questions posed in Berel Lang, 'Six Questions on or about Holocaust Denial', *History and Theory* 49 (2010), 157–68.

development of 'Revisionism' as a body of ideas. Instead, the cheerleaders comment journalistically on the legal repression, academic exclusion and social taboos provoked by Holocaust denial in an effort to stimulate interest in the belief system. As so few negationists engage in anything even vaguely resembling proper historical research, the output of the cheerleaders tends to dominate denier websites and journals, with the result that most articles produced by deniers amount to navel gazing, unwarranted victory dancing or hopelessly amateur attempts at doing history whose assertions are frequently at odds with the research output of past or present gurus. Thus, of 40 contributors to the *Inconvenient History* online journal since 2009, less than a quarter are even pretending to write history.[57] Similarly, the controversial Adelaide Institute in Australia, led by Frederik Töben, produces literally nothing that can be considered even pseudoscholarship, contenting itself with reprinting articles and news stories about 'Revisionism', the Holocaust, the Middle East conflict, or 9/11 conspiracy theories.[58]

With the demise of the IHR, the centre of gravity within the 'Revisionist' movement passed briefly to the Vrij Historisch Onderzoek (VHO) website, originally set up by Siegfried Verbeke[59] and then operated by Germar Rudolf until his arrest and extradition to Germany in 2005 after a failed attempt at claiming asylum in the United States.[60] The deportation of Ernst Zündel from Canada to Germany that same year relegated the once-significant Zündelsite to a position of near-irrelevance, while incompetence from the New York 'Revisionist' Michael Santomauro and German activists left in charge of VHO confirmed CODOH as the central clearing house for 'Revisionist' activism on the internet. In the early 2000s, VHO had already absorbed the French website L'Association des Anciens Amateurs de Récits de Guerres et d'Holocaustes (AAARGH), founded in 1996 by sometime Faurisson supporter Pierre Guillaume.[61]

Although a number of print journals and newspapers, including *The Barnes Review*, set up by Willis Carto after his ouster from the IHR, do occasionally feature 'Revisionist' content, the changes wrought by web 2.0 have more or less killed off denial within print culture.[62] More disturbing for the true believers is the manner in which 'Revisionism' has fallen out of fashion on much of the extreme right as a whole. In Europe, the majority of parties of the populist, radical or extreme right have formally distanced themselves from neo-Nazism, anti-Semitism or Holocaust

57 inconvenienthistory.com/index.php
58 Danny Ben-Moshe, 'Holocaust Denial in Australia', *Analysis of Current Trends in Anti-semitism* 25 (Jerusalem: SICSA, 2005), sicsa.huji.ac.il/acta25.pdf
59 A sometime member of the Flemish extreme-right party Vlaams Blok before its reformation as Vlaams Belang.
60 The failed asylum case and his two court cases in Germany are documented on his website at germarrudolf.com/persecution/, with virtually all relevant sources uploaded.
61 vho.org/aaargh/index.html. This sub-site has not been updated since May 2011.
62 On extreme-right print culture in the USA, see Chip Berlet, 'The Write Stuff: U.S. Serial Print Culture from Conservatives out to Neo-Nazis', *Library Trends* 56:3 (2008), 570–600.

denial, either to avoid prosecution under laws against incitement for racial hatred, or in order to repackage and 'mainstream' themselves. Open propagandising for Holocaust denial contributed to the lowest ever electoral results for the German National Democratic Party (NPD) under Günter Deckert, so that the NPD abandoned this tactic under Udo Voigt's chairmanship from 1996 to 2011,[63] while the British National Party (BNP) sought to distance itself from its neo-Nazi roots during the 2000s; in France, the Front National under Marine Le Pen has similarly tried to de-emphasise negationism.[64] Although Holocaust denial was undoubtedly a common 'metapolitical discourse' on the extreme right through to the 1990s,[65] it is debatable whether that is still really the case for far right or right-wing populist parties seeking to compete in open elections. The rise of Greece's Golden Dawn was somewhat tempered by the widespread condemnation of its leaders for advocating Holocaust denial, and is more the exception than the rule.[66]

Due to the two-party system in US politics, the extreme right in America has long tended towards 'groupuscularisation',[67] but even in white nationalist circles, 'Revisionism' is more and more seen as an unnecessary distraction. While David Duke remains a committed Holocaust denier and anti-Semite,[68] other prominent figures within white nationalism and 'race realism' either do not advocate denial or have openly queried its utility, *despite* remaining strongly committed to anti-Semitism. Thus, Kevin Macdonald, editor of the *Occidental Quarterly* and *Occidental Observer* journals and websites, refuses to promote denial on his websites, and allowed white nationalist Greg Johnson, editor of the Counter Currents website, to publish an article calling into question the relevance of 'Revisionism' to racialist politics,[69] inevitably provoking furious responses from diehards.[70] Other white nationalist bloggers have echoed this scepticism, labelling Holocaust denial 'strategic

---

63 Torauf Staud, *Moderne Nazis. Die neuen Rechten und der Aufstieg der NPD* (Jena: Kiepenheuer & Witsch, 2005).
64 Nigel Copsey, 'Changing Course or Changing Clothes? Reflections on the Ideological Evolution of the British National Party 1999–2006', *Patterns of Prejudice* 41:1 (2007), 61–82; Matthew J. Goodwin, 'Activism in Contemporary Extreme Right Parties: The Case of the British National Party (BNP)', *Journal of Elections, Public Opinion & Parties* 20:1 (2010), 31–54.
65 Roger Griffin, 'Interregnum or Endgame? Radical Right Thought in the "Postfascist" Era', *The Journal of Political Ideologies* 5:2 (2000), 163–78.
66 'Greek Gov't, Jews Slam Golden Dawn Chief for Holocaust Denial', Jewish Telegraphic Agency, 15 May 2012, www.jta.org/news/article/2012/05/15/3095476/greek-neo-nazi-head-condemned-for-holocaust-denial
67 Roger Griffin, 'From Slime Mould to Rhizome: An Introduction to the Groupuscular Right', *Patterns of Prejudice* 37:1 (2003), 27–50.
68 David Duke, *Jewish Supremacism: My Awakening to the Jewish Question* (Covington, LA: Free Speech Press, 2004), 267–314.
69 Greg Johnson, 'Dealing with the Holocaust', *Occidental Observer*, 20 July 2012, www.theoccidentalobserver.net/2012/07/dealing-with-the-holocaust/
70 Thomas Dalton, 'Nationalism and the Holocaust: A Reply to Greg Johnson', 31 July 2012, online at thewhitenetwork.com/2012/08/08/nationalism-and-the-holocaust-a-reply-to-greg-johnson/

buffoonery'.[71] While most on the extreme right remain emotionally and intellec-
tually wedded to anti-Semitism, other perceived threats, especially from Islam,
have even led some rightist intellectuals to reject anti-Semitism, as did the *nouvelle
droite* author Guillaume Faye.[72]

The ranks of cheerleaders for denial are therefore increasingly filled by
ex-members of far right parties, anti-Semites inspired by Christian or Islamic
traditionalism or fundamentalism, and a small number of secular anti-Zionists.
Ex-BNP activist Simon Shepperd was convicted in 2008 along with Luke O'Farrell
for content on the website heretical.com, including Holocaust denial expressed
with such virulent anti-Semitism that it violated the existing UK law against
incitement to racial hatred.[73] In Germany, the former Red Army Faction left-
wing terrorist-turned-neo-Nazi and ex-NPD member Horst Mahler and his partner, the lawyer Sylvia Stolz, were both convicted of incitement after
they harangued courts with a combination of overt Hitler-worship, extreme
anti-Semitism, and Holocaust denial.[74]

In the latter part of the 2000s, the endorsement of 'Revisionism' by Christian
or Islamic traditionalists and fundamentalists commanded much attention from
the media. Yet this has had virtually no effect on the visible growth of 'Holocaust
Revisionism'. The controversial remarks of the sedevacantist Bishop Richard
Williamson reflect a certain wellspring of support for negationism among traditionalist Catholics in France and elsewhere.[75] A number of 'Revisionist' movement activists, most notably Vincent Reynouard, also hail from a sedevacantist

71 Matt Parrott, 'Holocaust Denial as Strategic Buffoonery', *Occidental Dissent*, 7 July
    2010, www.occidentaldissent.com/2010/07/07/holocaust-denial-as-strategic-buffoon
    ery/#comments
72 Guillaume Faye, *La nouvelle question juive* (Chevaigné: Editions du Lore, 2007). Faye's
    'apostasy' was challenged by others on the 'new right' as well as, inevitably, by die-
    hard deniers. See the review by Michael O'Meara in *The Occidental Quarterly* 7:3
    (2007), 71–83, online at www.toqonline.com/archives/v7n3/7310OMearaFaye.pdf,
    as well as Jürgen Graf, '"The New Jewish Question", or The End of Guillaume
    Faye', CODOH, 29 October 2007, www.codoh.com/viewpoints/vpfaye.html
73 Dan Cohn-Sherbok, 'Neo-Nazism, Holocaust Denial and UK Law', *European Judaism*
    43:1 (2010), 105–15.
74 George Michael, 'The Ideological Evolution of Horst Mahler: The Far Left–Extreme
    Right Synthesis', *Studies in Conflict & Terrorism* 32:4 (2009), 346–66; Agence France
    Presse – German, 'Neonazi Horst Mahler soll Haft bis zum Schluß verbüßen – OLG
    hebt Aussetzung der Strafe zur Bewährung auf', 22 January 2016; Bürstädter Zei-
    tung, 'Haftstrafe für Nazi-Anwältin; Gericht Hitler als "Erlöser" bezeichnet', 11 May
    2009. See also Chapter 5 below.
75 Jean-Yves Camus, 'The French Extreme Right, Anti-Semitism, and Anti-Zionism
    (1945–2009)', *Holocaust. Studii și cercetări* 1:5 (2012), 175–89; J. Christopher Pryor,
    'Traditional Catholicism and the Teachings of Bishop Richard Williamson', *Journal
    for the Study of Antisemitism* 1:2 (2009), 233–52; on the PR disaster for the Vatican, see
    César García, 'Could it Happen Again? Catholic Church Image Repair Strategies in
    the Revocation of the Excommunication of the Four Lefebvrian Bishops', *Public
    Relations Review* 36:1 (2010), 70–2.

background. More problematic for Western 'Revisionists' has been the endorsement of denial by President Mahmoud Ahmadinejad of Iran and by other Islamist figures.[76] The so-called 'International Conference to Review the Global Vision of the Holocaust' in December 2006 turned into a complete disaster for 'Revisionism', as Iran failed to follow through with any significant further support, while the conference participants – including Robert Faurisson, Bradley Smith of CODOH, and the white nationalist politician David Duke – failed to capitalise on the platform by offering substantive work. Both Williamson and Ahmadinejad have also endorsed 9/11 conspiracy theories, further neutralising the propaganda benefit of their advocacy of either competing fringe belief. While Holocaust denial circulates widely in Islamic circles both in the Middle East and worldwide, this endorsement has hindered rather than helped the growth of the 'Revisionist' cause among non-Muslim audiences.[77] Thus, there has been very little mention on 'conventional' denier websites of Kaukab Siddique, associate professor at Lincoln University, Pennsylvania, a unique example of overtly Islamist Holocaust denial in American academia, and one of the very few endorsements by *any* US academic of 'Revisionism' in the past decade.[78]

The attitude of the secular anti-Zionist movement towards Holocaust denial confirms its relative uselessness as a weapon in the struggle to delegitimise the existence of Israel. Although left-wing supporters of Faurisson belonging to La Vieille Taupe were attracted to negationism because of their commitment to anti-imperialism and anti-Zionism,[79] exceedingly few anti-Zionists have subsequently followed suit. It is here, however, where one can find the few equally rare Jewish Holocaust deniers or 'fellow travellers', such as Paul Eisen,[80] Israel Shamir and Gilad Atzmon, many associated with Deir Yassin Remembered. When several deniers were expelled from the Palestine Solidarity Campaign, Atzmon regrouped with other sympathisers around the website Deliberation,[81] reprinting some negationist materials alongside the standard anti-Zionist fare.

Some of the negationist anti-Zionists have similarly found outlets in overtly conspiracist websites or been reprinted on 'conventional' denier websites; thus the

---

76 George Michael, 'Mahmoud Ahmadinejad's Sponsorship of Holocaust Denial', *Totalitarian Movements and Political Religions* 8:3 (2007), 667–71.

77 Meir Litvak and Esther Webman, *From Empathy to Denial: Arab Responses to the Holocaust* (London: Hurst & Co., 2009), especially 155–92; Gilbert Achcar, 'Assessing Holocaust Denial in Western and Arab Contexts', *Journal of Palestine Studies* 41:1 (2011), 82–95.

78 Dan Barrett, 'Academic Freedom and Holocaust Denial', *Inside Higher Education*, 26 October 2010, www.insidehighered.com/news/2010/10/26/siddique

79 See especially Yakira, *Post-Zionism, Post-Holocaust*.

80 Paul Eisen, 'My Life as a Holocaust Denier', January 2008, www.righteousjews.org/article27a.html

81 Francis Clark-Lowes, 'Questioning the Holocaust', 25 January 2012, http://web.archive.org/web/20140721033909/http://www.deliberation.info/questioning-the-holccaust/

writings of Daniel McGowan of Deir Yassin Remembered and professor emeritus of economics of Hobart and William College, can be found on rense.com as well as Germar Rudolf's website.[82] The conspiracist scene has in fact become one of the few potential growth areas for negationism in recent years, with a number of websites such as Veterans Today featuring the occasional poorly constructed article re-treading familiar old denier arguments.[83] Yet just as negationism has become virtually toxic on the extreme right and among anti-Zionists, the presence of Holocaust deniers has become extremely contentious within conspiracy theory circles, both inside the 9/11 Truth Movement as well as on the larger conspiracy forums such as Above Top Secret or David Icke's website. The Iranian government-sponsored website and TV station Press TV, a noted peddler of conspiracy theories, is one outlet that seems happy to reprint negationist material without blushing.[84]

The tolerance of conspiracist websites for denial is reciprocated in the tolerance of 'Revisionist' websites to welcome conspiracy theorists into the fold. In 2008, a 61-year-old British historian of astronomy, Nicholas Kollerstrom, wrote two articles for CODOH rehashing all the old claims surrounding Leuchter's 'chemical disproof' first tried over 20 years before, padding the pieces with internet clichés such as the Auschwitz swimming pool. Kollerstrom did not, however, confine his unconventional beliefs to Holocaust denial, as he is a classic example of so-called crank magnetism,[85] advocating astrology, crop circles, 9/11 Truth, as well as conspiracy theories about the London terrorist bombings of 7 July 2005. His harassment of survivors of the 7/7 bombings led bloggers to uncover his Holocaust-denying articles on CODOH, resulting in the loss of an honorary fellowship at University College London.[86] In 2013, the serial conspiracy theorist James Fetzer, professor emeritus of philosophy at the University of Minnesota, added Holocaust denial to his repertoire of theories regarding the assassination of John F. Kennedy, 9/11 and the Sandy Hook school shooting of December 2012. Fetzer subsequently contributed a foreword to Kollerstrom's book *Breaking the Spell*, and edited a collection of

82 Daniel McGowan, 'What does Holocaust Denial Really Mean?', 22 March 2007, rense.com/general75/viv.htm; Daniel McGowan, 'Galileo Revisited', posted on the front page of germarrudolf.com

83 J.B. Campbell, 'Behind the Holocaust', *Veterans Today*, 11 May 2011, www.veterans today.com/2011/05/11/jb-campbell-behind-the-holocaust/

84 Nicholas Kollerstrom, 'The Walls of Auschwitz', Press TV, 18 May 2008, edition. presstv.ir/detail/56287.html. Press TV subsequently lost its UK broadcasting licence in 2012.

85 Mark Hoofnagle, 'Crank Magnetism', 28 June 2007, scienceblogs.com/denialism/ 2007/06/28/crank-magnetism-1/

86 Nicholas Kollerstrom, 'The Auschwitz "Gas Chamber" Illusion' and 'The Walls of Auschwitz: A Chemical Study', both CODOH, May 2008. His UCL fellowship was unremunerated. Cf Nick Cohen, 'When Academics Lose their Power of Reason', *The Observer*, 4 May 2008.

articles featuring 'Revisionist' authors alongside moon-landing hoax theories and other fringe claims.[87]

The convergence of negationism and conspiracism can also be seen in the use of videos for propaganda purposes. In both cases, this resort to what is now known as '*argumentum ad YouTubium*' was preceded by the reliance on VHS videos in conspiracy theorist, white nationalist and negationist circles during the 1990s.[88] The novelty of YouTube, which was only founded in February 2005, as well as the advent of other social media in web 2.0, helped 9/11 conspiracy theories to go 'viral' in 2005–06 through the medium of video documentaries such as *Loose Change*.[89] Negationist efforts to exploit the viral-video phenomenon have met with mixed success. In 2006, 'Mike Smith', also known as 'denierbud', produced *One Third of the Holocaust*, 30 clips' worth of denial of the extermination camps of Belzec, Sobibor and Treblinka.[90] 'Denierbud' or 'Dean Irrebod' has since made two subsequent videos, on Buchenwald and Auschwitz, but recently declared he would probably not make further videos due to 'lack of financial contributions'.[91] Another younger 'Revisionist' video maker was Eric Hunt, who had previously received a two-year sentence in 2008 for attacking Holocaust survivor Elie Wiesel in a San Francisco hotel.[92] Hunt's four videos, produced between 2011 and 2016, are now hosted on other websites after a series of personal websites went offline, probably due to an inability to pay hosting charges.[93] In France, October 2010 saw the release of a video hagiography of Robert Faurisson, *Un homme*,[94] while

87 Nicholas Kollerstrom, *Breaking the Spell: The Holocaust, Myth & Reality* (Uckfield: Castle Hill, 2014), 9–14; Jim Fetzer and Mike Palecek (eds), *And I Suppose we Didn't Go to the Moon, Either? The Beatles, the Holocaust, and Other Mass Illusions* (United States: Moon Rock Books, 2015).

88 The IHR sold VHS videos of speeches at its conferences as well as other work from a fairly early stage, while the marketing of videos in militia circles is noted in Zeskind, *Blood and Politics*, and in UFO conspiracy theorist circles by Michael Barkun, *A Culture of Conspiracy. Apocalyptic Visions in Contemporary America* (Berkeley: University of California Press, 2003).

89 Jeremy Stahl, 'The Rise and Fall of the 9/11 Conspiracy Theory', *Slate*, 6–9 September 2011, www.slate.com/articles/news_and_politics/trutherism.html; for a brilliant analysis of the 'Truth Movement' see Ryan Mackey, 'The Great Internet Conspiracy: The Role of Technology and Social Media in the 9/11 Truth Movement' (November 2011), available at www.911myths.com/tgitc_1_0_final.pdf

90 Two websites archiving the videos, www.onethirdoftheholocaust.com and www.holocaustdenialvideos.com, are now both offline. The videos were swiftly debunked by amateur bloggers; see: holocaustcontroversies.blogspot.co.uk/2006/04/quick-links.html#debuv for commentaries.

91 'A Revisionist Video Maker's Confessions', 29 March 2012, barnesreview.org/wp/archives/395

92 Associated Press, 'Man Gets Two-Year Sentence for Accosting Elie Wiesel', *USA Today*, 18 August 2009, usatoday30.usatoday.com/news/nation/2008-08-18-wiesel-accosted_N.htm

93 A total of 13 videos are hosted on the 'Holocaust Handbooks' website. holocausthandbooks.com/index.php?main_page=2

94 This was available on the now-defunct website holocauste.com, as well as on YouTube.

Italian negationists released a video primer to 'Holocaust Revisionism' in the spring of 2012,[95] leading to a resurgence of calls to outlaw denial in that country.[96]

4 Social media and Holocaust denial

The defining hallmark of web 2.0 is the explosion of social media platforms and user-generated content, from discussion forums, blogs and social networks, to below-the-line comments threads on media sites, user reviews and video uploading sites, through to the microblogging platform Twitter. Holocaust deniers have taken to all of these platforms in an attempt to raise publicity for their ideas and drive traffic to their websites, while also using a variety of other tactics to propagate their belief system. Mirror sites, aggregator sites and astroturfing contribute to a seeming proliferation of 'Revisionist' content on the internet.

The results have been mixed. In many cases, especially on mainstream media websites, posts and comments from Holocaust deniers are deleted for violating community standards, while both YouTube and Facebook have inconsistently removed video uploads or usergroups for hate speech or copyright violations.[97] In some cases, such as the user-administered social network Reddit, deniers have successfully seized control of subreddits such as r/Holocaust,[98] and use the platform to spam their videos and articles while censoring all opposition.[99] Upvoting and downvoting on YouTube clips, such as the trailer for the David Hare-scripted film 'Denial', about the Irving-Lipstadt trial, can sometimes generate swarms of deniers, who 'disliked' one trailer 1,966 times in three months, compared to 728 'likes' and 120,989 views,[100] while another trailer was 'liked' 3,815 times against 2,562 'dislikes', out of 416,175 views.[101] Meanwhile, 'Revisionist' books on sale via Amazon are given a relatively small number of effusive reviews, while some titles in the 'Holocaust Handbooks' series have failed to attract a single user review.[102]

---

95 Marco Pasqua, 'Nella testa dei negazionisti "Shoah macabra leggenda"', *La Repubblica*, 4 May 2012, www.repubblica.it/cronaca/2012/04/05/news/nella_testa_dei_negazionisti-32798573/

96 'Italian Senate Debates Outlawing Negationism on Anniversary of WWII Roman Deportations', *European Jewish Press*, 22 October 2012, www.ejpress.org/article/62588. A bill criminalising denial in Italy was finally passed into law in June 2016.

97 On the debates over denial on Facebook, see Raphael Cohen-Almagor, 'Facebook and Holocaust Denial', *Justice* 57 (2016), 10–6.

98 www.reddit.com/r/Holocaust

99 William Allington, 'The Rise of Anti-intellectualism Online', *Honi Soit*, 15 August 2016, honisoit.com/2016/08/the-rise-of-anti-intellectualism-online/

100 www.youtube.com/watch?v=hYcx43AmAyY

101 www.youtube.com/watch?v=fG_qYZm2Is0

102 On the manipulation of online reviews, see Joseph M. Reagle, *Reading the Comments: Likers, Haters and Manipulators at the Bottom of the Web* (Cambridge, MA: The MIT Press, 2015).

How much traffic is driven towards 'Revisionist' websites by this online marketing effort? Web traffic analytics sites such as Alexa, Compete and Similarweb confirm a consistent pattern from 2010 to the present of significantly lower volumes of traffic for websites featuring exclusively 'Revisionist' content, compared to somewhat higher levels of traffic for websites that include denial alongside white nationalism, present-oriented anti-Semitism, or other conspiracy theories. A survey using Similarweb[103] in September 2016 found 21 defunct denier websites and blogs, six sites that could not be ranked at all due to low traffic, 26 ranked below 2 million globally, 11 ranked below 1 million, and six ranked below 275,000. The rankings of a comparative sample of 43 sites dedicated exclusively to propagating 9/11 conspiracy theories were strikingly similar. The same pattern is confirmed when analysing Twitter accounts: pure-denial accounts attract one-tenth or less of the number of followers compared to accounts promoting white nationalism, anti-Zionism or conspiracy theories more generally.[104]

Measured both in terms of membership as well as 'reach', the Stormfront forum is undoubtedly the largest website available to Holocaust deniers. Web traffic survey tools such as compete.com indicated a mass readership of between 175,000 and 318,000 visitors a month in 2009–10.[105] The 'History & Revisionism' sub-forum contained 182,477 posts as of mid-September 2016, up from 142,978 posts at the start of 2013, yet over a quarter (48,731) of the posts are to be found in a sub-forum on 9/11 conspiracy theories, while only a fraction of the discussions concerned 'pure' Holocaust negationism, with much discussion revolving around other traditional white nationalist and neo-Nazi interests.[106] As the former extreme right activist Jim Saleam has observed, 'typologically, neo-[N]azis share a fused set of ideological interests: Indo-Aryan pre-history, white race internationalism, Rudolf Hess's martyrdom, Holocaust-denial, Jewish-conspiracy ideology, Second World War historical revision, a Hitler-cult'.[107] This mixture of interests is mirrored in Stormfront's 'Revisionism' sub-forum.

The most prominent internet forum to dedicate itself solely to 'Revisionism' is the CODOH forum, active since November 2002.[108] In mid-September 2016, this contained 70,717 posts, up from 50,001 posts at the start of February 2013. While traffic analytics tools indicate the CODOH website attracts a considerable readership globally, with between 13,000 and 68,000 unique visitors per month,

103 www.similarweb.com
104 For a recent analysis of white supremacist Twitter accounts, see J.M. Berger, *Nazis vs. ISIS on Twitter: A Comparative Study of White Nationalist and ISIS Online Social Media Networks*, GW Program on Extremism (September 2016), online at cchs.gwu.edu/sites/cchs.gwu.edu/files/downloads/Nazis%20v.%20ISIS%20Final_0.pdf
105 Scott Darnell, *Measuring Holocaust Denial in the United States* (Harvard Kennedy School of Government, Policy Analysis Exercise, Spring 2010), 38: www.hks.harvard.edu/ocpa/pdf/HolocaustDenialPAE.pdf
106 www.stormfront.org/forum/f36/
107 James Saleam, *The Other Radicalism: An Inquiry into Contemporary Australian Extreme Right Ideology, Politics and Organization 1975–1995* (PhD, University of Sydney, 1999), 217.
108 forum.codoh.com

reader participation is far less extensive. Out of 1,171 CODOH forum members surveyed in August 2016, 288 had made no posts at all, 482 made between one and nine posts, 300 contributed between ten and 139 posts, leaving only 83 members ranked as 'contributors' with 140 to 599 posts, and just 19 'valuable assets' with more than 600 posts. Only 50 members had posted in the month preceding the survey. A similar survey conducted on 2 December 2012 also found only 50 members had posted in the previous 30 days, while only 189 had contributed in the previous 12 months. New members who contributed to discussions were added at a rate of between 36 and 92 per year over the course of 2003 to 2015, while between 22 and 80 members effectively dropped out of the discussion each year. While the use of 'handles' and pseudonyms masks the identities and origins of most members, at least one in six lives in Europe, with a smaller representation from Australasia, and a much larger cohort of North American posters.[109]

A tour of internet forums, blog and YouTube comment threads and other web 2.0 outlets inhabited by 'Revisionists' swiftly indicates that it is largely the exact same people who are trolling these venues. Moreover, the overlap in usernames and posters between dedicated 'Revisionist' forums and white nationalist forums such as Stormfront is fairly high. Ideologically, the CODOH forum membership includes overt neo-Nazis and white nationalists alongside minorities of Catholic traditionalists; the overwhelming majority express anti-Semitic and anti-Zionist sentiments.

The most striking hallmark of the CODOH forum membership is their age profile; the majority are evidently middle-aged or older still, with few members claiming to be in their teens or twenties.[110] Equally noticeable is the utter ignorance of either mainstream *or* 'Revisionist' literature displayed by the majority of members, especially among those who profess to have been converted by watching 'Revisionist' videos. Disagreements among members, either over tactics, the validity of other conspiracy theories, Hitler-worship, overt anti-Semitism or historical facts, flare up routinely. The forum is noticeably rigged in favour of a small inner circle of posters with any visiting non-deniers ruthlessly censored. Heavy-handed moderation and selective banning of the 'opposition' is far from unknown on other fringe forums, and helps to ward off cognitive dissonance and to reinforce in-group cohesion, but also causes – as with other sects and cults – disaffected members to quit or become inactive, thereby hampering the growth of the movement or the retention of once-enthusiastic would-be activists.

The proliferation of YouTube videos, blog articles and websites spamming the exact same arguments that were already in circulation 25 years ago has thus

---

109 In the 2 December 2012 sample, there were at least 20 Scandinavians, 25 British nationals, 32 Germans and half a dozen French; at least seven were from Australia or New Zealand.

110 See among other discussions the 'conversion narratives' related in the thread 'What made you first question the Holocaust?', forum.codoh.info/viewtopic.php?f=2&t=6441

arguably significantly undermined the coherence and effectiveness of Holocaust denial as a movement.[111] Reduced to a series of sound bites and dumbed-down claims, negationist propaganda in the era of web 2.0 simply does not equip 'Revisionists' to proselytise their case effectively, instead ensnaring a relatively limited number of converts in what amounts to a revolving-door cohort of increasingly ageing foot soldiers.

5 Conclusion

Since the *de facto* demise of the IHR in 2002 and the abandonment of negationism by the majority of vote-seeking far right parties, Holocaust denial has been cut loose to fend for itself as just one of many fringe conspiracy theories peddled on the internet. Its continued allure undoubtedly stems from the legal repression of denial as a form of incitement to racial hatred in a number of European countries, imbuing negationism with the appeal of an ultimate taboo. As a form of 'stigmatized knowledge', to borrow Michael Barkun's useful term,[112] negationism will likely continue to appeal to a small minority for the foreseeable future. Its wellsprings of support can be found on the extreme right, in certain fundamentalist or traditionalist religious circles, as well as increasingly among the contrarian conspiracist milieu.

Seven reasons can be adduced for the decline of Holocaust denial:

1   Consistent social disapproval
2   Its political ineffectiveness
3   The ease of finding other ways of expressing anti-Semitism or delegitimising Israel
4   Loss of 'market share' to other conspiracy theories
5   Inability to cope with the volume of recent Holocaust research
6   Lack of novelty
7   The ageing of the 'movement'

Indeed, at least 84 'Revisionist' authors, activists or prominent supporters have died since the turn of the millennium, including two of the most important organisers of the movement, Willis Carto and Bradley Smith, during the winter of 2015/16. Many other prominent figures from the heyday of 'Revisionism', such as Robert Faurisson, 87, or Ernst Zündel, 77, are now too old to contribute meaningfully to the belief system. While Mattogno and Graf are both now 65, and could well be producing their pseudoscholarship for some time to come, the

---

111 Similar arguments have been made about the coherence of 9/11 conspiracy theories. See in particular Steve Clarke, 'Conspiracy Theories and the Internet: Controlled Demolition and Arrested Development', *Episteme: A Journal of Social Epistemology* 4:2 (2007), 167–80.
112 Barkun, *A Culture of Conspiracy*, 15–38.

majority of their peers from the 1980s and 1990s have abandoned what Faurisson once called the 'intellectual adventure of the 21st Century', with few younger cadres emerging to replace the casualties. Thomas Kues, born in 1981 and thus one of the youngest 'Revisionist' authors of significance to publish since the turn of the millennium, quit the denier scene in July 2013 for personal reasons.[113]

While the rise of internet conspiracism has caused concern in some quarters, the failure of Holocaust denial to break out of its ghetto offers some hope more generally. As has been observed, pseudo-theories are always aimed over the heads of academics at an unsuspecting general public.[114] The transparency of the internet and the multiple outlets available in the age of web 2.0 might at first glance seem to encourage the spread of fringe ideas, as was seen in the mid-2000s with the 9/11 Truth Movement, and in President Barack Obama's first term with 'Birtherism'. Yet the self-same transparency also acts to expose advocates of fringe ideas as cranks, and to set firm limits on their growth, while also stimulating opposition to fringe ideas from ordinary internet surfers. The near-unanimous rejection of 'Holocaust Revisionism' by academic and intellectual opinion, in politics, the courts and in Western societies as a whole, has been reproduced on web 2.0 by a similar thumbs-down from the overwhelming majority of web surfers. With virtually all Holocaust denier activity now concentrated on the internet, a final twist can be noted: if one switches off the internet and walks away from the computer, Holocaust denial disappears entirely.

113   This news was confirmed belatedly by his co-author Jürgen Graf. See Jonathan Harrison, 'Thomas Kues is No Longer an Active Revisionist', 14 December 2015, holocaustcontroversies.blogspot.co.uk/2015/12/thomas-kues-is-no-longer-active.html
114   Garret G. Fagan, 'Diagnosing Pseudoarchaeology' in Fagan (ed.), *Archaeological Fantasies*, 29.

Part II

Holocaust and genocide denial around the world

Chapter 4

Silence and denial in Gulag testimonies

Listening for the unspeakable

Elisabeth Anstett

Throughout the socialist era, the use of forced labour, deportation and internal exile allowed successive Soviet governments to maintain a firm grip over their populations. Over the twentieth century, the Soviet Union built up a vast system of forced correctional labour camps, overseen by a central administration: the *Ispravitelno-Trudovoi Lager* (ITL), or *Gulag*. This concentrationary institution was used simultaneously as a tool of political control[1] and as an instrument of the country's economic transformation.[2]

As a result, between 1917 and 1989, more than 15 million Soviet citizens from all ethnic, religious and social backgrounds were sentenced to forced labour and detained within the concentrationary system. There is general agreement among contemporary historians that, in the USSR, one in six adult men experienced the Gulag during Stalin's rule.[3] This huge network of concentration camps spanned the length and breadth of the Soviet Union, and was involved in almost every area of the country's industrial infrastructure.

The experience of the Gulag occurred on so vast a geographical, historical and social scale that it raises a huge set of questions regarding the traces (or scars) left by this collective experiment in state violence. It was in order, then, to reveal and understand the legacy of the Gulag that I embarked in 2002 upon an investigation into the imprint left by these concentration camps in Russia, in the context of a wider enquiry into the legacy of mass violence in post-Soviet spaces.

The background to this research is somewhat unusual, in that no active policy has ever been adopted by Soviet or post-Soviet states with regard to the preservation of sites of detention or forced labour. Whether through their subsequent re-use or simply being abandoned to the ravages of time and a harsh climate, the original identity of these sites has been very effectively erased.[4] No national

---

1 J. Arch Getty and Oleg Naumov, *The Road to Terror: Stalin and the Self-Destruction of the Bolsheviks, 1932–1939* (New Haven: Yale University Press, 1999).
2 Galina Ivanova, *Labor Camp Socialism: The Gulag in the Soviet Totalitarian System* (London: ME Sharpe, 2000).
3 Nicolas Werth, *La terreur et le désarroi: Staline et son système* (Paris: Perrin, 2007).
4 Ivan Panikarov, 'Le chemin s'arrête-t-il là?' in Elisabeth Anstett and Luba Jurgenson (eds), *Le Goulag en héritage, pour une anthropologie de la trace* (Paris: Pétra, 2009), 131–41.

museum has been established to commemorate this concentrationary institution; only a few small, local and privately run museum spaces conserve any material evidence of the existence and activity of certain individual concentration camps.[5] More importantly still, before *Perestroika* and the legalisation of dissidence in the second half of the 1980s, the very mention of the Gulag in public was impossible.[6]

In Russia, then, along with the rest of the Soviet world, the act of forgetting for a long time displaced the more usual manifestations of memory. One must always keep in mind this delayed, distant and in many ways still problematic character of the memory of the Gulag.[7] Gaining an understanding of how a now post-Soviet Russia is negotiating with its concentrationary past was thus crucial. With the assistance of the Memorial Foundation, in 2002 I began fieldwork in a small provincial city with close links to the Gulag, aiming to observe how the former prisoners and former neighbours of one particular camp had come to terms with the material and symbolic traces of the Soviet concentrationary system.

I An ordinary Gulag

Officially designated at various points as *Volgolag*, *Volgostroi* and *Rybinlag*, the forced labour camps whose legacy I examine here existed as an autonomous administrative entity between 1935 and 1953. During this period, the *Volgolag* would spread over an area of more than 5,000 square kilometres, and over 150,000 prisoners would pass through it. Its headquarters was always situated in the city of Rybinsk, 380 kilometres north-east of Moscow, illustrating how the tentacles of the Soviet concentrationary system reached right into the most urbanised and densely populated parts of the USSR. Nikita Okhotin and Arseni Roginsky's edited volume, published in 1998,[8] allows the history of this Gulag to be traced in detail, so it will suffice here to recall the key events.

From 7 December 1935, the date of its creation under the name of *Volzhski ITL*, until 20 March 1942, it held up to 87,000 deportees per year.[9] It would primarily serve, in this first stage of its existence, to provide manpower for the construction of the dam and hydro-electric plant at Rybinsk. It would also provide logistical support (timber for construction, food) to the tens of thousands of people, prisoners and paid workers alike, involved in the *Bolshaia Volga* project,

5   Elisabeth Anstett, *Une Atlantide russe, anthropologie de la mémoire en Russie postsoviétique* (Paris: La Découverte, 2007).
6   Irina Sherbakova, 'The Gulag in Memory', *International Yearbook of Oral History and Life History*, vol. 1 (1992), 103–15.
7   Luba Jurgenson, *L'expérience concentrationnaire est-elle indicible?* (Monaco: Editions du Rocher, 2003).
8   Nikita Okhotin and Arseni Roginsky, *Sistema ispravitel'no-trudovyh lagerej v SSSR, 1923–1960: Spravochnik* (Moscow: Zven'ia, 1998).
9   Ibid., 189.

which aimed to control the seasonal flooding of the Volga. From the start, then, this Gulag combined a technical and agricultural character.

When the Rybinsk dam came into service on 14 April 1941, a considerable portion of the land used by the camp was covered by the newly formed reservoir. An important part of our Gulag thus disappeared beneath the rising waters in 1941. Rechristened *Rybinski ITL*[10] (or *Rybinlag*) in spring 1942, the establishment, re-centred on the city of Rybinsk, continued to function. It was now involved in industrial production as much as forestry, employing between 20,000 and 35,000 prisoners depending on the year in question, up until 26 February 1944. The Gulag was then reorganised as *ITL Volgostroi*,[11] holding between 15,000 and 25,000 prisoners in a given year, to concentrate on industrial activities (the production of arms, chemicals, pharmaceuticals).

Rechristened on 29 April 1946 as *Volzhski ITL MVD* to mark its coming under the direct control of the Interior Ministry (*Ministerstvo Vnutrennikh Del*, or MVD),[12] the establishment would henceforth hold a maximum of 15,000 deportees per year. Following Stalin's death in March 1953, it finally saw its command transferred to the Jaroslavl branch of the MVD, 80 kilometres away as, across the USSR, the slow dismantling of the Soviet concentrationary system began.

Our establishment, having lost its administrative independence, saw its functions progressively diminish until the 1960s, although a residual level of activity continued. For instance, Vladimir T., born in 1937, states in his biographical dossier placed with the Memorial Foundation[13] in Moscow that he was still subjected to the forced labour regime[14] while working in the *Volgolag* zone's hospital complex, next to the Rybinsk dam, between 1977 and 1980.

The long occupation of a single site by this Gulag raises various important issues, for the *Volgolag*, as I shall refer to it for the sake of convenience, existed in parallel with the urban development and demographic growth of the city of Rybinsk for several decades.

2 A provincial setting

I therefore chose Rybinsk to carry out my fieldwork. The setting for the study is that of a small provincial Russian city with 220,000 inhabitants. In the Soviet era, as well as being associated with the *Volgolag*, the city saw an important phase of economic expansion linked to the development of the military-industrial complex first established in the area in the 1930s. The city was therefore closed to foreigners until 1991.

---

10 Ibid., 369.
11 Ibid., 234.
12 Ibid., 191.
13 Archives of the Memorial Foundation, Moscow, Fond 1, opis 1, delo 216.
14 Stripped of identity papers and work documents, detainees were taken to their place of work under armed escort, and housed in wooden huts.

Rybinsk has undergone no fewer than seven changes of name since its foundation, four of which occurred in the second half of the twentieth century.[15] These onomastic convulsions reflect deep sociological and economic transformations, yet also help to fragment local memory. They also echo the innumerable name changes of the neighbouring Gulag. My study mainly concentrated on a zone in the west of the city, known as the *Perebory*, taken from the name of a former hamlet incorporated into Rybinsk with the advance of urbanisation. It was in the *Perebory* that the headquarters of the *Volgolag* was physically located. This was where new prisoners arrived by train before being assigned to different zones of the camp's territory. This was where the administrative, medical and cultural infrastructure of the Gulag was situated.

The *Perebory*, home to 7,000 inhabitants, are today the quiet and dilapidated suburbs of a very ordinary Russian provincial city. In many respects, the *Perebory* have lost out from de-Sovietisation: unemployment, depopulation and the deterioration of infrastructure have all taken their toll.

A significant number of former detainees of the *Volgolag* still live there. It was therefore in the *Perebory* that I chose to conduct a series of interviews with residents, including former prisoners and employees, but also neighbours (whether long-established or more recent arrivals) of these former zones of detention and forced labour.

3 Interview method

The methodological framework of this study focused on a qualitative approach to collective representations of the legacy of the Soviet camps. In addition to observing the ceremonies of commemoration for the victims of political repression held in Russia every year on 30 October,[16] between 2002 and 2007 I carried out a series of semi-guided interviews as and when the opportunity arose.

These interviews usually took place with both parties seated, in the interviewees' homes. Occasionally, however, they were conducted as we walked over the actual sites of the *Volgolag*. These walks were useful in both heuristic and methodological terms. On one level they made it possible to identify topographical traces left by these concentrationary spaces, as far as the knowledge of the local population allowed. These narrative walks (uniting physical movement and verbal narration) could also, however, in many cases bring forth words that were difficult or painful, and which were hard to express in a more formal or

---

15 Rybinsk was first renamed as *Shcherbakov* in 1946 in honour of Lieutenant-General Vladimir Ivanovitch Shcherbakov, a hero of the Great Patriotic War (World War II), before reverting to its original name in 1957. It was again, briefly, rechristened *Andropov* from 1990–91 in memory of the secretary-general of the Communist Party, long-serving director of the KGB and then short-lived successor to Brezhnev, before finally going back to *Rybinsk* with the collapse of the USSR.

16 Elisabeth Anstett, 'De la notoriété au déni. Les lieux de mémoire du Goulag à Rybinsk, ancienne capitale des Volgolag', *Gulag Studies* no. 1 (2008), 77–92.

indeed more intimate context. Not all the interviews could be recorded, given that it very soon became clear that certain interviewees felt great reticence and anxiety, and sometimes real panic at the prospect of having their words committed to tape.

Several factors seem to be involved here. The traumatic experience of interrogations at the hands of the Soviet judiciary obviously plays one part. It is a reminder that words can sometimes function as proof and judicial evidence. Nor can interviewees' scepticism as to the reliability of their interlocutor (a foreign woman, whose intentions are only partially understood, and who is too young to have known the camps) be discounted. It is possible that some of the interviewees' silences were attributable to their doubt that I would be able to understand what they were talking about. One must also acknowledge the fear, openly expressed by others, that speaking out would be interpreted as a militant act, associating them with those standard-bearers of memory who are regularly sought out by journalists for official commemorations.

Remaining as conscious as possible of all these difficulties, I therefore always concentrated on the open or semi-guided form of interview. Our discussions thus became 'conversation[s] with a purpose',[17] which ultimately aimed to reveal just what it means today to have been in contact with the Gulag. This study allowed me to assemble a wide range of testimony. Most of the accounts that were recorded are quite long, lasting two to three hours. It was possible in some cases to continue interviews over several sessions, with the result that the most intense among them could last up to ten hours.

4 Silence: an expected preliminary

Given the length of the testimony collected and the mass of documentation provided by the fund, Memorial, it might seem paradoxical to wish to examine the question of silence. It should be pointed out, however, that from the preparation stage onwards, silence was an expected feature of the testimony that this project sought to collect.

Several elements may be seen to come together in the production of silence. First, the nature of the subject, as the discourse of victims or witnesses to violence always contains an element of the unspeakable. Second, the distance in time from the events in question is also of importance, insofar as the passage of time leads to forgetting, and even more so when the memory is painful. Finally, the long and widespread use of secrecy by the Soviet state helped put in place a veritable policy of silence. The role played by the impossibility of publicly broaching the question of the Gulag before the advent of Perestroika cannot, in this respect, be overestimated. It was thus expected that silence would be a part of these interviews in various ways.

17 Colin Robson, *Real World Research* (Oxford: Blackwell, 1993), 228.

While preparing the project, however, a problem arose: the question of silence had been barely addressed by anthropology, to the extent that it constituted something of a blind spot. Of course, ever since the work of Sapir and Whorf, it had been understood that a cultural element in the meaning of informants' discourse could escape anthropologists. However, linguists working on macro-culturalist hypotheses and configurations had not taken into account elements such as, for example, intentional dissimulation or the reliability of the speaker. Yet these were all things reported by researchers, although most frequently placed under the heading of field anecdotes, despite their shedding an often uncomfortable light on the conditions of the production of ethnographic knowledge.

It was left to other disciplines, such as language sciences and their approach to the question of the unspeakable,[18] literary criticism and the notion of 'unreliable narration'[19] and the 'value of narrativity in the representation of reality',[20] or communication sciences with their 'studies of metaphoric structures in verbal exchange'[21] to shed some light on the role of silence within discourse. The edited volume by Jaworski[22] is in this respect one of the only studies to approach the notion of silence head-on. *Silence: Interdisciplinary Perspectives* allows us to draw up a preliminary typology of the different forms of silence, whether found in rhetorical figures, speech acts or interpretative contexts. While undoubtedly focusing on the question of silence, however, this book only brushes upon the social and cultural functions of silence, or the historical and ideological contexts revealed by different ways of silencing.

This diversity of disciplinary approaches left me relatively ill-prepared for interpreting the sense of the silences I encountered on the ground in the specific context of speaking about the traces of the Gulag in post-Soviet Russia. In the end, it was the work carried out by Stanley Cohen[23] on the subject of denial which allowed me to reach the hypothesis of silence as a symptomatic social manifestation, based on a correlation between the forms of silence and the practices of denial. The tissue of links between, on the one hand, various ways of silencing elaborated at the individual level and the different ways of denying reality produced at the collective level on the other, have proven an extremely fruitful area for exploration. Each of the three interviews selected here, for

18 Oswald Ducros, *Dire et ne pas dire. Principes de sémantique linguistique* (Paris: Hermann, 1998, original 1972).
19 Wayne C. Booth, *The Rhetoric of Fiction* (Chicago: The University of Chicago Press, 1983, original 1961).
20 Hayden White, 'The Value of Narrativity in the Representation of Reality', *Critical Inquiry* vol. 7, no. 1 (1980), 5–27.
21 James W. Fernandez (ed.), *Persuasions and Performances: The Play of Tropes in Culture* (Bloomington: Indiana University Press, 1986).
22 Adam Jaworski (ed.), *Silence: Interdisciplinary Perspectives* (Berlin: Mouton de Gruyters, 1997).
23 Stanley Cohen, *States of Denial: Knowing about Atrocities and Suffering* (Cambridge: Polity Press, 2001).

instance, illustrates how every personal way of (not) saying something relates directly to a shared way of silencing.[24]

5 Ways of saying, ways of silencing

5.1 Kim

Our first witness is a former deportee. Kim was sentenced to five years in the camps in 1943 when he was 17 years old, and was sent directly to Rybinsk from the region of Siberia where he had been born, several thousand kilometres away. Sentenced again following the war, he ended up spending more than ten years in the *Volgolag*. He has never really left it. The last time that I interviewed him, he was living with his second wife in an *isba* on a small island in the artificial lake created by the Rybinsk dam, less than five kilometres from the place of his imprisonment. Kim is a willing and engaging speaker. For this reason, he is regularly interviewed by journalists.

He finds it easy to talk about his period of imprisonment and about the camp itself. When he speaks about the *Volgolag*, the former detainee is happy to retrace its geography and layout. Part of a logging team for several years, he possesses a perfect knowledge of the Gulag's terrain, having covered every inch to clear it of trees. The camp space that he describes is nonetheless one in which everyday existence is punctuated by extreme violence in the form of forced labour, malnutrition, brutality and physical exhaustion.

The former detainee's speech is in this respect full of unrestrained violence. He employs a striking mixture of Soviet administrative language and camp slang (*blatnoe iazyk*). Every one of Kim's sentences, sprinkled with insults such as *sukha* (bitch) or *svoloch'* (bastard), combines the prisoners' harsh jargon with a lexicon taken straight out of Soviet newspeak.[25] The circumlocutions and incomprehensible metaphors that filled the socialist administrative lexicon[26] are placed next to crude epithets such as *sifilitik* ('the syphilitic one', for Lenin), *pogan* ('filth', for Stalin) or *prokhliataia gadost'* ('stinking scum', for most Soviet leaders). On a purely

---

24 Translator's note: the French text places in parallel the expressions 'façons de dire' and 'façons de taire' in a play on the title of Yvonne Verdier's study of rural French life in the second half of the twentieth century, *Façons de dire, façons de faire* (1979). The verb 'taire' means 'to silence', whether in relation to oneself (keeping silent, 'se taire') or to others ('faire taire quelqu'un'), but also has the sense of 'to hush up' ('taire une affaire').

25 Translator's note: in the French, the expression used is 'langue de bois', literally 'wooden language', a common term to express the clumsy, ugly character of official neologisms. Orwell's term places more stress on the mendacious character of totalitarian language.

26 In Soviet administrative language, 'spaces of privation of freedom' designates prisons, detainees die not of hunger but of 'pellagra' (niacin deficiency), and the *Volgostroi* signifies a Gulag. For an endless list of examples, see Jacques Rossi, *The Gulag Handbook, An Encyclopedia Dictionary of Soviet Penitentiary Institutions and Terms Related to the Forced Labor Camps* (New York: Paragon House, 1989).

formal level, Kim's discourse represents a powerful transgression of the polite and measured speech employed by other witnesses.

Yet his reconstruction of the concentrationary world still has its dark corners and its fair share of silence. For Kim does not speak about everything, or everybody. The universe that he describes is thus depicted in a Manichean, almost caricatured manner, based on a structural opposition between 'us' (the victims, the detainees) and 'them' (the persecutors, the political leaders of the Soviet era). 'Them' and 'us' nonetheless remain united in their anonymity, since Kim's long testimony only features a very small number of names.

Nor is any mention made of the grey zone thematised by Primo Levi[27] in the context of the Nazi camps. Kim does not speak of any dealings with free men within or outside the camp, or of the multitude of ruses and negotiations that enabled the prisoners of the Gulag to make their daily existence endurable, or indeed all of the survival strategies documented by numerous writers.[28] These ruses often involved collaborating with the camp staff, and frequently worked at the expense of weaker detainees. Nothing is said about any of this.

For Kim, speaking out is a social responsibility as much as the product of a personal commitment to reconstitute a truth hidden for too long. It is thus possible that the testimonial aspect of his discourse plays a role in perpetuating its intense, Manichean character. In this way, Kim's language is indeed highly performative: 'his verbal art is performance.'[29]

5.2 Vera

Our second witness is also a former deportee, this time a woman. Vera was 81 years old when I first met her. Born in central Russia, she was sentenced to five years' forced labour and sent to the *Volgolag* at the end of the 1930s when she was barely 20. After her release, she stayed in Rybinsk, where she was able to find work in a factory. She married and had a daughter.

Vera is a silent witness in the true sense of the term: the interviews I conducted with her were punctuated by long silences, not just in terms of words, but even of movement, as Vera is a very calm speaker who sometimes remains perfectly still for quite long periods. She is one of the people with whom it was easier to talk while walking than when sitting still. It seems to be particularly difficult – indeed impossible – for her to talk about her past as a detainee and the legacy of the

27 Primo Levi, *The Drowned and the Saved* (London: Michael Joseph, 1988), 22–51.
28 Varlam Shalamov, *Kolyma Tales* (London: Penguin, 1994); Eugenia Ginzburg, *Within the Whirlwind* (New York: Harcourt Brace Jovanovich, 1982); Aleksandr Solzhenitsyn, *The Gulag Archipelago, 1918–1956: An Experiment in Literary Investigation I–IV* (London: Fontana, 1976).
29 Richard Bauman, *Verbal Art as Performance* (Prospect Heights, IL: Waveland, 1977); Richard Bauman and Charles L. Briggs, 'Poetics and Performance as Critical Perspectives on Language and Social Life', *Annual Review of Anthropology* vol. 19, no. 1 (1990), 59–88.

camp where she was imprisoned while she is at home. Her testimony has not been recorded, as it would have been quite inappropriate to use a tape recorder given her reluctance to speak.

Physically and psychologically scarred by her years of imprisonment, Vera is still extremely frightened of the use that could be made of her testimony. She frequently goes back on what she has said in order to explain a particular situation, to give more details or clarify statements that she considers in retrospect to have been ambiguous. She is also very worried about her words being misinterpreted. In general terms, she does not wish to be associated with the public declarations of former deportees during ceremonies of commemoration, nor compared to those among them involved in campaigning for former detainees or other political activities.

During our narrative walks, Vera had less difficulty in speaking than when interviewed at home. At her own pace, she commented on the gradual transformation of the urban areas associated with the camp's operations and the now almost bucolic character taken on by the former sites of detention following their abandonment by the *Volgolag*'s administration. She recalled, in a quiet voice, almost a whisper, the boundaries of the camp, the buildings that had stood there, and compared these memories with what now remains.

Yet her account never leads us inside this zone, always leaving us at the gates of the Gulag. She never touched on the subject of the time she spent as a detainee in the camp, nor that of living near the *Volgolag* once she had been freed. She will say nothing about her relations with other deportees or camp guards, whether during her detention or after leaving the camp. She does not speak of what her experience of forced labour, of deportation and violence, has meant for relations with her family, her former colleagues or neighbours. Only once did she refer to having kept her past hidden for decades, by mentioning that each day she had carried '*klejmo pozora*' ('the stigma of shame').

Finally, it is interesting to note that, when speaking, Vera visibly experiences real difficulty in using collective grammatical subjects: she will say 'I', but rarely 'we' or 'they'. She is happier speaking descriptively, listing numerous details rather than explaining general situations. She does not wish to speak on behalf of a community or a group and she truly fears seeing her words exploited by journalists, campaigners or politicians. In this sense, it is possible that Vera is reacting directly against this 'economy of subtraction, where voices of the victims have become commodities in a transnational network of prestige', which Alejandro Castillejo Cuellar has described in the context of South Africa.[30]

5.3 Nina

Our third witness is a former neighbour of the Gulag. At the time of our last interview, Nina was an energetic 'iron lady' of 75, a retired headmistress who

30 Alejandro Castillejo Cuellar, 'Unraveling Silence: Violence, Memory and the Limits of Anthropology's Craft', *Dialectical Anthropology* vol. 29, no. 2 (2005), 159–80, 179.

retained a very clear memory of the Soviet period, wrote poems and sang in a choir with other retired people. Nina talks willingly and at length. The two interviews to which she agreed were recorded.

She has no difficulty in remembering these camps, having lived alongside them for almost ten years after arriving in Rybinsk, at the end of the war. She also clearly remembers the convoys of prisoners which she encountered daily while the *Volgolag* was operational. She talks with emotion of the hard labour that she shared on various occasions with certain groups of prisoners, when the oldest high school children had been sent out to help with the country's reconstruction following the war. She insists in this respect upon the shared destiny and suffering of the entire Russian people.

She tells with emotion of how the residents of Rybinsk had for a long time uncovered traces of the camp, in particular human bones, buried in the small plots of land given to them by their employers following the inauguration of the dam. She vigorously denounces the cruelty and indignity of leaving the dead without a proper burial.

She describes scenes in a very vivid and emotional fashion, and often makes references to great authors or even literary quotations to give weight to her words. The parallels she draws with the situations experienced and described by Shalamov, Solzhenitsyn (who was himself detained for a while in the *Volgolag*) and other writers, allow her to reiterate how similar the situation was throughout the entire country, and again refer to the collective scale of the tragedy and the suffering endured by the victims of the totalitarian state.

However, Nina's discourse also has its blind spots, its silent spaces. For instance, our retired teacher never broaches the subject of the fate of prisoners once they had been released, and of their return and reintegration into Soviet society. Likewise, she never mentions any personal contact, whether through being a neighbour, through work or even any friendship, that she may have had with detainees during or after their imprisonment. Nor are the camp guards, the NKVD[31] personnel present in great numbers in the city, or paid workers employed on site in the Gulag ever mentioned. It is therefore difficult to evaluate, on the basis of her account, how people actually lived their lives inside and in the immediate surroundings of the *Volgolag* while it was operational.

What Nina leaves unsaid is perhaps what Russian society as a whole has not yet learned, or really had the opportunity, to tell. This unspeakable element concerns not only the attribution of roles (victims, bystanders, perpetrators), and legal or moral responsibility, but also the assigning of defined collective identities.

6 Silence: forms and functions

Each of these three accounts thus contains examples of different forms of silence, whether linguistic for Kim, rhetorical for Nina or on the societal level for Vera. It

---

31 The *Narodnyi Komissariat Vnutrennikh Del* (NKVD), or People's Commissariat for Internal Affairs, was the law enforcement agency of the Soviet Union.

should be understood, however, that these various forms are not mutually exclusive. It would no doubt be possible to pick out occurrences of all three types in most of the testimonies collected for the project. What interpretation, then, should be placed on these silences? What do these ways of silencing tell us about the legacy of the Soviet concentrationary system?

6.1 Lexis, linguistic silence and literal denial

The first forms of silence one notices are purely linguistic. The jargon of the Soviet administration, which often serves to screen off a reality too stark to describe, is a prime example of this. These silences remind us that contemporary forms of expression and the terms we use to describe the Gulag today, often merge with older ways of speaking. From this perspective alone, it is important to bear in mind the historical burden carried by the Russian language, so thoroughly have the phraseology and rhetorical features of Soviet newspeak permeated even the most ordinary forms of speech.

With respect to the Gulag, then, it is always striking that the victims have no other choice but to use the (administrative) language of their tormentors to describe the concentrationary system and how it functioned. Despite its vivid inventiveness, camp slang is rarely used. In the absence of an alternative to Soviet bureaucratic jargon, then, the universe of the camps has usually been evoked in terms based on the point of view of its creators. These silent lexical forms, and other means of producing silence through language itself, can thus be seen as having a direct link to what Cohen terms 'literal denial'.[32] This first type of denial implies an inability even to acknowledge a fact. In the case of the Gulag, this denial has been transferred from the dominant symbolic space (that of the persecutors) onto that of Soviet society as a whole, through language.

6.2 Rhetorical strategies, discursive silence and interpretative denial

The second form of silence found in the accounts of the vast majority of witnesses to the past of the Soviet camps, such as Nina, is a feature of rhetorical strategies. This silence occurs at the more extended level of discourse. It shows us the predominant role played by literature in moulding narrative processes and, beyond this, in constructing the semantic frameworks of collective memory. In the Soviet context, then, major literary works provide pre-existing 'scripts', archetypal situations and emblematic characters for those who wish to give their testimony.

In Russia, literature has also been able to give a high degree of legitimacy to those wanting to speak out, providing a source of rhetorical techniques based on a total mastery of the language and the skilled use of tropes and figures such as periphrasis, antiphrasis and metaphor. These discursive 'silences' (in the sense that the witnesses in question do not use their own words) seem to be more closely

32 Cohen, *States of Denial*, 7.

linked to the form of denial that Cohen terms 'interpretative'.[33] For these feats of rhetorical virtuosity serve in the final analysis to mask the concrete specificity of the events they describe and the facts they recount, by associating them with other classes of facts and other types of events.

6.3 The loneliness of the narrator: social silence and implicatory denial

The final forms of silence that we have been able to identify truly reveal, in the Russian context, the loneliness of narrators like Vera. This loneliness, a product of the status of the camp witness in Soviet and post-Soviet societies, constitutes the foundation, one might say, of social forms of silence. This social silence throws a stark light on the problems of legitimacy associated with speaking out in a cultural and historical context in which talking about the Gulag is not yet a simple or everyday act.

One probable source of this problem is the way in which the former detainees of the Gulag had their status as victims recognised. First, it was possible for detainees, even in the Soviet period, to have their conviction annulled and their civil rights restored. However, this rehabilitation process, based on the recognition that there had been no reason for the conviction, did not involve any admission of error or wrongdoing on the part of the state. It was only after 1991, with the introduction of new legislation,[34] that former prisoners of the Gulags could have their status as victims of political repression recognised. As such, they can still claim financial compensation for material damages incurred as a result of their imprisonment. However, the possibility of claiming compensation for moral damages, which was envisaged in the original law of 1991, was removed by an amendment voted by the Russian Duma in 2007.

This enduring production of social silence regarding the victim status of former deportees to the Gulags seems to represent a form of implicatory denial as described by Cohen.[35] The latter defines implicatory denial as a technique of avoidance which allows wider social implications to be kept at arm's length, and dismisses the very idea of collective mobilisation. The case of Russia shows that the implementation of 'silencing' legislation can also very effectively help to perpetuate these forms of denial.

7 Conclusion

In the light of the examples provided by these actors in the legacy of the Soviet camps, we can, first of all, at a preliminary level of analysis, conclude that each

33 Ibid.
34 Arseni Roginsky and Nadine Marie-Schwartzenberg, 'Réhabilitation et législations', in Elisabeth Anstett and Luba Jurgenson (eds), *Le Goulag en héritage, pour une anthropologie de la trace* (Paris: Pétra, 2009), 57–70.
35 Cohen, *States of Denial*, 8.

form of silence constitutes a response to a particular danger, a particular threat. This threat is perceived by the speaker in more or less distinct terms within his or her social, political or symbolic environment. The linguistic games engaged in by the former detainees or neighbours of the camps whom I have interviewed are not always enough to neutralise these dangers.

To a similar extent to during the Soviet era, then, if in a different way, the act of speaking out in public continues to represent a risk in the post-Soviet context. Those who speak out therefore place limits on what they say. The violence of Kim's language is thus oriented towards the past: he insults Stalin and Lenin with gusto, but never says a word against the present Russian government. Nina, meanwhile, laments a tragic and painful collective past but will not say who was responsible for this collective tragedy. Vera, for her part, prefers not to speak out at all rather than risk her words being misinterpreted or misused by others.

The silences to which victims of the Gulags resort thus represent linguistic ways around some awkward questions. These silences shed light (to some extent negatively, through absence) on subjects that remain difficult to discuss in Russia, owing to a lack of social consensus as to how they should be dealt with. At the same time, these silences create spaces of powerful collective denial. For these ways of saying, which are also ways of silencing, prevent various elements that could give rise to an alternative debate from being analysed, commented upon, talked about or sometimes even named. Silence and denial, in this respect, overlap closely.

Yet if every form of silence maps onto a method of denial, it is essential to stress that the witnesses interviewed here are not always producers of denial, but often simply reproduce existing forms thereof. These language games and methods of denial are, in many instances, social constructions that long predate the context of this enquiry. These collective ways of producing denial can be seen, in this respect, as heavily influenced by political and ideological uses of discourse, such as the neologisms or propaganda that so typified the Soviet era. Their history has yet to be written.

Chapter 5

The presence of the past

On the significance of the Holocaust and the criminalisation of its negation in the Federal Republic of Germany[1]

Christian Mentel

There are few, if any, countries in the world for which history plays such an important role as for the Federal Republic of Germany (FRG) today. The number of exhibitions, books, movies, TV programmes, signs of remembrance in public space, the budget available to memorial sites and learning facilities, and the number of university courses give evidence for that. Also, particular importance is attributed to days of remembrance, large controversies on all kinds of historical issues are erupting periodically, and local grassroots initiatives digging into the often gloomy past of their neighbourhoods are valued as important for civil society. German politics are no exception to that. At least implicitly, the past is present in current debates no matter whether the subject is internet surveillance or a refugee crisis. In most cases it is a particular past: the Nazi past, and at its centre the Holocaust.

However, assuming that the Holocaust always had such a significance for FRG political and memory cultures would be wrong. To trace the transformation of its importance, we may count among the major indicators the manner in which attempts to negate or downplay the Holocaust have been dealt with over time.[2] Apparently, juridical actions and reactions in respect to negationism form the most important set of clues to what societal norms persisted in respect to the Holocaust, and how they were applied in respective times. Nevertheless, to interpret laws and jurisdiction in an isolated fashion would leave crucial questions unanswered, not least why the FRG took certain steps towards criminalisation of negationism at certain points in time, and what significance these steps both held and hold for society and State.

Based on previous findings by many scholars, it is the general assumption of this chapter that beyond their symbolic meaning, legislative processes, laws, litigation and court rulings hold utmost importance for the way post-1945 West German society dealt with the Nazi past. More specifically, I hold that juridical

1 I have benefited greatly from comments made by Paul Behrens, Olaf Jensen, Nicholas Terry and Richard Mullender; special thanks for critical readings of previous versions of this chapter are extended to Jacob S. Eder, Jan-Holger Kirsch and especially to Gideon Botsch.
2 Instead of the common term 'denial' I will use the more descriptive notion 'nega-tion'/'negationism'. Also, I am using the term 'Holocaust' in an analytical way, which is not to say that this was the case in respective times.

events occupied with negationism are standing even more in close, complex and reciprocal relationships with many other events, changes and transformations in respective times.

The many contexts that ought to be taken into account are already pointed out by practically all scholars working the field – jurists, historians, sociologists and others. Next to general political, cultural and societal factors are counted legal, legislative and jurisdictional traditions and perceptions, as well as historical experiences and mind-sets that resulted in the 'militant democracy' (*Streitbare Demokratie*) concept. Additionally, the capacity of legislation and jurisdiction as societal focal points of self-definition have been highlighted, both for the State and the population.[3] Though these studies which followed contextual and often comparative approaches have made important findings and gained crucial insights, it appears that their potential has not been fully exploited.

It is the aim of this chapter to offer a somewhat new perspective on the FRG's criminalisation of negationism. As a first step, I will provide a condensed synopsis of the path to the 1994 law that explicitly criminalised Holocaust negation. To do so, I will focus on the four major juridical events of the FRG's handling of the negationism phenomenon in 1960, 1979, 1985 and 1994. As a second step, I will review and analyse these instances in context in order to identify constants, similarities and differences between them, and in the significance that was attributed to the Holocaust and its negation in respective times. As will be seen, these juridical events follow a common pattern – despite the fact that they took place over the course of roughly 40 years and under very diverse conditions.[4]

I 'Incitement of the people' (1960)

The first landmark that has to be addressed is an amendment that created the crime 'incitement of the people' (*Volksverhetzung*) as §130 of the criminal code, and

3 Robert A. Kahn, *Holocaust Denial and the Law. A Comparative Study* (Basingstoke, 2004); Thomas Wandres, *Die Strafbarkeit des Auschwitz-Leugnens* (Berlin, 2000); Emanuela Fronza, 'The Criminal Protection of Memory. Some Observations About the Offense of Holocaust Denial', in Ludovic Hennebel and Thomas Hochmann (eds), *Genocide Denials and the Law* (Oxford, 2011), 155–81; Markus Bernhardt, 'Holocaustleugnung und Strafrecht als erinnerungskulturelles Phänomen', in Vadim Oswalt/Hans-Jürgen Pandel (eds), *Geschichtskultur. Die Anwesenheit von Vergangenheit in der Gegenwart* (Schwalbach am Taunus, 2009), 139–52; Eric Stein, 'History against Free Speech. The New German Law against the "Auschwitz" – and Other – "Lies"', *Michigan Law Review* 85 (1986), 277–324; Sergey Lagodinsky, *Kontexte des Antisemitismus. Rechtliche und gesellschaftliche Aspekte der Meinungsfreiheit und ihrer Schranken* (Berlin, 2013).
4 For an overview on periods and issues touched upon in the following, cf. Torben Fischer/Matthias N. Lorenz (eds), *Lexikon der 'Vergangenheitsbewältigung' in Deutschland. Debatten- und Diskursgeschichte des Nationalsozialismus nach 1945* (Bielefeld, 2015, 3rd edition); Norbert Frei, 'Deutsche Lernprozesse. NS-Vergangenheit und Generationenfolge 1945', in Norbert Frei, *1945 und wir. Das Dritte Reich im Bewußtsein der Deutschen* (Munich, 2005), 23–40; Gideon Botsch, *Die extreme Rechte in der Bundesrepublik Deutschland 1949 bis heute* (Darmstadt, 2012).

which became effective on 4 August 1960.[5] It covered offences that 'attack the human dignity of others' by means of insult and inciting hatred and violence. This provision neither mentioned Holocaust negation explicitly nor did it cover it completely – only when Holocaust negation was delivered as an attack on others could this paragraph be applied for prosecution. In contrast, this was not possible in case of a mere statement on history lacking vilification.[6]

It is crucial to bear in mind the general political framework of the time. On the one hand, the FRG and its Constitution were constructed as the counterpoint of the 'Third Reich', and Nazi ideology was segregated and condemned. On the other hand, the crimes during the Nazi period and the victims were excluded from the public focus; most West Germans shifted their share of accountability and guilt to a narrow group of Nazi leaders. The prevailing mood and popular demand was that the Nazi past should be 'cordoned off'. Correspondingly, Chancellor Konrad Adenauer and, with him, all of West German politics pursued a policy of integration which brought officials back to their desks and granted amnesty to convicted Nazi criminals, thus slowing down the willingness to prosecute other Nazi criminals.[7]

The congregation of these factors – that is, the way in which the Nazi past was mostly dealt with on the political, societal, juridical and personal levels – constitutes the main reason for the 1960 amendment. However, it was triggered by the so-called Nieland case. In 1957, Hamburg merchant Friedrich Nieland had sent a comprehensive anti-Semitic pamphlet to all ministers and members of parliaments in the FRG. In this brochure, Nieland ranted about 'World Jewry' preparing a Third World War, he claimed that Jews had themselves gassed in order to camouflage their crimes on Germany, and that he had discovered hidden messages when rearranging the characters of certain book titles.[8]

As crude and inciting as Nieland's pamphlet was, it earned its importance for national politics mainly because of the issues involved, which turned the case into a scandal even monitored abroad. First, there was the judiciary's reaction. Despite blatant anti-Semitism liable to prosecution, the Hamburg Regional Court dismissed the case in late 1958. If this were not enough, Judge Enno Budde argued that the pamphlet was not directed against Jews in general (thus, not against the Constitution), but only against 'a narrowly defined group of Jews, that is World Jewry'.[9] Second, not only did this reasoning seem to verify the Weimar topos that German judiciary is 'blind in the right eye', soon enough it became known that Budde as a judge in the Nazi era had praised anti-Jewish

---

5 For pre-existing criminal law provisions that did not rise to prominence, cf. Joachim Neander, 'Mit dem Strafrecht gegen die "Auschwitz-Lüge". Ein halbes Jahrhundert §130 Strafgesetzbuch "Volksverhetzung"', *Theologie Geschichte* 1 (2006), 275–325.
6 Benedikt Rohrßen, *Von der 'Anreizung zum Klassenkampf' zur 'Volksverhetzung' (§ 130 StGB). Reformdiskussion und Gesetzgebung seit dem 19. Jahrhundert* (Berlin/New York, 2009).
7 Norbert Frei, *Adenauer's Germany and the Nazi Past. The Politics of Amnesty and Integration* (New York, 2002).
8 JZ 1959, 414.
9 Ibid., 176. Translation by the author.

policies.[10] Third, the Nieland case was only one more in a whole series of anti-Semitic incidents that had occurred in the FRG since the mid-1950s. Unprecedented in terms of quality and quantity, these incidents started to encompass officials and ordinary citizens as well.[11]

The Nieland case indicated that the scope of anti-Semitism among the population was still wide, and even rising. In the eyes of politicians, not only did this mean danger for Jews, the youth, the still-young democracy and its reputation, but it also became obvious that this resurrection or persistence of anti-Semitism was connected to the continuous agency of officials with a Nazi past – not least judges, none of whom had ever been sentenced by a Federal court, and who in many cases proved to be extraordinarily soft on anti-Semites on trial after 1945. These implications as well as negative reactions abroad drove the cabinet to approve the amendment of §130 only five days after the Budde ruling became known in January 1959. A few days afterwards, it was even discussed in a parliamentary *Bundestag* debate on the judiciary.[12] However, it still took more than a year for the amendment finally to be approved.

In December 1959 a massive eruption of anti-Semitism in the form of graffiti and desecrations, mostly committed by youths and lasting for months, was witnessed all over the FRG. After even more right-wing extremist incidents, the authorities banned student and youth organisations that were held accountable. All of this influenced the controversial debate on the amendment. Critics – among them Hendrik G. van Dam, secretary-general of the Central Council of Jews in Germany – warned of establishing a 'national park' for Jews. Even though the law did not mention Jews specifically, it turned out to be exactly what van Dam warned against: a special 'Jew law'.[13]

Not least because of the outbursts of anti-Semitism and the corresponding debates, the 'period of silence' about the 'unresolved past' – as the 1950s are often called – approached its end and a self-reflective, critical public opinion started to emerge. The exhibition 'Ungesühnte Nazijustiz' (Unatoned Nazi Justice), which opened in November 1959 and was organised by students, provides one of the most important pieces of evidence for that.[14]

10 Rainer Hering, 'Der Fall "Nieland" und sein Richter. Zur Kontinuität in der Hamburger Justiz zwischen "Drittem Reich" und Bundesrepublik', *Zeitschrift des Vereins für Hamburgische Geschichte* 81 (1995), 207–22.

11 Werner Bergmann, *Antisemitismus in öffentlichen Konflikten. Kollektives Lernen in der politischen Kultur der Bundesrepublik 1949–1989* (Frankfurt am Main/New York, 1997), 187–277.

12 Ibid., 208–21. It may be added that Josef Schafheutle who in the Federal Ministry of Justice was in charge of the amendment, was already on post in the Reich Ministry of Justice's political criminal law department. On continuities between both ministries, cf. Manfred Görtemaker/Christoph Safferling, *Die Akte Rosenburg. Das Bundesministerium der Justiz und die NS-Zeit* (Munich, 2016).

13 Christoph Jahr, *Antisemitismus vor Gericht. Debatten über die juristische Ahndung judenfeindlicher Agitation in Deutschland (1879–1960)* (Frankfurt am Main/New York, 2011), 370–81.

14 Stephan Alexander Glienke, *Die "Ausstellung 'Ungesühnte Nazijustiz' (1959–1962)". Zur Geschichte der Aufarbeitung nationalsozialistischer Justizverbrechen* (Baden-Baden, 2008).

Thus, as much as the 1960 amendment and its prehistory indicate a major shift in terms of how West German society dealt with the Nazi past and its remnants, we have to be careful not to assume that this is true to the same extent for the particular issue of the Holocaust. It was only in the course of the high-profile Eichmann and Auschwitz trials of the early 1960s that the Holocaust rose to a certain prominence. Or, to be more precise, 'Auschwitz', because there was no such thing as the Holocaust yet, at least nothing synonymous with both what we subsume under the term and the significance we attribute to it today.[15] Accordingly, Holocaust negation was no prominent phenomenon. Just like Nieland with his pamphlet, rarely was the murder and its scope denied in its totality – instead, to have committed these acts personally, to have approved of, or to have had knowledge of them.

2 Holocaust negation as insult (1979)

Almost 20 years later, we can discern a second major step. In its ruling of 18 September 1979, the Federal Supreme Court laid out an interpretation of criminal law that was about to shape future jurisdiction and legislation. According to the judges, Holocaust negation – even when delivered as mere historical statements lacking racial vilification – was punishable as insult (§§185 et seq. of the criminal code) and all Jews living in the FRG were entitled to press charges on these terms.[16]

Just like the 1960 amendment, the 1979 court decision marks an important turning point. After a decade in which society's attention was mainly focused on the left and leftist terror, at the end of the 1970s the extreme right, the Nazi past and the question of how to deal with both of them returned to the agenda with force. As part of this and in contrast to the 1950s and 1960s, Holocaust negation obtained considerable public attention and reached its first peak. The title of one of the most infamous of the negationist brochures of the time – former *Schutzstaffel* (SS) man Thies Christophersen's 1973 'Die Auschwitz-Lüge' (The Auschwitz Lie) – quickly became the official term for the so far little-known phenomenon Holocaust negation.

The case the Federal Supreme Court had to decide upon goes back to an incident in 1975, when the defendant displayed a leaflet attached to his house, claiming that the murder of 6 million Jews was a 'Zionist swindle'. With this statement, the claimant (whose Jewish grandfather was killed at Auschwitz) saw his personal honour harmed. However, the Higher Regional Court Koblenz

15 Clemens Vollnhals, 'Zwischen Verdrängung und Aufklärung. Die Auseinandersetzung mit dem Holocaust in der frühen Bundesrepublik', in Ursula Büttner (ed.), *Die Deutschen und die Judenverfolgung im Dritten Reich* (Frankfurt am Main, 2003), 381–422; Dirk van Laak, 'Der Platz des Holocaust im deutschen Geschichtsbild', in Konrad H. Jarausch/Martin Sabrow (eds), *Die historische Meistererzählung. Deutungslinien der deutschen Nationalgeschichte* (Göttingen, 2002), 163–93.
16 NJW 1980, 45.

had dismissed the charge of insult because as a person born post-1945, the claimant was not a victim of Nazi persecution and hence not personally affected.[17]

Obviously, the generational aspect became important by the 1970s: the time of the 'Third Reich' was no longer a shared experience of all contemporaries. The next generation had come forth – also on the extreme right. Two aspects have to be mentioned to grasp the changes at hand. First, neo-Nazis now proved not only to be increasingly militant, but even committed acts of murder and terror. Second, they transformed negationism from a minor issue in 'general' anti-Semitic statements of old Nazis into an aggressive neo-Nazi propaganda strategy. The by far best-known of such propaganda efforts took place in 1978, when a small group of neo-Nazis marched through Hamburg while wearing donkey masks and with posters on their fronts such as '*Ich Esel glaube noch, daß in deutschen KZs Juden "vergast" wurden*' (I, donkey, still believe that in German concentration camps Jews were 'gassed'). It is no coincidence that the 22-year-old leader of this demonstration, Michael Kühnen, who subsequently rose to become one of Germany's major neo-Nazis, was the protégé of Christophersen.[18]

However, we should interpret these transformations on the extreme right only together with more general shifts in society, first and foremost the significance of Nazism in general and the Holocaust in particular. The broadcast of the TV miniseries 'Holocaust' in January 1979 is only the most obvious indicator of such transformations: West German society opened itself in an unprecedented way to what the extermination of Jews meant concretely, and increasingly the racial terror regime came into focus.[19] Facing this shift, Holocaust negation became attractive for neo-Nazis. First, because only by negating this crime could followers without genocidal intentions still be attracted. Second, mirroring the importance of the Holocaust for societal discourse, its negation gained an entirely new potential to provoke, and hence was well suited to propaganda.

The way in which negationism was delivered also became more diversified. The defendant tried to invoke these trends when he claimed that his leaflet constituted a legitimate revision of historiography.[20] Since the early 1970s, some of the more sophisticated negationist authors had started to present their writings as works of historical scholarship, rather than the previous style of mostly poorly written, hate-filled pamphlets. Now they contained hundreds of pages, footnotes, references to primary sources and seemed to be reasonably argued. The first major German book of this kind was 'Der Auschwitz-Mythos' (The Auschwitz Myth) by

---

17 Ibid., 45.
18 ID-Archiv im ISSG (ed.), *Drahtzieher im braunen Netz. Der Wiederaufbau der NSDAP* (Berlin/Amsterdam, 1993).
19 Harald Schmid, 'Die "Stunde der Wahrheit" und ihre Voraussetzungen. Zum geschichtskulturellen Wirkungskontext von "Holocaust"', *Historische Sozialforschung/ Historical Social Research* vol. 30, no. 4 (2005), 18–28.
20 NJW 1980, 45ff.

former Hamburg judge Wilhelm Stäglich.[21] Coincidence or not, the book appeared in March 1979, just days from a crucial *Bundestag* debate on the statute of limitations in respect to murder committed under Nazi rule. By contrast to the prior debates of 1965 and 1969, and under the distinct influence of the 'Holocaust' miniseries, only in 1979 would murder now cease to become time-barred.

Against this backdrop, the Federal Supreme Court in 1979 had to decide on appeal if the personal honour of the claimant of Jewish descent was harmed by Holocaust negation. The court argued that the fact that people of Jewish descent were persecuted and murdered by the Nazi State was not a distant historical fact like others, but still 'present' today in that it defined the relationship of 'Jews and Germans'. Denying that Jews were persecuted meant attacking 'one of the guarantees against repetition of such discrimination and a precondition of their lives in the Federal Republic'. Thus, the court considered not only Jews with first-hand experience of persecution as harmed and insulted by negationism, but whoever would have been persecuted as a Jew by the Nazis then. Applying the 1935 Nuremberg Race Laws, the court found the claimant to be of mixed race (*Mischling*) and hence part of this group.[22]

Whereas in 1960 considerable criticism was caused by a special law aimed at protecting Jews which would echo the legislative discrimination by the Nazis, the fact that in this case a German court effectively applied the Nuremberg Race Laws did not provoke many critical voices at all. Most commentators did not even mention this move by the court – the few who did (even if mostly in specialist literature and only years later) considered this unfortunate indeed, but emphasised instead the judges' good intentions, welcomed the general tenor of sympathy and support for Jews, and praised the end result: Holocaust negation was declared punishable.[23]

So, we may interpret the ruling's ambivalent content as a snapshot of a phase in which sensitivity towards Jewish suffering during the Nazi years and the Holocaust in particular was basically there, though still in a state of transformation, with the next step almost in sight.

3 The Nazi regime or another 'violent and arbitrary dominance' (1985)

Shortly after the 1979 Federal Supreme Court ruling began a process of parliamentary debate and legislation on how negationism should be dealt with. Despite the intentions of both coalition and opposition to create a separate Holocaust negation offence in the criminal code, eventually an amendment was approved

---

21 The first English edition appeared in 1986 as *Auschwitz. A Judge Looks at the Evidence*, published by the California-based negationist 'Institute for Historical Review' which itself was founded in 1978.

22 NJW 1980, 45ff. Translation by the author.

23 Wandres, *Die Strafbarkeit des Auschwitz-Leugnens*, 123–7.

that modified the legal situation on a procedural level only, becoming effective on 1 August 1985.

The origins of the 1985 amendment lay with the contexts already described in the previous section. On the one hand, the Holocaust was no longer a blind spot in public and scholarly discourses, and was becoming increasingly important to West German political and memory cultures. On the other hand, neo-Nazism was still growing and turning ever more violent, as can be seen in lethal arson attacks on the homes of asylum seekers and in the example of the Munich *Oktoberfest* bombing in 1980, an act of terrorism that killed 13 and injured over 200. The same year also witnessed the targeted murder of publisher Shlomo Lewin, a prominent member of the Jewish community, and his spouse Frida Poeschke, in Erlangen.[24] At the same time, the Federal government commissioned the first ever study on right-wing extremism and banned neo-Nazi associations and other extreme right-wing groups such as the paramilitary *Wehrsportgruppe Hoffmann*, whose members had been held accountable for the Munich and Erlangen attacks.

Against this backdrop, the 1979 Federal Supreme Court decision was deemed insufficient and unsatisfactory – it was held that the framework of laws concerned with personal honour falls short of the scope of the Nazi crimes against the Jews, a contention that was shared by all political parties.[25] Obviously, now negationism was beginning to be perceived as a phenomenon in its own right, though still of an anti-Semitic and neo-Nazi kind.

Thus, in September 1982, the government for the first time proposed a bill that explicitly outlawed the downplaying, approval of and denial of the Holocaust. Yet only days later, Chancellor Helmut Schmidt's government fell apart. Interestingly enough, after the end of the coalition between the Social Democrats and Liberals, the new coalition of Conservatives and Liberals under Chancellor Helmut Kohl put the bill to the vote without changes in the upper chamber (*Bundesrat*). However, the bill was turned down because it was considered questionable in terms of freedom of opinion. The Kohl government submitted the very same bill a second time, only to be turned down once more in April 1983. Even when in mid-1984 the *Bundestag* discussed the matter again, both government and opposition still proposed almost identical bills. However, to prevent the *Bundesrat* from turning down the almost unchanged bill a third time, the matter was referred to the legal committee for the time being.[26]

By early 1985, when the Social Democrat faction insisted on adopting a bill on negationism before the 40th anniversary of the end of World War II on 8 May 1945, the framework of FRG politics in respect to history had changed. Kohl's previous announcement that he would introduce a new way of dealing with the German past had by now been implemented. In late 1984, together with French President François Mitterrand, Kohl commemorated the start of World War I at

24 Botsch, *Die extreme Rechte*, 81ff.
25 Wandres, *Die Strafbarkeit des Auschwitz-Leugnens*, 110.
26 Ibid., 110ff.

Verdun, and on the occasion of the 40th anniversary of the end of World War II, together with US President Ronald Reagan, he was to visit a soldiers' cemetery at Bitburg for another highly symbolic act of reconciliation.[27]

While this is not to argue that the 1985 amendment is part of Kohl's politics of history, it is most important to be aware of its parallels and simultaneities to the Kohlian initiatives. As already hit upon by critics at the time, Kohl's baseline was to create a renewed positive identification with the German nation and to gain 'normality'. In order to accomplish this, Kohl stressed the West German democratic transformation after 1945, which inevitably meant de-emphasising the Nazi years. As can be seen in Kohl's politics of history and especially the scandal surrounding the visit to the Bitburg cemetery together with Reagan – where no US soldiers are buried, while *Waffen-SS* members are – there was a tendency to relativise, to abstract and to erase differences between perpetrators and victims.[28]

Some of these characteristics can be detected even in the phrasing of the law. Despite the original intentions of both coalition and opposition, no new offence was created; instead, the need for private petition for the insult charge was dropped. More importantly, shortly before approval, the legal committee inserted an addition. Now, prosecution would be initiated not only in cases of negation of the Holocaust and Nazi crimes, but also when crimes of another 'violent and arbitrary dominance' (*Gewalt- und Willkürherrschaft*) were negated. This insertion – which was meant to protect German expellees of the former Eastern territories from their fate being negated – tied in seamlessly with Kohl's other initiatives as touched upon above. Accordingly, parliamentarians, jurists and other observers heavily criticised this juxtaposition of the Holocaust with other crimes.[29] Thus, one could say that what was denounced by critics in 1960 – namely the legislative accentuation (or: the positive discrimination) of Jews – was desired by the critics of 1985.

It seems that while in the mid-1980s the significance of the Holocaust was at an abstract level commonly accepted, its concrete place – its 'singularity' and/or 'comparability' – was yet to be argued about. This can be observed also in the things to come, most notably during the *Historikerstreit* (historians' debate), which took off just one year later and perpetuated the already ongoing conflicts between two self-conceptions: on the one hand, the conservative Kohlian way of emphasising the post-1945 West German democratic transformation over the Nazi past; on the other hand, the left-liberal affirmation of the outstanding significance of

---

27 Jan-Holger Kirsch, '"Hier geht es um den Kern unseres Selbstverständnisses als Nation". Helmut Kohl und die Genese des Holocaust-Gedenkens als bundesdeutscher Staatsräson', *Potsdamer Bulletin für Zeithistorische Studien* no. 43/44 (2008), 40–9.

28 Werner Bergmann, 'Die Bitburg-Affäre in der deutschen Presse. Rechtskonservative und linksliberale Interpretationen', in Werner Bergmann/Rainer Erb/Albert Lichtblau (eds), *Schwieriges Erbe. Der Umgang mit Nationalsozialismus und Antisemitismus in Österreich, der DDR und der Bundesrepublik Deutschland* (Frankfurt am Main, 1995), 402–28.

29 Stein, 'History against Free Speech', 307ff; Wandres, *Die Strafbarkeit des Auschwitz-Leugnens*, 112ff.

the 'Third Reich'.[30] Ironically, as harsh as these conflicts were, they intersected with an agreement to outlaw negationism – because, as Lawrence Douglas has so rightly noted, the law 'serves not only to connect the present German state to its past incarnation, but also to sever such ties'.[31]

4 'Incitement of the people' reconsidered (1994)

Almost ten years after the 1985 amendment, the lawmakers took the last step on the path towards the explicit criminalisation of Holocaust negation. In mid-1994, after almost a decade without parliamentary debate on the issue, an amendment of §130 ('incitement of the people') was approved both by the Conservative-Liberal coalition and the opposition. For the first time, Holocaust negation became an explicit crime, effective from 1 December 1994.

With German unification in 1990, the framework of both German political and memory cultures as well as the general political context changed considerably. One of the most important backdrops to mention is the massive outburst of violence against foreigners, many among them asylum seekers. Not only were sentiments of xenophobia widespread in the early 1990s, but acts of physical violence and murder also reached all-time peaks. These were mostly perpetrated by neo-Nazis who encountered considerable support from 'ordinary citizens': numerous spectators applauded when arson attacks set living quarters of asylum seekers on fire.[32] Taken together with the fact that right-wing extremist parties succeeded in their efforts to get elected into state parliaments, this was interpreted as evidence that xenophobia in conjunction with right-wing extremist and/or neo-Nazi ideology was being disseminated into society at large. Accordingly, just as in the early 1960s and early 1980s, many right-wing extremist organisations were banned.

For many on the extreme right, the Holocaust now seemed to be the last main obstacle preventing united West and East German populations from turning to Nazism as a political alternative. Bela Ewald Althans, one of the most engaging neo-Nazi leaders at the time, laid out this strategy: 'Auschwitz must fall before man can accept what we want. The people all say, hey, that Althans, that's a nice guy, but Auschwitz … This is the problem.'[33] He and others drew heavily on a

---

30 On the *Historikerstreit* and its contexts, cf. Klaus Große Kracht, *Die zankende Zunft. Historische Kontroversen in Deutschland nach 1945* (Göttingen, 2005). On the connection of the 1985 amendment and the *Historikerstreit*, cf. the readers' letters in *Michigan Law Review* 87 (1989), 1026–32.

31 Lawrence Douglas, *The Memory of Judgment* (New Haven, 2001), 220.

32 Hermann Kurthen/Werner Bergmann/Rainer Erb (eds), *Antisemitism and Xenophobia in Germany after Unification* (Oxford, 1997).

33 Michael Schmidt, *The New Reich. Violent Extremism in Unified Germany and Beyond* (New York, 1993), 216. Althans made his remark during an interview in Schmidt's TV documentary 'The Truth Shall Make Us Free. Inside the Neo-Nazi Network' on which the book is based. Produced by Channel 1 of national Swedish TV, the programme premiered there on 18 September 1991, while it was first shown in Germany merely by regional TV station West 3 on 14 April 1992.

recent negationist strategy pioneered by the self-proclaimed American engineer Fred A. Leuchter, who argued that he had proven scientifically that the gas chambers in the Nazi extermination camps could not have been employed as means of mass murder. With his 'Leuchter Report', financed by Althans's mentor, Ernst Zündel – one of the most important neo-Nazi and negationist propagandists at the time – Leuchter constituted not only the decisive reason for the rise of negationism in the late 1980s and early 1990s, but also became the starting point for the 1994 amendment.

Because he had approvingly interpreted a Leuchter lecture during a meeting, Günter Deckert, leader of the extreme right-wing National Democratic Party (NPD), had been convicted in 1992 by the District Court of Mannheim of having committed 'incitement of the people'.[34] However, the trigger for the legislative process leading to the amendment was less the content of the speech than the way it was dealt with by the judiciary; to be more precise, by the judges. When Deckert's conviction was overturned by the Federal Supreme Court in March 1994 because the judgment was found to lack substantial reasoning, considerable public criticism erupted. While the Federal Supreme Court ruling itself constituted no change of course in terms of jurisdiction and reasoning, it had been presented in a way that made observers think the exact opposite. For them, the decision was not only a manual of how legally to negate the Holocaust, but also a 'perversion' in that it differentiated between 'simple' negation (mere historical statements) and 'qualified' negation (including racial vilification).[35]

It is noteworthy that this juridical differentiation, which had not caused criticism in prior years, now offended sensibilities in regard to the Holocaust. Obviously, after the controversies of the 1980s, by the 1990s the Holocaust had reached yet another level of significance – it may even be said that it was now embraced as the ultimate reference point of united Germany's memory culture. The whole attitude towards memorial sites had changed fundamentally, remembrance had intensified and countless Nazi-related societal focal points could be observed in the early and mid-1990s, among them the successful movie *Schindler's List* (opening in March 1994), the 50th anniversary of the liberation of Auschwitz and the end of World War II, the controversial *Wehrmacht* exhibition (all in 1995) and the Goldhagen debate of 1996.[36]

With this zeitgeist in mind, it is hardly surprising that the public controversy about the 1994 Federal Supreme Court ruling had considerable effects in the

---

34 Wolfgang Benz, 'Realitätsverweigerung als antisemitisches Prinzip. Die Leugnung des Holocaust', in Wolfgang Benz (ed.), *Antisemitismus in Deutschland. Zur Aktualität eines Vorurteils* (Munich, 1995), 121–39.

35 NJW 1994, 1421 ff.; for an overview on the criticism, cf. Gregor Peter Schmitz, *Geschichte per Gesetz? Die Debatten zum Umgang mit dem Phänomen der Holocaustleugnung in Deutschland, Großbritannien und den Vereinigten Staaten von Amerika*, Diss. University of Erfurt, 2007, 159–72.

36 Bill Niven, *Facing the Nazi Past. United Germany and the Legacy of the Third Reich* (London, 2002).

political sphere. Nevertheless, the speed of events may be called remarkable. Less than one month after the overturning of the verdict, for the first time in years, parliamentary discussions began on how to 'clarify' the legal situation. In little more than a month, the *Bundestag* legal committee approved unanimously a bill to amend §130 in order to explicitly criminalise Holocaust negation.[37] However, while the bill was still being discussed, the June 1994 verdict of the Deckert retrial generated even more attention, both in Germany and abroad. In their written opinion, the judges portrayed Deckert in positive terms only; they displayed compassion and sympathy for him and his ideas, and held that Deckert 'tried to strengthen the forces of resistance within the German people against Jewish demands derived from the Holocaust'.[38]

With this, a full-scale scandal erupted, one that displayed many similarities to the Nieland affair of the late 1950s. The judiciary as a whole was accused not only of being 'blind in the right eye', but of sharing an anti-Semitic attitude. Again, both the incidents and the reactions of the judiciary were assessed as serious for the FRG, both inwardly and outwardly.[39] In both the Nieland and Deckert cases, chancellors apologised and proclaimed their disapproval. Political and legislative actions at the national level were taken quickly, and the judges accountable were removed. Only one month afterwards the second Mannheim ruling became known and during the course of a tough national election campaign, an overwhelming majority in the *Bundestag* passed the bill, to be followed by the *Bundesrat* only two days later. Becoming effective in December 1994, anyone who approved of, denied or trivialised Nazi crimes could be sent to jail for up to five years.

Now it was no longer only Jews who were (more or less implicitly) conceded a special place in the code of law, but the Holocaust itself.

5 Constants, similarities and differences (1960–94)

When analysing in context the four juridical instances that have been presented, at first it may appear that their respective settings were quite different. Worlds lay between the situation of the late 1950s, when the Holocaust (and thus, its negation) was anything but the primary topic in public memory culture, compared to the early 1990s, when the Holocaust became its very centre. Also, negationism's bearers changed considerably. Whereas in the 1950s most negationists were to be counted among those old Nazis who stuck to their anti-Semitic beliefs, starting in the 1970s, negationism turned into a propaganda strategy of militant neo-Nazis born after 1945. Both means and strategies were also diversified. What was at first delivered in blatant anti-Semitic propaganda brochures was camouflaged as works of historical scholarship in the 1970s, and as scientific analyses by the late 1980s.

---

37 Wandres, *Die Strafbarkeit des Auschwitz-Leugnens*, 116–20.
38 NJW 1994, 2494–9. Translation by the author.
39 Schmitz, *Geschichte per Gesetz?*, 172–85.

Despite these differences, we may identify a common pattern. All four instances took place at times when in fact major shifts and transformations were occurring. The amendment of 1960 reflects the unprecedented anti-Semitic incidents of prior years and the fact that many of the Nazi elite were still to be found, unpunished, in high positions – all of which initiated a first period of critical reflection on the Nazi past. The ruling of the Federal Supreme Court in 1979 stood at a point in time when a generational change took place, neo-Nazism flourished and neo-Nazis committed terrorist attacks – and when, simultaneously, the whole picture of Nazism shifted and the Holocaust increasingly became seen as Nazism's major feature. The amendment of 1985, although rooted in the context of 1979, reflected Kohl's attempt to form a more positive way of dealing with the past, by (at least to some extent) equating crimes *of* Germans and crimes *against* Germans – which had considerable effects on the controversies of the 1980s about what significance the Holocaust should hold for the FRG. Finally, the 1994 amendment that criminalised negationism marked a period when not only neo-Nazi violence and the electoral successes of extreme right-wing parties reached all-time peaks, but also the Holocaust became accepted as the centre around which united Germany's memory culture was to revolve.

Thus, the main common denominator of these four steps towards criminalisation of Holocaust negation is their coincidence with upsurges of anti-Semitism and/or neo-Nazism. On the one hand, these upsurges started legislative and juridical debates on how to deal with the more or less new situation and led to corresponding adjustments. However, also executive measures were taken, like three major 'waves of repression' against the extreme right, most notably bans of youth organisations and other associations in the early 1960s, early 1980s and early 1990s. On the other hand, the upsurges generated broader societal debates not just on anti-Semitism and neo-Nazism, but on historical Nazism, to be more precise: on the state of 'facing', 'coping with' and/or 'working through' the Nazi past.

This entanglement of negationism, anti-Semitism, historical Nazism and neo-Nazism typical for Germany forced FRG society to define itself vis-à-vis the Nazi regime and the goals of neo-Nazism time and time again. Something similar occurred at the State level, in that the FRG repeatedly seemed to face the very same ideology that had destroyed its democratic predecessor, the Weimar Republic. Alongside this position of self-defence, another aspect should not be disregarded. By introducing anti-negationist laws and sentencing negationists, the State recognised its perpetration of the Holocaust as a crime. At least to some extent, this admission created a barrier against repetition – a threat that may arise considerably more easily when the State tolerates or even protects negation of its own crimes.

As with Holocaust negation, the shifts in anti-negationist legislation and jurisdiction mirror the rising significance of the Holocaust and Holocaust remembrance for society. This also seems to be the case in terms of special laws that both signal State recognition of Jewish suffering and mean repetition of discrimination, although in a positive way. Nevertheless, with the 1994 amendment of §130, the emphasis shifted from 'negationism as an attack on Jews' to 'nega-tionism as an attack on Holocaust remembrance', and indicates the Holocaust's grown importance for the nation as a whole. In that sense, §130 ceased to be a special law for Jews.

As the complexity of closely entangled events and transformations has shown, the rise of Holocaust awareness is not only due to prescription of provisions and jurisdiction. The law has not only been used 'from above' in order to send signals to societies in the FRG and abroad, to protect people from being insulted or to safeguard remembrance and the State's own democratic foundations. It has also constituted a reaction 'from below', for example when amendments were approved after – and because of – pressure by the media and the public. Here the law assumed the character of an *ex post facto* confirmation and amplification of values and norms already accepted and even called for by society. Moreover, applying these provisions seems to have contributed to confirming not only the appropriateness, but even the need for such laws in the eyes of observers. The latter can be seen in the late 2000s, when the prominent neo-Nazi negationists Sylvia Stolz and Horst Mahler spread anti-Semitism of the most brutal kind even in courtrooms.[40]

It follows that we best interpret negationism-related legislative and jurisdictional events in a two-fold way. On the one hand as shaping memory and political cultures, and on the other as being shaped by and being part of them as well.

---

40 Sylvia Stolz is an attorney who represented Ernst Zündel (see the text after n 33 above) in his trial before the Regional Court of Mannheim in 2005–07. As an example for her submissions in that context, see Antrag, 18 October 2005, Land-gericht Mannheim, 6 KLs 503 Js 4/96, www.voelkische-reichsbewegung.org/Schutz schrift_Sylvia%20Stolz.pdf (last accessed on 7 November 2008). Mahler, too, is an attorney. On his submissions on his own behalf, see, for example, Beweisantrag, 15 October 2008, Landgericht Potsdam, 24 KLs 42/05, recht-zur-verteidigung.org/BA_ Judaismus.pdf (last accessed on 7 November 2008).

Chapter 6

The prohibition of 'glorification of National Socialism' as an addition to the criminal provision on genocide denial

(Sect. 130 (4) of the German Criminal Code)

Björn Elberling and Alexander Hoffmann[1]

I Introduction

This chapter concerns itself not with Holocaust denial strictly speaking, but with a closely related phenomenon, namely the glorification of National Socialism. It is written from the perspective of practising lawyers who are also anti-fascist activists. Its focus is on Section 130 paragraph 4 of the German Criminal Code, which was introduced in April 2005, a few weeks prior to the celebrations of the 60th anniversary of the end of World War II in Europe. The new provision was added to Sect. 130 of the Criminal Code, entitled 'Incitement to Hatred' (*Volksverhetzung*), which in its para. 3 already codified the crime of Holocaust denial. Its wording is as follows:

> Whosoever publicly or in a meeting disturbs the public peace in a manner that violates the dignity of the victims by approving of, glorifying, or justifying National Socialist rule of arbitrary force shall be liable to imprisonment of not more than three years or a fine.[2]

Sect. 130 para. 4 is hardly ever put to use in its official capacity as a substantive criminal law provision: judicial statistics for the year 2013 show a total of six judicial proceedings against adults nationwide under this provision, of which three led to convictions, all fines. By contrast, a total of 300 judicial proceedings were

1 This chapter is based on a presentation at the workshop 'A Contextual View of Holocaust and Genocide Denial' at Leicester University, 23–24 September 2010. Many thanks are due to the organisers of the workshop, Paul Behrens and Olaf Jensen, as well as to the participants. Many thanks also to Lars-Arne Raffel for helpful comments. The usual disclaimer applies.
2 An English translation of the Criminal Code is available at www.gesetze-im-internet. de/englisch_stgb/.

conducted concerning the other parts of Sect. 130, of which 55 concerned the prohibition of Holocaust denial, and eight Holocaust deniers were sentenced to prison terms (albeit in all but one case suspended sentences).[3]

Rather than as a tool for individual prosecution, then, Sect. 130 para. 4 is mostly used as an instrument for the prohibition of (certain) neo-Nazi demonstrations. Under Sect. 15 para. 1 of the law on public demonstrations, a demonstration may be prohibited where there is an 'immediate danger to public security and order', and this includes the danger of a criminal act being committed.[4] Accordingly, a neo-Nazi demonstration may be prohibited where there is a danger that the crime of glorification of National Socialism will be committed by way of speeches, chants, leaflets, banners, etc.

This use has always been the main aim behind the provision, as already evidenced by its legislative history: it was introduced just shortly before the 60th anniversary of the end of World War II, following a parliamentary debate that focused mainly on the danger of neo-Nazis marching through the Brandenburg Gate on that day and of images of such a demonstration being broadcast all over the world.[5]

3 See the statistics provided by the Federal Statistical Office: Statistisches Bundesamt, Fachserie 10 Reihe 3–2013, Abgeurteilte und Verurteilte nach demographischen Merkmalen sowie Art der Straftat, angewandtem Strafrecht und Art der Entscheidung, available at: www.destatis.de/DE/Publikationen/Thematisch/Rechtspflege/StrafverfolgungVollzug/Strafverfolgung2100300137004.pdf.

4 The text of the Versammlungsgesetz is available, in German, at: www.gesetze-im-internet.de/versammlg. Following the so-called Federalism Reform of 2006, which shifted the jurisdiction for demonstrations from the federal level to the several Länder, some of the Länder have now passed their own laws on demonstrations. While all of these reproduce the text of Sect. 15 para. 1 of the federal code, some additionally contain further provisions prohibiting demonstrations based on their political contents – for the example of the Saxon law on demonstrations, see below, n 25.

5 The original proposal for a reform of Sect. 130 was presented by the governing Social Democrats and Greens on 14 February 2005 – see Deutscher Bundestag, Bundestags-Drucksache 15/4832 of 14 February 2005 – 'Entwurf eines Gesetzes zur Änderung des Versammlungsgesetzes und des Strafgesetzbuches', available at dip21.bundestag.de/dip21/btd/15/048/1504832.pdf. The law was passed, after an extremely speedy legislative process, on 24 March 2005. Besides introducing Sect. 130 para. 4, it also reformed the law on public demonstrations, adding a provision that allows for the prohibition of certain demonstrations close to certain public places such as the Holocaust Memorial in Berlin. The Christian Democrats had proposed instead to include the Brandenburg Gate in the 'no-protest zone' around the parliament (see Bundestags-Drucksache 15/4731 of – 'Entwurf eines Gesetzes zur Änderung des Gesetzes über befriedete Bezirke für Verfassungsorgane des Bundes', available at dip 21.bundestag.de/dip21/btd/15/047/1504731.pdf), a proposal which was rejected. For various references to a planned Nazi march through the Brandenburg Gate as the main occasion for the reforms, see the plenary protocols of parliamentary debates: Bundestag, Plenarprotokoll 15–158, 18 February 2005, available at dip21.bundestag.de/dip21/btp/15/15158.pdf, 14808 et seq.; Plenarprotokoll 15–164, 11 March 2005, available at dip21.bundestag.de/dip21/btp/15/15164.pdf, 15347 et seq. Some parliamentarians also referred to other demonstrations, such as the annual Hess

It should also be noted, however, that even the use of the new provision as a tool for the prohibition of Nazi marches has been somewhat limited. It has led to the prohibition and thus to the end of the Hess marches, commemorating the death of Hitler's deputy Rudolf Hess in the Allied prison in Spandau on 17 August 1987, which had taken place annually in the Franconian town of Wunsiedel where Hess was buried, and of a small number of additional demonstrations. Generally speaking, however, it has not made much of a dent in the full calendar of neo-Nazi marches in Germany. To give one prominent example, the annual marches in the city of Dresden, where up to 7,000 neo-Nazis from Germany and most of Europe met each year on the anniversary of the city's bombardment, were not prohibited under this provision.

Two more examples, both from the northernmost German state of Schleswig-Holstein, also show the limits of the use of Sect. 130 para. 4 as a provision against Nazi demonstrations: In 2010, i.e. after the ban of the Hess marches in Wunsiedel, neo-Nazis announced a demonstration in the town of Neumünster on 21 August, the weekend after the anniversary of Hess's death. In order to escape prohibition, they announced a commemoration of the death of King Frederick II of Prussia – who is hardly a mainstay of neo-Nazi demonstrations, but who conveniently also died on 17 August, in the year 1786. Despite the transparency of this ploy, the demonstration was not prohibited under Sect. 130 para. 4.[6] In 2012, the city of Lübeck banned a neo-Nazi march that had been held annually since 2006 in late March on the anniversary of the city's bombardment. The city based its decision *inter alia* on the danger that punishable acts of glorification of National Socialism would occur. The Administrative Court overturned that decision on the basis that the assertion of such danger was speculative – after all, not one marcher had been prosecuted under Sect. 130 para. 4 after any of the demonstrations in previous years.[7]

The main aim and use of Sect. 130 para. 4, then, is its usefulness in the prohibition of specific highly symbolic neo-Nazi demonstrations. It is for this reason that it has also been termed a 'lex Wunsiedel' after the location of the Hess marches. This gives rise to criticism from two distinct angles: the first concerns the relationship of this strategy to the politics of commemoration in modern-day

marches in Wunsiedel (Plenarprotokoll 15–158, pp. 14814–5 and 14819–20 (Dieter Wiefelspütz, Social Democratic Party); 14818 (Otto Schily, Social Democratic Party, Minister of the Interior); Plenarprotokoll 15–164, pp. 15351 (Silke Stokar von Neu-forn, Alliance 90/The Greens), 15352 (Max Stadler, Free Democratic Party), 15353 (Cornelie Sonntag-Wolgast, Social Democratic Party), 15354–5 (Günther Beckstein, Christian Social Union); 15360 (Otto Schily), 15364 (Hermann Bachmaier, Social Democratic Party)).

6 It was later partly prohibited for unrelated public order reasons.

7 *Verwaltungsgericht* Schleswig, Decision of 27 March 2012, case no. 3 B 39/12, available at www.ovgsh.de/ovg_sh/?4881. The Administrative Court of Appeal upheld that decision, but restricted the neo-Nazis to a largely stationary manifestation for unre-lated public order reasons – see *Oberverwaltungsgericht* Schleswig, Decision of 29 March 2012, case no. 4 MB 22/12, available at www.ovgsh.de/ovg_sh/?4780.

Germany (see below, section 2), the second the compliance of the resulting provision with constitutional law, particularly freedom of speech (below, section 3).

2 Glorification of National Socialism and modern German historiography

From the perspective of modern German historiography, it is to be deplored that government and parliament severely limited themselves in combating neo-Nazi activities. The use of Sect. 130 para. 4 only as an anti-demonstration provision, and its legislative history, invite the conclusion that they were mostly concerned with Germany's image in the global community, an image which might be threatened by pictures of Nazi marches on historic dates and/or in historic places being broadcast all around the world. That this is far from the only danger posed by neo-Nazis and Holocaust deniers, and that many in Germany rightfully feel that more needs to be done to combat the quite real and concrete dangers to the lives of those who do not fit into the worldview of the neo-Nazis, has recently been illuminated by the discovery that the murder of nine men of Turkish, Kurdish and Greek background between 2000 and 2006 – crimes which the police had until recently pinned on 'foreign organised criminals' – and of a policewoman in 2007, were all committed by the neo-Nazi terrorist group 'National Socialist Underground', members of which had apparently been aided in their crimes by at least one member of the extremist right-wing 'National Democratic Party' (NPD).[8]

Germany's rather timid approach may be contrasted with, for example, that of Austria, where a *Wiederbetätigungsverbot*, a provision criminalising attempts at re-forming the National Socialist Party and/or carrying on its policies, was introduced already in 1945 and is equal in rank to the Austrian Constitution.[9] By contrast, Sect. 130 para. 4 aims mainly at prohibiting certain symbolically important demonstrations of the German and European National Socialist movements. Some of these demonstrations are organised by individuals and groups which clearly continue in the footsteps of organisations that have been formally prohibited during the last three decades.[10] Nonetheless, they are mostly

8   For general information on the 'National Socialist Underground', see e.g. 'The Brown Army Faction. A Disturbing New Dimension of Far-Right Terror', Spiegel Online, 14 November 2011, available at www.spiegel.de/international/germany/ 0,1518,druck-797569,00.html. The authors are participating, as victims' counsel, in the trial against five accused members and supporters of the 'NSU' – for regular English-language updates on developments in the trial, see their blog, available at www.nsu-nebenklage.de/en/.

9   Verfassungsgesetz vom 8. Mai 1945 über das Verbot der NSDAP, as amended 1992, Sect. 3 et seq.; available atwww.ris.bka.gv.at/GeltendeFassung.wxe?Abfrage=Bundes normen&Gesetzesnummer=10000207.

10   On the 'Gesinnungsgemeinschaft der Neuen Front' (GdNF), a network of neo-Nazi leaders who have been active in a number of parties since the mid-1980s, see e.g. Jens Mecklenburg (ed.), *Handbuch deutscher Rechtsextremismus* (Berlin: Espresso, 1996), 269 et

able to continue in their political activities – with the exception of the aforementioned symbolic demonstrations.

On the other hand, this way of dealing with neo-Nazi marches does indeed fit quite well into other developments in German historiography and the way in which German elites deal with Germany's past, particularly the Third Reich. In our view, German views of recent history are changing towards one which, while not strictly revisionist in nature, still severely shifts the emphasis of how to think about Germany during the Third Reich.[11] On the one hand, there is a growing emphasis on the plight of Germans, on Germans as victims of the war – be it because of Allied bombardment of German cities, be it because of the expulsion of Germans from the eastern parts of the Reich and the formerly occupied parts of Eastern Europe. This is evidenced by countless books, both fiction and non-fiction, ever-popular TV movies on state television stations, and so on.[12] While often accompanied by statements acknowledging the responsibility of Nazi Germany for World War II and the Holocaust, this discourse nonetheless leads to an equation of those German crimes and of the plight of Germans suffered because of the response thereto, and thus in a way to a minimisation of the Holocaust and German war of aggression.

seq.; on their continuing influence on the NPD, see Jan Raabe, 'Wer ist das Dreigestirn aus der Kameradschaftsszene in der NPD?', in Fabian Virchow/Christian Dornbusch (eds), *88 Fragen und Antworten zur NPD: Weltanschauung, Strategie und Auftreten einer Rechtspartei – und was Demokraten dagegen tun können* (Schwalbach: Wochenschau Verlag, 2008), 193 et seq. Witness testimony in the 'NSU trial' revealed that the 'Thuringia Home Guard' ('Thüriner Heimatschutz'), i.e. the organisation from which hailed those neo-Nazis who would later form the 'NSU', also reported to the GdNF – see the authors' blog post available at www.nsu-nebenklage.de/en/2014/10/01/30-september1-october-2014/.

11   Of course, this is not meant to deny that the topos of German victimhood had been part of (particularly conservative) historiography since the end of World War II and even before that – many thanks to Olaf Jensen for reminding us of this aspect. In our view, what has changed is the extent to which this topos has been taken up by mainstream and even purportedly critical publications like *Der Spiegel*, and the way in which it has been combined with the topos of a 'renewed' Germany that has learned from its past.

12   Two prominent examples: in 2002, Jörg Friedrich published his book *Der Brand. Deutschland im Bombenkrieg 1940–1945* (Munich: Propyläen; English translation as *The Fire: The Bombing of Germany, 1940–1945*, New York: Columbia University Press, 2006), which became something of a bestseller. Friedrich referred to Allied bomber pilots as 'Einsatzgruppen' and to burning air raid shelters as 'crematoria' – words easily understood as references to Auschwitz. In February 2005, during a special session of the Saxon parliament on the occasion of the 60th anniversary of the bombardment of the city, NPD members of parliament did him one better by referring to the bombardment as a 'Bombing holocaust'. In 2006, public TV station ZDF broadcast the TV movie 'Dresden', in which historical facts about the bombardment are mixed with a dramatic love story. By focusing on its (German) protagonists, the movie shifts the focus on the fate of Germans as victims of war, mentioning the Holocaust and the German war of aggression only in passing and as 'context'.

There is also another thread, which began really to gain strength during the period of the Social Democrat/Green government, which was composed, to a large extent, of members of the generation of 1968, i.e. of those rebelling against the father generation still implicated in the National Socialist past. This thread emphasises that Germany has learned its lessons, has successfully dealt with (*aufgearbeitet*) its past, and that precisely because it has done so, it now has a specific 'obligation' towards other countries, an obligation sometimes cited in support of a new leadership position of Germany in the world. One classic example of such developments is the argument that Germany had to take part in the bombardment of Serbia in 1999 to combat the build-up of massive 'concentration camps' in Kosovo.[13]

In our view, at least the first wave of this historiographic discourse does indeed leave an open flank for neo-Nazi propaganda, a flank which neo-Nazis have amply attacked. One recent event that is a rather drastic example of the relationship between mainstream German historiography and neo-Nazi propaganda is the commemoration of the bombardment of the city of Dresden in February 1945:[14] for many years, this commemoration has been focused mostly or entirely on a celebration of German victimhood, referencing victims of the German war of aggression only as 'context'. Part of the commemoration has traditionally been held at the Forest Cemetery in Dresden, which contains a round monument of 14 stone pillars, each bearing the name of a city. Cities named include Coventry, Leningrad, Auschwitz, Bergen-Belsen, Lidice – and Dresden. In 2005, the official posters announcing the city's commemoration event even added a few more names to that list, among them New York, Sarajevo and Baghdad. In effect, then, Dresden was presented as just like any other city that had suffered armed violence, a victim of senseless war and terror.

And for almost a decade, it was accepted that the NPD and neo-Nazis could participate in the commemoration event side by side with democratic parties,

13 Two examples: Defence Minister Rudolf Scharping told the press on 31 March 1999 that there were 'serious indications' that Yugoslav forces had installed 'concentration camps' in Kosovo and were conducting 'selections' (*Selektionen*, a German word which recalls images of the 'selections' of newly arrived victims upon arrival at the historical death camps) ('Hinweise auf serbische Konzentrationslager', *Spiegel Online*, 31 March 1999, available at www.spiegel.de/politik/ausland/0,1518,druck-15424,00.html). Shortly thereafter, Foreign Minister Joseph Fischer stated in an interview with *Der Spiegel*: 'We are not at war, we are offering resistance, defending human rights, freedom and democracy. I am reminded of the Spanish resistance fighter "La Pasionara". "No pasarán" was the slogan of Republicans against the Franco regime – the fascists shall not pass' ('Spiegel-Gespräch – Milosevic wird der Verlierer sein', *Der Spiegel*, 19 April 1999, available at www.spiegel.de/spiegel/print/d-12137988.html) (translations by the authors).

14 Generally on the politics of commemoration in Dresden, see Henning Fischer, '*Erinnerung' an und für Deutschland: Dresden und der 13. Februar 1945 im Gedächtnis der Berliner Republik* (Münster: Verlag Westfälisches Dampfboot, 2011), as well as the various articles in analyse und kritik/Der Rechte Rand (eds), *Dresden Speciale 2012* (2012), available at www.akweb.de/ak_s/ak568/Dresden_Speciale_2012.pdf.

laying wreaths beside those of democratic parties and other organisations – a development which led to *inter alia* the Jewish community refusing to take part in the ceremony altogether. Beginning in 2000, the organised extreme right also staged marches every 13 February, which in the following years developed into the largest demonstration of the German and European Nazi movement, with up to 7,000 marchers. It was only this development – which was also noticed outside Germany – that led to more attention being paid by a broader public.

While the official politics of commemoration in Dresden has shifted somewhat in recent years (not least due to critical interventions by anti-fascist activists, who have organised mass protests and blockades against the Nazi marches and who have tried to shift the focus of historiography by organising walking tours 'following the footsteps of the perpetrators', focusing on places of National Socialist crimes in Dresden[15]), Dresden is nonetheless a good example of how the German elite's changing emphases in historiography have left an open flank for neo-Nazi propaganda.

3 Sect. 130 para. 4 and freedom of speech

Turning to the question of the constitutionality of Sect. 130 para. 4, this is mostly a question of its compatibility with the freedom of speech as protected by Art. 5 of the Basic Law (*Grundgesetz*), the German Constitution.[16] Now, it should be noted that this article, in the interpretation of the Constitutional Court and mainstream legal thought more generally, has always allowed a number of limitations of the freedom of speech – German constitutional law has never known such a thing as the 'first amendment absolutism' of US constitutional law. However, there have been two constants in the way German constitutional lawyers have dealt with Art. 5. First, value statements or expressions of opinion (*Meinungsäußerungen*) have always been entitled to a higher protection than claims of fact (*Tatsachenbehauptung*).[17] Second, where value statements were prohibited or otherwise sanctioned, this could only be done by way of a 'general', that is an 'opinion-neutral' law, in other words a prohibition could not be based on the specific content of an opinion being expressed, no matter how far from the mainstream that opinion was.[18]

---

15 For (German-language) documents documenting the various stops of the 2015 'Täterspuren' walking tour, see www.dresden-nazifrei.com/taeterspuren/700-redebei traege-zum-mahngang-taeterspuren-2015.

16 English translation available at www.gesetze-im-internet.de/englisch_gg/.

17 See e.g., Roman Herzog, in Roman Herzog/Rupert Scholz/Matthias Herdegen/ Hans H. Klein (eds), *Maunz/Dürig – Grundgesetz-Kommentar* (8th edn, as updated October 2011, Munich: C.H. Beck, 1999 et seq.), Art. 5, mn. 49 et seq. (with references and a criticism of the strict dichotomy); German Constitutional Court (Bundesverfassungsgericht), Decisions of the Federal Constitutional Court (BVerfGE), vol. 61, pp. 1, 8.

18 See e.g., Herzog, ibid., Art. 5, mn. 252 et seq.; BVerfGE, vol. 7, pp. 198, 209 et seq.; vol. 28, pp. 282, 292; vol. 71, 162, 175 et seq., vol. 93, pp. 266, 291.

Sect. 130 para. 3 of the Criminal Code, the prohibition of Holocaust denial, had already been subject to quite some criticism in the legal literature,[19] but the Constitutional Court had found it to be constitutional. The main argument was that Sect. 130 para. 3 concerned the denial of the undeniable fact that the Holocaust had happened, or in other words a demonstrably untrue *factual claim*, which deserves little to no protection under Art. 5 of the Basic Law.[20] Given that Sect. 130 para. 4, by contrast, prohibits the statement of an opinion based on its specific content, some mainstream legal commentators doubted whether the provision would survive scrutiny by the Constitutional Court.[21] Critical voices were, however, also raised by anti-fascist activists. They feared that if Sect. 130 para. 4 was upheld by the Constitutional Court, this might lead to a generally lowered protection for the freedom of expression, which might well then lead to laws directed against them.

Such fears also had a basis in the legislative history: the draft law presented by Social Democrats and Greens had proposed also to criminalise the approval and justification of genocide 'committed under another system of rule of arbitrary force if the act has been established by a final decision of an international court whose jurisdiction has been accepted by the Federal Republic of Germany'[22] – a provision meant to implement obligations under international law,[23] but which still raised concerns because it might, if broadly interpreted, have led to criminalisation of statements criticising German/Western policy in the Balkans – and this after German involvement in the bombardment of Yugoslavia in 1999 was precisely the first instance of the 'reformed' Germany using its history as a reason for military intervention in another country.[24]

Such fears of a generalised restriction of freedom of speech were also furthered by certain statements during the parliamentary debate which showed the influence of an 'anti-totalitarian' ideology equating the left and the right: Christian Democrat politicians had condemned certain left-wing demonstrations as just as bad as neo-Nazi marches, and had announced that further measures would become necessary against 'left extremists'.[25]

---

19 See Jürgen Schäfer, in Wolfgang Joecks/Klaus Miebach (eds), *Münchener Kommentar zum Strafgesetzbuch* (2nd edn, vol. 3, Munich: C.H. Beck, 2012), Sect. 130, mn. 77 with references.

20 BVerfGE, vol. 90, 241, 249 et seq.

21 See e.g., Christoph Enders, 'Die Freiheit der Andersdenkenden vor den Schranken des Bundesverwaltungsgerichts: Zum Urteil des BVerwG vom 25.6.2008 – Rudolf Heß-Gedenkmarsch', 63 *Juristenzeitung* (2008), 1092–9.

22 Bundestags-Drucksache 15/4832 (n 5), pp. 2–3.

23 Namely under the Council of Europe's Additional Protocol to the Convention on Cybercrime, concerning the criminalisation of acts of a racist and xenophobic nature committed through computer systems, of 28 January 2003, available at www.coe.int/en/web/conventions/full-list/-/conventions/treaty/189.

24 See above, text at n 13.

25 See e.g., Plenarprotokoll 15–158 (n 5), 14821 (Thomas Strobl); Plenarprotokoll 15–164 (n 5), 15350 (Wolfgang Bosbach), 15354–5, 15356 (Günther Beckstein). A more

Of course, anti-fascist activists at the time would not have had any concerns had Germany enacted an anti-National Socialist provision such as that in force in Austria. Rather on the contrary, the widely held view in the anti-fascist movement – summarised by the popular slogan 'fascism is not an opinion, but a crime' – is that such a provision is a necessary result of lessons to be drawn from German history.[26] However, there was some anxiety that were the Constitutional Court to uphold Sect. 130 para. 4, this would mean a lowering of the protection of freedom of speech generally.

The Federal Constitutional Court, in its decision of 4 November 2009,[27] surprised many legal commentators as well as many anti-fascist activists: it manages to uphold Sect. 130 para. 4 while still alleviating concerns that the protection of freedom of speech would be lowered across the board. The Court finds, first of all, that Sect. 130 para. 4 is not an opinion-neutral 'general law' as required under its constant jurisprudence on freedom of speech, given that it specifically prohibits the statement of a particular opinion.[28] However, in nonetheless upholding the provision, it does not give up the requirement of value neutrality generally, but only allows a restriction by special legislation in the exceptional case of National Socialism. Referring to the injustice and terror caused by the National Socialist rule, which escape general legal categories, the Court

detailed discussion of such 'anti-totalitarian' theories in mainstream German political thought is beyond the scope of this chapter. However, one example, which has become relevant in the context discussed here, deserves mention: on 25 January 2012, the government of Saxony, site of the annual Nazi marches in Dresden and a particular hotbed of 'anti-totalitarianism', passed the Saxon law on demonstrations. Its Sect. 15 allows a ban of demonstration at or near certain 'places of particular historical significance' – in contrast to e.g. the federal law on demonstrations, this concerns not only places of remembrance of National Socialist crimes, but also e.g. places commemorating persons who 'resisted against the National Socialist *or Communist* despotism' (emphasis added) or 'victims of war'. Accordingly, the list of such places includes the area around the rebuilt Frauenkirche, one of the main symbols of both German victimhood and of the 'reformed Germany'. See Gesetz über Versammlungen und Aufzüge im Freistaat Sachsen, Sect. 15 para. 2, Sächsisches Gesetz- und Verordnungsblatt, no. 2/2012, 1 February 2012, p. 54, available at www.sachsen-gesetze.de/shop/saechsgvbl/2012/2/read.

26 Some anti-fascist groups, as well as legal commentators, have also made the legal argument that such a provision is required by Art. 139 of the Basic Law, according to which the de-Nazification provisions passed by the Allies in 1945–9 are not affected by the provisions of the Basic Law. This reading of Art. 139 as a 'material value statement against National Socialist activities' has, however, been rejected by German constitutional law mainstream. See Matthias Herdegen, in Herzog *et al.* (n 17), Art. 139, mn. 12–4 with further references.

27 The decision has been published in the Court's official collection at BVerfGE, vol. 124, p. 300. An English translation is available on the Court's website at www.bverfg.de/e/rs20091104_1bvr215008en.html. For a commentary on the decision, see e.g. Uwe Volkmann, 'Die Geistesfreiheit und der Ungeist – Der Wunsiedel-Beschluss des BVerfG', 63 *Neue Juristische Wochenschrift* (2010), 417–20.

28 Decision of 4 November 2009 (n 27), mn. 53–61.

constructs an exception, which it considers to be inherent to Art. 5 para. (1) and (2) of the Basic Law, for provisions that set limits to the propagandistic approval of the historical National Socialist rule of arbitrary force. According to the Court, the Basic Law can to a large extent be regarded as a counter-concept to the totalitarianism of the National Socialist regime. Against this background, propaganda glorifying the historic National Socialist regime poses a special case which cannot adequately be grasped under the usual freedom of speech jurisprudence.[29] The Court is quick to note, however, that this exception does not 'restrict the material scope' of the right to freedom of speech generally, above all, that its judgment is not to be understood as reading into the Constitution a 'general anti-National Socialist principle' which would allow further restrictions of pro-National Socialist speech.[30]

This judgment, first of all, alleviated a lot of the fears concerning a potential reduction of the protection of free speech generally. More broadly speaking, it can probably be read in a number of ways – as simply acknowledging that the historical weight of the Holocaust and of National Socialism crimes generally required legal answers, as part of the discourse on the new, improved Germany which had learned its lessons from the past, or as simply an attempt to draft a narrow judgment which allowed the Court to uphold the 'lex Wunsiedel' without deviating too much from its general jurisprudence.

No matter which reading of the Constitutional Court decision is the right one, what remains is the criticism of the position of German elites, whose historiography provides some fodder to National Socialist propaganda, but who only seriously combat such propaganda (and more concrete neo-Nazi misdeeds) where it puts the global image of the German State at stake.

29 Ibid., mn. 63–6.
30 Ibid., mn. 67–8. The Court also rejects arguments for a general anti-National Socialist principle based on Art. 139 of the Basic Law (see above, text at n 26).

Chapter 7

Reckoning with the past?

Rwanda's revised Genocide Ideology Law
and international human rights law on
freedom of expression

Sejal Parmar

1 Introduction

Rwanda's 'Law Relating to the Punishment of the Crime of Genocide Ideology'
('Genocide Ideology Law' or the 'Law') has attracted significant global attention
over the years. Adopted in July 2008 as a direct response to the 1994 genocide of
more than 800,000 Tutsis and moderate Hutus, the justification for the Law was
clear and compelling.[1] The Law was further entrenched by Rwanda's penal code
of 2012, which penalises the crimes of 'negationism and minimization of the
genocide' as well as 'genocide ideology'.[2] Despite its apparently laudable aims,
the Law was subject to a barrage of criticism upon its adoption. An array of inter-
governmental authorities,[3] States,[4] non-governmental organisations (NGOs),[5]
media[6] and commentators in academic journals[7] condemned the original 2008

1 Law No. 18/2007 of 23 July 2008. Fred K. Nkusi, 'Rwanda Marks the 1994 Genocide: Is Never Again Possible?', Jurist Academic Commentary, 16 April 2014.
2 Articles 116 and 135, Law No. 01/2012/OL of 02/05/2012, Organic Law Instituting the Penal Code, published in the *Official Gazette* on 14/06/2012.
3 These include the African Commission of Human Rights, *Concluding Observations on
ninth and tenth reports of the Republic of Rwanda (2005–2009)*, adopted at its 47th ordinary
session of the African Commission of Human Rights, 12–26 May 2010, paras 31, 35
and 46.
4 For example, US Department of State, Bureau of Democracy, Human Rights and
Labor, 2010 Human Rights Reports on Human Rights Practices, Rwanda, 24 May
2012. See also European External Action Service, EU Annual Report on Democracy
and Human Rights in the World 2010, September 2011 at p. 128.
5 See, most notably, Amnesty International, *Safer to Stay Silent* (London: Amnesty International, 2010); Article 19, *Comment on the Law Relating to the Punishment of the Crime of
Genocide Ideology of Rwanda*, September 2009; Human Rights Watch, *Law and Reality:
Progress to Judicial Reform in Rwanda*, 25 July 2008.
6 'The difficulty of trying to stop it happening ever again', *The Economist*, 8 April 2009;
Peter Noorlander, 'How Paul Kagame has used the Law to Muzzle Rwanda's
Media', *The Guardian*, 9 August 2010; Stephen Kinzer, 'The Limits of Free Speech in
Rwanda', *The Guardian*, 2 March 2010; David Moshman, 'Fighting "Genocide Ideol-
ogy" in Rwanda', *The World Post*, 19 April 2016.
7 For academic literature on the original version of the Genocide Ideology Law, see
Pietro Sullo, 'Lois memorielles in Post-genocide Societies: The Rwandan Law on

Law – largely for its very broad and imprecise definition of the offence of 'genocide ideology' and harsh system of penalties, including for children – and urged the Rwandan government to repeal or urgently revise it according to international human rights standards.[8] Though the Law withstood such criticisms at first,[9] after signalling its intention to redraft the Law,[10] the Rwandan government proposed amendments in November 2012, and it was eventually amended in 2013.[11]

This chapter presents an international human rights law-based critique to the Genocide Ideology Law and, in doing so, considers the provisions of the original 2008 Law as well as the amended 2013 Law. Despite significant improvements in the Law, some of the key critiques levelled against the 2008 version remain relevant for

Genocide Ideology under International Human Rights Scrutiny' (2014) (27) 2 *Leiden Journal of International Law*, 419–45; Yakaré-Oulé (Nani) Jansen, 'Denying Genocide or Denying Free Speech? A Case Study of the Application of Rwanda's Genocide Ideology Laws' (2014) 12 (2) *Northwestern Journal of International Human Rights*, 191–212; Dominique E. Uwizeyimana, 'Aspects and Consequences of the Rwandan Law of Genocide Ideology: A Comparative Analysis' (2014) 23 (5) *Mediterranean Journal of Social Sciences*, 2370–9; Jennifer M. Allen and George H. Norris, 'Is Genocide Different? Dealing with Hate Speech in a Post-Genocide Society' (2011) 7 *Journal of International Law and International Relations*, 146–74; Casey Dalporto, 'Genocide Ideology Laws: Violation of Rwandan Peoples' "Peoples" Rights' (2012) 20 *Cardozo Journal of International and Comparative Law*, 875–909; Zachary Pall, 'Light Shining Darkly: Comparing Post-Conflict Constitutional Structures Concerning Speech and Association in Germany and Rwanda', (2010) 42 *Columbia Human Rights Law Review*, 5–26; Lars Waldorf, 'Revisiting Hotel Rwanda: Genocide Ideology, Reconciliation, and Rescuers' (2009) 11 (1) *Journal of Genocide Research*, 101–25.

8 The UN Independent Expert on Minority Issues, Gay McDougall, recommended that Rwanda's legislation concerning genocide ideology 'must be revised as a matter of urgency and safeguards should be implemented to guarantee that they are not used to silence dissent or restrict the legitimate activities of political opposition'. She went on: 'the legal standard of intentionality must be reflected clearly in the legislation'. Report of the Independent Expert on minority issues, Gay McDougall, Mission to Rwanda, 28 November 2011, A/HRC/19/56/Add.1, para. 89.

9 Amnesty International reported that the government had announced its intention to review the Genocide Ideology Law in April 2010, see Amnesty International, *Safer to Stay Silent, supra* note 5 at p. 8. On the negative consequences of the campaign, see Waldorf *supra* note 7.

10 During Rwanda's universal period review at the Human Rights Council, the 'delegation stated that Rwanda had agreed to review the Genocide Ideology Law because of the issues it had raised. A national group was therefore commissioned, foreign experts were consulted, and comments and input were sought from human rights groups and other interested parties'. Human Rights Council, *Report of the Working Group on the Universal Periodic Review: Rwanda*, Seventeenth session, A/HRC/17/4, 14 March 2011, para. 15. The Independent Expert on minority issues was also 'encouraged that the Government has stated its plan to re-draft the laws to respond to criticisms'. Report of the Independent Expert on minority issues, Gay McDougall, Mission to Rwanda, 28 November 2011, A/HRC/19/56/Add.1, para. 89.

11 Law No. 84/2013 of 11/09/2013, Law on the crime of genocide ideology and other offences, *Official Gazette* no. 43bis of 28/10/2013.

the amended 2013 Law.[12] While the potential value of an international law-based critique of the Law, as one that highlights individual rights, has recently been questioned from within the human rights paradigm from a group rights perspective, the position firmly taken in this chapter is that international law presents a positive framework for post-genocidal societies, as well as those which would like to safeguard against mass atrocities happening again.[13] Unlike earlier academic commentaries of the Law, this chapter both examines the Law as amended in 2013 and benefits from the 2016 Concluding Observations on Rwanda by the Human Rights Committee, as well as the 2015 Report of the Working Group on the Universal Periodic Review of Rwanda.[14] It shows how the Law, even in its amended form, undermines provisions of international human rights treaties on freedom of opinion and expression, particularly Articles 19 and 20 of the International Covenant on Civil and Political Rights (ICCPR). This chapter argues that the international legal framework on incitement, of which the Rabat Plan of Action on the prohibition of advocacy of national, racial or religious hatred that constitutes incitement to discrimination, hostility or violence ('Rabat Plan of Action') now forms an essential part, should provide the basic starting point for all societies, including and especially those who are coming to terms with the legacy of genocide or mass atrocities in their recent past, such as Rwanda.[15] While certain forms of speech ought to be prohibited under international law, meaningful reckoning with the past and building resilience for the future cannot be achieved in such societies without freedom of expression being allowed to flourish. As Francine Navarro wrote in 2014, 'can the nation truly heal without the freedom to discuss its past, present and future?'[16]

2 Critiques of the Genocide Ideology Law

This part examines the Genocide Ideology Law from an international law perspective. In doing so, it gauges the compatibility of the original text and also

12 Article 19, Individual Submission to the Universal Periodic Review of Rwanda for consideration at the 23rd session of the Working Group to be held in October/November 2015, 23 March 2015.
13 Rwanda ratified the African Charter on Human and People's Rights on 15 July 1983.
14 Human Rights Committee, *Concluding Observations on the fourth periodic report of Rwanda*, 2 May 2016 CCPR/C/RWA/CO/4; Report of the Human Rights Council, Working Group on the University Periodic Review, 18 December 2015 A/HRC/31/8.
15 See Rabat Plan of Action on the prohibition of advocacy of national, racial or religious hatred that constitutes incitement to discrimination, hostility or violence, Appendix in the *Annual Report of the United Nations High Commissioner for Human Rights*, A/HRC/22/17/Add.4, 11 January 2013. For commentaries, see Sejal Parmar, 'The Rabat Plan of Action: A Critical Turning Point in International Law on "Hate Speech"', in Peter Molnar (ed.), *Free Speech and Censorship Around the Globe* (Budapest: Central European University Press, 2015), 211–31.
16 Francine Navarro, 'W(h)ither free expression in post-genocide Rwanda?', Canadian Journalists for Free Expression (CJFE), 7 April 2014; 'A Hilly Dilemma', *The Economist*, 12 March 2016.

the amended version of the Law with key provisions of international human rights treaties. The criticisms of the Genocide Ideology Law, which were concentrated before its amendment in 2013, have focused upon its tensions with Rwanda's international legal obligations concerning freedom of expression, most notably under Articles 19 and 20 of the ICCPR. As a State party to the ICCPR, Rwanda is clearly obliged to implement into domestic law the rights contained therein,[17] including the right to freedom of opinion and expression as guaranteed by Articles 19 and 20 of that instrument.[18] The Law also fundamentally challenges Rwanda's obligations in other key international human rights instruments, most notably the Convention on the Prevention and Punishment of the Crime of Genocide of 1948 ('Genocide Convention'), but also the International Convention on the Elimination of Racial Discrimination of 1965 (ICERD) and the Convention on the Rights of the Child of 1989 (CRC).[19]

2.1 Constitutional identity v. international pressure

Understandably, the backdrop of the 1994 genocide fundamentally informs how the State of Rwanda is run and how it responds to the legacy of the genocide in particular. The government has, for instance, claimed its 'massive fight against the ideology of genocide and divisionism' is based upon the 'understanding that Rwandans know genocide better than anyone else and therefore have every legitimate responsibility to prevent its reoccurrence by all means'.[20] This 'we know genocide better' approach is coupled with the penalisation of 'genocide ideology' being firmly embedded in the State's constitutional and legal identity. Given the context, this central focus on combating the genocide is plausible. As Lars Waldorf, a leading commentator on the Rwandan genocide, has argued, in principle, 'Rwanda needs laws protecting the country from both genocide denial and "genocide ideology"', partly because of the 'vivid reminders that unrepentant *génocidaires* still live among the survivors'.[21] The United Nations (UN) Secretary-General had also observed 'lingering genocide ideology' and threats to the security of genocide survivors as challenges to the development of the country.[22] The

---

17 Articles 2(1)(b), 14(1) and 16, Vienna Convention on the Law of Treaties 1969.
18 Rwanda acceded on 16 April 1975.
19 Rwanda acceded to the Genocide Convention on 16 April 1975 and ratified the CRC on 24 January 1991.
20 Consideration of reports submitted by States parties under Article 40 of the Covenant, Fourth periodic reports of States parties due in 2013: Rwanda, 30 October 2014, CCPR/C/RWA/A/4 para. 88. See also Human Rights Council, *Report of the Working Group on the Universal Periodic Review: Rwanda*, Seventeenth session, A/HRC/17/4 14 March 2011, para. 15.
21 At the same time, for Waldorf, Rwanda's laws, including the Genocide Ideology Law, are 'too broadly drafted and open to political manipulation'. Waldorf, *supra* note 7 at 102.
22 The UN secretary-general noted that 'the right to security of the genocide survivors is threatened and there is a lingering genocide ideology as shown by the recent destruction of a banana plantation owned by genocide survivors in the district of

Rwandan government itself, in its national report for the second cycle of its Universal Periodic Review, justified the Law on the basis of research carried out by the parliament, that 'genocide ideology was still very much entrenched in the minds of ordinary Rwandans'. There was therefore 'a need to have a tough law against it … to completely deter people from harbouring or sharing a genocide ideology'.[23]

Such a law was viewed as necessary to complement relevant provisions of the Rwandan Constitution of 2003, which was revised in 2015.[24] The very first provision of Chapter III (ex Chapter II), which now deals with 'Fundamental Principles and Home-Grown Solutions' (ex 'Fundamental Principles'), commits the State to preventing and punishing 'the crime of genocide, fighting against denial and revisionism of genocide as well as eradication of genocide ideology and all its manifestations'. Article 38 (ex Article 34) of the Rwandan Constitution guarantees 'freedom of press, of expression and of access to information', but states that 'the conditions for exercising and respect of such freedoms are determined by law'. This limitation is problematic in itself because it leaves open the possibility of undercutting the constitutional protection on freedom of expression through legislation, including the Genocide Ideology Law. Consider that the Rwandan Supreme Court ruled in the case of Victoire Ingabire Umuhoza, that there is 'no contradiction between the genocide ideology law and the constitution' which grants 'freedom of expression and speech but the genocide ideology law puts limitations to avoid violations of the freedoms'.[25]

Thus, the political position, constitutional framework and an underpinning sense of moral imperative for the Law have stood as a formidable bulwark against any critical commentary of Rwanda's policies directed at preventing genocide. Indeed, notwithstanding the amendments of 2013, the characterising feature of the Genocide Ideology Law remains intact: it still assumes that 'genocide ideology' is definable and needs to be criminalised in order to minimise the risk of genocide reoccurring in Rwanda. At the same time, there is a tension between the entrenchment of 'genocide ideology' within Rwandan law and the Rwandan government's apparent desire to respond positively to the repeated recommendations of UN human rights bodies in particular to amend the Law. Indeed, the government seemed amenable to amending the Law, a move that could be

   Rusizi and attacks on genocide survivors who testified in court in the Northern Province of Rwanda'. General Assembly, *Report of the Secretary General on Assistance to survivors of the 1994 genocide in Rwanda, particularly orphans, widows and victims of sexual violence*, 20 August 2009 A/64/313, para. 9.
23 This justification was reflected in the State's national report for the second cycle of its Universal Periodic Review. See Human Rights Council, Working Group on the Universal Periodic Review, National report submitted in accordance with paragraph 5 of the annex to Human Rights Council resolution 16/21: Rwanda, 27 October 2015, A/HRC/WG.6/23/RWA/1, para. 65.
24 Constitution of the Republic of Rwanda of 2003 as revised in 2005, *Official Gazette*, 24/12/2005.
25 Rwanda News Agency, 'Supreme Court Upholds Genocide Law', 18 October 2012.

attributed to the accumulation of significant international pressure for the Law's improvement from NGOs and later, but critically, a range of UN human rights bodies. In 2011, the concept of 'genocide ideology' was considered as simply 'too broad' by the Committee on the Elimination of Racial Discrimination (CERD),[26] and 'problematic and ill-defined' and 'considerably beyond the limits to freedom of expression envisaged' in international law by the independent expert on minority issues, Gay McDougall.[27] During the first cycle of the Universal Periodic Review of Rwanda in March 2011, States such as Australia, Canada, Italy and the Netherlands expressed concerns about the Law's restrictions on freedom of expression.[28] At that stage, Rwanda had already accepted recommendations to 'accelerate the revision' of the Law to bring it in line with international standards and to ensure that its provisions were not 'manipulated or interpreted' to restrict freedom of opinion and expression – a commitment that it then had to meet.[29] At the second cycle of its Universal Periodic Review in October 2015, the Rwandan government recalled that given the Law 'had significant loopholes' and on the basis of 'research … among lawyers and judges', 'the law was amended to make it clearer and remove all ambiguity in the definition of the offence of genocide ideology'.[30] Most recently, in May 2016, the Human Rights Committee noted that the 2013 amended version of the Law 'introduced a more precise definition of the offence' of genocide ideology, but the Committee 'remains concerned at the vague definition of other related crimes, such as the crime of separatism'.[31]

26 Concluding Observations of the Committee on the Elimination of Racial Discrimination on Rwanda, 19 April 2011, A/HRC/WG.6/23/RWA/2, para. 14.
27 Report of the Independent Expert on minority issues, Gay McDougall, *supra* note 8, para. 89.
28 Human Rights Council, *Report of the Working Group on the Universal Periodic Review: Rwanda*, Seventeenth session, A/HRC/17/4, 14 March 2011, paras 69, 44, 62, 66.
29 See recommendations 79.3 of Switzerland, Austria, Italy and Belgium, as well as 79.4 of Australia and Canada; *Report of Working Group on Universal Periodic Review of Rwanda*, 27 January 2010, A/HRC/17/4.
30 This justification was reflected in the State's national report for the second cycle of its Universal Periodic Review. See Human Rights Council, Working Group on the Universal Periodic Review, National report submitted in accordance with paragraph 5 of the annex to Human Rights Council resolution 16/21: Rwanda, 27 October 2015, A/HRC/WG.6/23/RWA/1, para. 66. The national human rights institution, the National Commission for Human Rights of Rwanda, welcomed the revision of the law. Summary prepared by the Office of the High Commissioner for Human Rights, 17 August 2005, A/HRC/WG.6/23RWA/3.
31 It also recommended that Rwanda should 'refrain from prosecuting politicians, journalists and human rights defenders as a means of discouraging them from freely expressing their opinions and take immediate action to investigate attacks against them and to provide them with effective protection'. Concluding observations on the fourth periodic report of Rwanda, 2 May 2016, CCPR/C/RWA/CO/4, paras 39 and 40.

2.2 Definitions of 'genocide ideology' and related offences

The 2013 amended version of the Law begins with preambular paragraphs indicating that it is adopted pursuant to international treaties, specifically the Genocide Convention, the ICERD, the ICCPR and the African Charter on Human and Peoples' Rights.[32] This greater recognition on the part of the government of the relevance of international human rights treaties was undoubtedly prompted by the critiques of the original version of the Law. In another marked departure from the original Law, whose purpose was both to prevent and to punish the crime of genocide ideology, the amended version states that the purpose of the Law is to 'define the crime of genocide ideology and related offences' (Article 1), but this is not helpful in identifying the underpinning motivations for the adoption of the Law in the first place.

What is the meaning of 'genocide ideology' under the Law? The original version of the Law offered an extraordinarily broad definition which encompassed 'an aggregate of thoughts characterized by conduct, speeches, documents and other acts aiming at exterminating or inciting others to exterminate people basing on ethnic group, origin, nationality, region, color, physical appearance, sex, language, religion or political opinion, committed in normal periods or during war' (ex Article 2). The characteristics of genocide included 'any behaviour aimed at deshumanizing [sic] a person or a group of persons with the same characteristics' by: (1) 'threatening, intimidating, degrading through diffamatory [sic] speeches, documents or actions which aim at propounding wickedness or inciting hatred'; (2) 'marginalising, laughing at one's misfortune, defaming, mocking, boasting, despising, degrading createing [sic] confusion aiming at negating the genocide which occurred, stiring [sic] up ill feelings, taking revenge, altering testimony or evidence for the genocide which occurred'; (3) 'killing, planning to kill or attempting to kill someone for purposes of furthering genocide ideology' (ex Article 3). Such terms could be applied in a far-reaching and highly subjective manner. An Amnesty International report from 2010 found that neither the general public nor specialists in Rwandan law, such as lawyers and human rights workers, were able precisely to define 'genocide ideology'.[33] Even judges found the law difficult to apply because of its abstract nature.[34] The effect of an absence of a common and clear definition was that many specialists 'chose to restrict their areas of work and self-censor to avoid falling foul' of the law.[35]

The 2013 amended version of the Law markedly improves on the original version's definitions of terms (Article 2) and definition of the crime of 'genocide ideology' (Article 3). The definition of 'genocide' directly draws on the international meaning of the term under Article 2 of the Genocide Convention (Article 2(1)). It is interesting to note that the genocide of the Tutsi from 1 October 1990 to 31

---

32 Law No. 84/2013 of 11/09/2013, Law on the crime of genocide ideology and other offences, *Official Gazette* no. 43bis of 28/10/2013, preambular paras 4–7.
33 See Amnesty International, *Safer to Stay Silent, supra* note 5 at 17–18.
34 See Amnesty International, *Safer to Stay Silent, supra* note 5 at 18.
35 See Amnesty International, *Safer to Stay silent, supra* note 5 at 18.

December 1994 as well as 'any other genocide recognized by the United Nations' are identified in the same provision (Article 2(2) and (3)). The offence of genocide ideology is defined as 'any deliberate act committed in public whether orally, written or video means or by any other means which may show that a person is characterized by ethnic, religious, nationality or racial-hatred with the aim to: (1) advocate for the commission of genocide; (2) support the genocide' (Article 3). The narrowed scope of the offence means that only proven intentional acts and statements committed in the presence of two other persons (Article 2(4) and (5)) could qualify as 'genocide ideology'. This a positive step, reducing the possibility of abusive prosecutions. However, the essential definition of 'genocide ideology' as encompassing statements that aim to 'advocate for the commission of' or, even more ambiguously, 'support the genocide' remains very broad and open to interpretation, and, as will be shown below, incompatible with international human rights law.

The 2013 amended Law goes on to define 'genocide related offences' including 'incitement to commit genocide' (Article 4), which is defined as 'any act committed in public with the intent to encourage, influence, induce or coerce another person to commit genocide', a more specific and hence potentially narrower definition than Article 3(c) of the Genocide Convention which prohibits 'direct and public incitement to genocide'. The Law then goes on to define other prohibited speech-related offences including the 'negation of genocide' (Article 5), 'the minimization of genocide' (Article 6) and 'justifying genocide' (Article 7), as well as other criminal offences such as 'concealment or destruction of evidence of genocide or of other crimes against humanity' (Article 8), 'theft or destruction of remains of victims of genocide' (Article 9), 'demolishing a memorial site or cemetery for the victims of genocide' (Article 10), 'violence against a genocide survivor' (Article 11). In this way, the Law sweeps a broad range of offences up, from those concerning discussion of alternative views about the genocide to physical attacks on persons who survived the genocide themselves.

However, there are deeper challenges concerning the scope of 'genocide related offences', which mirror the criticisms that were levelled at the earlier version of the Law. This section criminalises acts, including statements, which: '[state or explain] that genocide is not genocide', 'deliberately [misconstrue] the facts about genocide for the purpose of misleading the public', or '[support] a double genocide theory for Rwanda', '[state or explain] that genocide was not planned' (Article 5 on 'negation'); or 'downplay the gravity or consequences of genocide', or the 'methods through which [it] was committed' (Article 6 on 'minimization'); or 'glorify', 'support' or 'legitimize' genocide (Article 7 on 'justifying'). The continued existence of these offences curtails the potential for serious and critical public discussion about the 1994 genocide, as well as academic inquiry and research into its causes.

2.3 International human rights approaches to 'genocide ideology'

As indicated above, through the preamble and definitions of genocide and 'incitement to commit genocide', the 2013 Law bears the influence of international sources. Yet this does not mean that there is any concept of 'genocide ideology' itself or obligation upon States to fight it within international law. What do international treaties and their authoritative interpretations say about speech that might cause or lead to genocide? There are a range of international human rights treaties and other sources which are relevant to the prohibition and criminalisation of harmful speech. Before these are assessed, it is noted that the amended 2013 Genocide Ideology Law engages and infringes the child's right to freedom of expression as contained in Article 13 of the CRC,[36] but also the child's right to education as contained in Articles 28 and 29 of the CRC.[37] This is because its provisions clearly impact upon classroom debates and discussions on recent Rwandan history and society. In May 2012, the US State Department noted that '[a]uthorities frequently suspended secondary and university students for divisionism or engaging in genocide ideology'.[38] There is therefore real evidence that the Law frustrates the intellectual freedom of younger generations and their ability to talk freely about issues related to the 1994 genocide.

2.3.1 Genocide Convention

The most directly relevant international instrument is obviously the Genocide Convention. That instrument imposes no obligation upon States to criminalise 'genocide ideology'; indeed, it makes no reference to the concept of 'genocide ideology' at all.[39] Not even in the years following the Holocaust was this concept considered a matter for international law. It should also be noted that provisions of international criminal law – namely Article 25(3)(e) of the 1998 Rome Statute of the International Criminal Court, Article 4(c) of the 1993 Statute of the International Criminal Tribunal for the Former Yugoslavia (ICTY), and Article 2 (3) of the 1994 Statute of the International Criminal Tribunal for Rwanda (ICTR) – follow the same approach in prohibiting direct and public incitement to genocide. From these perspectives, if Rwandan law should target any form of expression specifically related to genocide, it should be the type of expression that falls within this narrow category of speech which can lead to the severest consequences.[40] In the leading judgment on the issue of incitement to commit genocide, *Nahimana*, the Appeals Chamber of the ICTR considered that a person may be found guilty of the crime of direct and public incitement to genocide if he or she directly and publicly incited the commission of genocide and had the intent directly and publicly to incite others to commit genocide.[41] The court emphasised

---

36 The wording of this provision reflects Article 19 ICCPR.
37 See in particular Article 29(1) CRC.
38 US State Department, *supra* note 4 section 2 on Press Freedom and Cultural Events.
39 Article 19, Comment, *supra* note 5 at para. 11.
40 See Article 19, 'Hate Speech Pyramid' in Article 19, '"Hate Speech" Explained: A Toolkit' (2015).
41 *Ferdinand Nahimana, Jean-Bosco Barayagwiza and Hassan Ngeze v. The Prosecutor* (Case ICTR-99-52-A), Judgment of the Appeals Chamber of 28 November 2007 at para. 677.

that incitement to commit genocide 'assumes that the speech is a direct appeal', 'has to be more than a mere vague or indirect suggestion' and may 'be preceded or accompanied by hate speech', though it is distinct from it.[42] The Appeals Chamber also held that the specific context is a factor to consider in deciding whether discourse constitutes direct incitement to commit genocide, that the crime is an inchoate offence, punishable even if no act of genocide has actually resulted from it.[43] Through the criminalisation of 'genocide ideology' and every one of the offences in Chapter III except incitement to commit genocide, the amended Genocide Ideology Law goes manifestly far beyond the types of speech targeted by the Genocide Convention and international criminal law.

2.3.2 ICCPR

Under the ICCPR, the Rwandan State authorities may sanction a broader range of speech than that which falls into the category of 'direct and public incitement to commit genocide'. Any such regulation of speech must meet the thresholds contained in Articles 19 and 20 of the ICCPR on the protection of freedom of opinion and expression, however. Article 19 of the ICCPR provides that:

1   Everyone shall have the right to hold opinions without interference.
2   Everyone shall have the right to freedom of expression; this right shall include freedom to seek, receive and impart information and ideas of all kinds, regardless of frontiers, either orally, in writing or in print, in the form of art, or through any other media of his choice.
3   The exercise of the rights provided for in paragraph 2 of this article carries with it special duties and responsibilities. It may therefore be subject to certain restrictions, but these shall only be such as are provided by law and are necessary:

   a   For respect of the rights or reputations of others;
   b   For the protection of national security or of public order (ordre public), or of public health or morals.

Article 20 of the ICCPR then states:

1   Any propaganda for war shall be prohibited by law.
2   Any advocacy of national, racial or religious hatred that constitutes incitement to discrimination, hostility or violence shall be prohibited by law.

---

42 Ibid., para. 692 of judgment and footnote 1658.
43 See also Article 25(3)(b) of the Statute of the International Criminal Court which provides that any person who 'orders, solicits or induces' the commission of a crime falling under the jurisdiction of the Court shall be individually responsible for such a crime 'which in fact occurs or is attempted'. However, Article 25(3)(e) of the Statute of the International Criminal Court provides that a person may incur responsibility for direct and public incitement to commit genocide and it does not require the commission or attempted commission of such a crime.

General Comment 34, which was adopted by the Human Rights Committee in July 2011, clarifies the meaning of Article 19 of the ICCPR and, in doing so, elucidates its interrelationship with Article 20 of the ICCPR.[44] General Comment 34 emphasises that Articles 19 and 20 are compatible with and complement each other. As the Human Rights Committee states, the 'acts that are addressed in article 20 are all subject to restriction pursuant to article 19, paragraph 3' and '[a]s such, a limitation that is justified on the basis of article 20 must also comply with article 19, paragraph 3'.[45] The Committee indicates that 'it is only with regard to the forms of expression indicated in article 20 that States parties are obliged to have legal prohibitions'.[46] Yet the notion of 'genocide ideology' as contained in Article 3 of the 2013 version of the Law, which does not contain any notion of 'incitement', does not meet the standard of Article 20(2).[47]

While the Genocide Ideology Law could not be justified on the basis of Article 20(2) of the ICCPR, the restrictions on freedom of expression that potentially flow from it could violate Article 19(2) and (3) of the ICCPR. Indeed, it is highly unlikely that the Law would survive any scrutiny under Article 19(3) of the ICCPR. Although the 2008 and 2013 versions of the Genocide Ideology Law would be deemed to meet the criterion of 'provided by Law',[48] and Rwanda's State

44 Human Rights Committee, General Comment No. 34, CCPR/C/GC/34, 11 September 2011. Although it does not constitute binding international law, the General Comment may be considered 'secondary treaty law, deriving its authority from the binding nature of [the ICCPR] and the implied consent of states to it'; Christine Chinkin, 'Sources' in Daniel Moeckli, Sangeeta Shah and Sandesh Sivakumaran (eds), *International Human Rights Law* (Oxford: Oxford University Press, 2010), at 109–10. Alternatively, it may be considered as 'a species of international soft law'; Yogesh Tyagi, *The Work of the Human Rights Committee under the ICCPR* (Cambridge: Cambridge University Press, 2010). See also Gerd Oberleitner, *Global Human Rights Institutions* (Cambridge: Polity, 2007), at 100–1. See also Human Rights Committee, General Comment 11 on the prohibition of propaganda for war and inciting national, racial or religious hatred (Article 20), 29 July 1983.
45 General Comment No. 34, ibid. para. 50; see communication No. 736/1997, *Ross v. Canada*, Views adopted on 18 October 2000. Mendel has argued that 'a law properly designed to implement Article 20(2) would automatically serve the aim of protecting the rights of others, specifically to equality, thereby satisfying the … test for restrictions on freedom of expression'. Toby Mendel, *Study on International Standards Relating to Incitement to Genocide or Racial Hatred* prepared for the UN Special Advisor on the Prevention of Genocide, April 2006 at 31.
46 General Comment No. 34, ibid. para. 52. See also Human Rights Committee, *General Comment 11 on the Prohibition of propaganda for war and inciting national, racial or religious hatred* (Article 20), 29 July 1983, para. 2.
47 See generally, Jeroen Temperman, *The Prohibition of Religious Incitement in International Law* (Cambridge: Cambridge University Press, 2015).
48 The Human Rights Committee has stated: 'For the purposes of paragraph 3, a norm, to be characterized as a "law", must be formulated with sufficient precision to enable an individual to regulate his or her conduct accordingly and it must be made accessible to the public. A law may not confer unfettered discretion for the restriction of freedom of expression on those charged with its execution. Laws must provide sufficient guidance to those charged with their execution to enable them to ascertain what

authorities would likely invoke the rights of others not to be discriminated against on the grounds of ethnicity as the legitimate basis for the Genocide Ideology Law, it is doubtful that in any particular case the authorities could 'demonstrate in specific and individualized fashion the precise nature of the threat' and 'the necessity and proportionality of the specific action taken, in particular by establishing a direct and immediate connection between the expression and the threat'.[49]

An additional consideration is that, in applying the principle of proportionality to the Genocide Ideology Law, the potentially high public interest value of the speech in expressions concerning the genocide in Rwanda would need to be taken into account. General Comment 34 states that 'the value placed by the Covenant upon uninhibited expression is particularly high in the circumstances of public debate in a democratic society concerning figures in the public and political domain'.[50] Moreover, General Comment 34 expressly indicates that Article 19 is deemed to cover a broad range of expression, including political discourse, commentary on public affairs, discussion of human rights, journalism, cultural and artistic expression and teaching. It also embraces speech that may be 'regarded as deeply offensive', including presumably controversial or upsetting views about genocide which fall short of incitement.[51] Finally, the Genocide Ideology Law's criminalisation of speech about the 'Genocide committed against the Tutsi' and any 'other genocide recognized by the United Nations' as historical facts also falls foul of the Human Rights Committee's authoritative interpretation of Article 19 in a very direct way. Paragraph 49 of the comment states, in no uncertain terms:

> Laws that penalize the expression of opinions about historical facts are incompatible with the obligations that the Covenant imposes on States parties in relation to the respect for freedom of opinion and expression. The Covenant does not permit general prohibition of expressions of an erroneous opinion or an incorrect interpretation of past events. Restrictions on the right of freedom of opinion should never be imposed and, with regard to freedom of expression, they should not go beyond what is permitted in [Article 19] paragraph 3 or required under article 20.

sorts of expression are properly restricted and what sorts are not'. See General Comment No. 34, *supra* note 44 at para. 25. See also General Comment No. 27, CCPR/C/21/Rev.1/Add.9 2 November 1999.

49 General Comment No. 34, *supra* note 44 at para. 35. The Committee observed in General Comment No. 27 that 'restrictive measures must conform to the principle of proportionality; they must be appropriate to achieve their protective function; they must be the least intrusive instrument amongst those which might achieve their protective function; they must be proportionate to the interest to be protected ... The principle of proportionality has to be respected not only in the law that frames the restrictions but also by the administrative and judicial authorities in applying the law'. General Comment No. 27, ibid. at para. 49.

50 General Comment No. 34, *supra* note 44 at para. 34.

51 General Comment No. 34 *supra* note 44 at para. 11.

2.3.3 ICERD

The ICERD requires a broader range of speech to be criminalised than the ICCPR.[52] Article 4 ICERD requires States parties to 'condemn all propaganda and all organisations which are based on ideas or theories of superiority of race or group ... or which attempt to justify or promote racial hatred and discrimination in any form, and undertake to adopt immediate and positive measures designed to eradicate all incitement to, or acts of, such discrimination'. States are required to 'declare as punishable by law' a number of offences including 'the dissemination of ideas based on racial superiority or racial hatred, incitement to discrimination' and incitement to acts of racially motivated violence (Article 4(a)). States are also obliged to declare illegal and prohibit organisations and activities that promote and incite racial discrimination and make it an offence punishable by law to participate in such organisations and/or activities (Article 4(b)). Finally, public authorities are forbidden from inciting racial discrimination (Article 4(c)).

In relation to any potential tension between freedom of expression and Article 4, it is important to note that Article 4 states that measures taken under its terms should have due regard for the principles set out in the Universal Declaration of Human Rights (UDHR), which includes freedom of expression. Article 4 ICERD may be distinguished from Article 20 ICCPR, principally because 'advocacy of hatred' is not a necessary component of proscribed speech under Article 4, but it is under Article 20 ICCPR.[53] This is hardly surprising given the instrument's entire focus on measures to eradicate racial discrimination. The 2013 Genocide Ideology Law's definition of 'genocide ideology', however, may not even be justified under this broader range of criteria for proscribed speech under the ICERD because the CERD had explicitly stated that Article 4 should be read compatibly with freedom of expression under Article 19 of the ICCPR based on Article 5(d) (viii) of ICERD itself.[54] Moreover, General Recommendation No. 35 of the CERD of 2013, reinforces the position of the Human Rights Committee in stating that 'public denials or attempts to justify crimes of genocide and crimes against humanity, as defined by international law, should be declared as offences

---

52 For analyses of the Committee on the Elimination of Racial Discrimination's approach to issues of freedom of expression and hate speech, see Patrick Thornberry, 'Forms of Hate Speech and the Convention on the Elimination of All Forms of Racial Discrimination', Conference Room Paper 11 presented at OHCHR Expert seminar on the links between articles 19 and 20 of the International Covenant on Civil and Political Rights (ICCPR): Freedom of expression and advocacy of religious hatred that constitutes incitement to discrimination, hostility or violence, 2–3 October 2008, Geneva; José A Lindgren Alves, 'Race and Religion in the United Nations Committee on the Elimination of Racial Discrimination', (2008) 41 *University of San Francisco Law Review*, 941–82 at 970.

53 As noted by Toby Mendel, *Study on International Standards Relating to Incitement to Genocide or Racial Hatred, supra* note 45.

54 General Recommendation 15 on organised violence based on ethnic origin, 23 March 2003 A/48/18, paras 2 and 4.

punishable by law, provided that they clearly constitute incitement to racial violence or hatred', and underlining that 'the expression of opinions about historical facts' should not be prohibited or punished.[55]

2.3.4 Soft law and NGO standards on 'incitement'

As indicated above, the Genocide Ideology Law criminalises a whole range of speech besides 'incitement to genocide'. General Comment No. 34 offers some guidance on the content of Article 20 of the ICCPR, but addresses the provision only insofar as it relates to Article 19 of the ICCPR. Moreover, the meaning of incitement under Article 20 of the ICCPR is not comprehensively addressed by the jurisprudence under Articles 19 and 20 of the ICCPR either.[56] A more honed interpretation of the term 'incitement' has emerged, however, through the Rabat Plan of Action which was adopted in October 2012. The Rabat Action Plan is not binding upon States, yet it offers a 'global blueprint' for all States and key non-State actors, such as the media, on the implementation of their international obligations and responsibilities concerning incitement under Article 20 of the ICCPR, in particular.[57] Its legitimacy and credibility derive both from the deliberative and participatory process that led to its drafting, as well as the nature of its substantive content.[58] As a soft law instrument, the Rabat Plan of Action could be especially relevant for Rwanda, as a post-genocidal State in developing its response to harmful speech.[59]

55 Committee on the Elimination of Racial Discrimination, General Recommendation No. 35 on 'Combating racist hate speech', 26 September 2013, CERD/C/GC/35, para. 14.
56 Communication No. 736/97, *Ross v. Canada*, Views adopted on 18 October 2000; Communication No. 550/93, *Faurisson v. France*, Views adopted on 8 November 1996; Communication No. 104, 1981, *J R T and the W G Party v. Canada*, Views adopted on 6 April 1983. In *Ross v. Canada* the State party relied on Article 20 (2) of the ICCPR to justify the restrictions on the author's expression. The case concerned a teacher who had been removed from his teaching position because of various instances of his public anti-Semitic speech. In deciding that there was no violation of Article 19, the Committee noted that restrictions on 'statements which are of a nature as to raise or strengthen anti-semitic feeling, in order to uphold the Jewish communities' right to be protected from religious hatred … also derive support from Article 20(2) of the Covenant'. In making its decision, the Committee also considered a number of factors that may be seen as relevant to whether the statements by the author constituted incitement: the advocacy of contempt of those of the Jewish faith and ancestry; the 'special duties and responsibilities' of the speaker, a teacher in the school system; and a causal connection (which the domestic court drew) between 'the expressions of the author and the "poisoned school environment" experienced by Jewish children'.
57 Rabat Plan of Action, *supra* 15. Sejal Parmar, 'The Rabat Plan of Action: A Global Blueprint for Combating "Hate Speech"', (2014) 1 *European Human Rights Law Review*, 21–31.
58 Ibid., 25–31.
59 The plan draws together the conclusions and recommendations emanating from four regional expert workshops that took place in Vienna (for Europe), Nairobi (for

Interestingly, the Rabat Plan of Action's origins lie in international efforts against racism stretching back to the 2001 World Conference Against Racism, Racial Discrimination, Xenophobia and Related Intolerance, held in Durban and, more directly, the 2009 Durban Review Conference held in Geneva[60] – efforts that were crucially informed by the recent background of the Rwandan genocide, as indicated by the participation of Rwandan survivors and reflections on the Rwandan example during the Durban Review Conference,[61] including a statement from its president.[62] In its introduction, the plan also alludes to the role played by certain types of statements in creating an atmosphere that is conducive to the worst forms of human rights abuse, including genocide, through the statement, '[v]irulent and hate-laden advocacy can trigger the worst of crimes'.[63] Notwithstanding these general points, the Rabat Plan of Action is particularly germane for the Rwandan situation for a number of reasons. It provides the most elaborated, if not the strongest basis for how the legal framework around 'genocide ideology' and related offences should be reformed.

Africa), Bangkok (for Asia/Pacific) and Santiago (for the Americas) during 2011 organised by the OHCHR in 2011. Each workshop brought together experts, a number of treaty body members and special procedures mandate holders and others, most notably a consultant who would undertake a substantive regional review of legislation, judicial practices and policies on the prohibition of incitement to national, racial or religious hatred in advance of each of the workshops. See also *Report of the Office of the United Nations High Commissioner for Human Rights on the Expert Seminar*, 2–3 October 2008, Geneva, Palais des Nations, Room XXIA HRC/10/31/Add.3.

60 *Report of the World Conference Against Racism, Racial Discrimination, Xenophobia and Related Intolerance*, Durban 31 August–8 September 2001, A/CONF.189/12; Durban Review Conference, 20–24 April 2009, Outcome Document, para. 134.

61 In addition, the representative of Rwanda made a statement on 23 April 2009 at the Durban Review Conference, 20–24 April 2009; Report of Durban Review Conference, Geneva 20–24 April 2009 A/CONF.211/8. A survivor of the genocide, Berthe Kayites, participated at the OHCHR-convened discussion, 'United Against Racism', which was intended 'as a reminder and an inspiration to participants of the daily suffering and courage of so many around the world whose lives are affected by racism, racial discrimination, xenophobia and related intolerance'.

62 'We reaffirm that genocide is the most serious manifestation of racism, racial discrimination, xenophobia and related intolerance. The 1994 genocide committed against the Tutsi in Rwanda, which claimed 1 million innocent lives as the entire world watched, still haunts our collective conscience and must never be forgotten. The International Criminal Tribunal for Rwanda and the 1948 Convention on the Prevention and Punishment of the Crime of Genocide send an unequivocal message that the world will not tolerate impunity for genocide. Today, 15 years later, we recognize that there are attempts to diminish the gravity and seriousness of this genocide, through its negation and trivialization. This is a serious impediment to efforts for the prevention of genocide and for bringing justice to and fostering reconciliation for the people of Rwanda. We, therefore, hereby urge the international community to make all efforts to combat negation and trivialization of the genocide committed against the Tutsi in Rwanda'. *Report of the Durban Review Conference, supra* note 60, para. 10.

63 *Supra* note 15 at para. 2.

First, Rwanda's 'domestic legal framework on incitement' should be guided by express reference to Article 20 of the ICCPR, and '[include] robust definitions of key terms like hatred, discrimination, violence, hostility among others'. Such definitions should be drawn from the Camden Principles on Freedom of Expression and Equality ('Camden Principles').[64] While these are not fleshed out in the Rabat Plan of Action as such, Principle 12.1 of the Camden Principles defines '"hatred" and "hostility" to refer to intense and irrational emotions of opprobrium, enmity and detestation towards the target group', '"advocacy" ... as requiring an intention to promote hatred publicly towards the target group' and '"incitement" [as referring] to statements about national, racial or religious groups which create an imminent risk of discrimination, hostility or violence against persons belonging to those groups'. Significantly, Principle 12.2 of the Camden Principles also emphasises that States can only 'prohibit the condoning or denying of crimes of genocide ... where such statements constitute hate speech as defined by Principle 12.1'.[65]

Second, in terms of the threshold for incitement to be applied in specific cases, the Rabat Plan of Action emphasises that 'Article 20 of the ICCPR requires a high threshold because, as a matter of fundamental principle, limitation of speech must remain an exception'.[66] It then proposes a six-part threshold test for determining when speech should be considered as criminal incitement. This test should be instructive for Rwanda's prosecutors, defence lawyers as well as judges in arguing and adjudicating cases. The following elements of this threshold test, which are cumulative, draw upon Article 19's Policy Brief, *Prohibiting incitement to discrimination, hostility and violence*, which elaborates on each element in much greater detail:[67]

- *Context*: Context is of great importance when assessing whether particular statements are likely to incite to discrimination, hostility or violence against the target group and it may have a bearing directly on both intent and/or causation. Analysis of the context should place the speech act within the

---

64 Rabat Plan of Action, *supra* note 15 at para. 21. *The Camden Principles on Freedom of Expression and Equality* were prepared by Article 19 on the basis of multi-stakeholder discussions involving international human rights law on freedom of expression and equality issues. See *The Camden Principles on Freedom of Expression and Equality*, April 2009.

65 As Article 19 highlighted in their analysis of the 2008 Law, the Genocide Ideology Law did not meet the robust definitions of Principle 12 of the Camden Principles in failing, for example, to spell out the requirement for an intention to promote hatred publicly or an imminent risk of discrimination, hostility or violence. Article 19, *Comment on the Law Relating to the Punishment of the Crime of Genocide Ideology of Rwanda, supra* note 5.

66 *Supra* note 15, para. 22.

67 Article 19, *Policy Brief: Prohibiting incitement to discrimination, hostility or violence*, December 2012. See also Article 19, '"Hate Speech" Explained: A Toolkit' (2015).

social and political context prevalent at the time the speech was made and disseminated.

- *Speaker*: The position or status of the speaker in the society should be considered, specifically the individual's or organisation's standing in the context of the audience to whom the speech is directed.
- *Intent*: Article 20 of the ICCPR requires intent. Negligence and recklessness are not sufficient for an Article 20 situation which requires 'advocacy' and 'incitement' rather than mere distribution or circulation. In this regard, it requires the activation of a triangular relationship between the object and subject of the speech as well as the audience.
- *Content or form*: The content of the speech constitutes one of the key foci of the court's deliberations and is a critical element of incitement. Content analysis may include the degree to which the speech was provocative and direct, as well as a focus on the form, style, nature of the arguments deployed in the speech at issue or in the balance struck between arguments deployed, etc.
- *Extent of the speech*: This includes elements such as the reach of the speech, its public nature, magnitude and the size of its audience. Further elements are whether the speech is public, what the means of dissemination are, considering whether the speech was disseminated through one single leaflet or through broadcasting in the mainstream media or internet, what was the frequency, the amount and the extent of the communications, whether the audience had the means to act on the incitement, whether the statement (or work of art) was circulated in a restricted environment or widely accessible to the general public.
- *Likelihood, including imminence*: Incitement, by definition, is an inchoate crime. The action advocated through incitement speech does not have to be committed for that speech to amount to a crime. Nevertheless some degree of risk of resulting harm must be identified. It means the courts will have to determine that there was a reasonable probability that the speech would succeed in inciting actual action against the target group, recognising that such causation should be rather direct.[68]

Third, the Rabat Plan of Action envisages a holistic approach to targeting incitement to discrimination, hostility and violence, which should urge Rwanda's State, non-State and inter-governmental actors to think more imaginatively about the best way of tackling incitement and fostering a harmonious society. This approach includes 'criminal sanctions ... as last resort measures to be only applied in strictly justifiable situations', but also 'civil sanctions and remedies ... including pecuniary and non-pecuniary damages, along with the right of correction and the right to reply' and 'administrative sanctions and remedies ... including those identified and put in force by various professional and regulatory bodies'.[69] Such legal responses also include 'comprehensive anti-discrimination legislation

---

68   *Supra* note 15, para. 29.
69   *Supra* note 15, para. 34.

that includes preventive and punitive action to effectively combat incitement to hatred'.[70] At the same time, the Rabat Plan of Action indicates that non-legal responses, specifically 'policies, practices and measures nurturing social consciousness, tolerance and understanding change and public discussion' should also be adopted by States to '[create] and [strengthen] a culture of peace, tolerance and mutual respect among individuals, public officials and members of the judiciary ... [to render] media organizations and religious/community leaders more ethically aware and socially responsible'.[71] Such initiatives are based on the premise that '[S]tates, media and society have a collective responsibility to ensure that acts of incitement to hatred are spoken out against and acted upon with the appropriate measures in accordance with international human rights law'.[72]

The Rabat Plan of Action makes a number of other policy recommendations, many of which variously also draw on the Camden Principles, including: for 'teacher training on human rights values and principles by introducing or strengthening intercultural understanding as part of the school curriculum for pupils of all ages'; for 'a public policy and regulatory framework which promotes pluralism and diversity of the media, including new media' and 'which promotes universal and non-discrimination in access to use of means of communication'; for political parties to 'adopt and enforce ethical guidelines in relation to the conduct of their representatives, particularly with respect to public speech'; and for the media 'to play a role in combatting discrimination and in promoting intercultural understanding' by, amongst other things, 'taking care to report in context and in a factual and sensitive manner, while ensuring that acts of discrimination are brought to the attention of the public'.[73] The Rabat Plan of Action also urges UN human rights bodies, including the Office of the High Commissioner for Human Rights (OHCHR) and the Office of the Special Advisor on the Prevention of Genocide to 'enhance their cooperation in order to maximize synergies and stimulate joint action'.[74]

2.4 Penalties

2.4.1 2008 Law

The original 2008 version of Genocide Ideology Law established a harsh regime of penalties that encompasses both heavy fines and prison sentences for those individuals convicted of genocide ideology. Anyone convicted of genocide ideology

---

70 *Supra* note 15, para. 26.
71 *Supra* note 15, para. 35.
72 Ibid.
73 *Supra* note 15, paras 44, 48, 57, 58.
74 *Supra* note 15, para. 53. Together with the Special Advisor on the Responsibility to Protect, the Special Advisor on the Prevention of Genocide has developed a 'Tool for Prevention' in order to assess the risk of genocide as well as war crimes and crimes against humanity. *Framework for Analysis of Atrocity Crimes: A Tool for Prevention* (United Nations, 2014).

could be sentenced to an imprisonment of 10–25 years and a fine of 200,000 to 1 million Rwandan francs (ex Article 4). In the case of recidivism, that penalty was to be doubled. Anyone found guilty of genocide ideology who was also convicted of genocide could be sentenced to life imprisonment (ex Article 5). Current or former leaders in public or private administrative organs, political organisations or NGOs, or religious leaders convicted of the crime of genocide ideology, could be sentenced to harsher sentences than ordinary people, 15–25 years and a fine of 2 million to 5 million Rwandan francs (ex Article 6). Those who were convicted of disseminating genocide ideology in public through documents, speeches, pictures and other media could be sentenced to 20–25 years' imprisonment and a fine of 2 million to 5 million Rwandan francs (ex Article 8). Anyone who kills another, conspires or attempts to kill basing on the ideology of genocide could be sentenced to a life imprisonment, a crime for which there were no mitigating circumstances (ex Article 12). Anyone found guilty of making false accusations of genocide ideology is liable to punishment under the Penal Code (ex Article 13). Penalties were also harsh for associations and organisations.[75] Any association, political organisation or non-profit making organisation convicted of the ideology of genocide could be punished through its dissolution or a fine of 5 million to 10 million Rwandan francs without prejudice to individual liability of any participant in the commission of the crime (ex Article 7). Thus Rwandan associations and organisations, including NGOs in Rwanda, risked bankruptcy for overstepping the low bar for 'genocide ideology'. These penalties, particularly the high level of fines and prison sentences possible under the law, were clearly disproportionate and therefore incompatible with international human rights law, particularly Article 19(3) of the ICCPR. In General Comment 34, the Human Rights Committee reiterated its earlier stated position that restrictions on freedom of expression 'must conform to the principle of proportionality'.[76] It emphasised that '[care] should be taken by States parties to avoid excessively punitive measures and penalties … [T]he application of the criminal law should only be countenanced in the most serious of cases and imprisonment is never an appropriate penalty'.[77]

The provisions concerning the penalties possible for children were also very alarming. Any child found guilty of genocide ideology could be taken to a rehabilitation centre for up to 12 months, if he or she is under 12 (Article 9). If he or she is between 12 and 18 years, he or she could receive half the sentences referred to in Article 4 of the Law. Part or all of the sentence may be served in the rehabilitation centre. The follow-up procedures for children sent to such rehabilitation

---

75 The International Criminal Tribunal of Rwanda gave a life sentence to Alfred Musema, a director of a tea plantation who allowed trucks to be used to hunt down and exterminate civilians, after it found him criminally responsible under international law for genocide and crimes against humanity. Musema took no steps to prevent the participation of the tea factory employees or the use of vehicles in the relevant crimes. Alfred Musema Case ICTR-96-13-T, Judgment of 27 January 2000.
76 General Comment No. 34, *supra* note 44, para. 34.
77 General Comment No. 34, *supra* note 44, para. 47.

centres were supposed to be governed by a government minister responsible for the centres. Troublingly, these provisions suggested criminal responsibility could be appropriately attributed to someone below the age of 12. Furthermore, whilst those under 12 convicted of genocide ideology could serve their sentence at a rehabilitation centre, those between 12 and 18 only have the possibility of serving their sentence at a rehabilitation centre and may go to an adult prison for a conviction under the Law. Although it may be argued that the provisions took some account of the age of children, the CRC requires that *all* those under the age of 18 are entitled to be treated within the criminal justice system in a manner that takes due account of their age. Such individuals enjoy, among other things: the right to be detained separately from adults, except where this is not in the child's best interests;[78] the right to privacy at all stages of the criminal proceedings;[79] and the right to be detained or sentenced to imprisonment as a last resort and for the shortest appropriate time.[80] Moreover, any system of juvenile justice requires that children have basic guarantees against arbitrary detention and procedural protections ensuring fair trial[81] and that there are in place special laws, procedures and institutions for determining the criminal liability of children.[82]

Penalties could also be awarded to parents and to other guardians of children found guilty of 'genocide ideology'. '[I]n case it is evident that the parent of the child referred to in Article 9 of this Law, the guardian, the tutor, the teacher or the school headmaster of the child participated in inoculating the genocide ideology' (ex Article 11), these individuals shall be sentenced to 15 to 20 years' imprisonment. A teacher or a director referred in the preceding paragraph therefore could not be reintegrated into his teaching career. This provision criminalised parents, guardians and teachers for encouraging children to engage in critical thinking about issues relating to the 1994 genocide.[83] In doing so, it contradicted the State's obligations under Article 14(2) of the CRC on the child's right to freedom of thought, conscience and religion which provides that States 'shall respect the rights and duties of the parents, and, when applicable, legal guardians, to provide direction to the child in the exercise of his or her right in a manner consistent with the evolving capacities of the child'.

2.4.2 2013 Law

The 2013 Law revised and simplified the system of penalties for the crime of genocide ideology under an amended version of the Rwandan Penal Code,[84]

78 Article 37(c) CRC.
79 Article 40(2)(b)(vii) CRC.
80 Article 37(b) CRC.
81 Articles 37 and 40 CRC.
82 Article 40(3) CRC. See also the UN Standard Minimum Rules for the Administration of Juvenile Justice (the 'Beijing Rules') adopted by the UN General Assembly in 1985.
83 Article 14 CRC and Article 18 ICCPR.
84 Articles 135 *Official Gazette* No. Special of 14 June 2012.

repealing the regime of sanctions contained in the 2008 Law.[85] Article 135 of the Code provides that any person who commits the crime of genocide ideology and other related offences shall be liable to a prison sentence of five to nine years and a fine of 100,000 to 1 million Rwandan francs. Under Article 116, the crimes of negationism and minimisation of the genocide against the Tutsi attract the same prison sentences. These amendments radically cut back on the maximum prison sentence for 'genocide ideology' from 25 years to nine years, and reduce the maximum fine five-fold. One could argue that they serve to bring the Law closer to the standards in Article 20(2) of the ICCPR and the Genocide Convention. Yet, as suggested before, there should be no penalty for and no criminalisation of the offence of 'genocide ideology' in the terms of international human rights law. Indeed, Article 19 remains concerned that 'by retaining the broad concept of "genocide ideology", as distinct from "incitement to genocide", there remains scope for this law to be abused to silence critical voices or commentary on important matters in the public interest'.[86] The organisation has warned that the revised Law should not be 'manipulated or interpreted in a manner that restricts the exercise of freedom of opinion, expression or association', but rather should interpret the offence in line with Articles 19 and 20(2) of the ICCPR and the Genocide Convention.[87] This would mean the interpretation would obviate its apparent aims which clearly aim to sanction a broader range of speech beyond incitement.

2.5 Impacts

Apart from the normative problems with the original and amended versions of the Genocide Ideology Law, there is a major concern that the offence of 'genocide ideology' as such has been applied to crack down on real or suspected government opponents and critical journalists. The 2008 Law in particular was shown to lead to politically motivated charges, prosecutions and convictions. In perhaps the most notorious example, on 30 October 2012, Victoire Ingabire, president of the United Democratic Forces (FDU) opposition party, was charged with offences including on the basis of the 2008 Law and sentenced to eight years' imprisonment for genocide denial and conspiracy against the government. Ingabire had questioned why Hutu moderates who died in the genocide were not mentioned alongside ethnic Hutu victims.[88] The Supreme Court increased this sentence to 15 years. Human Rights Watch and Ingabire's lawyer have argued that her first instance trial was flawed given, in particular, the reliability of the evidence and statements upon which Ms Ingabire was convicted.[89] In another case, in April

---

85   Article 14, Repealing provision of the 2013 Law, *supra* note 1.
86   Article 19, *supra* note 12, para. 11.
87   Article 19, *supra* note 12, para. 28(iii).
88   Human Rights Watch, 'Eight-year Sentenced for Opposition Leader', 30 October 2012; *The Economist*, 'Rwandan Justice: Fairness on Trial', 3 November 2012.
89   Rwanda, 'Eight Year Sentence for Opposition Leader', Human Rights Watch, 30 October 2012; Reuters, 'Rwanda Opposition Leader Sentenced to 8 years', 30 October 2012.

2012, Epaphrodite Habarugira, a presenter at Radio Huguka, a community station in Rwanda's second largest city, Gitarama, was arrested and detained for three months having accidentally mixed up the Kinyarwandan words for 'victims' and 'survivors' while reading a morning news report about commemorations of the 18th anniversary of the genocide. Though prosecutors initially sought a prison sentence of 20 years and a fine, on 28 May 2014, the Rwandan High Court finally acquitted Habarugira of the charges of 'minimizing the genocide' and 'spreading genocide ideology'.[90]

In order to determine in a more systematic fashion the impact of the Law, it would be useful to have access to data about its application over the eight years since its adoption. NGO publications covering the first years following 2008 suggest that the actual figure of prosecutions actually far exceeds official statistics.[91] In March 2016, the executive director of the National Commission for the Fight Against Genocide (CNLG) stated that there were 180 cases reported in 2013, 138 in 2014, and 192 in 2015, while there has been an 84% drop in 'genocide ideology' overall in Rwanda since 1994.[92] As official information and data about cases and prosecutions under the Law are inconsistently gathered, it is difficult to draw conclusions from the most recent years since the Law was adopted and especially since it was amended in 2013. The National Public Prosecution Authority (NPPA) offers limited statistical information on its site at the time of writing.[93]

According to US Department of State human rights reports, which rely on NPPA data: from January to September 2010, there were 236 registered cases of genocide ideology as well as violence against genocide survivors, 96 of which were filed in court or suspended;[94] from January to June 2011, there were 103 cases of genocide

---

90 Media Legal Defence Initiative, 'Rwandan Acquitted of Genocide Ideology', 4 June 2014.
91 According to Article 19, 912 people were in prison on genocide ideology charges in July 2010. Article 19's submission to the UN Human Rights Council Universal Periodic Review: The Republic of Rwanda, 6 July 2010. Amnesty International's August 2010 Report, *Safer To Stay Silent: The Chilling Effect of Rwanda's Law on 'Genocide Ideology' and 'Sectarianism'*, suggests that there were 1,034 prosecutions connected to 'genocide ideology which were prosecuted as assassination, murder, poisoning, aggravated assault, arson, damage to goods and cattle, negationism, revisionism, discrimination and threats' *even before* the promulgation of the law in October 2008. See Amnesty International, *Safer to Stay Silent, supra* note 5 at 15–8. Some other sources suggest that as many as 1,300 such cases were initiated in the Rwandan courts in the 2007/08 judicial year. See 'The Genocide in Rwanda: The Difficulty of Trying to Stop it Happening Ever Again', *The Economist*, 8 April 2009; *Human Rights Watch World Report*, Country Chapter on Rwanda, January 2009; Human Rights Watch, *Law and Reality: Progress in Judicial Reform in Rwanda*, 24 July 2008.
92 Athan Tashobya, 'Rwanda: Kwibuka22: Govt to Engage Diaspora on Genocide Ideology', *The New Times* (Kigali), 31 March 2016.
93 See the website of the National Public Prosecution Authority (NPPA), nppa.gov.rw/ikaze/, where only the most recent report (July 2015 to March 2016) could be found.
94 US Department of State, Bureau of Democracy, Human Rights and Labor, *2010 Human Rights Reports on Human Rights Practices, Rwanda*.

ideology, 56 of which ended in conviction;[95] from January to September 2012, there were 167 registered cases of genocide ideology, of which 64 were filed in court, 31 were dismissed, ten were reclassified, and 62 were pending investigation (and in the same period, across 59 cases (concerning 63 individuals), the courts convicted 52 and acquitted 11);[96] from July 2012 to July 2013, there were 772 prosecutions for 'genocide ideology-related crimes' and divisionism, signifying a 33% increase in such prosecutions, compared with the same period the previous year;[97] from January to August 2014, there was apparently a decrease in cases of 'genocide ideology-related crimes' and divisionism with just 20 prosecutions;[98] and the same is indicated for the period from January to August 2015, which is somewhat surprising.[99] According to the latest report of the NPPA itself, between July 2015 and March 2016 there were 59 received cases of 'genocide ideology' and 54 of those were 'handled'.[100]

In any event, the Law has had a broader social impact stretching beyond those who have been actually charged, prosecuted and punished. The regime of penalties of the 2008 Law certainly added to 'the culture of fear surrounding the law'.[101] The US State Department has stated that the Law coupled with the laws prohibiting divisionism and genocide denial have '[discouraged] viewpoints that might be construed as promoting societal divisions'[102] as well as 'debate or criticism of the government'.[103] The deleterious effects of the law are exacerbated by the Rwandan government's broader 'campaign against genocide ideology'[104] as well as intimidation and harassment of opposition parties and media.[105] The shrinking or even completely absent political space, which is due in part to the Genocide Ideology Law,[106] stands in

95 US Department of State, Bureau of Democracy, Human Rights and Labor, *2011 Human Rights Reports on Human Rights Practices, Rwanda*.
96 US Department of State, Bureau of Democracy, Human Rights and Labor, *2012 Human Rights Reports on Human Rights Practices, Rwanda*.
97 US Department of State, Bureau of Democracy, Human Rights and Labor, *2013 Human Rights Reports on Human Rights Practices, Rwanda*.
98 US Department of State, Bureau of Democracy, Human Rights and Labor, *2014 Human Rights Reports on Human Rights Practices, Rwanda*.
99 US Department of State, Bureau of Democracy, Human Rights and Labor, *2015 Human Rights Reports on Human Rights Practices, Rwanda*.
100 Quarterly Report of the National Public Prosecution Authority (NPPA), July 2015– March 2016, May 2016.
101 Article 19's submission to Human Rights Council's universal periodic review of Rwanda, 6 July 2010.
102 US Department of State et al., *supra* note 95.
103 *Supra* note 96 (2012), Section 3 on 'Elections and Political Participation'.
104 This has included the enforcement of another law on sectarianism, Law No. 47/2001 on 18 December 2001 on Prevention, Suppression and Punishment of the Crime of Discrimination and Sectarianism. This law has been criticised on similar grounds as the Genocide Ideology Law. See Amnesty International, *Safer to Stay Silent*, *supra* note 5 at 15–8; Waldorf, *supra* note 7.
105 Timothy P. Longman, 'After Genocide, Stifled Dissent', *The New York Times*, 29 June 2012; *The Economist*, 'Rwandan Justice: Fairness on Trial', 3 November 2012.
106 The Human Rights Committee has noted 'with concern reports that journalists who have criticized the Government are currently subjected to intimidation or to acts of

contrast to Rwanda's apparent progress towards what the economist Paul Collier identifies as the 'hat-trick' of 'rapid growth, sharp poverty reduction and reduced inequality'.[107] In recent years, the Rwandan government has also been putting more effort into engaging the Rwandan diaspora in fighting 'genocide ideology', allowing for the problems associated with the Law to be exported abroad.[108] Human Rights Watch has noted that 'in addition to the repression of critical voices inside Rwanda, dissidents and critics outside the country have been attacked and threatened', even though the Rwandan government has consistently denied any involvement in these cases.[109] The particular freedom-related challenges presented by the Law therefore need to be seen against the backdrop of more general concerns about the state of democracy, the protection of human rights and the rule of law in Rwanda under the leadership of its president, Paul Kagame.

3 Conclusion

For a number of years, the Genocide Ideology Law has provided a focal point for international authorities and NGOs to criticise Rwanda on its human rights record, specifically on freedom of expression. This international attention undoubtedly nudged the Rwandan government to revise the Law in 2013 and in doing so considerably improve its terms. Yet any openness to international criticism shown by the Rwandan government was curtailed by the exceptionalist 'we know genocide better' stance, a parochial rootedness to the idea of genocide prevention in a nation's psyche. The trauma and scale of the Rwandan genocide thus explains Rwanda's ongoing attachment to the concept of 'genocide ideology' through law, but should not justify politically motivated application of the Law to target government opponents, critics and the media. Beyond this, however, the existence of the offence of 'genocide ideology' itself stands at odds with the authoritative interpretation and elaboration of relevant international law on incitement by the UN human rights system, including through the Rabat Plan of Action, which provides a range of strategies well suited to serving the objective of genocide prevention in Rwanda. The airing and sharing of views and questions about Rwanda's history of legacy of genocide are both natural and necessary if Rwanda is to reckon fully with its still-recent past, as immensely challenging a process as that was always going to be.

aggression by authorities of the State party and that some have been charged with "divisionism"', in its 2009 Concluding Observations on the periodic report of Rwanda. Concluding Observations of the Human Rights Committee, 31 March 2009, CCPR/C/RWA/CO/3, para. 20.
107 Paul Collier, 'The Economics of Isolation and the Role of Aid', *Social Europe Journal*, 15 February 2012
108 Athan Tashobya, 'Rwanda: Kwibuka22: Govt to Engage Diaspora on Genocide Ideology', *The New Times* (Kigali), 31 March 2016.
109 Human Rights Watch, *Submission to the Human Rights Committee in advance of the fourth periodic review of Rwanda*, 12 February 2016.

Chapter 8

A view of the impact of genocide denial laws in Rwanda

Niamh Barry

1 Introduction

Post-genocide Rwanda is a State struggling to move forward from its horrifying past through the collective processes of combating impunity, rehabilitation and national reconciliation. It is from this delicate minefield of challenges that the issue of genocide denial laws emanates. The question arises of whether such use of State power ultimately impacts upon society in a positive or negative manner. First, this chapter will take a look at Rwanda's obligations under international law in relation to the right to freedom of speech. Second, it will look at the three legislative instruments, which for the purposes of this chapter I refer to collectively as the 'denial laws', and which combine to create the impenetrable protection afforded to the 'memory of the genocide' in Rwanda. This chapter will then look at what is the 'official truth' or 'collective memory' for which protection is sought and the reasoning behind the legislation. This discussion aims to highlight some key areas that have displayed themselves as being most affected by the legislation in question. Accepting that the state of Rwanda and its people face a monumental task of transforming a divided nation into a unified and reconciled country, the question to be assessed is whether the genocide denial laws as currently operated are achieving this.

2 Legislation

2.1 Relevant international legal obligations of Rwanda

Rwanda is a party to the International Covenant on Civil and Political Rights (ICCPR), under which it has an obligation to respect the right to freedom of speech, including the right to hold opinions without interference and the right to freedom of expression.[1] Restrictions on these rights are permissible where provided by law and are necessary: (a) For respect of the rights or reputations of

---

1 Art.19 ICCPR.

others, and (b) For the protection of national security or of public order (ordre public), or of public health or morals.[2]

Rwanda also acceded to the African Charter on Human and People's Rights. Under the African Charter, 'every individual shall have the right to receive information' and 'every individual shall have the right to express and disseminate his opinions within the law'.[3] The African Charter does not explicitly list permissible restrictions on the right to freedom of expression. However, all rights within the Charter are subject to general restrictions and limitations. The preamble refers to the duties associated with rights.[4] It lists among them that 'every individual shall have duties towards his family and society, the State and other legally recognised communities and the international community'.[5] A further limitation on the right is that it 'shall be exercised with due regard to the rights of others, collective security, morality and common interest'.[6] Individuals must also exercise their rights under a 'duty to respect and consider his fellow beings without discrimination, and to maintain relations aimed at promoting, safeguarding and reinforcing mutual respect and tolerance'.[7]

2.2 Relevant legal instruments in Rwanda

The Constitution of Rwanda of 2003 was recently revised and came into force in December 2015. The provision dealing with freedom of speech and freedom of the press now exists in an amended form, in particular by the inclusion of the term 'expression'. It states that: 'Freedom of press, of expression and of access to information are recognised and guaranteed by the State'; however, it goes on to prescribe that such freedoms shall 'not prejudice public order, good morals, the protection of the youth and children, the right of every citizen to honour and dignity and protection of personal and family privacy'.[8]

Denial, negation or revisionism of genocide[9] were criminalised under article 13 of the Rwandan Constitution of 2003.[10] The offence was set out under article 4

---

2 Art.19(3) ICCPR.
3 Art.9(1) and (2), African Charter on Human and Peoples' Rights, 27 June 1981, O.A. U. Doc. CAB/LEG/67/3 rev.5, 21 I.L.M. 58 (1982) [hereinafter African Charter].
4 Preamble, African Charter.
5 Art.27, African Charter.
6 Ibid.
7 Art.28, African Charter.
8 Art.38, The Constitution of the Republic of Rwanda (*Official Gazette* no. Special of 24/12/2015).
9 For a discussion on the meaning of the terms 'denial, negation and revisionism', see Emanuela Fronza, 'The Punishment of Negationism: The Difficult Dialogue Between Law and Memory', (2006) 30 *VLR* 609; and Pascale Bloch, 'Response to Professor Fronza's The Punishment of Negationism', (2006) 30 *VLR* 62; see also Yakaré-Oulé (Nani) Jansen, 'Denying Genocide or Denying Free Speech? A Case Study of the Application of Rwanda's Genocide Denial Laws', (2014) 12 *Nw. J. Int'l Hum. Rts.* 191.
10 Art.13 of the 2003 Constitution also stated that '[t]he crime of genocide, crimes against humanity and war crimes do not have a period of limitation'.

of law No. 33n bis/2003,[11] which provided a penalty of between ten and 20 years where a person 'negated', 'rudely minimised' or 'attempted to justify or approve' the genocide.[12] The revised Constitution of 2015 removed article 13 in its previous form and instead committed the State, in its preamble, to 'preventing and punishing the crime of genocide, fighting genocide negationism and revisionism, eradicating genocide ideology and all its manifestations, divisionism and discrimination …' This is again repeated in article 10, which contains a set of 'Fundamental Principles' that the State of Rwanda is committed to upholding and ensuring respect for.

While not explicitly related to genocide denial, the following laws have been used to similar effect, essentially implicating an individual as being a denier of the genocide. Genocide ideology was punishable under law No.18/2008[13] (now repealed). The crime of genocide ideology was deemed to be 'characterized in any behaviour manifested by facts aimed at dehumanising a person or a group of persons' by, *inter alia*, threatening, intimidating or degrading defamatory speeches aimed at 'producing wickedness or inciting hatred', 'laughing at one's misfortune', or 'mocking' or 'boasting'.[14] Discrimination and sectarianism are criminalised under Law No. 47/2001.[15] Discrimination is that which is 'aimed at depriving a person or groups of persons of their rights as provided by Rwandan law and by International Conventions to which Rwanda is a Party'.[16] Sectarianism is defined as 'the use of any speech, written statement or action that divides people, that is likely to spark conflicts among people, or that causes an uprising which might degenerate into strife among people …'[17]

Due to widespread criticism of the denial laws, a process of reform was embarked upon in 2010. In 2012 a new Penal Code was adopted, article 116 of which provided for the punishment of the crime of 'negationism and minimisation of the genocide against the Tutsi'.[18] The provision closely mirrors article 4 of law No. 33n bis/2003. In 2013, Law No. 18/2008 relating to the crime of Genocide Ideology was replaced by Law No. 84/2013[19] amending the definition of, and the acts that constitute, the crime of genocide ideology.[20] Most notable is the

11 Law No. 33n bis/2003 Repressing the Crime of Genocide, Crimes Against Humanity and War Crimes, 6 September 2003.
12 Art.4, Law No. 33n bis/2003, n 11.
13 Law No. 18/2008 of 23/07/2008 Relating to the Punishment of the Crime of Genocide Ideology.
14 Ibid., Art.3.
15 Law No. 47/2001 of 18/12/2001 Instituting Punishment for Offences of Discrimination and Sectarianism.
16 Ibid., Art.1(1).
17 Ibid., Art.1(2).
18 Law No. 01/2012/OL, Instituting the Penal Code, *Official Gazette* of Rwanda, 14 June 2012.
19 Law No. 84/2013 of 11/09/2013 Law on the crime of genocide ideology and other related offences.
20 Art.3, Law No. 84/2013.

inclusion of a 'public' element to the offence and that it must be a 'deliberate act'. While this aspect of the new law appears a welcome improvement, on closer inspection the definition of what constitutes in 'public' is any place accessible by two or more people.[21] The 'related offences' set out in the law of 2013 include, *inter alia*, 'incitement to commit genocide', 'negation of genocide', 'minimization of genocide' and 'justifying genocide'.[22] Negation of the genocide now includes any deliberate act in public aimed at 'stating or explaining that genocide is not genocide', 'deliberately misconstruing the facts about genocide for the purpose of misleading the public', 'supporting a double genocide theory for Rwanda', and 'stating or explaining that genocide committed against the Tutsi was not planned'.[23] Minimisation of the genocide includes 'downplaying the gravity or consequences of genocide' or 'downplaying the methods through which genocide was committed'.[24]

What is 'deliberate' for the purposes of the new law is set out in article 2(2)(5) and states that it is 'willingly and with an intent to promote genocide ideology'. Thus, to prove the crimes of negation and minimisation, it must be proven that the accused committed a specified act with 'an intent to promote genocide ideology'. The definition provided for what constitutes genocide ideology remains vague, and as such the law is left in as much of a precarious position as it was prior to the revision that took place.

3 Purpose of the legislation

The laws discussed in this chapter are intended to protect the government-supported 'official truth' that genocide occurred within Rwanda in 1994 – a genocide carried out against Rwandan Tutsis by Rwandan Hutus. Genocide denial laws generally serve many varied purposes.[25] In Rwanda, the legislature has specifically stated the aims of the aforementioned laws to be as follows: to repress the crime of genocide, crimes against humanity and war crimes;[26] to prevent and punish the crime of genocide ideology;[27] and to punish any person guilty of the crime of discrimination and sectarianism.[28] The preamble to the instrument criminalising discrimination and sectarianism is interesting in that it specifically refers to the wrongs of the past which they seek to address. It refers to

21 Art.2(4), Law No. 84/2013.
22 Law No. 84/2013, Chapter III.
23 Art.5, Law No. 84/2013.
24 Art.6, Law No. 84/2013.
25 For a discussion on the legitimacy of genocide denial laws see generally Fronza, (n 9); Bloch (n 9); and Peter R. Teachout, 'Making "Holocaust Denial" a Crime: Reflections on European Anti-Negationist Laws from the Perspective of U.S. Constitutional Experience', (2006) 30 *VLR* 655.
26 Art.4, Law No. 33n bis/2003, n 11.
27 Art.1, Law No. 18/2008, n 13.
28 Art.2, Law No. 47/2001, n 15.

the history of Rwanda and notes that 'certain political leaders used discrimination so as to find a way of favouring certain people while being injust [sic] to others'.[29] It further states: 'Considering that since regaining its independence, on 1st July 1962 up to the setting up of the Government of National Unity on July 19, 1994, Rwanda has been ruled by political regimes characterized by discrimination and sowing of divisions among Rwandans.'[30] These statements set the backdrop for justification of the invocation of genocide denial laws and related legislation.

While the purposes of the combined legislative instruments appear to be meritorious, their structure and application have rendered them vulnerable to criticism. There was much disapproval of the law relating to the crime of genocide ideology, particularly its vague and ambiguous nature. The freedom of expression organisation Article 19 describes the genocide ideology law as 'counter-productive to its apparent objectives ... Its current application suggests that it presents a catalyst for, rather than a barrier against, future human rights atrocities in Rwanda'.[31] While the intention behind the instrument is understandable, many have called for clarification on the constituent elements of the offence.[32] For example, the use of terms such as 'laughing at one's misfortune' and 'stirring up ill feeling' were ambiguous and ripe for abusive treatment. These terms are not the clear and precise legal language required by a criminal law instrument. While the revised law of 2013 has omitted the aforementioned terms, it fails to particularise the offence with any greater certainty. The offences of genocide ideology, negationism and revisionism as set out in the 2013 law are similarly wanting in terms of definition and specificity.[33]

4 Impacted areas

This section will focus on five key areas of impact in order to give a brief overview of the issues that have manifested. It will attempt to display some of the reasons behind the criticism.

4.1 Education

In education, problems arise most specifically in the area of teaching history, the true account of which is contentious and politically charged. There are conflicting

29 Ibid., Preamble.
30 Ibid.
31 Article 19 Global Campaign for Free Expression, Comment on the Law Relating to the Punishment of the Crime of Genocide Ideology of Rwanda, p. 3, available at www.article19.org/.../rwanda-comment-on-the-law-relating-to-the-punishment-of-the-crime-of-genocid.pdf.
32 See Human Rights Watch, 'Law and Reality, Progress in Judicial Reform in Rwanda', July 2008, chapter 7, available at: www.hrw.org/sites/default/files/reports/rwanda0708webwcover.pdf; Amnesty International, *Safer to Stay Silent*, 31 August 2010, pp. 17–8, available at: www.amnesty.org/en/library/info/AFR47/005/2010.
33 See generally Yakaré-Oulé (Nani) Jansen, n 9.

accounts espoused by different ethnic groups. One commentator insists that 'it is clear that the history of Rwanda has yet to be written'.[34] One version claims that the Tutsi emigrated to modern-day Rwanda from the horn of Africa, subjugating the 'native' Hutu and Twa. The other version asserts that the Hutu, Tutsi and Twa lived together peacefully until the arrival of colonialism, following which the Tutsi were placed in a position of elitism and control. The latter version is the one which is supported by the current government of Rwanda. The former is maintained by the Hutu *génocidaires*.[35] The distinctions are more rigid than ever in the aftermath of the 1994 genocide. The position promulgated by the Rwandan Patriotic Front (RPF)-created government is that the 'white man' caused the strife and division among Rwandans and they should now unite to build a strengthened Rwanda.[36] A leading scholar in the area, Eugenia Zorbas, professes that this is creating a problem within the country. The various versions of history are not being challenged or debated and instead the RPF-endorsed version is unilaterally imposed.

The Rwandan government placed a moratorium on teaching history within schools in 1994. It was not until five years later in 1999 that the government suggested that history be taught for two hours a week.[37] However, no textbooks or manuals were provided. In 2006 a collaboration between the National University of Rwanda, the National Curriculum Development Centre of the Rwandan Ministry of Education, the Human Rights Centre of the University of California, Berkeley, and the non-governmental organisation (NGO) Facing History created a resource book for teaching history in Rwanda, entitled *The Teaching of History of Rwanda: A Participatory Approach*.[38] However, in looking at the guidebook, the outline for teachers does not include the period from 1990 onwards. The project acted as a guide and an attempt to open up the space to write the history of Rwanda. Unfortunately, the climate of fear surrounding the use of the denial laws is an inhibitive factor which will prevent any such progress.

It is evident that the topic of history and what to teach is a sensitive one and for the moment the position is simply to avoid all discussion on the matter. One cannot refer to different ethnicities as there is only one 'Banyarwanda' now. To

34 Nigel Eltringham, *Accounting for Horror: Post-Genocide Debates in Rwanda* (Pluto, London 2004), 149.
35 Eugenia Zorbas, 'Reconciliation in Post-Genocide Rwanda', (2004) 1 *AJLS* 42; see the Official Website of the Government of Rwanda, www.rwanda1.com/government/
36 See Zorbas, n 35, at 42 citing a Famous RPF song.
37 See Anna Obura, 'Never Again: Educational Reconstruction in Rwanda' (2003, International Institute for Educational Planning) available at: unesdoc.unesco.org/images/0013/001330/133051e.pdf, 18, 99.
38 The resource book was published by the Rwandan Ministry of Education in 2008. However, in 2011 the government had still not introduced the resource book into schools as part of the curriculum; see Lyndsay McLean Hilker, 'The Role of Education in Driving Conflict and Peace Building – The Case of Rwanda' (2010, Background Paper Prepared for UNESCO for the EFA Global Monitoring Report, 2011), available at: unesdoc.unesco.org/images/0019/001913/191301e.pdf, p. 14.

contest the state-supported version of history, to question, debate or suggest otherwise, puts oneself at risk of allegations of divisionism or, worse still, revisionism. Classroom discussions or constructive dialogues surrounding the history of Rwanda are consequentially inhibited. The result is manifested in poor development of the critical thinking skills needed for independent thought.[39]

4.2 Politics

The State of Rwanda has held two presidential elections since 1994, the first in 2003 and the second in 2010.[40] Allegations of persecution against political opposition and manipulation of the law by the present government, in pursuit of the retention of power, surrounded the most recent elections held on 9 August 2010. Human rights organisations have consistently expressed concern that the denial laws were being utilised for the benefit of the current government.[41]

In April 2010, Victoire Ingabire, an opposition politician who sought to run against Kagame in the 2010 presidential elections, was arrested and charged with genocide ideology, minimising the genocide and divisionism. Government officials claimed that comments made by Ingabire at the Gisozi Genocide Memorial on 16 January 2010 amount to 'genocide denial' and 'divisionism', promoting ethnic division.[42] She called for prosecution of the war crimes and crimes against humanity committed against Hutus by the RPF and the commemoration of Hutu victims killed during the war. Amnesty International stated in its report, entitled 'Safer to Stay Silent',[43] that it considers that the content of the speech cannot reasonably be construed as hate speech. The prosecutor-general of Rwanda stated that 'the issue is the philosophy behind it. It is not one of criminality, it's one of philosophy'.[44] Aside from the fact that Amnesty International condemns this freedom for the government to focus on the perception of an underlying philosophy as opposed to the statements at issue, they also claim that the timing of the accusations against Ingabire strongly suggest a political motivation.[45] Ms. Ingabire unsuccessfully challenged the constitutionality of provisions of the 2008

39 See McLean Hilker, n 38, p. 3.
40 Paul Kagame was re-elected for a seven-year term on 9 August 2010, winning 92.9% of the votes. See www.bbc.co.uk/news/world-africa-10935892.
41 Human Rights Watch, 'Rwanda: Silencing Dissent Ahead of Elections', 2 August 2010, available at: www.hrw.org/news/2010/08/02/rwanda-silencing-dissent-ahead-elections; Amnesty International, 'Pre-election Attacks on Rwandan Politicians and Journalists Condemned', 5 August 2010, available at: www.amnesty.org/en/latest/news/2010/08/pre-election-attacks-rwandan-politicians-and-journalists-condemned/.
42 Amnesty International, 'Rwanda Urged to Ensure Opposition Leader Receives Fair Trial', 28 April 2010, available at www.amnesty.org/en/news-and-updates/rwanda-urged-ensure-opposition-leader-receives-fair-trial-2010-04-28.
43 Amnesty International, Safer to Stay Silent, n 32.
44 See Amnesty International, Safer to Stay Silent, n 32, p. 21.
45 The European Parliament noted that many observers considered the trial to be politically motivated in its Resolution of 23 May 2013 on Rwanda: Case of Victoire

genocide ideology law before the Rwandan Supreme Court in 2012. The decision has been questioned for its seemingly contradictory finding, whereby it upholds the constitutionality of the laws in question, while simultaneously noting that they require clarification.[46]

Bernard Ntaganda, the leader of the Ideal Social Party (PS-Imberakuri),[47] was called before the Rwandan Senate in late 2009 to respond to genocide ideology accusations. On 24 June 2010, the first day that presidential candidates could register for the elections, Bernard Ntaganda was arrested. Amnesty International claims the timing of this incident suggests a political motivation. He was ultimately convicted of threatening State security and 'divisionism' in relation to his speeches criticising government policies.[48]

In January 2011, former senior government and army officials Faustin Kayumba Nyamwasa,[49] Patrick Karegeya,[50] Gerald Gahima and Théogène Rudasingwa, were tried in absentia by a military court in Kigali and found guilty of endangering State security, destabilising public order, 'divisionism', defamation, and forming a criminal enterprise. Human Rights Watch noted that although the government publicly accused the four men of forming an armed group and of being behind a spate of grenade attacks in Rwanda in 2010, the trial did not deal with these allegations, but rather it dealt with criticism of the government and Kagame.[51]

The law that punishes discrimination and sectarianism is utilised to implicate people as *génocidaire* sympathisers. All Rwandans must be referred to as 'Banyarwanda'. Faustin Twagirimungu, a Hutu who himself lost family members during

Ingabire, (2013/2641 (RSP)), para. J, available at: www.europarl.europa.eu/docu ment/activities/cont/201306/20130620ATT68096/20130620ATT68096EN.pdf.

46 See Yakaré-Oulé (Nani) Jansen, n 9, p. 211, referring to the judgment: *Le Ministère Public v. Ingabire, Judgment* No. RP 0081-0110/10/HC/KIG (High Ct. of Kigali 20 October 2012).

47 The only new opposition party to secure registration.

48 Amnesty International, *Rwandan Opposition Politician Jailed for Exercising Rights*, 14 February 2011, available at: www.amnesty.org/en/news-and-updates/rwandan-oppo sition-politician-jailed-exercising-rights-2011-02-14; this conviction and sentence was upheld on appeal to the Supreme Court in its judgment of 27 April 2012, see Human Rights Watch, 'Rwanda, Opposition Leader's Sentence Upheld, Bernard Ntaganda, Journalists in Prison for Expressing Critical Views', 27 April 2012, available at: www. hrw.org/news/2012/04/27/rwanda-opposition-leaders-sentence-upheld.

49 An assassination attempt was made on General Nyamwasa, in South Africa on 19 June 2010, while living in exile. Four men were found guilty for the attempt on his life by a South African Court on 29 August 2014, see BBC News Report, 'Rwandan Nyamwasa Murder Plot: Four Guilty in South Africa', available at: www.bbc.com/ news/world-africa-28981317.

50 Patrick Karegeya is since deceased, having been murdered in mysterious circumstances in South Africa on 31 December 2013, see BBC New Report by Gabriel Gatehouse, 'Patrick Karegeya: Mysterious Death of a Rwandan Exile', 26 March 2014, available at: www.bbc.com/news/world-africa-26752838.

51 Human Rights Watch, *Rwanda: Prison Term for Opposition Leader*, 11 February 2011, available at: www.hrw.org/news/2011/02/11/rwanda-prison-term-opposition-leader.

the genocide for his opposition to it, and former prime minister of the post-genocide transitional government, was labelled a *génocidaire* sympathiser while attempting to run against Kagame in the 2003 presidential elections. Academic researcher Elisabeth King notes that the offence of 'divisionism', 'while meant to eradicate "genocide ideology," increasingly seems to mean simply disagreeing with the government'. In an interview with one Rwandan woman she stated that 'Rwandans have become liars. We can't say anything because they'll imprison us or kill us'.[52] In May 2007, a senior adviser with Human Rights Watch's Africa division and an expert on Rwanda stated that several judges who had convicted accused persons of divisionism were unable to provide their researchers with a definition of the crime. It was further noted that at the time of the 2003 election the government even applied this term 'divisionist' to the Liberal Party, a political party strongly identified with survivor groups, because it appealed to survivors to vote for it instead of for the dominant RPF.[53] The National Unity and Reconciliation Commission[54] argued that female supporters were in contravention of the law by encouraging women to vote for the only female presidential candidate on the basis of gender alone. The Parti Démocrate Chrétien and the Parti Démocratique Islamiste changed their respective names because of a fear they would be labelled divisionist through name alone. A survey conducted in 2002 by Gakuzi and Mouzer to gauge the numbers of the various ethnicities in positions of power within Rwanda displayed how the 'RPF have used the defence of *Banyarwanda* identity to mask a "Tutsification" of power in Rwanda'.[55] As a result of the inability to assess or determine openly the proportion of each ethnicity in positions of power, it is asserted that the government is essentially using this as a tool to hide the true nature of post-genocide Rwanda. It has been noted that Hutu personalities have been steadily leaving what, at least in the first few years after 1994, seemed to be a government with genuine power-sharing ambitions.[56]

Due to the broad and unrestrictive nature of the denial laws they are vulnerable to profitable interpretation and politically motivated enforcement. Legitimate peaceful political dissent has essentially become criminalised.

52 Elisabeth King, 'From Data Problems to Data Points: Challenges and Opportunities of Research in Postgenocide Rwanda', (2009) 52 *ASR* 3, 132.

53 Correspondence between Human Rights Watch and the Research Directorate, Immigration and Refugee Board of Canada, *Rwanda: Legislation Governing Divisionism and its Impact on Political Parties, the Media, Civil Society and Individuals* (2004–June 2007), 3 August 2007, available at: www.unhcr.org/refworld/docid/474e895a1e.html

54 Created under Art.178 of the Rwandan Constitution of 2003.

55 A.E. Gakusi and F. Mouzer, *De la Révolution Rwandaise à la Contre-révolution: Contraintes structurelles et gouvernance 1950–2003* (L'Harmattan, 2003), 28: 'Tableau 2: Appartenance ethnique au politique de hauts fonctionnaires et de responsables d'entreprises', as cited in Zorbas, n 35, p. 44.

56 See Zorbas, n 35, footnote 49.

4.3 Freedom of the press

The media in Rwanda were strictly controlled by the RPF-led government in the aftermath of the events of 1994. An independent institution called the High Council of the Press was established under the Constitution of Rwanda.[57] The functions, organisation and operation of the body were determined by law.[58] New laws promulgated in 2009 gave the institution a new name – the Media High Council – and a wider mandate as a broadcasting and print media regulator.[59] There was much criticism of this institution and its powers.[60] At the United Nations (UN) Human Rights Council in 2011 the State promised to revise the media law prior to and during its Universal Periodic Review. However, Article 19 claims that while some progress has been made, the revised version[61] does not go far enough in safeguarding freedom of the press.[62]

The denial laws as currently interpreted are preventing the media from carrying out their legitimate investigative and reporting duties. Every criticism of the government, perceived or otherwise, will leave the press vulnerable to allegations of genocide ideology or divisionism at a minimum. Rwanda has a very limited independent media and following the closure of *Umuvugizi* and *Umuseso* for six months prior to the 2010 presidential election, the independent media within Rwanda was rendered almost non-existent.[63]

Agnès Uwimana Nkusi, editor of the privately owned *Umurabyo*, was arrested on 8 July 2010 and charged with inciting civil disobedience, insulting the president, spreading false rumours and denying the Tutsi genocide. The publications on which the charges were based raised questions on the murder of Jean-Léonard Rugambage, editor of *Umuvugizi*, and on the attempted murder of Gen. Kayumba Nyamwasa, an exiled former Rwandan military officer who was once close to the present government. The articles also made reference to the prevailing sense of insecurity prior to the elections in 2010 and contended there were growing divisions within the security forces. Agnès Uwimana Nkusi was found guilty of

57 Art.34, Constitution of Rwanda.
58 First by the Press Law No.18/2002 of 11/05/2002, and second, Presidential Decree No. 99/01 of 12/11/2002.
59 Law No. 30/2009 of 16/9/2009 and Law No. 22/2009 of 12/08/2009 on media available at: www.mhc.gov.rw.
60 See Article 19's Submission to the UN Universal Periodic Review in February 2011, available at: www.article19.org/data/files/pdfs/submissions/rwanda-article-19-s-submission-to-the-un-universal-periodic-review.pdf.
61 Law No. 02/2013 of 08/02/2013 Regulating Media.
62 Article 19, 'Rwanda: Media Law Does Not Go Far Enough', 18 March 2013, available at: www.article19.org/resources.php/resource/3665/en/rwanda:-media-law-does-not-go-far-enough.
63 The Media High Council suspended *Umuvugizi* and *Umuseo* for a period of six months on the 13 April 2010, alleging that some publications constituted a threat to national security. See Human Rights Watch, 'Rwanda: Stop Attacks on Journalists, Opponents', 26 June 2010, available at: www.hrw.org/news/2010/06/26/rwanda-stop-attacks-journalists-opponents.

threatening state security, genocide ideology, divisionism and defamation[64] and deputy editor Saidati Mukakibibi was found guilty of threatening state security. On appeal to the Supreme Court, Agnès Uwimana Nkusi was acquitted on the charges of minimisation and divisionism for lack of intent.[65]

The impact of the genocide denial laws has been felt not only within Rwanda by domestic journalists but also by international media. In 2009, the BBC Kinyarwanda service was suspended as a result of a trailer advertising a programme that was intended for airing, which discussed forgiveness after the genocide. The trailer included Faustin Twagiramungu opposing attempts to have all Hutu apologise for the genocide as he said not all had participated in it. A man of mixed ethnicity is also heard speaking on the fact that the government had not allowed relatives of those killed by the government to grieve.[66] More recently, the Rwanda Utilities Regulatory Authority (RURA), now the *de facto* media regulator in Rwanda,[67] imposed an indefinite ban on BBC broadcasts in the local Kinyarwanda language, which many have called to be lifted.[68]

4.4 Human rights advocacy

In relation to human rights advocacy, the denial laws have been utilised in much the same way as matters affecting political life and freedom of the press. Criticism of the government and their policies are generally not tolerated and NGOs are

64 Agnès Uwimana Nkusi was previously sentenced to a year's imprisonment in 2007 for a publication entitled 'You have Problems if you Kill a Tutsi but you Go Free if you Kill a Hutu'. She was charged with creating divisions, sectarianism and defamation.
65 Argument surrounded the meaning of the word 'gutemagurana'. Ms. Uwimana-Nkusi argued the term should be read as meaning 'killing each other with machetes'. The prosecution, however, insisted that the term implied that a 'civil war' had occurred, rather than genocide. The Supreme Court held that the term did minimise the genocide but decided the case based on intent. See Yakaré-Oulé (Nani) Jansen, n 9, pp. 201–5.
66 See Human Rights Watch, 'Rwanda: Restore BBC to the Air', 27 April 2009, available at: www.hrw.org/news/2009/04/27/rwanda-restore-bbc-air.
67 This assertion was made by Reporters Without Borders, see 'What Lies Behind the Indefinite Ban on the BBC', 2 June 2015, available at: en.rsf.org/rwanda-what-lies-behind-the-indefinite-02-06-2015,47958.html. This is despite the fact that the New Media Law enacted in 2012 provided for self-regulation, and in furtherance of which a regulatory body was established. However, on 27 October 2014 BBC Kinyrwanda radio service was suspended by RURA after BBC TV aired the documentary 'Rwanda, The Untold Story', without consulting the self-regulation authority. See Article 19 Submission to the Universal Periodic Review of Rwanda (23 March 2015), para. 22, available at: www.article19.org/data/files/medialibrary/37903/ARTICLE-19-Individual-Submission-to-the-UPR-of-Rwanda.pdf.
68 Announced on 29 May 2015. The ban includes radio broadcasts in Kinyarwanda, despite the fact that the broadcast in issue was a BBC TV broadcast from London. See Reporters Without Borders, n 67; *The Guardian*, Dugald Baird, 'UK Urges Rwanda to Lift BBC Broadcasting Ban', 19 March 2015, available at: www.theguardian.com/media/2015/mar/19/uk-urges-rwanda-to-lift-bbc-broadcasting-ban.

not exempt from this intolerance. Human Rights Watch, Amnesty International, Trocaire, CARE International, Norwegian People's Aid and more have come under verbal attack by the government of Rwanda and have even been accused of 'sowing division among the Rwandan population'.[69] Included in the Amnesty report on the situation was a statement from a representative of an international NGO working in Rwanda saying that '[g]enocide ideology leads to general self-censorship'.[70] Such self-censorship is an inherently dangerous position for human rights organisations to operate under and prohibits them from working effectively.

Christian Davenport of the University of Notre Dame and Allan Stam of the University of Michigan were accused of revisionism of the genocide. Davenport stated that what is contained in the leaked UN report[71] concerning the Rwandan government is consistent with their findings. Stam stated that '[i]n the Rwanda civil war case, a genocide against the Tutsi took place, but it was part of a broader and far longer lasting civil war in which there were large numbers of victims on both sides'. Stam says the problem in Rwanda today is that to simply observe this fact puts one on the wrong side of the law. Both Davenport and Stam had their visas revoked.[72]

Elisabeth King noted the authoritarian nature of post-genocide Rwanda and the implications this had on her ability to conduct research in the country. Interviewing an individual was a complex issue and had to be conducted one-on-one because of the 'potentially politically sensitive nature' of the findings.[73] King also expressed the difficulties with the state orthodoxy of there being 'one people', the Rwandan people. It rendered it difficult in her research to obtain an equal representation of both Hutu and Tutsi, as she could not ask one's ethnic identity. One 16-year-old boy told her 'we know [people's ethnicities], but if you speak of that they put you in jail'.[74]

In 2004, a parliamentary commission laid accusations of divisionism and called for the disbandment of the Rwandan League for the Protection of Human Rights in Rwanda (Ligue Rwandaise pour la Promotion et la Défense des Droits de l'Homme, LIPRODHOR), which is described as one of the very last independent human rights NGOs operating in Rwanda. Consequently, the organisation's leadership fled the country, after which LIPRODHOR acquired a new board of directors that is sympathetic to the government, and which issued a public

69 See Amnesty International, *Safer to Stay Silent*, n 32, p. 32.
70 Ibid., p. 27.
71 See *The Guardian*, Chris McGreal, Xan Rice and Lizzy Davies, 'Leaked UN Report Accuses Rwanda of Possible Genocide in Congo', 26 August 2010, available at: www. theguardian.com/world/2010/aug/26/un-report-rwanda-congo-hutus.
72 Aprille Muscara, 'Rwanda: Genocide Ideology and Sectarianism Laws Silencing Criticism?' 31 August 2010, available at: allafrica.com/stories/201009010007.html; see generally Christian Davenport and Allan C. Stam, 'What Really Happened in Rwanda', available at: www.miller-mccune.com/politics/what-really-happened-in-rwanda-3432/.
73 See Elisabeth King, n 52, at 129.
74 Ibid., at 136.

apology for the organisation's past 'erring'. The authorities subsequently placed those accused members of the organisation who had not fled the country under house arrest.[75]

In November 2004, the minister of justice refused to grant legal status to the Community of Indigenous Peoples of Rwanda (Communauté autochtones rwandais, CAURWA), on the basis that it advocated on behalf of Rwanda's Batwa minority population, and that this promoted divisionism. The Observatory for the Protection of Human Rights Defenders notes that this was likely a retaliatory accusation as CAURWA had submitted a shadow report to the African Commission on Human and Peoples' Rights (ACHPR), which had caused the Ministry of Justice to come under scrutiny.[76]

4.5 Refugees

Amnesty International documents an emerging pattern of Rwandans being prosecuted under the denial laws for statements they made in exile or as part of asylum proceedings abroad.[77] In one particular case a man was arrested at Kigali airport on 'genocide ideology' and forgery charges, following his deportation from Germany as a result of a failed asylum application. The Rwandan authorities found documents on his person relating to his asylum claim. He was reportedly told there was a great deal of 'genocide ideology' on his file. The man had claimed that the RPF had killed his family but only one side was being judged before Gacaca courts. Following his arrest, he retracted his statement and said his family were still alive. The Prosecution continued with the charge of 'genocide ideology'; however, the court did not recognise the charge but convicted him for using forged documents as part of his asylum claim abroad.[78]

A diplomat representing a donor state indicated to Amnesty International that revision of the 'genocide ideology' law in line with international standards could be an important prerequisite for movement towards declaring 'cessation' of refugee status for Rwandans in the Great Lakes Region.[79] As a result of the unpredictable nature and selective application of the laws at issue, many Rwandan refugees fear return to their home country. This is a situation of which Rwandan development partners are acutely aware.[80] Despite the existent threat, the UN High Commissioner for Refugees (UNHCR), at the request of the Rwandan authorities, set an aspirational date of 30 June 2013 for the invocation of the

---

75 See Amnesty International, *Safer to Stay Silent*, n 32, p. 27.
76 Rwanda: Legislation governing divisionism and its impact on political parties, the media, civil society and individuals (2004–June 2007), Publication of the Canadian Immigration and Refugee Board.
77 See Amnesty International, *Safer to Stay Silent*, n 32, p. 22.
78 Ibid., p. 23.
79 Ibid.
80 Ibid.

cessation clause.[81] This was revisited on 2 October 2015 at a ministerial meeting convened at UNHCR Headquarters in Geneva to discuss the state of implementation of the Comprehensive Solutions Strategy for Rwandan Refugees, and it was agreed that the strategy for cessation would be complete by December 2017 at the latest.[82]

5 Conclusion

While the use of legislation prohibiting certain forms of speech is often controversial, limitations on the right to free speech are permissible under Rwanda's obligations under international law. What is required is a clearly defined legal instrument, breaches of which are foreseeable. Any limitations must be necessary for the specified reasons contained in the clauses of the international and regional treaties to which Rwanda is a party. The instruments must only be used for the aforementioned specified purposes and not for any politically motivated or other purpose.

It is clear from the examples provided in this chapter that Rwanda is showing calculated disregard for some basic human rights principles and must act quickly to rectify this situation. The space for discussion of history in classrooms must be opened. Legitimate political dissent must be permitted and political opposition must be unimpeded. Freedom of the press must be tolerated and facilitated. Human rights advocates require unrestricted mobility and voice within the remit of their duties. Rwanda is in a unique position and is entitled to work towards reconciliation as it sees most appropriate. However, if the chosen avenue follows the path of restricting the right to free speech, Rwanda must adhere to international legal obligations and principles that safeguard the core of this right. To do otherwise would be to create a repressive society which will inevitably foment rebellion.

---

81 UNHCR, 'UNHCR Working to Help Conclude Three African Refugee Situations', Briefing Notes, 7 February 2012, available at: www.unhcr.org/4f3125cc9.html.
82 UNHCR Press Release, 'Ministerial Meeting on the Comprehensive Solutions Strategy for Rwandan Refugees Joint Communiqué', 2 October 2015, available at: www.unhcr.org/560eb74c6.html.

Chapter 9

Confronting genocide denial

Using the law as a tool in combating genocide denial in Rwanda

Freda Kabatsi

I Introduction

Rwanda, like other countries,[1] has enacted and used laws to contend with genocide denial. There is indeed general consensus that what happened in Rwanda in 1994 is genocide.[2] Nonetheless, the fact that genocide occurred is often denied, negated, minimised and even justified.[3] This is not only the case with the Rwandan Tutsi genocide (hereinafter Rwandan genocide) but other genocides including the Holocaust.[4] Claims will range from disputing that an intention to exterminate a particular group existed, that the numbers of those killed are exaggerated, the victims are to blame, it was a tribal war, and so forth.[5]

Therefore, countries like Rwanda have found that there is a need to enact laws against denial, the main purpose of which is to stem activity that would ultimately result in another genocide. Such measures have been heavily criticised, with

1 For instance, Belgium enacted the Negationism Law (1995, Amendments of 1999), Israel Denial of Holocaust (Prohibition) Law, 5746-1986, Luxembourg Denial of Holocaust (Prohibition) Law, 5746-1986. However, many other countries will deal with denial under laws relating to hate speech as well as expressions based on racial and other discrimination.

2 The United Nations International Criminal Tribunal for Rwanda (ICTR) in 1998 found Jean-Paul Akayesu guilty of genocide. Judgment available at unictr.unmict.org/en/cases/ictr-96-4 (accessed 10 January 2016).

3 An example is Antoine Nyetera. On the occasion of a colloquium held in the French Senate on 4 April 2002, Nyetera flatly stated that 'although massacres happened, there was no genocide'; see René Lemarchand, 'Rwanda: The State of Research', Online Encyclopaedia of Mass Violence [online], published on 27 May 2013, www. massviolence.org/RWANDA-THE-STATE-OF-RESEARCH,742 (accessed 10 January 2016).

4 In *Irving v. Penguin Books Limited and Deborah E. Lipstadt* [2000] EWHC 115 (QB) (11 April 2000), available at www.bailii.org/ew/cases/EWHC/QB/2000/115.html (accessed 5 December 2015); At [13.161], the Hon. Mr Justice Gray noted, 'Irving displays all the characteristics of a Holocaust denier. He repeatedly makes assertions about the Holocaust which are offensive to Jews in their terms and unsupported by or contrary to the historical record'.

5 Gregory H. Stanton, 'The 12 Ways to Deny a Genocide', www.genocidewatch.org/aboutgenocide/12waystodenygenocide.html (accessed 12 January 2016).

critics raising pertinent issues, for instance, that these laws may infringe on freedom of speech and freedom of the media.[6]

It must be noted that genocide, being the crime of crimes, must be accorded the seriousness it deserves. The results of genocide are far reaching, leaving communities with the arduous task of rebuilding broken societies, as well as forging and fostering harmony. Laws certainly should not premise on coercing people to like each other, because that is impossible. However, they should ensure everyone lives in an environment free from fear of extermination simply based on who they are. The purpose of denial laws is not, and should not therefore be, to monopolise one version of events or promote hidden political motives, but to check speech or other activity that would create tension or an environment where genocide would thrive – to prevent the spiral of speech which may innocently or otherwise appear to be one's expressed opinion but is actually a catalyst to invoking sentiments that would catalyse the extinction of a particular group of people.

However, it is equally important to note that laws on denial must meet the delicate balance required when put up against inviolable human rights such as freedom of expression and of the media. To ignore or set aside these rights would certainly be heavily detrimental to any society. Freedom of expression is an essential foundation for any democratic society and one of the basic conditions for its progress.[7] Therefore limiting this right must be done only when it is necessary and within the parameters acceptable by law in a free and democratic society.

2 Background of genocide ideology laws in Rwanda

In 1994 over 800,000 Rwandans, for the most part Tutsi Rwandans, and moderate Hutu Rwandans were killed in one of the worst tragedies of modern history.[8] It has been estimated that 11% of the population was wiped out, of whom 84% were Tutsi.[9] It is now over 20 years since the genocide. For Rwanda, recovering from the genocide has been very challenging to say the least. From the

6 See, Yakaré-Oulé (Nani) Jansen, 'Denying Genocide or Denying Free Speech? A Case Study of the Application of Rwanda's Genocide Denial Laws', 12 NWJ, INT. HUM. RTS, 191 (2014). Available at scholarlycommons.law.northwestern.edu/cgi/viewcontent.cgi?article=1172&context=njihr (accessed 12 January 2016).

7 In *Burundian Journalists Union v. The Attorney General of Burundi*, Ref. 7/2013; available at eacj.org/wp-content/uploads/2015/05/Reference-No.7-of-2013-Final-15th-May-2c-2015-Very-Final1.pdf (accessed 10 January 2016), par. 76. The East African Court of Justice adopted the view that freedom of expression is the lifeblood of an open and democratic society.

8 The Rwanda Constitution of 2003 (as Amended, 2015) specifically refers to it as the 'genocide against the Tutsi' and not simply the Rwandan genocide. Available at www.inteko.gov.rw/parliament/DF_DocumentViewer.aspx?id… (accessed 12 January 2016).

9 Jared Cohen, *One Hundred Days of Silence: America and the Rwanda Genocide* (Rowman & Littlefield Publishers, 2007), 1.

intricate task of uniting a people who were suspicious and harboured so much hate for each other, to ensuring democracy, respect for human rights, justice for all and reconciliation, as well as making certain the country grows economically is much to ask of any nation. The country has made considerable and commendable steps in attaining the above – but, as with everything, not all the steps have been perfect.

As earlier stated, laws on genocide denial are not unique to Rwanda. Following the 1994 genocide in Rwanda, a number of laws were enacted, some broadly on genocide and other acts with a connotation of genocide denial/ideology. The aim of these laws has been to ensure justice as well as to ensure that the genocide, in the much-used phrase, will 'never again' occur.

The Constitution of Rwanda under Article 10 (1) provides that one of the country's fundamental principles is to prevent and punish the crime of genocide as well as its denial, revisionism, ideology in all their manifestations.[10] Earlier on in 2001, Law No. 47/2001 – the Law on Prevention, Suppression and Punishment of the Crime of Discrimination and Sectarianism – was enacted. It was under this law that cases of genocide ideology were prosecuted before the 2008 Genocide Ideology Law which specifically provided for crimes related to denial.[11]

In 2008 Rwanda enacted a law against genocide denial: Law No. 18/2008, the Law Relating to the Punishment of the Crime of Genocide Ideology. This law has since been reviewed;[12] however, to put the background of genocide ideology in Rwanda into perspective, a brief discussion is necessary. This law faced heavy criticism. Several non-governmental organisations, scholars and foreign governments had issues with this law, arguing that it was harsh, vague, broad and open to abuse.[13] The Rwandan government had always defended this law although it had also hinted that it would review it,[14] which it has since done.[15]

It is to be noted that much of the pressure to review the Genocide Ideology Law was from foreign governments and organisations, which was not appreciated by many people in Rwanda who felt that these were the same actors who had abandoned them in 1994. Gerald Caplan captures this sentiment: 'To make matters worse, only months after the genocide ended many of the foreigners who came to help the country begun to argue that Rwandans ought to get on with the task of rebuilding their society, "quit dwelling on the past and get on with future" yes the genocide happened, but it is time to

10 See note 8.
11 See Lars Waldorf, 'Instrumentalizing Genocide', in Scott Strauss and Lars Waldorf (eds), *Remaking Rwanda: State Building and Human Rights after Mass Violation* (The University of Wisconsin Press, 2011), 54.
12 Reviewed by Law No. 84/2013; On the Crime of Genocide Ideology and other Related Offences. Available at www.minijust.gov.rw/fileadmin/Laws_and_Regula tions/INGENGABITEKEREZO.pdf (accessed 2 December 2015).
13 Amnesty International, June 2011 Report, *Unsafe to Speak; Restrictions on Freedom of Expression in Rwanda*, pp. 2, 3, www.amnesty.org/en/documents/AFR47/002/2011/en/ (accessed 2 December 2015).
14 Ibid.
15 See note 12.

get over it and move on.'[16] To Rwandans who suffered the genocide and perhaps to many of those whose wounds were yet to be healed, such sentiments were taken as not only in bad taste but also cruel.

It is also to be remembered that those who were on the ground like Roméo Antonius Dallaire, Commander of the United Nations (UN) peacekeeping force, United Nations Assistance Mission for Rwanda (UNAMIR), which was in Rwanda at the time of the genocide, expressed stern warnings on ignoring reckless utterances by the press; you ignore the press at your own peril, he said.[17] He went on to state that, '[t]he local media, particularly the extremist radio station Radio-Télévision Libre des Milles Collines (RTLM), were literally part of the genocide. The *genocidaires* used the media like a weapon. The haunting image of killers with a machete in one hand and a radio in the other never leaves you'.[18] In a Note Verbale in reply to the European Union (EU) concerns on Rwandan laws vis-à-vis freedom of expression, the Rwandan government said:

> in 1994 some governments in the western world were begged to use their technological advances to silence the infamous Radio-Télévision Libre des Milles Collines (RTLM) which was calling for exterminations of Tutsis. The unequivocal answer was that silencing this terrible radio would be an infringement to the freedom of expression and/or press of those who were using RTLM. Rwanda cannot subscribe to this liberal interpretation of the freedom of expression and freedom of press.[19]

Sixteen years after the genocide, Rwandan Foreign Minister Louise Mushikiwabo in an interview said:

> You will see in our 2003 Constitution the word 'unity' repeated so many times. What that means is you can be critical; you can bring up any subject for discussion, but please do not bring [up] anything that's going to divide us again. That's a decision that was made by the citizens of Rwanda, and that is not something that would make sense in other places. We cannot be rushed into allowing any kind of discourse, [especially] when it takes us back to where we were 16 years ago. I think that [policy] is something most people have said is being manipulated. It's not. We've been working on so many competing priorities in the last 16 years to rebuild the country, to make sure people live peacefully together, to reconcile after genocide. These are

16 Gerald Caplan, 'Rwanda: Walking the Road to Genocide', in Allan Thompson (ed.), *The Media and the Rwanda Genocide* (Pluto Press, Fountain Publishers and International Development Research Centre, 2007), 30.

17 Roméo Antonius Dallaire, 'The Media Dichotomy', in Allan Thompson (ed.), *The Media and the Rwanda Genocide* (Pluto Press, Fountain Publishers and International Development Research Centre, 2007), 17.

18 Ibid., p. 12.

19 See note 11.

processes that take time. We do as a government welcome dissenting voices and different views, but we have a responsibility to preserve the kind of stability, the kind of unity, we've been working on very hard for the last 16 years.[20]

Such sentiments are shared by many Rwandans – especially those who assert they do not want to return to 1994. It is therefore not surprising that the laws on genocide ideology would reflect this.

With that said, freedom of expression is a very important right in a society that considers itself free and democratic.[21] It is provided for in national laws of countries as well as the most important international conventions. Article 19(1) and (2) of the International Covenant on Civil and Political Rights, 1966 (ICCPR), to which Rwanda is party, provides *inter alia* that everyone is entitled to hold opinions without interference and shall have the right to freedom of expression – Article 19(3) and Article 20 provide for exceptions.

Many countries including Uganda, Kenya, Canada, Papua New Guinea, Namibia, Zimbabwe, Nigeria, Zambia and others have included in their constitutions this right stating that limitations to it must conform to what is acceptable and demonstrably justifiable in a free and democratic society.[22] The International Criminal Tribunal for Rwanda (ICTR) in a landmark case now dubbed the 'The Media Case', states that there is a titanic struggle between the right to freedom of expression and abuse of that right.[23]

So, the important question was whether this particular Rwandan law fell within the envisaged exceptions to freedom of expression.

It may be that Rwanda was looking to Articles 19(3) and 20(2) of the ICCPR and other exceptions to absolute freedom of expression when it drafted this law against genocide denial. It clearly gives a State leverage to enact laws to restrict freedom of expression, albeit within certain strict parameters. Laws to prevent advocacy of national, racial or religious hatred that constitutes incitement to discrimination, hostility or violence are acceptable.

20 europe.newsweek.com/louise-mushikiwabo-defends-genocide-ideology-law-74831?rm=eu (accessed 28 January 2016).
21 See *Charles Onyango Obbo and Another v Attorney General* (Constitutional Petition No. 15 of 1997) [2000] UGCC 4 (21 July 2000), where the Supreme Court of Uganda thoroughly discussed the concept of freedom of expression; available at www.ulii.org/node/15792 (accessed 27 January 2016). This case has been widely quoted in a number of judgments in the East African region.
22 For instance, under Article 24(1) of the Constitution of Kenya, 2010, 'A right or fundamental freedom in the Bill of Rights shall not be limited except by law, and then only to the extent that the limitation is reasonable and justifiable in an open and democratic society based on human dignity, equality and freedom, taking into account all relevant factors …'
23 *Ferdinand Nahimana, Jean-Bosco Barayagwiza and Hassan Ngeze v The Prosecutor* (Case ICTR-99-52-A), Judgment of the Appeals Chamber of 28 November 2007, 381.

It must also not be forgotten that all laws, especially criminal laws, must be drafted with utmost clarity and their objective be manifestly apparent. It must be said that any law enacted to combat denial, incitement to genocide and ultimately genocide, must fulfil these requirements.

3 Law No. 18/2008 of 23/07/2008 Relating to the Punishment of the Crime of Genocide Ideology[24]

In its 2010 Report on Rwanda, Amnesty International reported:

> Although the Law covers some acts that can constitute hate speech, it requires no link to any genocidal act and is extremely vague. For example, it penalizes people with a 10- to 25-year prison term for 'dehumanizing' a group of people by 'laughing at one's misfortune' or 'stirring up ill feelings' … It penalizes young children with sentences of up to 12 months at a rehabilitation centre, and those aged 12 to 18 with prison sentences of between five and twelve and a half years.[25]

The above is really a summation of the problems of this law. To give a clear picture of what this law is, its strengths and weaknesses, it is necessary to consider some of the provisions of this law, for instance Articles 1, 2 and 3 as they appeared in the law books.[26]

There is no doubt that Rwanda strives to ensure that democratic principles are part and parcel of the nation. In a constitutional case premised on the right to freedom of expression, the Ugandan Supreme Court noted (quoting other decided cases) that:

> A law which seeks to limit or derogate from the basic rights of the individual on grounds of public interest will be saved by Article 30(2) of the Constitution … only if it satisfies two essential requirements: First, such a law must be lawful in a sense that it is not arbitrary. It should make adequate safeguards against arbitrary decisions and provide effective controls against abuse by those in authority … by those using the law. Secondly the limitation imposed by such a law must not be more than is reasonably necessary to achieve the legitimate objective. This is what is also known as the principle of proportionality. The principle requires that such a law must not be drafted too widely so as to net everyone including even the untargeted members of society. If a law which

---

24 Currently reviewed, see note 12 above. Available at www.refworld.org/docid/4acc9a 4e2.html (accessed 10 January 2016).

25 Ibid.

26 Article 1 provided for the purpose of the law, Article 2 defined genocide ideology, and Article 3 gave the characteristics of genocide ideology; available at www.refworld. org/docid/4acc9a4e2.html (accessed 10 January 2016).

infringes a basic right does not meet both requirements, such a law is not saved by Article 30(2) of the Constitution, it is null and void.[27]

To give a fair critique of the relevant Rwandan law, it is perhaps important to see where the Rwandan people are coming from. Although the occurrence of the 1994 genocide is well established, before 1994 there were several series of killings connected to what finally culminated in the 1994 genocide. From the 1960s and also in October 1990, January 1991, February 1991, March 1992, August 1992, January 1993, March 1993 and February 1994, scores of Tutsi Rwandans were killed.[28] After the 1994 genocide, the government set up a number of Parliamentary Commissions to investigate a number of matters relating to genocide.[29] The fourth Commission identified cases of 'genocide ideology' which manifested in schools in the form of hurtful comments and tracts against survivors, destroying or stealing school materials of survivors and defecating in the beds of survivors.[30] Henceforth, with the additional abuse survivors endured the government found it imperative to deal with these issues by enacting laws.[31] It is not surprising that the ideology law includes phrase such as laughing at another's misfortune, defaming, mocking, boasting, despising. Perhaps this was exactly what was going on on the ground and the government included these acts in the law verbatim.

However, Chapter 1 of the 2008 law, which defined genocide ideology and enunciated the characteristics of genocide ideology, was poorly phrased; it was too broad and vague, whereas it had been the intention of the lawmakers to prevent and punish the crime of genocide ideology and conversely ensure that no genocide recurs. By broadening this definition, Articles 2 and 3 of the Genocide Ideology Law appeared to be extending to acts that would not be related to genocide as envisaged by the 1948 Convention on the Punishment and Prevention of Genocide. Certain phrases may also be at risk of being too open to interpretation or indiscernible, for instance, the phrase, 'propounding wickedness' as used in Article 3 of this old Genocide Ideology Law. Is it to put forward or suggest revealing one's evil intentions, or to depict a person's poisonous, sinister nature? Another unclear phrase was, 'confusion aiming at negating the genocide' in Article 3 (2), which is confusing in itself. It is appreciated that these may be direct translations from Kinyarwanda; however, if that is the case, the translations may need to be revised or the confusing terms omitted, to provide clarity.

Articles 4–13 dealt with penalties. The main criticism here had not been on the vagueness or ambiguity but the disproportionate nature of the penalties.[32] There was indeed serious fault with penalties given to children below the age of 12 and

27 See note 21.
28 See note 16, p. 29.
29 See note 24, p. 11.
30 Ibid.
31 Ibid.
32 www.article19.org/data/files/pdfs/analysis/rwanda-comment-on-the-law-relating-to-the-punishment-of-the-crime-of-genocid.pdf (accessed 29 December 2015), p.10.

those aged between 12 and 18, which were quite severe.[33] Since the law had been enacted several years after 1994, those who would potentially serve these sentences were not even born at the time of the genocide. Article 28 of the Rwandan Constitution states that, '[e]very child is entitled to special measures of protection by his/her family, society and the State that are necessary, depending on the status of the child, under national and international law'.[34] The Convention on the Rights of the Child of 1989 protects the rights of children and cements the principle of a child's best interests. The penalties in this law were not in conformity with this. Perhaps other methods such as sensitisation, further education on tolerance and the like would have been more favourable.

The other Articles (5–13) provided for sentences such as life imprisonment and prison sentences ranging from 15 and 25 years. Other laws criminalising genocide denial do not impose such severe punishment. In Belgium, the Negationism Law (1995, amendments of 1999) imposes a prison sentence ranging from eight days to one year, and a fine ranging from 26 francs to 5,000 francs. In Germany the prison terms do not exceed five years.[35] The reason for this may be that laws on Holocaust denial came long after the Holocaust, whereas for Rwanda they came much sooner – at a time of transition but also at a time when the scars of the 1994 genocide were still vivid. Nonetheless the Rwandan laws are the most severe and this may be taking an extremely precautionary and not correctional attitude.

Article 12 was noteworthy; it provides for a mandatory sentence of life imprisonment with no mitigating circumstances for a murderer, conspirator or attempted murderer who has based his or her actions on genocide ideology. To rule out mitigating factors completely is moving away from the good principles governing sentencing.

However, it does appear from Articles 4–13 that there was some rationale for giving various sentences to different groups of people. It is to reflect the level of responsibility different groups had by action or omission during the 1994 genocide. For instance, Jean-Paul Akayesu, who was the first person found guilty of genocide by the ICTR, was a former teacher, school inspector and at the time of the genocide, mayor of a commune where scores of Tutsi Rwandans were killed under his watch.[36] Hence, Article 6 specifically awarded penalties to persons who were leaders in public administrative organs, political organisations, private

---

33 'Article 9: Penalties awarded to children guilty of the crime of genocide ideology. In case a child under twelve years (12) of age is found guilty of a crime of genocide ideology, he or she shall be taken to a rehabilitation centre for a period not exceeding twelve (12) months. In case a child who is found guilty of the crime of genocide ideology is between twelve (12) and eighteen (18) years, he or she shall be sentenced to a half of the penalty referred to in Article 4 of this Law, without prejudice to the possibility that a part or whole of the sentence may be served in the rehabilitation centre.'

34 Article 28, the Rwandan Constitution, 2003 (as amended).

35 § 130 Public Incitement (1985, Revised 1992, 2002, 2005).

36 ICTR judgment available at www.unictr.org/Portals/0/Case%5CEnglish%5CAka yesu%5Cjudgement%5Cakay001.pdf (accessed 4 January 2016).

administrative organs, or non-governmental organs, as well as religious leaders who hold influential positions. In addition, the long incarceration period is perhaps envisaged to keep those away from the public who were intent on inciting or spreading propaganda in the form of ideology that could culminate in serious acts leading to genocide.

Another law that was employed to criminalise denial was Law No. 33bis/2003, Repressing the Crime of Genocide, Crimes against Humanity and War Crimes. Article 4 of this law specifically criminalised genocide denial.[37] This particular article was subjected to scrutiny by the High Court and Supreme Court of Rwanda in a case that attracted a lot of media attention both nationally and internationally and generated the new revised law – the case of Nkusi and Mukakibibi.

4 The case of Agnes Uwimana Nkusi and Saidat Mukakibibi[38]

At the centre of the case were two female journalists employed by the Rwandan newspaper *Umurabyo*.[39] They were arrested and charged with various crimes ranging from defaming the president, endangering national security to divisionism based on articles written in their newspaper.[40] Ms. Nkusi was additionally charged with genocide denial contrary to Article 4 of the law against denial.[41] This was as a result of what she had written in issue 21 of *Umurabyo*, where she stated: 'Rwandans lived for a long time with this hatred until they ended up killing each other after [former President] Kinani [Habyarimana]'s death.'[42] Ms. Uwimana Nkusi had used the Kinyarwanda (Rwandan national language) word, *gutemagaruna* (killing each other) in her publication; according to her this was to be construed as, 'killing each other with machetes', while the Prosecution insisted that this was to be perceived as there having been a civil war and not genocide.[43] The High Court agreed with the Prosecution and found her guilty of minimising the genocide. However, the Supreme Court acquitted her on this charge.

---

37 Article 4 provides: 'Shall be sentenced to an imprisonment of ten (10) to twenty (20) years, any person who will have publicly shown, by his or her words, writings, images, or by any other means, that he or she has negated the genocide committed, rudely minimised it or attempted to justify or approve its grounds, or any person who will have hidden or destroyed its evidence. Where the crimes mentioned in the preceding paragraph are committed by an association or a political party, its dissolution shall be pronounced.'
38 Case No. RPA *0061/11/CS* (S.C. Apr. 4, 2012), see also Yakaré-Oulé (Nani) Jansen, note 6, p. 203.
39 Ibid.
40 Ibid.
41 Ibid.
42 www1.umn.edu/humanrts/wgad/25-2012.pdf (accessed 12 February 2016), p. 4.
43 See Yakaré-Oulé (Nani) Jansen, note 6, p. 202.

In their assessment of what genocide minimisation meant, the Supreme Court said:

> This article does not explain clearly the acts constituting the crime of genocide minimisation. It only shows the denial of genocide can be punished when it is made public either through speech, writing, image or photo or any other way. The Supreme Court has never taken a decision in a trial explaining what it means to minimise the genocide. The Rwanda dictionary also does not give an explanation of what is 'the minimization of genocide'.[44]

The Court went on to add:

> However, in the current language of Kinyarwanda *gupfobya* means giving something minimal worth it does not deserve. This idea is developed in the law project on the criminalisation of genocide ideology in which it says: 'The minimisation of genocide is any behaviour exhibited publicly and intentionally in order to reduce the weight or consequences of the genocide against Tutsis, minimise how the genocide was committed, alter the truth about the genocide against the Tutsis in order to hide the truth from the people; asserting that there were two genocides in Rwanda: one committed against the Tutsis and the other against Hutus.'[45]

It is evident from the above that the crime of genocide minimisation as a concept was unascertainable.[46] It is indeed one of the important tenets of criminal law that offences must be properly defined – and therefore the drafters of these laws must ensure this. Possibly the offence of genocide minimisation was established in good faith, but the questions it raises did not make the law tenable.

5 The new law: No. 84/2013 on the Crime of Genocide Ideology and other Related Crimes[47]

This law amended the controversial 2008 law on genocide ideology. It seeks to streamline the crime of genocide denial. Noticeable is that the provision on the inclusion of culpability of children was deleted. The penalties have been softened and an attempt to clarify the law further has been made.

Article 6 of this new law, for instance, has attempted to clarify what constitutes minimisation. It reads:

---

44 Ibid.
45 Ibid.
46 Ibid., p. 205.
47 Available at www.moh.gov.rw/fileadmin/templates/HLaws/RFMA_Law_Published. pdf, p. 32.

Minimization of genocide

Minimization of genocide shall be any deliberate act, committed in public, aiming at:

1   downplaying the gravity or consequences of genocide;
2   downplaying the methods through which genocide was committed.

Any person who commits an act provided for by the preceding paragraph commits an offence of minimization of the genocide.

This is a positive step towards clarifying what minimisation is. It is more specific and provides more clarity. It is yet to be tested and tried by the courts – perhaps then its sustainability will be measured.

Furthermore, under the new 2013 law, the definition of genocide ideology sheds more light on what constitutes ideology. Article 3 defines what constitutes genocide ideology: 'it is a deliberate act committed in public advocating for the commission of genocide or supporting genocide.'[48] The article thus provides the important nexus of the said act to the crime of genocide. Thus the restriction is within the greater common good and henceforth the parameters of necessity are met. Article 5 deals with negation, Article 6 with minimisation, and Article 7 with justification. All of them are phrased in clearer terms.[49] The penalties have been reconsidered. The penalties are cross-referenced to the provisions of the Penal Code[50] and considerably more lenient than those in the 2008 old law, which is a positive step.

The question of whether or not this law meets the threshold of what is accepted in a free and democratic society is important to consider. It must be noted that there are some who support the view that genocide denial laws in general cannot be an acceptable exemption to freedom of expression.[51] The courts have held otherwise;[52] they have, however, applied strict tests on a

48   Ibid.
49   Ibid.
50   It refers to the Penal Code, Law no. 01/2012, Articles 135, provides for a term between five and nine years. Available at www.ilo.org/dyn/natlex/docs/SERIAL/93714/109657/F1967095662/RWA-93714.pdf (accessed 10 February 2016).
51   See debate, www.debate.org/opinions/should-holocaust-denial-be-a-criminal-offense (accessed 10 January 2016).
52   Case no. 275110/08; *Perinçek v Switzerland (2015)*. Available at hudoc.echr.coe.int/eng#{%22itemid%22:[%22001-158235%22]} (accessed 22 December 2015), para. 209. The Grand Chamber referred to *Nachtmann v Austria* (no. 36773/97, Commission Decision of 9 September 1998, unreported) and other cases, and noted that '[i]n those cases the Commission was faced with statements, almost invariably emanating from persons professing Nazi-like views or linked with Nazi-inspired movements, that cast doubt on the reality of the persecution and extermination of millions of Jews under the Nazi regime; claimed that the Holocaust was an "unacceptable lie" and a "Zionistic swindle", contrived as a means of political extortion; denied the existence of the concentration camps or justified it; or claimed either that the gas chambers in

case-by-case basis. For instance, denial of the Armenian genocide in Switzerland may be acceptable.[53] European jurisprudence seems to put a harder stance of denial of the Holocaust especially to countries that were more closely affected by it.[54] In the same breath, denial laws in Rwanda would probably be given more credence than if, for instance, there were laws prohibiting the denial of the Rwandan genocide in Nigeria. This is important because denial in Nigeria would not have the same impact as denial in Rwanda.

The limitations to freedom of expression are not abstract. Freedom of the press, expression and access to information are guaranteed under Article 38 of the Rwandan Constitution.[55] Article 41 of the same Constitution provides for limitation of rights but states that the limits must be provided for by law, aimed at ensuring recognition and respect of other people's rights and freedoms, including public morals, public order and social welfare which generally characterise a democratic society.

The limitation, however, must be strictly construed with leverage given to freedom of expression when a balancing act is conducted. Offensive, false, abusive speech is therefore acceptable and protected under this right.[56]

The European Court of Human Rights sitting as the Grand Chamber has pointed out – with regard to Holocaust denial – that its denial, even if clothed as impartial historical research, must be seen as antidemocratic and anti-Semitic, and it carries a particular danger in states that have suffered Nazi horrors.[57] Similarly, denial in a society like Rwanda, which has suffered the horror of genocide, should be outlawed. Laws on genocide denial are indeed not unique to Rwanda and have been upheld in a number of similar democratic societies.

6 Conclusion

The government of Rwanda is taking many positive steps towards rebuilding a nation that was ravaged by genocide. It is not surprising that laws criminalising

those camps had never existed or that the number of persons killed in them was being highly exaggerated and technically impossible. The Commission, frequently referring to the historical experience of the States concerned, described such statements as attacks on the Jewish community and intrinsically linked to Nazi ideology, which was antidemocratic and inimical to human rights. It regarded them as inciting to racial hatred, anti-Semitism and xenophobia, and was on that basis satisfied that the criminal convictions in respect of them had been "necessary in a democratic society". In some of those cases the Commission relied on Article 17 as an aid in the interpretation of Article 10 § 2 of the Convention, and used it to reinforce its conclusion on the necessity of the interference.'

53 Ibid., para. 281.
54 Ibid., paras 242–8.
55 The Rwandan Constitution 2003 (as amended 2015). See also Articles 19 (3) and 20 of the ICCPR, 1966.
56 *Supra*, note 52.
57 *Supra*, note 52, para. 243.

denial/ideology have been enacted. However, these laws must be drafted in clear terms so that ultimately their objective is attained and they do not trample over inviolable human rights like freedom of expression and of the media.

It also must be remembered that Rwanda is in a transitional period. It is not unique for countries to use transitional laws to address immediate and pressing issues for the purposes of building a nation and ensuring peace. Nonetheless, these essentially should be clear, unambiguous and not prone to abuse by those who would take advantage of their poorly drafted nature. However, as this concerns genocide which is the crime of all crimes, they must be stern and tailored towards preventing any further genocide.

Chapter 10

Srebrenica and genocide denial in the former Yugoslavia

What has the ICTY done to address it?

Dejana Radisavljević and Martin Petrov

1 Introduction

In the summer of 1995, over 7,000 Bosnian Muslim men and boys were executed in the small Bosnian town of Srebrenica, at the hands of members of the Bosnian Serb Army – the worst massacre witnessed in Europe since the Second World War.[1]

The United Nations International Criminal Tribunal for the former Yugoslavia (hereinafter 'ICTY' or 'Tribunal'), established two years earlier by the United Nations Security Council (UNSC) on 25 May 1993, was created 'for the sole purpose of prosecuting persons responsible for serious violations of international humanitarian law committed in the territory of the former Yugoslavia'.[2] The ICTY has 'invested a great deal of time and effort in investigating what happened in Srebrenica and bringing those responsible to justice'.[3] Over 1,000 witness testimonies have been heard relating to Srebrenica. It has indicted 20 individuals for crimes related to the events in Srebrenica, convicted 14, and rendered one acquittal. In 2004, the ICTY found beyond reasonable doubt that the Srebrenica massacre amounted to the crime of genocide under international criminal law.[4] In 2007, the International Court of Justice similarly concluded that the crimes committed in Srebrenica in July 1995 amounted to genocide under the Convention on the Prevention and Punishment of the Crime of Genocide.[5]

Yet, categorisation of the massacre as genocide remains contentious in the region of the former Yugoslavia. Media outlets, academics, politicians, religious leaders and heads of state still publicly deny the categorisation of what happened

1 UNICTY Outreach Office, *Facts about Srebrenica* (October 2005), www.icty.org/x/file/Outreach/view_from_hague/jit_srebrenica_en.pdf (accessed 28 January 2016).
2 UNSC Res 827 (25 May 1993) UN Doc S/RES/827.
3 See n 1.
4 *Prosecutor v Krstić* (Appeals Judgment) ICTY-98-33-A (19 April 2004), confirming the finding of genocide established by the Trial Chamber in this case on 2 August 2001.
5 *Case Concerning the Application of the Convention on the Prevention and Punishment of the Crime of Genocide (Bosnia and Herzegovina v Serbia and Montenegro)* (Merits) [2007], para. 297.

in Srebrenica as genocide. This chapter will look at the 'culture of denial'[6] prevalent in areas of the former Yugoslavia relating to the genocide in Srebrenica and examine the work of the ICTY to break through the wall of denial. The authors will argue that despite its ground-breaking work, the ICTY has failed to respond effectively to denialism. More than a critique of the first international criminal tribunal since the Nuremberg and Tokyo trials, the aim of this chapter is to provide a lessons-learned inventory of the ICTY's experience, for future international genocide prosecutions.

Throughout, this chapter will examine genocide denial particularly in Republika Srpska[7] and Serbia, both as places where the denial is most notable and as areas where the ICTY has made continuous efforts to communicate its work to the local population. This chapter will only consider denial of genocide in Srebrenica – the crimes which the ICTY's Trial and Appeals Chambers unequivocally characterised as genocide and on the basis of which the Tribunal convicted several individuals. As such, any reference to genocide or genocide denial in this chapter does not include the accusations of genocide in different municipalities in Bosnia and Herzegovina, the instances where genocide charges were dropped, nor the allegations of genocide made by Croatia and Serbia before the International Court of Justice. Rightly or wrongly, there has been no judicial finding of genocide in these examples and, as such, they fall outside the scope of the present chapter. In addition, the chapter is limited to discussing genocide denial in the former Yugoslavia, where the ICTY has sought to make a contribution to the restoration of peace and reconciliation. Accordingly, whilst genocide denial is by no means restricted to the former Yugoslavia, this chapter will not consider denial outside this region.

2 The ICTY's findings of genocide in Srebrenica

Based on the Convention on the Prevention and Punishment of the Crime of Genocide, Article 4 of the ICTY's Statute defines genocide as:

> any of the following acts committed with intent to destroy, in whole or in part, a national, ethnical, racial or religious group, as such: (a) killing members of the group; (b) causing serious bodily or mental harm to members of the group; (c) deliberately inflicting on the group conditions of life calculated to bring about its physical destruction in whole or in part; (d) imposing measures intended to prevent births within the group; (e) forcibly transferring children of the group to another group.[8]

6 As described during an interview with Jadranka Jelenčić (Belgrade, 24 November 2006), reported by Diane F. Orentlicher, 'Shrinking the Space for Denial: The Impact of the ICTY in Serbia' (Open Society Justice Initiative, 2008).
7 A predominantly Serb administrative entity in Bosnia and Herzegovina.
8 Updated Statute of the International Criminal Tribunal for the former Yugoslavia (September 2009), www.icty.org/x/file/Legal%20Library/Statute/statute_sept09_en.pdf (accessed 28 January 2016).

The crime of genocide consists thus of an *actus reus*, contained in provisions (a) to (e), and a *mens rea*, 'the intent to destroy'.

On 2 August 2001, the ICTY became the first international criminal tribunal to render a conviction for the crime of genocide committed in Europe.[9] In the case of Radislav Krstić, Chief of Staff and Deputy Commander of the Drina Corps of the Bosnian Serb Army, the ICTY undoubtedly found that the massacre committed in Srebrenica constituted genocide.[10] The finding of genocide was upheld by the Appeals Chamber, although Krstić's mode of liability was altered from perpetrator to aider and abettor of genocide because 'the Trial Chamber had failed to supply adequate proof of Krstić's genocidal intent'.[11] Subsequently, the ICTY Appeals Chamber has found three accused persons guilty of having committed genocide and sentenced them to life imprisonment: Zdravko Tolimir,[12] Vujadin Popović and Ljubiša Beara.[13] Drago Nikolić, a co-accused of Vujadin Popović and Ljubiša Beara, was found guilty of aiding and abetting genocide and sentenced to 35 years' imprisonment.[14] In its most recent case, the ICTY Trial Chamber rendered its highest ranking conviction in finding Radovan Karadžić, the former President of Republika Srpska and Supreme Commander of its armed forces, guilty of genocide.[15]

These judicial findings of the ICTY are important not only for the development of international criminal law, but also in bringing justice to the victims and their families in the former Yugoslavia. Notably, through such judicial findings – and more broadly through its judicial work[16] – the ICTY was also meant to 'contribute to the restoration and maintenance of peace' in the region.[17] Or at least,

---

9   The Nuremberg trials and the Tokyo trials did not prosecute the crime of genocide. The ICTY's sister tribunal, the ICTR, rendered the first genocide conviction in history on 2 September 1998 against Jean Paul Akayesu.

10 *Prosecutor v Krstić* (Trial Judgment) ICTY-98-33-T (2 August 2001).

11 *Prosecutor v Krstić*, n 4, para. 134. Krstić's sentence was accordingly reduced from 46 to 35 years' imprisonment.

12 *Prosecutor v Tolimir* (Appeals Judgment) ICTY-05-88/2-A (8 April 2015).

13 *Prosecutor v Popović, Beara, Nikolić, Miletić and Pandurević* (Appeals Judgment) IT-05-88-A (30 January 2015).

14 The other co-accused, Radivoje Miletić, was not charged with genocide, and Vinko Pandurević was found not guilty of genocide. Initially, the cases against Ljubomir Borovčanin and Milan Gvero were added to this case, but Milan Gvero died after the Trial Judgment against him was rendered and Ljubomir Borovčanin did not appeal his conviction. Neither Borovčanin nor Gvero were convicted of genocide.

15 *Prosecutor v Karadžić* (Trial Judgment) IT-95-5/18-T (24 March 2016).

16 In its over 20 years of existence, the ICTY has indicted 161 individuals, completed trials for 149 accused and acquitted 18 individuals. Among those indicted are heads of state, prime ministers, government officials and army chiefs-of-staff. According to its website, the ICTY's workload has included hearing 4,650 witnesses and producing 2.5 million pages of transcripts. At the time of writing, there are ongoing proceedings for 12 individuals – four accused are at trial and eight individuals are currently before the Appeals Chamber.

17 UNSC Resolution 827, n 2; *Prosecutor v Erdemović*, Sentencing Judgment (IT-96-22-Tbis), 5 March 1998, para. 21.

this was the intention of the Tribunal's founders back in 1993. They seem to have expected that by hearing witnesses in court, establishing the truth about historical events and individualising guilt as a result of a fair and impartial trial, the Tribunal would contribute to reconciliation in the region after a devastating war. According to the former ICTY President Judge Theodor Meron, 'the remarkable achievements' of the Tribunal include its contribution to 'bringing peace and reconciliation to the countries of the former Yugoslavia' and 'forging a new international culture of accountability'.[18] If this is the case, why are parts of the population still denying that what happened in Srebrenica was genocide? Or was the bar of expectations placed too high for the ICTY (or, for that matter, any other court of law)?

3 Why then is genocide denial so widespread?

Genocide remains a particularly contentious term in the former Yugoslavia. Despite the jurisprudential findings of the ICTY, establishing that genocide was committed in Srebrenica in 1995, that over 7,000 Muslim boys and men were killed at the hands of the Bosnian Serb Army, this is not an acceptable fact for certain individuals in the region.

Published in a report of the Open Society Justice Initiative, Diane Orentlicher's studies in the region confirmed the Bosniak[19] public's perception that the ICTY's 'finding that what happened at Srebrenica was genocide is the most important achievement and without the ICTY this would not be possible'.[20] Whilst Orentlicher's interviewees claim that 'evidence adduced in The Hague has significantly "shrunk the public space" in which political leaders can credibly deny key facts about notorious atrocities',[21] as discussed below, public denial persists.

In its plainest form, denial means refusing to admit the truth or existence of something, but it can be an altogether subtler affair. Thus, denial may also come in the form of 'giving the facts a different meaning from what seems apparent to others', or 'denying or minimising the implications that conventionally follow'.[22] The sociologist Stanley Cohen writes that:

> One common thread runs through the many different stories of denial: people, organisations, governments or whole societies are presented with information that is too disturbing, threatening or anomalous to be fully

18 *Address of Judge Theodor Meron, President of the International Criminal Tribunal for the former Yugoslavia to the United Nations General Assembly*, 15 October 2012, www.icty.org/x/file/ Press/Statements%20and%20Speeches/President/121015_pdt_meron_un_ga_en.pdf (accessed 28 January 2016).
19 The term 'Bosniak' refers to the Bosnian Muslim population of Bosnia and Herzegovina.
20 See n 6, 14.
21 See n 6, 19.
22 Martin Shaw, *War and Genocide: Organised Killing in Modern Society* (Polity, 2003), 119.

absorbed or openly acknowledged. The information is therefore somehow repressed, disavowed, pushed aside or reinterpreted. Or else the information 'registers' well enough, but its implications – cognitive, emotional or moral – are evaded, neutralized or rationalized away.[23]

In the case of Srebrenica, a number of studies have demonstrated that the most prevalent form of denial in the former Yugoslavia is the second form referred to by Cohen – interpretative denial.[24] Thus, those denying the Srebrenica genocide are generally not doubting that crimes were committed but are giving them a meaning different from what would seem obvious to others. During fieldwork in Bosnia and Herzegovina, Janine Natalya Clark found that her Bosnian Serb interviewees claimed 'that those killed in Srebrenica were combatants and there-fore legitimate military targets; that no genocide occurred because only males were targeted; and that Bosnian Muslims had greatly inflated the number of deaths'.[25] Linked to this was a clear mistrust for what had been established as facts – the truth according to these individuals is that the so-called victims are 'in reality alive and well and living abroad'.[26] Disturbingly, Clark found that those living in closest proximity to Srebrenica 'were most prone to denial'.[27] It cannot be said that these individuals are ignorant that crimes at such a scale were com-mitted, if only due to their proximity. Instead, Clark remarks that the key point in understanding this denial lies in recognising that there is 'a critical disconnect between the legal meaning of genocide and the way in which lay people may understand and utilise the term in support of their own ethnic narratives of suf-fering'.[28] As lay persons, these same individuals are most often unable to give the legal definition of genocide. Yet, their reaction to the term is so strong, pre-sumably because of the stigma attached to it and the ensuing disbelief that 'our army' would have committed such heinous crimes. Moreover, in the context of a highly polarised war and post-war rhetoric about the opposing ethnicity, accepting that genocide took place is felt by many as an acceptance of collective guilt for the underlying events, despite the fact that the ICTY prosecutes solely on the basis of individual criminal responsibility.

Denial extends to the platform of prominent political figures and local media, which is exacerbated by the rhetoric of certain religious leaders in the region.

23 Stanley Cohen, *States of Denial: Knowing about Atrocities and Suffering* (Polity, 2001), 1.
24 Janine Natalya Clark, 'Religion and Reconciliation in Bosnia & Herzegovina: Are Religious Actors Doing Enough?' (2010) 62(4) *Europe Asia Studies* 671, 681; Paul B. Miller, 'Contested Memories: The Bosnian Genocide in Serb and Bosnian Minds' (2006) 8(3) *Journal of Genocide Research* 311, 313; Human Rights Watch, *Selling Justice Short: Why Accountability Matters for Peace* (2009), 121, www.hrw.org/sites/default/files/reports/ij0709webwcover_1.pdf (accessed 28 January 2016).
25 Janine Natalya Clark, 'The "Crime of Crimes": Genocide, Criminal Trials and Reconciliation' (2012) 14(1) *Journal of Genocide Research* 55, 67.
26 Ibid.
27 Ibid.
28 Ibid., 69.

Thus, rather than promote reconciliation, Janine Natalya Clark has found that 'religious actors are instead employing denial and/or minimising war crimes'.[29] Government representatives, notably those in Serbia and Republika Srpska, have successively denied genocide. Despite efforts to move forward made by his predecessor, the newly elected President of Serbia, Tomislav Nikolić, stated during a televised interview that 'there was no genocide in Srebrenica'.[30] Although issuing an apology for the crimes committed in Srebrenica a year after this interview, the Serbian President fell short of calling the crime one of genocide.[31] Similarly, statements calling into doubt the findings of the ICTY on genocide are not an uncommon element of the politics of Milorad Dodik, President of Republika Srpska. Christian Nielsen notes that Dodik 'has increasingly obliged Bosniak critics by engaging in nationalist rhetoric and questioning the status of Srebrenica as a genocide – and to some extent by permitting those around him to argue that the Serbs were themselves the victims of genocide'.[32] The government of Republika Srpska not only issues press statements denying genocide, but has issued a report making such claims[33] and rejected the adoption of a resolution condemning the crimes committed in Srebrenica. Unsurprisingly, denial from within Bosnia and Herzegovina is particularly damaging, especially when it derives from the government and a prominent politician. Such rhetoric effectively negates efforts to stabilise Bosnia and Herzegovina and move beyond the tension and 'negative peace' in evidence thus far.

So is genocide denial in the former Yugoslavia the fault of the ICTY? The Tribunal established that genocide was committed in Srebrenica and found several individuals guilty of that crime beyond reasonable doubt. Many ICTY judges share the view that this is all that a court of law can and should do – render judgments, which speak for themselves. While this may be true for domestic courts dealing with standard criminal offences, an international criminal tribunal

---

29 See n 24, 691.
30 Statement by Tomislav Nikolić, President of Serbia, during a televised interview in Montenegro on 1 June 2012. Reported widely, including www.aljazeera.com/news/europe/2012/06/201262161913498413.html; www.lefigaro.fr/flash-actu/2012/06/01/97001-20120601FILWWW00497-pas-de-genocide-a-srebrenica-nikolic.php>; <www.bbc.com/news/world-europe-18301196 (accessed 8 January 2016).
31 President Nikolić apologised on live television during an interview with *Radio-Televizija Bosne i Hercegovine*. Reported widely, for example www.aljazeera.com/news/europe/2013/04/2013425102523848273.html (accessed 28 January 2016).
32 'Surmounting the Myopic Focus on Genocide: The Case of the War in Bosnia and Herzegovina' (2013) 15(1) *Journal of Genocide Research* 21, 30.
33 Darko Trifunović, 'Report About Case Srebrenica (the first part)' (Banja Luka: Documentation Centre of Republic of Srpska for War Crimes Research and the Bureau of Government of RS for Relation with ICTY, 2002), www.slobodan.milosevic.org/documents/srebenica.pdf (accessed 28 January 2016). The report created outrage internationally, and was subsequently repudiated in a second report in 2004. The current government of Republika Srpska has since repudiated the 2004 report and repeated claims that a genocide was not committed in Srebrenica.

has, in the view of the authors, special responsibilities to promote its work and bring it closer to the public directly affected by its judgments.

4 The ICTY's extra-judicial activities: a genuine effort or the bare minimum?

To repeat an old dictum, justice must not only be done; it must also be seen to be done. How can justice be seen to be done if the community most affected by the judicial decisions has little confidence in the court pronouncing them, and has difficulty understanding the judgments because they discuss complex legal concepts over hundreds of pages in a language the community does not understand?

It took the ICTY six years to conclude that communication with the public in the former Yugoslavia was a necessary component of its work. In an address to the General Assembly, the then ICTY President, Judge Gabrielle Kirk McDonald, announced the creation of the Outreach Programme, in recognition of the fact 'that the Tribunal must work harder to communicate with the peoples of the former Yugoslavia'.[34] Explaining the need for such a programme, President Judge McDonald referred to the people of the former Yugoslavia as the ICTY's 'constituents', who nevertheless 'often have little idea of what the Tribunal is doing except from what they learn via distorted news coverage and state-controlled propaganda'.[35]

Indeed, the ICTY had recognised the need to engage with the peoples of the former Yugoslavia proactively – to disseminate information about its proceedings, but also to counter misinformation about its work which was commonplace in parts of the region. Since its creation, the ICTY's Outreach Programme has held numerous conferences, seminars and visits to schools and universities in the former Yugoslavia. It has hosted visits by government representatives, legal professionals, non-governmental organisations (NGOs), journalists and students, among others, and organised peer-to-peer exchanges between the ICTY and local judges and prosecutors as part of capacity-building efforts. It has also published press releases and various other materials in the local languages, and its representatives have appeared in local media, including in public debates. Last but not least, the Outreach Programme has made a number of documentaries on the work of the Tribunal, including on the circumstances surrounding its establishment, its ground-breaking work on sexual violence, the experience of victims and witnesses before the ICTY, and most recently, a series of documentaries on crimes in specific regions of Bosnia and Herzegovina. The ICTY's communication efforts were bolstered further in 2010 with more ambitious outreach strategies,[36]

---

34 www.icty.org/en/press/address-united-nations-general-assembly-judge-gabrielle-kirk-mcdonald-president-international (accessed 28 January 2016).
35 Ibid.
36 Kristin Xuequin Wu, 'Experiences that Count: A Comparative Study of the ICTY and SCSL in Shaping the Image of Justice' (2013) 9(1) *Utrecht Law Review* 60, 64.

including outreach activities with the youth of the former Yugoslavia and the creation of ICTY accounts on social media, ensuring wider access to the general public, both within and outside the former Yugoslavia. The ICTY's outreach work is truly pioneering, if only for its existence. It may now seem evident that the work of an international court can hope to have but minimal impact without effective communication of its judgments to the communities directly affected by it, but this was still a novel idea when the ICTY was created. Today, there is no international or hybrid criminal court or tribunal that does not have an outreach programme. The question posed today is therefore not whether an international court needs to communicate its work, but to what extent and how.[37] This, in itself, is a remarkable achievement.

Unfortunately, much of the ICTY's efforts came too late. Official documents and press releases in the so-called Bosnian/Croatian/Serbian language, as it is referred to by the ICTY, were not available until seven years after the ICTY's creation. This contributed to the fact that, for a long time, the population in the former Yugoslavia knew very little about the ICTY, and what it did know was largely based on a deliberate misrepresentation of the facts.[38] As a consequence, the Tribunal's delayed efforts could only hope to have a limited impact. As a former ICTY outreach officer correctly notes, '[i]t is much more difficult to dismantle already established misperceptions and propaganda than it would have been to start from the outset with updated and accurate information about the Tribunal'.[39] In fact, between the ICTY's establishment and the creation of the Outreach Programme, the public in the former Yugoslavia received information on the Tribunal almost exclusively as it was represented in the local media. Influential parts of the media were still under the power of the political and military elite, themselves under investigation by the ICTY.[40] It is thus unsurprising that the media, loyal to the political elite, 'did all they could to convince their subjects that the Tribunal was biased and hostile towards their state and ethnic groups'.[41] While things have changed since then and journalistic pluralism and objective reporting in more recent years have contributed to a better understanding of the facts surrounding the crimes committed in Srebrenica, the picture painted by

37 See for example International Bar Association, *ICC Monitoring and Outreach Programme: First Outreach Report* (2006), 8, www.ibanet.org/ICC_ICL_Programme/Reports.aspx# 2012. The International Bar Association in its first report on the International Criminal Court's Outreach Programme recognised that international criminal tribunals 'cannot rely on the states concerned to portray the structure, mandate, functions and findings of the ICC objectively and accurately. As a result, the ICC must take the lead in public information and outreach'.
38 Jasna Šarčević, 'Interview with Mirko Klarin: Systematic Difficulties for Denial' (2006) 2 *Justice in Transition: Media and Crime*, www.tuzilastvorz.org.rs/html_trz/ (CASOPIS)/ENG/ENG02/639.pdf (accessed 28 January 2016).
39 Diane F. Orentlicher, n 6, 22.
40 Mirko Klarin, 'The Impact of the ICTY Trials on Public Opinion in the Former Yugoslavia' (2009) 7 *Journal of International Criminal Justice* 89, 90.
41 Ibid.

the propaganda machine in the early years, unopposed by the ICTY, may be among the factors influencing the 'public's understanding and collective memory of the events'.[42]

Would a communication tool within the region have resulted in a more favourable public opinion of the Tribunal and its work, in particular in Serbia and Republika Srpska? Whilst it is doubtful that the ICTY could have effectively overcome the distortions of its work put forth by the political elite in the absence of the Outreach Programme, some believe that 'it might have blunted their force', particularly in the post-Milošević transition.[43] Others, well versed in the political situation both during and post-conflict in the former Yugoslavia, have argued that the ICTY was incapable of changing public opinion.[44]

The authors believe that this is too simplistic a view. It is well known that public opinion of the ICTY has always been largely dependent on the local media's portrayal. It is contended that the ICTY's most damaging shortfall lies not in the delay in creating an Outreach Programme, but in its half-hearted and inconsistent use over the years. The extent of the ICTY's communication with the people in the former Yugoslavia has always been largely dependent on the ICTY leadership at a given time. That is to say that each new ICTY President can, and often does, make choices on the extent and nature of communication with the public in the region, regardless of whether it contrasts with the strategy of his or her predecessor. Although perhaps not something clearly visible outside the organisation, this inconsistency is evident in the ICTY's response or lack thereof in the face of genocide denial, despite its judicial findings to the contrary. In a rare moment of openness, the ICTY issued a press statement in response to a publication by Serbian daily *Glas Javnosti* denying the genocide. Refik Hodžić, as ICTY spokesperson at the time, responded stating that 'the piece in question represents shameful denial of the facts that this court has established beyond reasonable doubt about the genocide committed in Srebrenica [...] in the judgments by the Trial and Appeals Chambers in the case against Radislav Krstić'.[45] Despite subsequent convictions for genocide, more recent examples of public genocide denial have not been denounced by the Tribunal. The authors' interviews with relevant ICTY staff suggest that as a matter of policy, the ICTY has preferred not to engage in this discussion and leave it to NGOs in the region to tackle and explain the Tribunal's jurisprudence on the matter. Such an inconsistent approach and passing of responsibility, it is argued, is particularly problematic in feeding mistrust among the people of the former Yugoslavia.

---

42 Mirza Velagić and Zlatka Velagić, 'Do Court Rulings Matter? International Courts and Journalists' Framing of the Srebrenica Genocide' (2013) 8(4) *Journalism Practice* 421.

43 Diane F. Orentlicher, n 6, 22.

44 Jasna Šarčević, n 38.

45 ICTY Press Weekly Briefing (14 March 2007) www.icty.org/x/file/About/Reports%20and%20Publications/ICTYDigest/icty_digest_10_en.pdf (accessed 28 January 2016).

The authors' interviews also indicate that the ICTY's silence is in large part linked to the ICTY judiciary's refusal to issue any statements regarding the genocide until all pending genocide cases are completed. It would appear that this policy was instituted out of fear that to do so might taint the findings of future Trial and Appeals Chambers or create a perception of partiality. The authors do not see such a risk. If an ICTY Chamber has found an individual is guilty of genocide – no matter the mode of liability – the Chamber's finding also confirms that the crime of genocide was committed within the temporal and geographical scope of the indictment. As such, once the judgment has been pronounced, the ICTY offices tasked with informing the public should be able to respond to genocide denial claims by referring to the relevant ICTY judgments. Of course, the ICTY should not engage in a political debate, but this does not mean that it therefore has to remain silent when its judgments and judicial findings are negated. Silence on the part of the court in these circumstances not only leaves its work untold, but also damages its reputation in the eyes of many for whom the ICTY was the only hope to get justice. In the context of the years of misrepresentation of its work in the local media, the Tribunal's silence in the face of genocide denial has limited the impact of its judicial findings and has made it easy for politicians all too ready to bolster their political strength by scaremongering among ethnic lines.

Another example of the ICTY not using the full potential of outreach and communication tools to cement the Tribunal's legacy is the significant reluctance of some to broadcast graphic images of the crimes in Srebrenica as part of the audio-visual material created by Outreach. Whilst certainly uncomfortable to watch, it is precisely for this reason that such images must be shown. Facing the crimes head-on leaves little room for their denial.

Further evidence of the half-hearted engagement with outreach is the crippling lack of funds experienced by the Outreach Programme. From the start, the Outreach Programme has not been part of the regular Tribunal budget and has had to rely on external funding and on local NGOs to continue its work and implement activities in the region, which it cannot finance. The fact that the Outreach Programme does not form part of the ICTY's budget is indicative of the place it is given in the overall work of the Tribunal. Yet that work is expected to contribute to peace and reconciliation in the region. For the judgments rendered by a distant court to have such an impact on the region, there must be a sense of ownership of the court's work – the community needs to see that justice is being delivered in their name as opposed to being imposed by a foreign institution. This sense of ownership certainly involves engaging with local NGOs, among others, but does not remove the primary responsibility of the institution to educate the public on its work. Outreach should therefore be recognised as a core function of every international court.

Finally, research has repeatedly concluded that one of the first steps to a positive impact, including combatting genocide denial, is managing the stakeholders' expectations. ICTY Outreach staff and academics alike are quick to note the important divergence between local expectations and what the ICTY could reasonably have achieved within its powerful, yet limited, mandate. In the authors' view, the ICTY erred in not making the limits of its jurisdiction, capacity and objectives clear to the people of the former Yugoslavia until very recently, when it was perhaps too late.

Was it unrealistic to expect the ICTY to contribute to the restoration of peace and reconciliation in the former Yugoslavia? The UN Security Council Resolution establishing it utilised these terms and its former President believes the Tribunal has met this objective. It is hard to tell how much the Tribunal has contributed to peace and reconciliation in the region, but one thing is clear: the Tribunal was never expected to be the sole tool in achieving this goal. Through its judicial work and with the most proactive outreach strategy, the Tribunal always would have had limited jurisdiction and a limited ability to deal with all the crimes committed during the war in the former Yugoslavia. Given the nature of the crimes prosecuted, the Tribunal's judgments always would have left one side in the conflict unsatisfied, yielding praise by some and criticism by others who will use them as grounds to challenge the Tribunal's credibility within their constituency. Had the ICTY made its limitations clear from the start, there would have been less room for political leaders to utilise these false promises to build mistrust and spread misrepresentations of its work.

5 The legacy of the ICTY

The ICTY is now in its final stages, soon to be closing its doors in 2017. The United Nations Mechanism for International Criminal Tribunals (hereinafter 'MICT') was established to assume the ICTY's residual judicial and administrative responsibilities, together with those of the ICTY's sister Tribunal for Rwanda. It is, however, not too late for the ICTY (or the MICT for that matter) to improve the ICTY's impact on genocide denial. There is an ongoing need for the ICTY to actively promote its legacy and reach out to the local communities. One interviewee noted that the ICTY has a tendency to shy away from engaging face-on with its critics, noting that it is easy for the Tribunal to reach out to NGOs and groups that are supportive of its work, but it also needs to approach those that are antagonistic and even negate its findings.

Second, the ICTY outreach work with the youth in the region, in particular, is very important. Such projects can be extended to educating children living in rural Bosnia and Herzegovina, where the majority of the population lives, where children are more likely to leave education at an earlier age, have limited access to objective information, and where division amongst different ethnic or religious groups is most evident. Whilst the Outreach Programme does engage with the local youth, these projects need more engagement – a single one-hour, two-hour visit to a school is simply not enough to make a lasting mark. The purpose of such outreach activities is to encourage children to question what they are hearing and what they think they know, which can be achieved by prolonged engagement with the region's rural population.

6 Conclusion

The Srebrenica genocide was committed more than 20 years ago. The ICTY, mandated to prosecute those individuals most responsible for serious violations of international humanitarian law committed in the former Yugoslavia, has rendered five convictions for genocide. Yet, as this chapter has illustrated, denial of genocide, particularly in Serbia and Republika Srpska, is not uncommon, whether by members of the public, religious leaders or the political elite. For years, the local media, under the power of the political elite, built mistrust in the work of the ICTY. Opinions against the ICTY were already strong by the time the ICTY created its Outreach Programme. However, more than this, this chapter has argued that when it did finally create an Outreach Programme, the ICTY did not do so effectively. The ICTY's biggest shortfall in responding to genocide denial resides in its inconsistent and half-hearted approach to communicating proactively with the people in the former Yugoslavia. Despite the remarkable range of activities that the Outreach Programme has undertaken since its creation, the authors' research suggests that the Tribunal has grown more reluctant to engage effectively in outreach activities and to communicate its work proactively. This is partly due to the general reluctance of the judiciary to engage in explaining its judgments and to counter misinformation about them. This is typical for criminal courts generally, and not just international judicial institutions. While this approach is understandable for national courts which form part of a homogeneous judicial system and are part of the governance structure of the State, this is not the case for international criminal courts, which often sit outside the country, apply special rules, and render judgments in a different language from that of the country concerned.

An international criminal court therefore has special responsibilities to promote its work and bring it closer to the public directly affected by its judgments. If an international court is to contribute to the restoration of peace and justice in the affected region, its 'constituents' need access to full and impartial information on its judgments. This is the first step to combatting denial. The ICTY, despite its many successes, did not address genocide denial effectively. First, it allowed the local propaganda machine to paint unopposed a picture of what did and did not occur in Srebrenica in the early years. Second, once it did start presenting its work to the people of the former Yugoslavia, it did so selectively and somewhat reluctantly. Perhaps in view of the nascent nature of international criminal justice, the ICTY's shortfalls were predictable, but as it closes its doors, the ICTY's experience is offering a learning opportunity for future courts. This chapter has underlined, in particular, the following lessons that can be learned from the ICTY's experience:

- Do respond when the facts established by the court are negated or misrepresented. A serious, clear and consistent communication strategy is needed in the face of genocide denial.

- Recognise outreach as a core function of an international criminal court and fund it accordingly.
- The court's communication and outreach strategy should not be affected by changes in leadership.

Inconsistency and silence breed the grounds for genocide denial. If crimes such as those committed in Srebrenica are to be prevented, international courts have to gain the trust of the post-atrocity communities. This they will never achieve only by rendering judgments. Outreach is the key.

Chapter 11

Holocaust denial in Iran
Ahmadinejad, the 2006 Holocaust conference and international law

Paul Behrens

1 Ahmadinejad and denialist discourse: the 2006 Holocaust conference

Mahmoud Ahmadinejad had been in office as president of Iran for barely four months, when he made headlines with statements not uncommon in denialist discourse. In December 2005, he was quoted as saying he did not believe that 6 million Jews had died at the hands of the Nazis,[1] and that the killing of the Jews had been a 'myth'.[2] In the following year, a 'Holocaust cartoon contest' took place in Tehran.[3] Then, in December 2006, a conference was hosted in Tehran under the title 'Review of the Holocaust: Global Vision'.[4] The event, based on an initiative by Ahmadinejad,[5] was attended by 67 participants from 30 countries, including David Duke, a former Ku Klux Klan leader,[6] Robert Faurisson, a former French academic who had previously spoken of the 'myth of the gas chambers' and had been found guilty in France of denial of crimes against humanity,[7] and Frederick Toben, sentenced by a German court after he had denied that gas chambers for human beings had been in operation in Auschwitz.[8]

---

1 BBC Online, 'Holocaust Comments Spark Outrage', 14 December 2005, news.bbc. co.uk/2/hi/middle_east/4529198.stm.
2 Ibid.; Gregory Gordon, 'From Incitement to Indictment? Prosecuting Iran's President for Advocating Israel's Destruction and Piecing Together Incitement Law's Emerging Analytical Framework', 98 *Journal of Criminal Law and Criminology* (2008), 868.
3 Edgar Lefkovits, 'Iran Paving Way for Another Holocaust', *Jerusalem Post*, 12 December 2006. The exhibition was apparently not well attended by the Iranian population, Martin Beck Matuštík, 'Velvet Revolution in Iran?', 9 *International Journal for Not-For-Profit Law* (2006), 31.
4 *National Post* (Canada), 'Inside the Mind of a Holocaust Denier', 12 December 2006.
5 Nasser Karimi, 'Holocaust Deniers Gather in Tehran for Conference Casting Doubt on Nazi Genocide', *Associated Press Worldstream*, 12 December 2006.
6 Ali Akbar Dareini, 'Ahmadinejad Tells Holocaust Deniers Israel will be "Wiped Out" Like the Soviet Union', *Associated Press*, 12 December 2006.
7 Human Rights Committee, *Robert Faurisson v France*, Communication No. 550/1993, UN Doc. CCPR/C/58/D/550/1993 (1996), paras 2.6 and 2.7.
8 BGH 1StR 184/00, at A.II.2.

At the conference, Toben reportedly said that the railroad to the Auschwitz camp 'did not have enough capacity to transfer large numbers of Jews'.[9] Duke called the Holocaust 'the device used as the pillar of Zionist imperialism, Zionist aggression, Zionist terror and Zionist murder'.[10] Ahmadinejad himself was quoted as stating, on the second day of the meeting, that the 'Zionist regime will be wiped out soon the same [as] the Soviet Union was'.[11]

That an event of this kind would provoke strong international reactions is hardly surprising[12] – not least because of its potential consequences. In the words of a speaker of Yad Vashem, the conference represented 'an effort to mainstream Holocaust denial'.[13] It is, in that regard, of some importance that its organisation had fallen to the 'Institute of Political and International Studies' (part of the Iranian Foreign Ministry).[14] The opening speech was given by the head of the Institute, who stated that the conference sought 'to provide an appropriate scientific atmosphere for scholars to offer their opinions in freedom about a historical issue'.[15]

Not that this attempt to give the conference a scholarly veneer fooled the experts in the field.[16] Yet it carried some significance: in a part of the world in which knowledge of the facts of the Holocaust is reported to be generally poor,[17] the danger cannot be dismissed that the views of deniers, if presented as 'scholarly discourse', will in the minds of the population take the place of an accurate understanding of the Nazi crimes.[18] There is also reason to believe that the style of the presentation of the relevant views can carry meaning for their legal

---

9   Karimi, 'Holocaust Deniers Gather' (n 5 above).
10 Dareini, 'Ahmadinejad Tells Holocaust Deniers' (n 6 above).
11 Ibid.
12 See US Fed News/Israel Project, 'Top Academics, Political Leaders Seek "Incitement to Genocide" Charges Against Iran, President Ahmadinejad', 12 December 2006; Dareini, 'Ahmadinejad tells Holocaust Deniers' (n 6 above).
13 Karimi, 'Holocaust Deniers Gather' (n 5 above).
14 Lefkovits, 'Iran Paving Way' (n 3 above).
15 Nasser Karimi, 'Iran Opens Holocaust Conference, Saying it Will See Whether Genocide Took Place', *Associated Press*, 11 December 2006.
16 The historian Wolfgang Benz was quoted as noting on this occasion that these activities were 'about politics ... not about scholarship'. Karimi, 'Holocaust Deniers Gather' (n 5 above).
17 According to the Alan D. Leve Center for Jewish Studies at UCLA, the Holocaust had not been taught in Iranian schools since 1979, the year of the Iranian revolution. UCLA Alan D. Leve Center for Jewish Studies, The 1939 Society, 'Holocaust Events 2014–2015. The Holocaust in Farsi', www.cjs.ucla.edu/holocaust-studies/. See also Roya Hakakian, 'Holocaust Denial and Tehran', *Wall Street Journal*, 3 November 2007; and Ali Arouzi, 'What Do Everyday Iranians Know About the Holocaust?', NBC News, 16 October 2013, at www.nbcnews.com/news/other/what-do-every day-iranians-know-about-holocaust-f8C11401975.
18 See on this also Shane Croucher, 'Holocaust Memorial Day 2015: Why Denial of Jewish Genocide Thrives in the Arab World', *International Business Times*, 25 January 2015, at www.ibtimes.co.uk/holocaust-memorial-day-2015-why-denial-jewish-genocide-thrives-arab-world-1484903 (with reference to Gilbert Achcar).

assessment – as the recent case of *Perinçek* before the European Court of Human Rights (ECtHR) has indicated.[19]

The significance of the conference was also founded on the dangerous potential that denialism, especially before the backdrop of a volatile context, carries. At the time of the Tehran conference, Yosef Lapid, chairman of the Yad Vashem Council, noted that the event was an attempt to 'pave the way psychologically' for the West to accept that another Holocaust was a possibility.[20]

These aspects – the gravity of denial, its potential impact on an audience that does not necessarily have sound knowledge of the facts, and its creation of a dangerous climate – raise the question whether conduct of this kind has entered the awareness of the international community and if it has been countered with the tools of international criminal law. In the case of Ahmadinejad, there certainly had been attempts to initiate the criminal prosecution of the Iranian president, focusing, however, on incitement rather than on denialism.[21]

The following sections will examine two particular aspects of the way in which denialism has been addressed by international law: its treatment as an independent crime (section 2), and its potential significance as a form of hate speech, in particular within the system of international criminal law (section 3). The role that denialism plays with regard to the crime of incitement to genocide is explored in more detail in Chapter 14.

2 Denialism in transnational and international criminal law

International law has struggled with the matter of genocide denial. Its treatment where State obligations are concerned is illuminating for the difficulty in this regard. There is no universal duty on States to criminalise denial, and efforts in that direction were not borne by the entire international community. In January 2007, the United Nations General Assembly passed a resolution urging UN members 'unreservedly' to reject 'denial of the Holocaust as a historical event',[22] but stopped short of calling for criminalisation. Even so, the resolution was passed with 'only 103 votes from among the 192 member States'.[23]

Multilateral treaties dealing with offensive speech tend not to refer specifically to genocide denial. Article 20 of the International Covenant on Civil and Political Rights (ICCPR), for instance, prohibits more generally certain forms of advocacy of hatred.[24] In 2011, the Human Rights Committee (HRC) expressed the view

---

19   ECtHR Grand Chamber, *Perinçek v Switzerland* (Application no. 27510/08), (2016) 63 EHRR 6, Judgment, 15 October 2015, at paras 13 and 22.
20   Lefkovits, 'Iran Paving Way' (n 3 above).
21   Gordon (n 2 above), 855–6.
22   United Nations General Assembly, Resolution 61/55 'Holocaust Denial', 26 January 2007.
23   *Perinçek* (Grand Chamber) (n 19 above), para. 13.
24   International Covenant on Civil and Political Rights (ICCPR) (adopted 16 December 1966; in force 23 March 1970), 999 UNTS 171, Art 20.

that laws penalising 'the expression of opinions about historical facts' were incompatible with ICCPR obligations regarding freedom of expression.[25] This observation courted controversy,[26] but it is reflective of the gulf that exists within the international community on restrictive measures affecting the written and spoken word.[27] At the European Union (EU) level, Framework Decision 2008/913/JHA on Combating Certain Forms and Expressions of Racism and Xenophobia by Means of Criminal Law was adopted on 28 November 2008. That instrument, too, obliges member States to criminalise forms of denialism – in particular, denial relating to crimes 'defined in Article 6 of the Charter of the International Military Tribunal'[28] (i.e. the Nuremberg War Crimes Tribunal).[29] And it is indeed within the European region that States have shown particular willingness to resort to criminalisation: in *Perinçek*, the ECtHR referred to 20 European States in which the denial of the Holocaust, Nazi crimes, communist crimes or genocides in general had been made a crime.[30] Outside Europe, examples of criminalisation are rarer. Israel bans the denial of 'acts committed in the period of the Nazi regime, which are crimes against the Jewish people or crimes against humanity', if there is an intent to 'defend the perpetrators of those acts or to express sympathy or identification with them',[31] and laws against the denial of specific historical crimes have also been adopted by Rwanda in 2008[32] and the Ukrainian parliament in 2006.[33]

Among laws that focus on denialist statements relating to the Holocaust, certain common themes are identifiable. The relevant conduct is described as 'denying'

25 HRC General Comment No. 34, CCPR/C/GC/34 (2011), para. 49.
26 See on this *Perinçek v Switzerland* (Application no. 27510/08), ECtHR Chamber, Judgment 17 December 2013, Joint Partly Dissenting Opinion of Judges Vučinić and Pinto de Albuquerque, para. 22, fn 26.
27 This divide within the international community is also apparent in the difficulty which the implementation of Article 20 ICCPR encountered and in similar challenges arising in the context of Article 4 of the International Convention on the Elimination of All Forms of Racial Discrimination (adopted 21 December 1965, entry into force 4 January 1969) 660 UNTS 195. See, on the whole, Paul Behrens, *Diplomatic Interference and the Law* (Hart, 2016), 178–9.
28 Framework Decision 2008/913/JHA, Art 1(1)(d). See also ibid., Article 1(1)(c). The Decision is discussed in more detail in Chapter 13.
29 See also Article 6(1) of the Additional Protocol to the Convention on Cybercrime, concerning the criminalisation of acts of a racist and xenophobic nature committed through computer systems (adopted 28 January 2003, entry into force 1 March 2006), ETS No. 189, but see, on the difficulties regarding its implementation, *Perinçek* (Grand Chamber), n 19 above, para. 74.
30 *Perinçek* (Grand Chamber), n 19 above, para. 256.
31 Jaqueline Lechtholz Zey, 'The Laws Banning Holocaust Denial – Revised from GPN', 9 *Genocide Prevention Now Original* (2012) at n 28.
32 *Rwanda: Law No. 18/2008 of 2008 Relating to the Punishment of the Crime of Genocide Ideology* [Rwanda], 23 July 2008, available at www.refworld.org/docid/4acc9a4e2.html. On the law, see also above, Chapters 7–9.
33 Deutsche Presse-Agentur, 'Ukraine Parliament Classifies 1930s Famine as "Genocide"', 28 November 2006. See also below, Chapter 13.

or 'contradicting'[34] the events, but there are also (to a lesser degree) references to behaviour that seeks to diminish their proportions[35] or which in some form approves of them.[36] Several States also specify that the relevant statements must have been given a certain measure of publicity.[37] From the analysis of these provisions, it is possible to identify a certain concept of denial which can claim the widest degree of criminalisation: i.e. the making of statements that deny or contradict the Holocaust and do so in a public manner. Ahmadinejad's public reference to the killing of the European Jews as a 'myth' certainly qualifies under these parameters, and there is little doubt that by initiating the Tehran conference, he assisted in the public commission of denialist activities.

At the level of international criminal law, however, the question remains whether such conduct meets with a direct ban. In that regard, the general divide between States on the regulation of speech[38] reappears: there is no mention of denialism or denial in the statutes of international criminal courts and tribunals or other instruments of international criminal law. If a direct ban is to be established at all, it has to find its basis in customary international law.

Domestic legislation would be an acceptable strand of evidence for State practice as an element of customary international criminal law,[39] but such practice must be shown to be 'extensive'[40] and 'generally consistent'.[41] Proof of that can be a challenge: even if the practice of those States were included whose law addresses the denial of 'any' genocide,[42] the total number of States resorting to criminalisation represents only a limited section of the international community.

---

34 See, for Austria, Verbotsgesetz (1945), s 3(h); Belgium: Negationism Law 1995 (as amended in 1999); Czech Republic: Law Against Support and Dissemination of Movements Oppressing Human Rights and Freedoms (2001), s 261(a); Germany: Strafgesetzbuch s 130(3); Israel: Denial of Holocaust (Prohibition) Law 5746-1986, s 2; Luxembourg: Criminal Code, s 457-3; Poland: Act on the Institute of National Remembrance – Commission for the Prosecution of Crimes against the Polish Nation (1998), s 55; Romania: Emergency Ordinance No. 31 of 13 March 2002, s 6. The provisions according to Lechtholz Zey (n 31 above), at n 14–31.
35 Thus the laws of Israel, similarly Austria, Belgium, Germany, Luxembourg. Ibid.
36 See Austria, Belgium, Czech Republic, Germany, Luxembourg. Under the laws of some States, it is sufficient that the perpetrator put the relevant events in doubt: see on this Czech Republic, and arguably France (Law No. 90–615, s. 9). Ibid.
37 See Austria; Czech Republic; Hungary; Israel; Poland; Romania. See also Belgium (publicly or 'in the presence of the offended person and in front of witnesses'); Germany ('publicly or in a meeting'). Ibid.
38 See above, text at nn 25–7.
39 See on this, for instance ICTY (Appeals Chamber), *Prosecutor v Dusko Tadić*, Case No. IT-94-1-AR72, Decision on the Defence Motion for Interlocutory Appeal on Jurisdiction, 2 October 1995, paras 130–4; ICTY (Appeals Chamber), *Prosecutor v Stanislav Galić*, Case No. IT-98-29-A, Judgment, 30 November 2006, paras 95–8.
40 *North Sea Continental Shelf Cases (Germany v Denmark; Germany v Netherlands)* (Judgment), [1969] ICJ Rep. 3, para. 74.
41 *Case Concerning Military and Paramilitary Activities in and against Nicaragua (Nicaragua v United States of America)* (Judgment) [1986] ICJ Rep. 14, para. 186.
42 See text at n 30.

Even within Europe, an entirely uniform picture does not emerge: a certain number of European States have not resorted to criminalisation.[43] In light of this divergence of legislation, the ECtHR Grand Chamber in *Perinçek* in 2015 was unable to find that there was a rule under customary international law obliging States to criminalise genocide denial.[44] The same consideration holds true where the assumption of criminalisation of the relevant conduct under customary international criminal law is concerned.

That does not mean that the situation will remain immutable. A dissenting opinion in *Perinçek*, joined by seven members of the Grand Chamber, considered the possibility of custom emerging at least within the area of the EU;[45] instruments such as the Framework Decision of 2008 make that line of reasoning particularly tempting.[46] Yet the majority pointed out that that Decision had not been fully implemented by member States,[47] and even the dissenting judges did not go as far as to conclude that local custom existed, but merely noted that it might be 'gradually emerging'.[48]

If denialist discourse is not directly addressed under conventional or customary international criminal law, the possibility still exists that it forms, at least under certain conditions, part of conduct with which this legal system already deals. It is a consideration that plays a particular role if denialism can be understood as a form of hate speech and thus be subject to the liability of international criminal law which may attach to conduct of this kind.

3 Denialism, hate speech and the crime of persecution

Any analysis of hate speech encounters the fundamental problem that the concept lacks authoritative definition.[49] Certain statements by international courts and institutions, however, provide assistance in that regard. Within the Council of Europe, the Committee of Ministers in 1997 adopted a recommendation in which 'hate speech' was understood as 'covering all forms of expression which spread, incite, promote or justify racial hatred, xenophobia, anti-Semitism or other forms of hatred based on intolerance'.[50] In *Gündüz v Turkey*, a case concerning punishment for hate speech, the ECtHR stated that it might be considered necessary in some societies to prevent 'all forms of expression which spread,

---

43 See *Perinçek* (Grand Chamber), n 19 above, para. 256.
44 Ibid., para. 266.
45 Ibid., Joint Dissenting Opinion of Judges Spielmann et al., para. 10.
46 See above, at n 28.
47 *Perinçek* (Grand Chamber), n 19 above, para. 266.
48 Ibid., Joint Dissenting Opinion of Judges Spielmann et al., para. 10.
49 See on this Anne Weber, *Manual on Hate Speech* (Council of Europe Publishing, Strasbourg, 2009), 3.
50 Council of Europe, Committee of Ministers, *Recommendation No. R (97) 20 of the Committee of Ministers to Member States On 'Hate Speech'* (adopted 30 October 1997). ECtHR, *Gündüz v Turkey* (2005) 41 EHRR 5, Judgment of 4 December 2003, para. 22.

incite, promote or justify hatred based on intolerance'.[51] Other authorities adopt a somewhat more restrictive view,[52] but the wider concept is certainly better aligned with the ordinary understanding of the term.[53]

These conceptual difficulties may account for some of the debate on the classification of denial as part of this category. In *Faurisson*, France referred to a statement by her former minister of justice, noting that denial of the Holocaust was a 'contemporary expression of racism and anti-semitism'.[54] The Spanish Constitutional Court, on the other hand, distinguished between 'mere denial' of a crime and 'other types of conduct in which specific values adhere to the criminal act', finding that it could not be stated that 'denial of conduct legally defined as a crime of genocide objectively pursues the creation of a social climate of hostility' against persons belonging to a group that had been victim of a specific crime of genocide.[55]

A third opinion places emphasis on the context in which the relevant statement appeared. The HRC in *Faurisson*, for instance, noted that Faurisson's remarks, 'read in their full context' were 'of a nature as to raise or strengthen anti-semitic feelings',[56] and in *Perinçek*, the Grand Chamber of the ECtHR accorded significance to the context to support a finding in the opposite direction. Perinçek had been prosecuted by Switzerland after he had stated, *inter alia*, that 'the allegations of the "Armenian genocide" [were] an international lie'.[57] In the eyes of the Court, however, his remarks, 'read as a whole and taken in their immediate and wider context', could not be seen 'as a call for hatred, violence or intolerance towards the Armenians'.[58]

The significance of the context also manifests itself where the assessment of the objective purpose of the remarks is concerned – a factor that is arguably a constituent element of hate speech.[59] When the ECtHR analysed the applicant's statement in *Jersild* – the case of a journalist prosecuted in Denmark for hate speech after he had conducted a TV interview with young people who had voiced racist views – context was clearly of importance. In the Court's opinion, the

51 *Gündüz v Turkey* (n 50 above), para. 20.
52 See Organization of American States, *Annual Report of the Inter-American Commission on Human Rights 2004*, Chapter VII: Hate Speech and the American Convention on Human Rights, 2004 IACHR 161 (OAS), 2004 WL 3392078, 1 ('designed to intimidate, oppress or incite'). See also *Perinçek* (Grand Chamber), n 19 above, para. 204.
53 See on this *Oxford English Dictionary*, 'hate, n 1, Draft additions July 2002', at www.oed. com
54 *Faurisson v France* (n 7 above), para. 8.8 (paraphrasing by HRC).
55 Spanish Constitutional Court, Judgment No. 235/2007, of 7 November (unofficial translation), at www.tribunalconstitucional.es/es/jurisprudencia/restrad/Paginas/JCC2352007en.aspx
56 *Faurisson v France* (n 7 above), para. 9.6. See also ibid., Concurring Opinion of Prafullachandra Bhagwati.
57 *Perinçek* (Grand Chamber), n 19 above, paras 13 and 22.
58 Ibid., 239.
59 See on this Organization of American States (n 52 above) 13, para. 42.

feature could not have appeared to have the purpose of spreading racist views:[60] it emphasised that the broadcast had been introduced with references to a recent public discussion on racism and that its aim ('to address aspects of the problem') had been announced.[61] The interview was also part of a 'serious news programme'.[62] The composition of the viewers mattered, too: the programme had been 'intended for a well-informed audience'.[63] According to the Court, attempts had been made to 'counterbalance' the opinions expressed by the interviewees: Jersild had described them as 'a group of extremist youths' and had not left all of their statements unopposed.[64]

It is illuminating to consider the situation that arose from the Tehran Holocaust conference in light of the same parameters. The result would be quite different: the presentation of the conference was fashioned in such a way as to be favourable to its participants, whom the organisers sought to portray as 'scholars' given an opportunity to offer their views on an historical matter.[65] Instead of a 'well-informed audience',[66] there was real danger that the messages would reach people who were poorly informed about the Holocaust.[67] There was no reported attempt to counteract the messages: on the contrary, the context of the conference was formed by statements and events that underlined an identifiable hostile purpose.[68]

These approaches towards the concept of hate speech do not yet lead to an evaluation of the relevant conduct under international criminal law. The statutes of the international criminal courts and tribunals do not directly refer to 'hate speech'. But, the conduct has entered judicial discourse: both the International Criminal Tribunal for the former Yugoslavia (ICTY) and the International Criminal Tribunal for Rwanda (ICTR) had to deal with it in the context of crimes against humanity.[69]

---

60 ECtHR, *Jersild v Denmark* (1995) EHRR 1, Judgment of 23 September 1994, para. 33. The objective purpose of the programme mattered to the Court in particular in the context of its investigation into the alleged necessity of the Danish state to interfere with the applicant's freedom of expression under Article 10 of the Convention for the Protection of Human Rights and Fundamental Freedoms 213 UNTS 222 (adopted 4 November 1950, entry into force 3 September 1953) [ECHR]. However, it is suggested that purpose also matters for the very concept of hate speech itself: once conduct is positively identified as hate speech, it would not fall under the protection of Article 10 to begin with. *Gündüz v Turkey* (n 50 above), para. 41.

61 *Jersild v Denmark* (n 60 above), para. 33.

62 Ibid., para. 34.

63 Ibid.

64 Ibid., para. 34.

65 See above, text at n 15.

66 See above, text at n 63.

67 See n 17 above and accompanying text.

68 BBC Online, 'Iranian Leader Denies Holocaust', 14 December 2005, at news.bbc.co. uk/1/hi/world/middle_east/4527142.stm; and Lefkovits, 'Iran Paving Way' (n 3 above), and see above, at nn 1–3 and 11.

69 See Art 5(h) Statute of the International Criminal Tribunal for the Former Yugoslavia (adopted 25 May 1993 by SC Res 827) [hereinafter ICTYSt]; Art 3(h) Statute of

When Dario Kordić, a Bosnian Croat political leader, was charged with per-secution,[70] the Prosecution substantiated the charge, *inter alia*, with the finding that he had engaged in 'encouraging, instigating and promoting hatred, distrust and strife on political, racial, ethnic or religious grounds'.[71] It is a concept of hate speech that may appear more restrictive than that used by the Committee of Ministers.[72] Even so, it encountered difficulties: the Trial Chamber found that the act did not constitute 'by itself' persecution; it was not 'enumerated as a crime elsewhere' in the Statute of the ICTY, did not 'rise to the same level of gravity as the other acts enumerated in Article 5', and its criminalisation had 'not attained the status of customary international law'.[73]

A different direction appeared to be taken by the ICTR Appeals Chamber in the *Media Case* – the case of individuals involved in the Rwandan Radio Télévision Libre des Milles Collines (RTLM) and the Kangura newspaper respectively.[74] Mass media had played a decisive role in the killings in Rwanda in 1994[75] – partly through their use of hostile language, partly also through direct calls for violence.[76] The Appeals Chamber did find that certain hate speeches broadcast by RTLM constituted persecution.[77] Yet even in that case, the categorisation of hate speech as a crime against humanity was subject to criticism.[78]

A particular difficulty arises from the fact that persecution requires a dis-criminatory act or omission that denied or infringed a fundamental right.[79] That act need not itself be a crime against humanity.[80] That it could consist in hate

the International Criminal Tribunal for Rwanda (adopted 8 November 1994 by SC Res 955) [hereinafter ICTRSt].

70 ICTY, *The Prosecutor v Dario Kordić and Mario Čerkez*, Case No. IT-95-14/2, Amended Indictment, 30 September 1998, para. 36.

71 Ibid., para. 37(c).

72 See above, at n 50.

73 ICTY (Trial Chamber), *The Prosecutor v Dario Kordić and Mario Čerkez*, Case No. IT-95-14/2-T, Judgment 26 February 2001, para. 209.

74 ICTR (Trial Chamber), Case No. ICTR-99-52-T, *The Prosecutor v Ferdinand Nahimana, Jean-Bosco Barayagwiza, Hassan Ngeze*, Judgment 3 December 2003.

75 See on the whole situation William Schabas, 'Hate Speech in Rwanda: The Road to Genocide', 46 *McGill Law Journal* (2000), 141.

76 See, for instance, ICTR (Appeals Chamber), Case No. ICTR-99-52-A, *Ferdinand Nahimana, Jean-Bosco Barayagwiza, Hassan Ngeze v The Prosecutor*, Judgment, 28 November 2007, para. 756 [hereinafter '*Media Case* (Appeals Chamber)'].

77 Ibid., para. 995. See also ICTR (Trial Chamber), Case No. ICTR-01-72-T, *The Prosecutor v Simon Bikindi*, Judgment 2 December 2008, para. 390.

78 *Media Case* (Appeals Chamber), n 76 above, Partly Dissenting Opinion of Judge Meron, in particular paras 3–21.

79 ICTY (Appeals Chamber), *Prosecutor v Miroslav Deronjić*, Case No. IT-02-61-A, Judgment 20 July 2005, para. 109. Where hate speech is concerned, the 'fundamental right' is often considered to lie in the dignity of members of the targeted group, see *Media Case* (Appeals Chamber), n 76 above, para. 986. See also *Bikindi* (Trial Chamber), n 77 above, para. 392.

80 ICTY (Trial Chamber), *Prosecutor v Blagoje Simić, Miroslav Tadić, Simo Zarić*, Case No. IT-95-9-T, Judgment 17 October 2003, para. 48. The Elements of Crime to the

speech, however, was, to one of the judges, a step too far: while not denying the offensive character of hate speech, Judge Meron felt that speech falling 'on the non-criminal side' of the balance between conflicting liberties, enjoyed 'special protection', and the majority, by permitting 'protected speech to serve as a basis for a conviction for persecution' was, 'in essence, criminali[sing] non-criminal speech'.[81]

At the same time, the international criminal tribunals do impose a cap on the acceptance of conduct as 'underlying acts': such acts, if they are not listed in the statute of the tribunal, must be of 'the same level of gravity' as the enumerated crimes against humanity.[82]

The majority in the Appeals Chamber in the *Media Case* had not lost sight of that requirement. Hate speech was not considered in isolation: context, once again, played a role. The Appeals Chamber thus drew attention to the fact that the relevant speeches were 'accompanied by calls for genocide' and took place 'in a context of a massive campaign of persecution'. It was not necessary to ascertain the gravity of each act in isolation; it was indeed only by consideration of the speeches 'as a whole and in their context' that the Chamber was able to establish such gravity.[83]

Hate speech which is to attract liability for the crime of persecution also has to be accompanied by the relevant subjective element of the crime. In this regard, persecution presupposes the existence of a specific motive: the statutes of ICTY and ICTR speak of 'political, racial' or 'religious grounds' which must have given rise to the relevant conduct.[84] For persecution under the jurisdiction of the International Criminal Court (ICC), the perpetrator must have targeted the victims on 'reason of the identity of a group or collectivity' or must have 'targeted the group or collectivity as such', and must have done so on grounds that were 'universally recognized as impermissible under international law'.[85] As with all crimes against humanity, evidence must also be adduced as to the contextual element that characterises this crime category.[86]

<hr/>

ICCSt do, however, make clear that the conduct must have been committed in con-nection with one of the crimes against humanity listed in Article 7 ICCSt or with 'any crime within the jurisdiction of the Court', Elements of Crime (adopted 9 September 2002), UN Doc PCNICC/2000/1/Add.2, Article 7(1)(h), para. 4. See also *Media Case* (Appeals Chamber), n 76 above, para. 985 and *Bikindi* (Trial Chamber), n 77 above, para. 397.

81 *Media Case* (Appeals Chamber), Meron Opinion, n 78 above, para. 16.
82 *Simić, Tadić and Zarić* (Trial Chamber), n 80 above, para. 129. See also n 80 above for the link to crimes against humanity or other crimes under the jurisdiction of the ICC which the Elements of Crime establish.
83 *Media Case* (Appeals Chamber), n 76 above, para. 988. See also *Bikindi* (Trial Cham-ber), n 77 above, para. 394.
84 Art 5(h) ICTYSt, n 69 above; Art 3(h) ICTRSt, ibid.
85 Elements of Crime, n 80 above, Article 7(1)(h), paras 2 and 3.
86 See on this ibid., paras 5 and 6.

The bar for a conviction of persecution is therefore set high. Given the stigma that liability for crimes against humanity incur and given the grave consequences of a conviction, the burden on the prosecution does not appear unreasonable.

And yet, if the conceptual requirements of persecution are fulfilled, there is no reason why hate speech should be excluded from the scope of the norm. The *Bikindi* Trial Chamber was not far off the mark when it spoke of a 'discernable hierarchy of expressions', compelling it to deal with 'different forms of expression differently' and when, on that basis, it declined to treat statements that formed the seeds of future international crimes in the same manner 'as any other act of expression'.[87]

4 Concluding thoughts

The challenges which the evaluation of denial encounters and which thus impact on the situation that arose from Ahmadinejad's conduct, are symptomatic of a considerable divide within the international community. Among a growing number of States, denialism raises concerns in view of its potential harmful consequences. Other States are unwilling to withdraw even speech of this kind from the remit of freedom of expression.

It is not a new development,[88] but the divide informs the position of international law to the present day and impedes a finding that customary international law criminalising hate speech and negationism has come into existence. That, in turn, has raised criticism where the evaluation of hate speech as part of the crime against humanity of persecution is concerned. But in that regard, the international criminal tribunals have supported the view that, once the relevant elements of this concept are in place, hate speech can indeed qualify as an 'underlying act' on which the crime can be based.

Context has emerged as a crucial factor where the evaluation of various emanations of speech is concerned. It not only can lend support to the finding that hate speech has come into existence in the first place; it also plays a decisive role where its assessment as persecution is concerned, for contextual factors may allow for the finding that the gravity of such forms of speech equals that of the enumerated crimes against humanity.

In the case of Ahmadinejad and the Tehran conference, a contextual consideration can hardly be expected to favour the initiator of the event. Coming, as it did, one year after the Iranian president had referred to the killing of the European Jews as a 'myth' and a few months after the 'Holocaust cartoon' exhibition, the context of the conference was quite clear. This was not the act of a schoolboy

---

87 *Bikindi* (Trial Chamber), n 77 above, para. 396.
88 On the positions taken by different States during the drafting stage of the Genocide Convention when attempts had been made to outlaw certain forms of hate speech, see Schabas, n 75 above, 163–7.

who parrots Holocaust denial found on the internet. It was intentional support of negationist discourse in an already volatile situation.

It is the significance of this event, the fact that it received official sanction by an incumbent president, and its potential for the creation of a discriminatory mindset among the likely audience, which leads to challenges to the position of States that maintain their silence in situations of this kind. There may be good reasons for a critical view towards criminalisation of denialist conduct – not least in view of the questionable efficiency of measures of this kind.[89] Nor is recourse to criminal law the only option available even at the international level. But the view that action is indicated only when 'clear and present danger' emanates from the relevant statements[90] is difficult to maintain. Once this stage is reached, once hate speech is no longer needed to prepare the ground, but appears as one of many discriminatory acts adopted in addition to the commission of international crimes, it will often be too late for the international community to come to the aid of the victims. The arch of injustice does not begin when the first shot is fired and the first person deported. It begins with the deprivation of the dignity of the victims. Its endpoint is all too well known.

89 See on this below, Chapter 15.
90 See, for instance, Schabas n 75 above, at 150, with reference to the US view at the drafting stage of the Genocide Convention.

Chapter 12

A centenary of denial

The case of the Armenian genocide

Nariné Ghazaryan

I Introduction

On 24 April 2015, Armenia commemorated the 100th anniversary of the Armenian genocide. On the same day, the Turkish government marked the centenary of the battle of Gallipoli in World War I, even though the actual landing of the Allied forces took place on 25 April 1915. Far from being a mere coincidence, this overlap might be seen as a continuation of the tactics of successive Turkish governments, aimed at distracting attention from the recognition of massacres as genocide, at trivialising and restricting the debate, and at distorting the historical record. The main achievement of the Turkish government in this respect has been to foment a perception that historic events of the early twentieth century are disputed, despite the extensive documentation and reporting of mass extermination of Armenians by Ottoman Turkey. Turkey is keen, thus, on steering the debate from the realm of political and legal into the domain of 'disputed past'.

This does not necessarily mean that scholars or others in Turkey are free to express their opinions qualifying the Armenian massacres as genocide. Only recently Turkey prided itself as epitomising tolerance on the European continent by accommodating almost 2 million Syrian refugees.[1] Various issues related to its minorities, however, continued to be a matter of incessant concern, even more so now given the political crackdown following the attempted military coup. The issue of the Armenian genocide is merely one such example with legal and political taboos created around it. In fact, the denial of the Armenian genocide is an official State policy, entrenched in the internal legal framework but also institutionalised in Turkey's foreign policy through its diplomatic relations and representations. The official Turkish position and the attempts at the recognition of the Armenian genocide worldwide most certainly left an imprint on Turkish foreign policy. Internally, the subject of the Armenian genocide is a matter of legal taboo due to the existing restrictions on freedom of expression. Turkey efficiently criminalises any speech suggesting that the massacres of Armenians amounted to genocide

---

1 See for instance the remarks of the Turkish Prime Minister Davutoğlu on his visit to Brussels in 2015, 'Turkish PM: If Europe Persists in its "Holy Roman Attitude", it is over', *Euractiv*, 16 January 2015.

under international law, adding yet another complexity to its poor record in the area of freedom of expression. The denialist attitude of the Turkish State is motivated primarily by the commitment of the State to guarding Turkish national identity and avoiding any discussion of possible consequences of the recognition of genocide.

Although this chapter mentions the substantive aspects of the denialist position of Turkey, it is aimed primarily at placing genocide denial within the legal and political context of the Turkish State. The chapter thus explores a number of inter-related issues. First, the denialism by the Turkish State, its rationale and its forms are explored to provide an historical and political narrative of the debate. Linked to this is the transposition of the denialism to the foreign policy of Turkey considered next. Finally, the legalisation of the genocide denial within Turkey will be considered, with particular reference to freedom of expression and Turkey's international obligations. The chapter will be concluded with a brief summary of findings.

2 Genocide denialism and Turkish national identity

The 1948 United Nations (UN) Convention on the Prevention and Punishment of the Crime of Genocide of 1948 is considered to be the 'centrepiece' of any debate on genocide.[2] This does not, however, suggest that events that occurred prior to the adoption of Convention cannot be qualified as genocide.[3] According to lawyers, it rather signifies that individual or State responsibility for these events cannot be imposed by the Convention without preventing the qualification of certain past events as genocide under international law.[4] It is commonly acknowledged that when Lemkin penned the term of 'genocide' the massacres of Armenians in the early twentieth century were well on his mind.[5] The Turkish Republic has persistently refused to recognise the overwhelming evidence of survivors, international archives and scholarly works, which showed that the annihilation of more than 1 million Armenians in their historical homeland between 1915 and 1922 was organised by the 'Young Turks' government with an intention to

2 (1951) 78 UNTS 277; W.A. Schabas, *Genocide in International Law: The Crime of Crimes* (Cambridge University Press, 2009), 3.
3 The Applicability of the United Nations Convention on the Prevention and Punishment of the Crime of Genocide to Events which Occurred during the Early Twentieth Century, Legal Analysis prepared for the International Centre for Transitional Justice, 10 February 2003, www.armenian-genocide.org/Affirmation.244/current_category.5/affirmation_detail.html (accessed 15 May 2016).
4 G. Robertson QC, 'Was there an Armenian Genocide?', Opinion, 9 October 2009, 26 groong.usc.edu/Geoffrey-Robertson-QC-Genocide.pdf (accessed 15 May 2016); W. Schabas, 'Crimes Against Humanity as a Paradigm for International Atrocity Crimes', *Middle Eastern Critique* 20:3 (2011), 253, 269.
5 R. Lemkin, 'Le Crime de Génocide', *Revue de Droit International, des Sciences Diplomatiques et Politiques* (1946), 213; H.T. King Jr, 'Genocide and Nuremberg' in R. Henham and P. Behrens (eds), *Criminal Law of Genocide: International Comparative and Contextual Aspects* (Ashgate, 2008), 29; Robertson, 'Was there an Armenian Genocide?', 4–5.

destroy the group.[6] Some consider that genocide denial contributes to the act of violence itself,[7] and is 'inevitably a phase of the genocidal process'.[8]

In one of the classifications of genocide denial that he developed, Charny considers the denial by the Turkish government to be 'the outstanding and most persistent case of denial by non-perpetrators'.[9] It is distinct from a more 'usual' instance of denial when the perpetrator government stays in power.[10] In fact, in the case of the Armenian genocide the State of Turkey *is* the 'instigator of the denial',[11] having 'fully institutionalised' it.[12] The denial here is therefore primarily characterised not by individual statements from historians, politicians or other individuals, but rather is a matter of State policy endorsed by Turkey internally and externally. A question arises as to why the modern State of Turkey, created in 1923 – that is after the genocide – would vehemently deny the crimes of its predecessor State, the Ottoman Empire.

According to Lemarchand, like historical revisionism, denial 'involves the manipulation of historical facts in order to promote a political agenda'.[13] This political agenda in the case of Turkey is linked to the foundations of the Turkish Republic. The denial of the Armenian genocide was one of the precepts of the homogenised vision of Turkey, which rested *inter alia* on the recognition that there was 'no Armenian genocide; such a thing never happened'.[14] The Republic was to accord Turkey with a new identity, distinct from the Ottoman Empire, allowing the former to distance itself from past crimes. The founders of the new Republic were focused on the building of the future by discarding and rewriting the past, omitting the atrocities committed against the minorities prior to 1919 from the official historiography.[15] Yet the new State identity was premised on the

6 R.G. Hovannisian, *The Armenian 'Genocide': History, Politics, Ethics* (Macmillan, 1992), xvii.
7 R.W. Smith, E. Markuse, R.J. Lifton, 'Professional Ethics and the Denial of Armenian Genocide', *Holocaust and Genocide Studies* 9:1 (1995), 14.
8 I.W. Charny, 'Innocent Denials of Known Genocides: A Further Contribution to a Psychology of Denial of Genocide', *Human Rights Review* 15:1 (2000), 37.
9 I.W. Charny, 'A Classification of Denials of the Holocaust and Other Genocides', *Journal of Genocide Research* 11:5 (2003), 15.
10 L. Kuper, *Genocide: Its Political Use in the Twentieth Century* (Penguin, 1981), 113.
11 M. Imbleau, 'Denial of the Holocaust, Genocide, and Crimes against Humanity: A Comparative Overview of Ad Hoc Statutes' in L. Hennebel and T. Hochma (eds), *Genocide Denials and the Law* (Oxford University Press, 2011), 235–77, 244.
12 R.G. Hovannisian, 'Denial: The Armenian Genocide as a Prototype' in J.K. Roth and M. Maxwell (eds), *Remembering for the Future: The Holocaust in an Age of Genocide* (Palgrave, 2001), 796–812, 796.
13 R. Lemarchand (ed.), *Forgotten Genocides: Oblivion, Denial and Memory* (University of Pennsylvania Press, 2011), 14.
14 T. Akçam, *From Empire to Republic: Turkish Nationalism and the Armenian Genocide* (Zed Books, 2004), 231.
15 F.M. Göçek, 'Reading Genocide: Turkish Historiography on 1915' in R.G. Suny, F. M. Göçek and N.M. Naimark (eds), A *Question of Genocide: Armenians and Turks at the End of the Ottoman Empire* (Oxford University Press, 2011), 42–52.

transition of the governing elite from the Ottoman Empire to the Turkish Republic, with many of those incriminated in the Armenian genocide taking up positions in the new government.[16]

The identity of the Turkish Republic is supported by strong nationalism prevalent in the country. Some brand it as 'state endorsement of nationalism ... sanctioned' in the country's Constitution.[17] Turkey's reactions to international debates or recognition have demonstrated that any possible admittance of responsibility for the fate of the Armenians at the hands of the Ottoman authorities would be considered a stain on Turkish identity. Hence, debates on genocide are persecuted in Turkey under the heading of 'denigrating Turkishness' discussed below. Indeed, denialism is rooted in the national education system, in which history textbooks present the events as a case of rebellion, disloyalty and violence by Armenians, prompting a justified response from the Turkish government.[18] Thus, the ordinary Turkish citizen is brought up to think of an Armenian not as a victim of historical injustice, but rather as the aggressor.

Bolstered by the aforementioned rationale, the Turkish denialism took on particular characteristics, including belittling the number of Armenian deaths, countercharging the Armenians and their allies and disavowing any intention of the government to exterminate the Armenian population, to name but a few.[19] Consequently, the Turkish official position does not deny the fact of loss of life but posits alternative plausible explanations and presents the tragedy as one of many others, each equivalently tragic.[20] According to Göçek, at the time of 'the transition from the Ottoman to the Turkish nation-State, the official attribution of responsibility for the crimes gradually shifted from the perpetrators to the victims'.[21] Thus, the denialist strategy has a protean nature: it transforms from one of recrimination of others to internal and external censorship, and it engenders a shift in perception by promoting a different version of long-established and documented events as 'the other side of the story'.[22] Various lines of such arguments where, *inter alia*, the blame is apportioned to the Armenians or their allies,

16 Akçam, *From Empire to Republic*, 237–41; E.J. Zürcher, 'Renewal and Silence: Postwar Unionist and Kemalist Rhetoric on the Armenian Genocide' in Suny, Göçek and Naimark (eds), *A Question of Genocide*, 306–16.

17 N. Schrodt, *Modern Turkey and the Armenian Genocide: An Argument About the Meaning of the Past* (Springer, 2014), 278.

18 R. Bilali, 'National Narrative and Social Psychological Influences in Turks' Denial of the Mass Killings of Armenians as Genocide', *Journal of Social Issues* 69:1 (2013), 16, 19.

19 See further R.G. Hovannisian, 'Denial of the Armenian Genocide in Comparison with Holocaust Denial' in R.G. Hovannisian (ed.), *Remembrance and Denial: The Case of the Armenian Genocide* (Wayne State University Press, 1999), 205–19; Hovannisian, 'Denial: The Armenian Genocide as a Prototype', 796–809; Kuper, *Genocide*, 113–5.

20 Göçek, 'Reading Genocide', 52.

21 Ibid., 42.

22 Smith et al., 'Professional Ethics', 3–4; Hovannisian, 'Denial: The Armenian Genocide as a Prototype', 796–7.

have been refuted by scholars.[23] It should be noted that such tactics of revisionism as the minimisation of the number of victims, rejection of the role of the State and disputing the accuracy of memory, including that of the victims, are seen as 'generic features of the arguments of those who deny *any* episode of mass atrocity' of which the Armenian genocide is just one example.[24] At the same time, the development of the 'other side of the story' should be seen in the wider context of the 'state-sponsored rewriting of Armenian and Turkish history' attempting to distort the history of the Armenian people which had inhabited the Ottoman territories from ancient times.[25]

In addition to the fear of tainting the national identity, the Turkish reaction is coupled with territorial concerns, as well as the issue of possible reparations.[26] The Armenian genocide occurred *inter alia* as a consequence of Ottoman inse-curity about the crumbling empire,[27] where the losses of geographic territories motivated Turkey in denying autonomy to national minorities.[28] The Turkish Republic can be seen to have inherited this fear of loss of territory, known as the 'Sèvres Syndrome': the 1920 Treaty of Sèvres attempted to partition the Ottoman Empire among the European powers.[29] The modern Turkish perception affiliated with the 'Sèvres Syndrome' is said to be reinforced by the fact that Armenia has not officially recognised Turkey's eastern borders.[30] Turkey has issued official statements calling on Armenia to eradicate from its Independence Declaration and Constitution any articles citing territorial claims as a precondition for estab-lishing normal diplomatic relations.[31] Turkish insecurity might have some grounds as far as the position of the Armenian diaspora is concerned, which

23 V.N. Dadrian, 'The Signal Facts Surrounding the Armenian Genocide and the Turkish Denial Syndrome', *Journal of Genocide Research* 5:2 (2003), 269, 274–5; C.J. Walker, 'World War I and the Armenian Genocide' in R.G. Hovannisian (ed.), *Armenian People from Ancient to Modern Times Volume II* (St Martin's Press, 2004), 239–73.

24 L. Douglas, 'From Trying the Perpetrator to Trying the Denier and Back Again: Some Reflections' in Hennebel and Hochmann (eds), *Genocide Denials and the Law*, 49–74, 63.

25 D. Bloxham, *The Great Game of Genocide: Imperialism, Nationalism, and the Destruction of the Ottoman Armenians* (Oxford University Press, 2005), 209. Cf. C. Foss, 'The Turkish View of Armenian History: A Vanishing Nation' in R.G. Hovannisian (ed.), *The Armenian Genocide: History, Politics, Ethics* (Palgrave, 1992), 250–79; Hovannisian, 'Denial: The Armenian Genocide as a Prototype', 797.

26 Bloxham, *The Great Game of Genocide*, 208.

27 See R.G. Suny, *'They Can Live in the Desert but Nowhere Else': A History of the Armenian Genocide* (Princeton University Press, 2015).

28 Dadrian, 'The Signal Facts', 270–1.

29 See further, F. Keyman and S.A. Duzgit, 'Democratization and Human Rights in Turkey' in E. Lagro and K.E. Jørgensen (eds), *Turkey and the European Union: Prospects for Difficult Encounter* (Palgrave, 2007), 80.

30 A. Akçakoca, F. Cameron and E. Rhein, 'Turkey-Ready for the EU', European Policy Centre, Issue Paper No.16, 28 September 2004, 12.

31 'Statement by the Turkish Ambassador to Russia', *REGNUM News Agency*, 30 October 2007.

continues to pursue territorial claims,[32] but the assumption is not justified in relation to the official Armenian position. Whereas the 1990 Declaration of Independence of the Republic of Armenia alluded to 'restoration of historical justice', and declared its support for 'the task of achieving international recognition of the 1915 Genocide in Ottoman Turkey and Western Armenia',[33] neither of these references found their way to the 1995 Constitution of Armenia.

The Preamble of the Constitution, nevertheless, makes a reference to the Declaration of Independence recognising the national aspirations set therein. In 2007, noting that the European Union (EU) accession process would assist Turkey in correctly assessing its past, the then President of Armenia Robert Kocharyan confirmed that by no means was the recognition of the genocide bound with the claim for land.[34] The recognition of Turkish borders as established in the Treaty of Kars was also a precondition in the Roadmap for improving the relations between the two countries, discussed below. Signed in 1923 between the Grand National Assembly of Turkey and Soviet Georgia, Soviet Armenia and Soviet Azerbaijan, the Treaty of Kars established a new border between Turkey and Soviet Armenia. Major territorial concessions were made to Turkey by surrendering territories previously acquired by Russia and the new border was defined along the Aras and Akhurian Rivers. Some observers have linked the territorial concerns to wider Turkish preoccupations with possible consequences, which could include the payment of reparations.[35]

As a result, Turkey is against any 'judicial settlement', and keen for the debate to be confined to the historical realm,[36] and devoid of legal qualifications. Hence, Turkey does not only officially support revisionism, but also actively encourages and funds it. Often, this is viewed in a positive light, demonstrating the openness of the Turkish government towards the subject. In 2005, the Turkish prime minister invited the Armenian president to jointly examine the relevant Turkish archives in order to establish a consensus on the historical facts. The Armenian president responded with a proposal to establish diplomatic relations without preconditions but rejected the idea of a commission of historians as redundant due the 'self-evident' character of the Armenian genocide.[37] The lack of recognition of the genocide nonetheless appears to be one of the insurmountable

32 'Recognition of the Armenian Genocide by Turkey is a Secondary Issue', *REGNUM News Agency*, 10 October 2010.
33 The Supreme Council of the Armenian Soviet Socialist Republic, 23 August 1990.
34 'Turkey's Joining EU will Force it to Correctly Assess its Past', *Panarmenian Network*, 27 April 2007.
35 V. Avedian, 'State Identity, Continuity, and Responsibility: The Ottoman Empire, the Republic of Turkey and the Armenian Genocide', *European Journal of International Law* 23 (2012), 797, 799.
36 E. Oktem, 'Turkey: Successor or Continuing State of the Ottoman Empire?', *Leiden Journal of International Law* 24 (2011), 561, 582.
37 'Events of 1915 Can be Treated Differently', *REGNUM News Agency*, 30 October 2007.

obstacles in the process of normalisation of diplomatic relations between Turkey and Armenia.

3 The Armenian genocide as a component of Turkish foreign policy

In the Armenian political history the genocide recognition has not always been on State agenda. The first Armenian Republic was merely preoccupied with its survival: established in 1918, it was short-lived and was torn by wars and inter-ethnic violence, culminating in its Sovietisation in 1920.[38] Due to the 1925 Treaty of Friendship between the Soviet Union and Kemalist Turkey and the official Soviet policy of forgetting the past, in the first few decades of the existence of Soviet Armenia, the issues of human and territorial losses were largely ignored with the exception of Stalin's failed territorial claims against Turkey in the 1940s.[39] The Armenian genocide resurfaced decades later due to the national awakening in Soviet Armenia, the activity of the Armenian diaspora and international recognition in some countries, as well as infamous Armenian terrorist attacks.[40] However, it was not until the emergence of the independent Armenia that the issue of the genocide acquired prominence.

As noted above, the 1990 Declaration of Independence of the Republic of Armenia openly raised the issue of the international recognition of the genocide. The first Armenian government was nevertheless in favour of normalising relations with Turkey and did not wish to set the recognition as a precondition for Turkish-Armenian relations.[41] The next government of President Robert Kocharyan, which came to power in 1998, was more vocal on the issue of recognition.[42] The proactive approach of the Armenian State on this matter is currently endorsed in its 2007 National Security Strategy: 'Armenia aspires for the universal recognition and condemnation, including by Turkey, of the Armenian Genocide, and sees it both as a restoration of an historical justice and as a way to improve the overall situation in the region, while also preventing similar crimes in the future.'[43]

In its attempts to normalise the relations with Armenia at the end of 2000s, Turkey took its preferred stance of steering the matter towards historical discourse. In April 2009, under pressure from the United States and Russia, and with the mediation efforts of Switzerland, Armenia and Turkey agreed to a 'Roadmap' to normalise their strained relations. Despite a strenuous negotiating process, two protocols were agreed in the Roadmap, including on the recognition

38 C.J. Walker, *Armenia: The Survival of a Nation* (2nd edn, Routledge, 1990), 256–90, 303–30; Bloxham, *Great Game of Genocide*, 101–5.
39 T. De Waal, *Great Catastrophe: Armenians and Turks in the Shadow of Genocide* (Oxford University Press, 2015), 109.
40 Walker, *Armenia*, 379.
41 De Waal, *Great Catastrophe*, 202.
42 Ibid., 207–9.
43 Republic of Armenia, National Security Strategy, 26 January 2007.

of Turkish borders and the establishment of an historical commission to commonly explore the past,[44] a condition which Armenia previously refused to accept. The suggestion regarding historical investigation was seen as a cynical and futile act by the diaspora Armenians. Despite the signing of the Protocols constituting the Roadmap, the latter have not been ratified in either the Turkish or the Armenian Parliaments to date.

While the Roadmap focused on the normalisation of bilateral Turkish-Armenian relations, the opening of the borders was vehemently opposed by Turkish Prime Minister Erdogan in view of the Nagorno-Karabakh conflict involving Armenia and Azerbaijan.[45] A close ally of Azerbaijan, Turkey closed its borders with Armenia as well as shut its airspace in 1993 in response to the Armenian territorial advance during the armed conflict. Most recently, in the so called 'April Fool's War' in Nagorno-Karabakh lasting four days at the beginning of April 2016, the Turkish President vowed to support Azerbaijan 'to the end'.[46] Turkey's unequivocal support for Azerbaijan in the Nagorno-Karabakh conflict, coupled with the lack of recognition of the genocide, continues to fuel the existing perception of the 'Turk' as a threat.[47] Such a state of affairs not only prevents the normalisation of relations between Turkey and Armenia, but also undermines the possible solution of the Nagorno-Karabakh conflict contributing to regional instability.

The issue of the Armenian genocide, however, transgresses bilateral and regional affairs. In fact, it is a permanent fixture of Turkish foreign relations. The latter actively pursues a policy of influencing the position of other States, or even international organisations such as the United Nations, on this matter.[48] This policy is particularly telling in the cases of countries abstaining from recognising the Armenian genocide. Despite the growing number of States that have recognised the Armenian genocide to date,[49] the United States and Israel are 'two most notable exceptions' in the words of Suny.[50] The lack of recognition on the part of some notable countries can be linked not only to their self-restraint motivated by strategic, military and economic interests, but also the pressure exerted by Turkey willing to manipulating those interests. Some examples have been explored in literature where Turkey openly or covertly put pressure on various States to abort attempts at recognition and commemoration or even holding

44 De Waal, *Great Catastrophe*, 214–34.
45 Ibid., 220–3, 228–9, 233.
46 'Azerbaijan-Armenia Conflict is a Reminder of Europe's Instability', *The Guardian*, 3 April 2016.
47 Azeris are often referred to as 'Turks' in Armenia due to the common Turkic ethnicity of Turks and Azeris.
48 Charny, 'A Classification of Denials', 15.
49 See the website of the Ministry of Foreign Affairs of Armenia, www.mfa.am/en/recognition/ (accessed 15 May 2016).
50 R.G. Suny, 'Writing Genocide: The Fate of the Ottoman Armenians' in Suny, Göçek and Naimark (eds), *A Question of Genocide*, 15–41, 23.

relevant debates. An example of self-restraint is explored by Geoffrey Robertson QC regarding non-recognition by successive British governments: the latter have been keen to ensure that important British interests are not jeopardised by the prospect of genocide recognition.[51]

Mueller, for instance, explores the case of the withdrawal of Resolution 596 from deliberation in the US House of Representatives in 2000.[52] This was due to Turkish threats to cease US-Turkish military cooperation and rekindle relations with Iraq.[53] This episode should be seen as part of the bigger picture in US-Turkish relations since the 1970s: Turkey's significance as a US ally in the Cold War continuously prevented the latter from official recognition of the massacres as genocide.[54] It has been noted that at times statements made in the chambers of US Congress 'came straight out of the denial literature produced by the Turkish embassy, the Institute of Turkish Studies ... and by the Association of Turkish American Associations'.[55] Auron notes that the failure of a number of efforts in the US Congress in 1980s could also have been linked to a pressure from Israeli officials and lobby advancing the Turkish cause in the United States.[56] A dichotomy should be noted here between the frequent willingness of Congress and the caution of the executive branch. For instance, in 1996 the House of Representatives voted to withdraw aid to Turkey until it recognises the geno-cide.[57] It should be noted that parliaments are the leaders in the recognition process worldwide, often against the judgement of their executives. For instance, the French bill recognising the Armenian genocide was passed into law in 2001, overriding a presidential veto.[58]

For Israel, Turkey is an important strategic ally, the relations with which should not be undermined by recognition of the genocide. While it is perceived that the claim of uniqueness of the Holocaust is one of the reasons for lack of Israeli recognition, Israel's strategic interests and the safety and the preservation of the Jewish community, including in Turkey, are cited among the others.[59] In the early 1980s, for instance, Israel was wary of upsetting relations with Turkey when the latter served as an escape route for Jewish refugees fleeing Syria and

---

51 Robertson, 'Was there an Armenian Genocide?', 22–37.
52 A.G. Mueller, 'Affirming Denial Through Preemptive Apologia: The Case of the Armenian Genocide Resolution', *Western Journal of Communication* 68:1 (2004), 24.
53 Ibid., 34–5.
54 De Waal, *Great Catastrophe*, 170, 173–4; Bloxham, *Great Game of Genocide*, 221.
55 Hovannisian, 'Denial: The Armenian Genocide as a Prototype', 806.
56 Y. Auron, *The Banality of Indifference: Zionism and the Armenian Genocide* (Transaction, 2000), 355; Y. Auron, *The Banality of Denial: Israel and the Armenian Genocide* (Transaction, 2004), 103–18.
57 Auron, *The Banality of Denial*, 57.
58 D. Fraser, 'Law's Holocaust Denial: State, Memory, Legality' in Hennebel and Hochma (eds), *Genocide Denials and the Law*, 3–48, 42.
59 E.B. Aharon, 'A Unique Denial: Israel's Foreign Policy and the Armenian Genocide', *British Journal of Middle Eastern Studies* 42:4 (2015), 638, 652–3; Auron, *The Banality of Denial*, 64–6.

Iran.[60] As a result, the Israeli government put pressure on the organisers of a conference on the topic of the Holocaust and genocide in 1982 in Tel Aviv, where few panels on the Armenian genocide were to be held, to prevent the discussion of the Armenian genocide.[61] Auron notes other examples, such as prevention of commemoration of the Armenian genocide and film screenings with the involvement of the Israeli government, Turkish officials and diplomatic representation, the Jewish community in Turkey and other parties.[62]

Turkish pressure, then, extends beyond affecting the official position of third countries and stretches to influence various sectors of public life to silence the debate beyond its borders. In an early example, the Turkish government successfully exerted pressure on the US State Department and Metro-Goldwyn-Mayer film studios to suppress a 1935 film project based on the novel by Franz Werfel, *The Forty Days of Musa Dagh*, depicting a true story of Armenian resistance to Turkish forces over a period of 40 days before rescue by Allied naval forces.[63] The funding of biased research is a tried and tested method of propagandising alternative versions of events.[64] A letter signed by 69 academics questioning the genocide and published as an advertisement in 1985 in leading US newspapers provides an infamous example, as the advertising campaign was sponsored by the Turkish government.[65] Another example is the Turkish-funded Institute of Turkish Studies in Washington, DC, established in 1982, the research activities of which are *inter alia* focused on the denial of the Armenian genocide.[66]

Not only does Turkey actively seek the cooperation of others in this respect, but it also promotes a reactionary policy towards the recognition of the Armenian massacres as genocide. An example includes the case of genocide recognition by the French Parliament which led to diplomatic and economic reactions, including the recalling of the Turkish ambassador and the cancelling of a multi-million satellite contract with a French company.[67] More recently, Pope Francis referred to the Armenian massacres as the first genocide of the twentieth century, which led to the summoning of the papal ambassador to Ankara and the recalling of the Turkish ambassador from the Vatican.[68] At times, even single statements by State officials can provoke a Turkish reaction. Auron notes an example of the mention

60 Ibid., 647, 652.
61 Ibid., 646–9; Auron, *The Banality of Denial*, 217–26.
62 Auron, *The Banality of Indifference*, 352–3.
63 D. Bloxham, 'The Roots of American Genocide Denial: Near Eastern Geopolitics and the Interwar Armenian Question', *Journal of Genocide Research* 8:1 (2006), 27, 44.
64 Smith et al., 'Professional Ethics', 3–4.
65 Charny, 'Innocent Denials of Known Genocides', 17–19.
66 R.W. Smith, E. Markusen, R.J. Lifton, 'Professional Ethics and the Denial of Armenian Genocide' in R.G. Hovannisian (ed.), *Remembrance and Denial: The Case of the Armenian Genocide* (Wayne State University Press, 1999), 274–85; Bloxham, *Great Game of Genocide*, 220.
67 Auron, *The Banality of Denial*, 121–2.
68 'Pope Boosts Armenia's Efforts to have Ottoman Killings Recognised as Genocide', *The Guardian*, 12 April 2015.

of the word 'genocide' in relation to the Armenian massacres by an Israeli minister of education, Yossi Sarid, in 2000, which led to the summoning of the Israeli
chargé d'affaires in Ankara: Israel had to confirm that the statement did not
signify a change in its official position.[69]

Furthermore, efforts to criminalise the denial of the genocide also can harm
bilateral relations with Turkey. Marrani notes the example of Sarkozy's proposal
on the introduction of a new bill criminalising the Armenian genocide as affecting
relations not only with Turkey, but also with Azerbaijan.[70] Turkey in particular
threatened to boycott French imports and cancel projects in energy and other
sectors.[71] Reprisal measures were taken against France and French businesses also
in 2006 following an earlier legislative attempt to criminalise the denial of the
Armenian genocide.[72] This is notwithstanding the fact that Turkey is a candidate
country for EU membership and is a member of a customs union with the EU.[73]

Yet more significant for Turkey's political life is the domestic criminalisation
of debates on the genocide, leading to breaches of Turkey's international
obligations.

4 The Armenian genocide and the freedom of expression in Turkey

The issue of Armenian massacres organised by Ottoman Turkey is one that
demands a revision of the sensitive topic of national identity. For each generation
of Turks, the task of coming to terms with the country's past and the crimes of
their ancestors has been successfully suppressed. Those members of Turkish
society seeking openness in this matter risk public condemnation, or worse, face
criminal persecution. For instance, the organisers of a conference on the subject
of the genocide in 2005 were accused of treason by the justice minister, leading to
its postponement.[74] This is despite the official line of encouraging historic
debates. As regards criminal prosecutions, they take place primarily on the basis
of the infamous Article 301 of the Turkish Criminal Code. Under the earlier
version of the article, those accused of 'publicly degrading Turkishness' could be
imprisoned for a period of three years. The effect of Article 301 is to criminalise
anyone who expresses the opinion that the events of 1915–22 amounted to a

69 Auron, *The Banality of Denial*, 195–6.
70 D. Marrani, 'France: Conseil Constitutionnel Declares Genocide Denial Law
    Unconstitutional', *Public Law* (2012), 573.
71 'Turkey Set for Spat with France Over "Genocide" Bill', *Reuters*, 21 December 2011.
72 Schrodt, *Modern Turkey*, 17.
73 Turkey was granted a candidate status in 1997, and the accession negotiations have
    been progressing very slowly since. A customs union was established between the EU
    and Turkey in 1995.
74 'Turkish Protest Over Genocide Conference', *The Guardian*, 26 September 2005; R.G.
    Suny and F.M. Göçek, 'Introduction: Leaving it to the Historians' in Suny, Göçek
    and Naimark (eds), *A Question of Genocide*, 3–11, 7.

genocide of the Armenian population orchestrated by the Ottoman Empire. The vagueness of the notion of 'denigrating' or 'insulting Turkishness' was criticised as creating a wide scope for misinterpretation.[75] This provision has been condemned by Turkish and international organisations as threatening freedom of expression in the country.[76]

Article 301 has been instrumental in prosecuting journalists, historians, writers and publishers. The Nobel Prize winner Orhan Pamuk was prosecuted for an interview to the foreign press where he had referred to the events of the murder of 30,000 Kurds and 1 million Armenians on the territory of the Ottoman Empire. After eliciting international condemnation, including from the EU within the framework of Turkey's EU accession process, Pamuk's case was dropped.[77] While the charges against Taner Akçam were similarly dropped, the historian responded by bringing a case against his prosecution to the European Court of Human Rights (ECtHR).[78] The fiction writer Elif Shafak and her publisher were charged for denigrating Turkishness for a work of fiction: in her book *The Bastard of Istanbul*, Shafak explored the theme of the Armenian genocide. Another, tragic episode pertains to the prosecution of Hrant Dink, a Turkish-Armenian editor of the bilingual Turkish and Armenian weekly newspaper, *Agos*. Dink was prosecuted under Article 301 three times for 'denigrating Turkishness' in his writings on Armenian identity and the issue of genocide recognition: he was acquitted once, convicted once and was still under investigation at the time of his death.[79] In the case resulting in his conviction, a group of experts, called upon by the court to testify, exonerated Dink, yet he was convicted and given a suspended sentence of six months' imprisonment.[80] This is commonly believed to have led to his targeting by radical nationalists, culminating in his assassination in January 2007.

Dink's son Arat subsequently took over his father's journalistic role at the paper, only to face a new prosecution, again under Article 301, for reiterating Dink's earlier views on the Armenian massacres. The judge in the case explained that 'talk

---

75 E. Shafak, 'Turkey's Home Truth' in D. Hayes, *Turkey: Writers, Politics and Free Speech*, The Open Democracy Quarterly Series 1, Volume 2, 58.

76 'Dissenting Voices: Freedom of Expression and Association in Turkey', Fact-finding Mission Report, September 2005, Kurdish Human Rights Project, Bar Human Rights Committee of England and Wales, 21–42; 'Turkey: Legal Reforms Fall Short on Freedom of Expression', Amnesty International, 30 April 2013, www.amnesty.org/en/latest/news/2013/04/turkey-legal-reforms-fall-short-freedom-expression/ (accessed 15 May 2016); 'Turkey: Government Amendments Will Not Protect Free Speech: Article 301 Should Be Abolished', Human Rights Watch, 16 April 2008, www.hrw.org/news/2008/04/16/turkey-government-amendments-will-not-protect-free-speech (accessed 15 May 2016).

77 'Court Drops Turkish Writer's Case', BBC, 23 January 2006.

78 *Altuğ Taner Akçam v. Turkey* (27520/07), 25 October 2011.

79 I. Hilton, 'Hrant Dink: An Open Democracy Tribute' in D. Hayes, *Turkey: Writers, Politics and Free Speech*, The Open Democracy Quarterly Series 1, Volume 2, 15.

80 Case Comment, 'Right to Life: Assassination of a Journalist: Armenian Genocide – Prosecution for "Denigrating Turkishness"' *EHRLR* (2011), 101.

about genocide, both in Turkey and in other countries, unfavourably affects national security and national interest. The claim of genocide … has become part of and the means of special plans aiming to change the geographic, political boundaries of Turkey'.[81] Thus, instead of providing a credible assessment of the extent to which such debates might 'denigrate' Turkish identity, the judge appeared to advocate their banishment in principle as a matter of conspiracy against Turkey.

It is to be expected that such a state of affairs raises concerns regarding freedom of expression in Turkey. Freedom of expression and freedom of the media are, as far as human rights in Turkey are concerned, among the most sensitive of controversies.[82] As a signatory to the International Covenant on Civil and Political Rights, Turkey is bound under Article 19(2) to guarantee freedom of expression for everyone to 'seek, receive and impart information and ideas of all kinds, regardless of frontiers, either orally, in writing or in print, in the form of art, or through any other media of his choice', although restrictions can be imposed without undermining the essence of the right in limited circumstances.[83] As a member of the Council of Europe, Turkey is also bound by Article 10 of the European Convention on Human Rights (ECHR), subject to the jurisdiction of the ECtHR. Under Article 10 ECHR, Turkey is obligated to uphold the right of everyone to freedom of expression, which shall include 'freedom to hold opinions and to receive and impart information and ideas without interference by public authority and regardless of frontiers'. Figures released in 2014 show that complaints on this issue against Turkey top the list of all the cases brought to the ECtHR.[84]

In its 2010 judgment on Turkey's failure to prevent Dink's murder, the ECtHR stated that various judgments against Dink under Article 301 had taken place without the presence of a pressing social need and therefore violated his right to free expression under applicable international conventions.[85] Under the ECtHR's previous case law, restrictions of freedom of expression had to satisfy a number of conditions, including prescription by law, pursuit of a 'legitimate aim', and being considered 'necessary in a democratic society'. Focusing on the element of necessity, the Court found none in the case of Dink's conviction leading to a finding of a breach of Article 10 ECHR. Following the murder of Dink, it was

81 G. Lewy, *Outlawing Genocide Denial: The Dilemmas of Official Historical Truth* (The University of Utah Press, 2014), 136–7.
82 'PACE President, Ending Visit: Turkey is more Essential than Ever', Parliamentary Assembly of the Council of Europe, 10 April 2015, www.assembly.coe.int/nw/xml/News/News-View-EN.asp?newsid=5519&lang=2&cat=15.
83 Siracusa Principles on the Limitation and Derogation of Provisions in the International Covenant on Civil and Political Rights, Annex, UN Doc E/CN.4/1985/4 (1985), Principle 2; Communication Ballantyne, Davidson, McIntyre v Canada, no. 385/1989: Canada, 05/05/93, CCPR/C/47/D/359/1989, (Jurisprudence) para. 11.4.
84 'ECtHR Releases 2014 Figures: Turkey's Violations Account for more than the Other 46 States Combined', *Sunday's Zaman*, 30 January 2015.
85 *Dink v Turkey* (2668/07) Unreported, 14 September 2010.

revealed that the Turkish police had been warned about the dangers he faced yet failed to act on the information provided, violating Article 2 ECHR (the right to life). The role that the 'denigration of Turkishness' prosecution played in the fatal events was noted by the Council of Europe Parliamentary Assembly, which made reference to the incitement of nationalist sentiments.[86] Some went further to suggest that 'Article 301 killed Hrant Dink'.[87]

The outcry about Dink's murder and the subsequent international pressure led to a number of amendments to Article 301 in April 2008. In spite of the pressure, however, its wording was changed only slightly to stipulate a new requirement for prosecutors to receive permission from the Justice Ministry in order to initiate inquiries relating to Article 301, together with a reduction of the upper threshold of the penalty. Thus, 'denigrating Turkishness' was replaced with 'denigration of the Turkish nation' alongside the State of the Republic of Turkey, the Turkish Parliament, the government of the Republic of Turkey and the legal institutions of the State. It is not surprising that these reforms have been viewed as merely cosmetic and unambitious in upholding freedom of expression in the country.[88] The ECtHR revised the legality of the post-2008 reformed version of the article in the case of *Altuğ Taner Akçam v Turkey*. The Court found that a 'system of prior authorisation by the Ministry of Justice in each individual case is not a lasting solution which can replace the integration of the relevant Convention standards into the Turkish legal system and practice'.[89] The Court noted that 'despite the replacement of the term "Turkishness" (*Türklük*) by "the Turkish nation", there seemed to be no change or major difference in the interpretation of these concepts because they have been understood in the same manner' by the national court, and that the 'legal proceedings against those affirming the Armenian "genocide" had continued unabated'.[90]

It should be noted that the amendments to Article 301 were introduced *inter alia* due to pressure from the EU. Although the EU accession framework has never been used to include genocide recognition as part of membership conditionality,[91] despite the call from the European Parliament in its 1987 resolution recognising the genocide to include this issue within the 'framework of relations between Turkey and the [then] Community',[92] freedom of expression in Turkey is a thorny matter in the Turkish accession process. As a candidate country since

---

86 'Right to Life', 102.
87 'Freedom of the Media in Turkey and the Killing of Hrant Dink', Trial Observation Report, September 2007, Kurdish Human Rights Project, Bar Human Rights Committee of England and Wales, Index on Censorship, Article 19.
88 'Turkey: Decriminalise Dissent. Time to Deliver on the Right to Freedom of Expression', Amnesty International, 2013, 11.
89 *Altuğ Taner Akçam v Turkey* (27520/07), 25 October 2011, para. 77.
90 Ibid., paras 58, 92.
91 See further N. Ghazaryan and J. Kenner, 'Turkey's Accession to the European Union: A Pathway to a New Relationship between Turkey and Armenia?', *Armenian Yearbook of International and Comparative Law* 1 (2013), 78.
92 European Parliament Resolution on a Political Solution to the Armenian Question [1987] OJ C190/119, para. 1.

1997, Turkey must respect the values of the EU listed in Article 2 of the Treaty on European Union, including democracy, the rule of law and human rights.[93] In particular, Article 11 of the Charter of Fundamental Rights of the EU establishes freedom of expression as one of the tenets of the human rights regime in the EU.[94] The issue of freedom of expression in Turkey, including the arbitrary prosecutions under Article 301, has been regularly emphasised by the EU institutions, including the European Commission and the European Parliament.[95] In December 2007, an extension of the accession talks to key areas of justice and human rights was made conditional upon amendments to Article 301.[96] The amendments noted above were criticised by the European Commission, in particular noting the similarity of the wording and the scope for 'political consideration' inherent in the system of prior authorisation.[97]

Although Article 301 is no longer used in a systematic way following the amendments, prosecutions still continue.[98] For example, in June 2008 Ragıp Zarakolu, the Turkish publisher of an Armenian book by a British author, was convicted under Article 301.[99] Prosecutions continue on the basis of opinions suggesting that Dink was murdered not because of his ethnicity, but because of his views on the issue of genocide, as in the case of the writer Temel Demirer.[100] The amendments have ultimately failed to alter the essence of this provision, and its role as an impediment to freedom of expression remains the same. Officials from the Ministry of Justice have revealed to Amnesty International that in 2011, permission was given for eight investigations, out of a total of 305 requested by prosecutors, to proceed.[101]

Article 301 is not the only avenue for suppressing freedom of expression when it comes to debates on the Armenian genocide. For instance, Article 306 of the Criminal Code prohibiting acting against fundamental national interests could also be used to prosecute those who express a view that genocide took

93   (2012) OJ C326.
94   (2010) OJ C83/02.
95   European Parliament resolution on Turkey's progress towards accession 27 September 2006, P6_TA(2006)038, paras 10–11; European Parliament resolution of 12 March 2009 on Turkey's progress report 2008, P6_TA(2009)0134, para. 13; see European Commission annual progress reports, ec.europa.eu/enlargement/countries/detailed-country-information/turkey/index_en.htm (accessed 15 May 2016).
96   Olli Rehn, EU Commissioner for Enlargement, The Commission's 2007 Enlargement Reports, SPEECH/07/736, 21 November 2007.
97   Turkey 2008 Progress Reports, Commission Staff Working Document, SEC (2008) 2699, 15–16.
98   Turkey 2011 Progress Report, Commission Staff Working Document, SEC (2011) 1201, 12 October 2011, 25.
99   Lewy, Outlawing Genocide Denial, 137.
100 International PEN, International Publishers Association and Index on Censorship (NGOs in Consultative Status with ECOSOC), Contribution to the 8th session of the Working Group of the Universal Periodic Review, Submission on Turkey, 9 November 2009, 3.
101 'Turkey: Decriminalise Dissent. Time to Deliver on the Right to Freedom of Expression', Amnesty International (2013), 10.

place.[102] A foreign academic who criticised the Turkish government's attitudes towards matters related to Armenian and Kurdish minorities was expelled and subsequently banned from re-entering Turkey on the basis of a law on the status of foreigners.[103] The ECtHR found this to be a breach of Article 10 ECHR, as Turkey failed to prove that the claimant's views were harmful to Turkey's national security. Most recently, in its 2013 resolution, the Council of Europe Parliamentary Assembly called for the repealing of Article 301 and other provisions of the Criminal Code restricting freedom of expression.[104]

It appears that the silencing of the debates on the Armenian genocide in Turkey will persist not only due to the limited legislative amendments, but also due to the increasingly nationalist atmosphere and intolerance of the authorities towards any dissent.[105]

5 Conclusion

Even after 100 years, the rationale for the Turkish denial of the Armenian genocide remains rooted in the foundations of the modern Turkish Republic. A recognition of the genocide would prompt a questioning of the very tenets of the State and a coming to terms with some of the least glorious pages of its history. It is therefore not surprising that the main legal provision criminalising any possible debates on the issue of recognition concerns 'denigrating' Turkish identity, rejecting out of hand the idea that Turkey, even Ottoman Turkey, could have committed such acts. This prohibition *inter alia* is one of the reasons for criticism directed at the state of affairs in Turkey in relation to freedom of expression.

In the current atmosphere of heightened nationalism and the eradication of opposition and dissent, one can hardly expect a change of heart on the issue of the Armenian genocide. The recent crackdown on journalists and academics in Turkey demonstrates that the influence of international organisations, most importantly that of the EU, is diminishing. In this context, the prospect of improvement in Turkish-Armenian relations is far from promising. Turkey's position on the Armenian genocide, coupled with the unequivocal support for Azerbaijan in the Nagorno-Karabakh conflict, fuels Armenia's historic and current existentialist fears, further undermining regional stability. Given Turkey's importance in the current international context, including the refugee crisis and various conflicts in the Middle East, its position on the Armenian genocide, internally or externally, will continue to remain unchallenged.

---

102   C. Overson Hensler and Mark Muller, 'Freedom of Expression and Association in Turkey', November 2005, Kurdish Human Rights Project, Bar Human Rights Committee of England and Wales, 48.
103   *Cox v Turkey* (2933/03), 20 May 2010, para. 20.
104   Resolution 1925 (2013), para. 11.
105   'President Erdogan Says Freedom and Democracy have "No Value" in Turkey Amid Arrests and Military Crackdown', *The Independent*, 15 January 2016.

Part III

Dealing with Holocaust and genocide denial

Chapter 13

From introduction to implementation

First steps of the EU Framework Decision 2008/913/JHA against racism and xenophobia[1]

Paolo Lobba

1 Introduction

The European Union's (EU) Framework Decision 2008/913/JHA (hereafter 'FD')[2] entered into force after protracted negotiations among Member States which reflected the controversial nature of the issues addressed therein. Although the FD has its origins in anti-racism policies pursued by the EU since the mid-1980s, it foresees for the first time criminal provisions seeking to ban not only the denial, justification and gross trivialisation of the Holocaust, but also that of most other core international crimes – conduct termed here 'denialism' or 'negationism'.

On 28 November 2010 the deadline set for the FD to be implemented by EU Member States expired. On 27 January 2014, the EU Commission published a report assessing the compliance of the Member States with the requirements laid down in the FD.[3] It emerged that most legal systems in Western Europe have not adopted significant measures of execution as of yet. As regards the countries previously included within the Soviet bloc, instead, the FD reinforced a drive for a wave of legislation dealing with past atrocities. Notably, they introduced measures to ban denial related to the crimes committed by former communist regimes.

The FD covers a wide range of measures designed to counter racism and xenophobia, including the criminalisation of public incitement to racial violence and hatred, liability and penalties for legal persons, and rules ensuring a broad

---

1 This chapter expands and updates an article I published in the *New Journal of European Criminal Law* 5:1 (2014), 58–77.

2 Council Framework Decision 2008/913/JHA of 28 November 2008 on combatting certain forms and expressions of racism and xenophobia by means of criminal law, O. J. L 328/55, 6 December 2008.

3 See Report from the Commission to the European Parliament and the Council on the implementation of Council Framework Decision 2008/913/JHA [...], Brussels, 27 January 2014, COM(2014) 27 final ('Commission Report on Implementation').

exercise of jurisdiction. This chapter, however, focuses upon its provisions on denialism. After the criminalisation of denialism promoted by the FD is contextualised, this chapter examines its requirements and sketches the main legal issues that need to be addressed by EU Member States during the transposition phase.

The chapter then moves on to address a more general question, namely the expansion of the crime of denialism beyond Holocaust denial. This tendency, fostered by the FD, raises a number of concerns relating to both the principle of legality – due to the vagueness in the crime's definition – and the right to freedom of speech and historical research – caused by the unqualified prohibition of a wide spectrum of conduct. In conclusion, it is argued that denialism should only be punished, if at all, where it falls within existing hate speech crimes.

2 The Framework Decision's legal background

2.1 European instruments against racism and xenophobia

The EU's anti-racism policy, to which the FD comes as a latest step, dates back to the 1980s and includes a number of declarations, actions, campaigns and legislation.[4] From a normative viewpoint, the FD descends from, and repeals, the Joint Action of 15 July 1996 concerning action to combat racism and xenophobia,[5] which represents the first EU-wide attempt to harmonise the criminal response to denialism. The Joint Action purported *inter alia* to strengthen judicial cooperation around the offences of 'public condoning, for a racist or xenophobic purpose, of crimes against humanity and human rights violations' and 'public denial of the crimes defined in Article 6 of the Charter of the International Military Tribunal [of Nuremberg]'.[6]

This European act failed, however, to have a substantial impact on advancing the harmonisation of legislation on denialism. For one thing, the binding effect of joint actions as such was dubious at best, so much so that this uncertainty led to their replacement with the instrument of framework decisions.[7] Second, the call

---

4 See e.g. the Joint Declaration by the European Parliament, the Council and the Commission Against Racism and Xenophobia, 11 June 1986 (O.J. C 158, 25 June 1986); Council Regulation (EC) No. 1035/97 of 2 June 1997; Article 19 of the Treaty on the Functioning of the European Union ('TFEU') (ex Article 13 of the Treaty establishing the European Community); European Parliament resolution No. B5-0766/2000, 21 September 2000 (O.J. C 146, 17 May 2001).
5 Joint Action 96/443/JHA, 15 July 1996, (O.J. L 185, 24 July 1996) ('Joint Action').
6 Joint Action, Title I, A(b) and (c).
7 Consolidated Version of the Treaty on European Union (O.J. C 325/7, 24 December 2002), Articles 29, 31(1)(e) and 34(2)(b) (laying down the legal regime of framework decisions after the Treaties of Amsterdam and Nice).

for the prohibition of denialism was restricted to those expressions 'includ[ing] behaviour which is contemptuous of, or degrading to, a group of persons defined by reference to colour, race, religion or national or ethnic origin'.[8] It was for each State, therefore, to decide whether to introduce an express provision banning denialism, or punish it only insofar as it amounted to contemptuous or degrading behaviour. The latter choice permitted States, in effect, not to take any measures in implementation of the Joint Action, considering that these general provisions against hate speech were already widely in force throughout Europe.

As a result European domestic systems remained fundamentally divided between the express prohibition of denialism and general provisions against hate speech under which denialism may be implicitly punished. This dichotomy of approach emerged also in relation to the Additional Protocol to the Convention on Cybercrime, adopted by the Council of Europe.[9] While Article 6(1) requires States parties to introduce the crime of denialism, Article 6(2) allows them to restrict the scope of the prohibition to the acts committed with the intent to incite hatred, discrimination or violence, or otherwise to reserve the right not to apply Article 6(1), in whole or in part. Nevertheless, the limited progress in the domestic implementation of the Additional Protocol shows once more the cautiousness of States in this field.[10]

2.2 Domestic legal frameworks

The same split among European States is reflected in domestic legislation on denialism, with which the FD is destined to interact. In addition to such '*summa divisio*' between explicit and implicit prohibition, there is a further distinction to be drawn. Some systems – like France[11] and Austria[12] – punish Holocaust denial as such, that is, without any additional requirements. Others limit the scope of the offence by introducing a wide range of conditions aimed at restricting the contours of criminal responsibility to the most harmful conduct.

In the field of express criminalisation, States differ not only with regard to the additional elements embedded into the basic form of the crime, but also, and most significantly, in relation to which historical facts are banned from being denied or justified. While some systems restrict the scope of the prohibition to the

---

8 Joint Action, Title I, A(c).
9 Additional Protocol to the Convention on Cybercrime, 28 January 2003, ETS No. 189.
10 At the time of research, 20 out of 47 Council of Europe's members have ratified the Protocol and eight of them entered declarations or reservations aiming at restricting the scope of Article 6 (source: conventions.coe.int).
11 Law on Freedom of Press of 29 July 1881 as amended by Law No. 90-615, 13 July 1990 ('Loi Gayssot'), Article 24 bis.
12 Law against national-socialist activities in Austria ('Verbotsgesetz'), effective 18 February 1947, as amended on 26 February 1992 (*Federal Gazette* 148/1992), Section 3(h).

Holocaust only,[13] others outlaw the denial of genocide, crimes against humanity and war crimes.[14]

A further development has been on prominent display in an ongoing dispute engaged by a number of Eastern European countries. In an effort to deal with their common past of Soviet control, legislation has been passed to proscribe the denial, justification or approval of crimes committed by 'communists' or by 'totalitarian regimes'.[15] Such policies mark the attempt by these States to place the Nazi and communist crimes on the same level, overcoming a different normative treatment perceived as unfair. The issue was raised also in the course of negotiations on the FD, but ultimately such demand remained unsatisfied. Despite the pressure exercised for the inclusion of the crimes committed by communist regimes, the most the Eastern European States were able to achieve was the Council's 'deploration' of such crimes and its commitment to re-examine the matter in two years.[16] In 2010, the European Commission finally brought the controversy to an end by declaring that, due to the different measures adopted even among Member States with similar experiences of totalitarian regimes, the conditions for extending the Framework Decision's scope of application did not exist.[17]

13 See e.g. in addition to France and Austria, Belgium (Law of 23 March 1995, Article 1), Romania (Emergency Ordinance No. 31, 13 March 2002, Article 6) and Germany (Criminal Code, Section 130). See, for a comprehensive panorama, R. Kahn, *Holocaust Denial and the Law. A Comparative Study* (New York: Palgrave Macmillan, 2004); EU Network of Independent Experts on Fundamental Rights, 'Combating Racism and Xenophobia Through Criminal Legislation: The Situation in the EU Member States', Opinion No. 5–2005, 28 November 2005; Institut Suisse de Droit Comparé, 'Étude comparative sur la négation des génocides et des crimes contre l'humanité', 19 December 2006.

14 See e.g. Spanish Criminal Code, Article 510(1)(c) (against denial, justification and gross trivialisation of genocide, crimes against humanity and war crimes); Luxembourgian Criminal Code, Article 457–3 (targeting Holocaust and other genocides), Liechtenstein's Criminal Code, Section 283(1)(5) (genocide or other crimes against humanity, but see the defence provided for by Section 283(3)); Swiss Criminal Code, Article 261 bis(4) (genocide and crimes against humanity); Slovenian Criminal Code, Article 297 (genocide, crimes against humanity and war crimes).

15 See e.g. Czech Criminal Code, Section 405; Polish Law of 18 December 1998 Establishing the Institute of National Remembrance, Articles 1 and 55; Hungarian Criminal Code as amended in June 2010, Article 269(c); Slovak Criminal Code, Article 422(d); Lithuanian Criminal Code as amended on 15 June 2010, Article 170–2.

16 Council of the European Union, Addendum to Draft Minutes, 16395/08 ADD 1, PV/CONS 75, 27 January 2009, Item 45, Statement by the Council. See also, ibid., Statement by Latvia (advocating that the denial, condoning and gross trivialisation of totalitarian communist crimes should also be punished); L. Cajani, 'Criminal Laws on History: The Case of European Union', *Historein* 11.1 (2011), 19–48, at 31 (reporting of the request advanced by the three Baltic countries, Poland and Slovenia that the Soviet crimes be included in the FD).

17 Report from the Commission to the European Parliament and to the Council: The memory of the crimes committed by totalitarian regimes in Europe, Brussels, 22 December 2010, COM(2010) 783 final, at 10.

3 Overview of the Framework Decision as regards the crime of denialism

3.1 The legal definition of denialism

The highly contentious nature of the crime of denialism is further confirmed by the lengthy and troubled seven-year negotiating history of the FD. Though the first draft had been proposed by the Commission in 2001, unanimous agreement could not be achieved before April 2007, and the decision was finally issued on 28 November 2008 in a much less stringent form, carefully worded to settle the concerns of all Member States.[18]

Article 1 of the FD stipulates that Member States make punishable the conduct of publicly condoning, denying or grossly trivialising the following international crimes: (a) genocide, crimes against humanity and war crimes as defined in the Statute of the International Criminal Court;[19] and (b) the crimes defined in Article 6 of the Charter of the Nuremberg Tribunal.[20] Therefore, the FD does not merely concern the Holocaust or the acts committed by the Nazi regime, but rather extends to most core international crimes. Concerns about excessive restrictions upon free speech voiced by many States, however, caused the final version of the FD to be diluted by introducing additional clauses that attenuate its potential impact on domestic legal systems.

To begin with, the public condoning, denial or trivialisation of an international crime is required to be punished only insofar as 'the conduct is carried out *in a manner likely to incite to violence or hatred*' against a group (or one of its members) defined by reference to race, colour, religion, descent, or national or ethnic origin (Article 1(1)(c) and (d)).[21] This definition does not bind Member States to make negationism punishable *per se*. Rather, it seems that, in its current wording, the crime of denialism is subsumed under the broader crime of incitement to hatred or violence provided for under Article 1(1)(a) of the FD. In other words, the FD requires criminalisation of denialism only to the extent that an expression

18 See e.g., for general comments on the FD, L. Pech, 'The Law of Holocaust Denial in Europe: Towards a (Qualified) EU-wide Criminal Prohibition', in L. Hennebel, T. Hochmann (eds), *Genocide Denials and the Law* (Oxford: Oxford University Press, 2011), 185–234; B. Renauld, 'La décision-cadre 2008/913/JAI du Conseil de l'Union Européenne: du nouveau en matière de lutte contre le racisme?', *Revue trimestrièlle des droits de l'homme* 21.81 (2010), 119–40; J.J. Garman, 'The European Union Combats Racism and Xenophobia by Forbidding Expression: An Analysis of the Framework Decision', *University of Toledo Law Review* 39.4 (2008), 843–60; J.C. Knechtle, 'Holocaust Denial and the Concept of Dignity in the European Union', *Florida State University Law Review* 36.1 (2008), 41–66; M. Bell, *Racism and Equality in the European Union* (Oxford: Oxford University Press, 2008), 164–8.
19 FD, Article 1(1)(c).
20 FD, Article 1(1)(d) (the reference to Article 6 of the Charter of the Nuremberg Tribunal indicates, in short, the crimes committed by the Nazi regime and thus, among them, the Holocaust).
21 Emphasis added.

amounts to a public incitement to hatred or violence. Therefore, denialism appears to be defined as a sub-species of the latter conduct.

This interpretation inevitably calls into question the autonomous meaning of Article 1(1)(c) and (d) and, accordingly, apparent European support for an express prohibition of denialism. Considering that the conduct of denialism as drafted in the FD is already punishable in all Member States under other more general provisions against hate speech, the FD's legal impact is likely to be minor. This relatively low degree of cogency might increase in the near future, given that non-compliance with the obligations stemming from framework decisions may now be subject to penalties in the EU legal system.[22]

3.2 The optional elements of crime and other restrictive clauses

In addition to this significant restriction deriving directly from the crime's defini-tion, the FD includes another two clauses allowing States to further reduce the range of punishable expressions when implementing the FD in their own national systems. They operate as optional elements that each State *may* decide to add to the domestic definition of the crime. The goal pursued by the drafters was to enable States to confine punishment to conduct carried out in a manner that threatened or damaged a protected interest such as public order or the reputation of others.

The first optional element draws from German legislation. This provision per-mits States to choose whether 'to punish only conduct which is […] carried out in a manner likely to disturb public order'.[23] It is not clear whether this clause is capable of effectively restricting the scope of punishable expressions to those in which the harmful effect is actually demonstrated. As an example, whereas German legislation criminalises only conduct that poses a threat to public peace – a notion akin to public order – German courts adopted an interpretation according to which, in effect, any denial or minimisation of the Holocaust fulfils *per se* this requirement.[24] In so doing, judges have *de facto* obliterated an element

---

22 TFEU, Articles 258–60 read in conjunction with Protocol No. 36 appended to the Treaty of Lisbon, Title VII, Articles 9–10 (infringement procedures for framework decisions are possible from 1 December 2014).

23 FD, Article 1(2).

24 Bundesgerichtshof (Federal High Court of Germany), 8 August 2006, 5 StR 405/05, in *Neue Zeitschrift für Strafrecht* 27.4 (2007), 216, at 217; Bundesgerichtshof, 12 Decem-ber 2000, 1 StR 184/00, in *Entscheidungen des Bundesgerichtshofes in Strafsachen* 46 (2001), 212, at 219 et seq. (qualifying the crime as '*Abstrakt-konkrete Gefährdungsdelikte*'). See T. Lenckner, D. Sternberg-Lieben, *sub* Section 130, in *Strafgesetzbuch Kommentar* (Munich: Beck, 28th edn, 2010), 1405, at 1418 (noting that, in relation to the denial of the Holocaust, the disturbance to public peace requirement is fulfilled by the fact that such utterances are capable of reviving a feeling of insecurity among German living descendants of genocide victims); T. Fischer, *Strafgesetzbuch* (Munich: Beck, 60th edn, 2013), *sub* Section 130, 969, at 976 ff. See also L. Pech, note 18 above, at 193; Institut Suisse de Droit Comparé, note 13 above, at 12; E. Stein, 'History Against

aimed at restricting the scope of the crime to expressions that – upon an assessment of the circumstances of the case – could be considered as likely to endanger public order.

While in Germany this requirement has in effect been annulled by judicial interpretation, it might still play a valuable role if introduced in other systems that stick to its original function as an element that must be established on a case-by-case basis. In this regard, it may become useful especially in respect of expressions whose dangerous character is not considered self-evident, such as the denial of the Armenian or Srebrenica genocides. A restriction on free speech thus could only be upheld as a consequence of a genuine and case-specific assessment of the case as a whole. Ultimately, the capacity of this optional element to strike a reasonable balance between the opposing interests of freedom of speech and public order is dependent on the judicial interpretation given to it by domestic courts.

According to the second optional element, Member States may elect to confine criminal punishment to the denial or gross trivialisation of the crimes that have been established by a final judicial decision,[25] similarly to the French *loi Gayssot*. Although, unlike the public order limitation, this clause permits a State to tailor precisely the desired scope of the crime, its main shortcoming is that it fails to ensure the equal treatment of victim groups. It encompasses, for instance, the crimes committed during the Holocaust, given that they were established by the Nuremberg International Tribunal, and yet excludes the Armenian massacre merely because it has never been adjudicated by a court of law.

This is not to say that the scope of the crime of denialism ought to be expanded to include a vast group of events in addition to the Holocaust. The goal here is simply to highlight the unfair consequences to which this clause may lead, when it is transplanted from the French legal context – where the reference to the Nuremberg judgment limits the scope of the crime to Holocaust denial only – to the FD – in which punishment is encouraged with regard to the denial of any international crime. Admittedly, the inequality issue might be considered

Free Speech: The New German Law Against the "Auschwitz" – and other – "Lies"', *Michigan Law Review* 85.2 (1986), 277–324, at 293 (examining West Germany's courts' case law dealing with Holocaust denial prior to the 1994 and 2005 amendments. Notably the author refers to the German Supreme Court judgment in a case concerning anti-Semitic leaflets, in which it was found that public peace did not require proof of an actual breach, because the conduct under scrutiny, in light of historical experience, shatters *per se* the confidence in legal security). However, see, more recently, Bundesverfassungsgericht (Federal Constitutional Court of Germany), 4 November 2009, 1 BvR 2150/08 (assigning to the public peace ingredient a vital 'corrective' role, aimed at making sufficiently precise – and thus in accordance with constitutional principles – the crime of approval, glorification or justification of the National Socialist rule of arbitrary force, envisaged under Section 130(4) of the German Penal Code).

25 FD, Article 1(4) ('only if the crimes […] have been established by a final decision of a national court of this Member State and/or an international court, or by a final decision of an international court only').

negligible in countries that restrict criminal punishment to the denial of the Holocaust – like France and Germany – due to the extraordinary (perhaps unique) magnitude of the Holocaust which might justify the special protection accorded to it. However, this problematic aspect cannot be overlooked in systems where a higher number of crimes, in addition to the Holocaust, may or may not be given protection against denial, depending on whether or not they had been established by a court. The circumstance of their having been the subject of legal proceedings has nothing to do with their victims' need of protection, but is rather determined by accident. Hence the excluded victims' feeling of frustration and their forceful demands for equal treatment.

As a further guard against excessive encroachments on free speech, the FD contains a peculiar constitutional-like provision. Article 7 declares that the FD shall not have the effect of modifying Member States' obligations to respect fundamental rights – in particular, freedom of expression and association as enshrined in the Treaty on European Union and in Member States' constitutional principles.[26] This provision seems quite atypical and legally unnecessary, considering that EU framework decisions could never prevail over the European constitutive treaties, to which they are hierarchically subordinate. Apart from the symbolic form of reassurance that Article 7 might represent, its actual impact remains uncertain. At most, it may imply a greater weight that domestic constitutional principles are to be accorded in future cases before the Court of Justice of the European Union. In any event, this provision cannot but confirm, yet again, the difficulties in the negotiations and the intention to restrict the FD's influence in a field in which States clearly desire to retain the power to choose the form of criminalisation best suited to their domestic policies.

4 The implementation of the Framework Decision

4.1 The 2014 Commission Report on Implementation and the Commission's subsequent position

As required under Article 10(2) of the FD, the Commission prepared a report outlining the extent to which EU Member States, over three years after the deadline set for implementation expired, have complied with the requirements of the FD. The analysis of the Commission revealed a complex and diversified legal panorama, in which numerous Member States did not transpose verbatim the provisions of the FD into their national laws, but preferred to rely on pre-existing legislation and case law.[27] The language used in different systems and the scope

26 FD, Article 7 and recital 14.
27 For example, the government of the United Kingdom (UK) declared that, in spite of the absence in the UK of an explicit criminalisation of any form of denialism, its national legislation combined with common law provisions complied with the requirements of the FD. In any event, the UK elected to opt out *en masse* of most of the pre-Lisbon criminal law measures, including the FD, which accordingly ceased to apply to the UK on 1

of the relevant crimes thus remain quite heterogeneous. This outcome, as argued elsewhere in this chapter, was not unforeseeable, in light of the loose formulation of the requirements contained in the FD. As a result, it is hard to gauge whether, in reality, the FD succeeded in creating minimum standards – that is, ensuring that the same conduct constitutes an offence throughout the EU.

Nevertheless, there are areas in which there is a closer harmonisation than others. For example, most Member States punish incitement to hatred or violence and take the racist motivation into account in the sentencing phase.[28] Conversely, a split may still be observed between States where the denial of the Holocaust, without more, is an offence and those where a specific criminal prohibition is lacking, or where punishment of denialism is subject to conditions.[29]

Of particular note is that numerous Members of the European Parliament pushed the Commission into taking action against some EU Member States in which the implementation of the FD was believed to be inadequate.[30] The Commission consistently responded that it is holding 'bilateral dialogues' with Member States in order to ensure that the FD is properly and fully transposed into domestic legislations.[31] After having received the replies from the Member States to its administrative letters, the Commission is now presumably signalling to each national government the areas of the FD that still lack proper implementation, promoting legislative measures to fill the gaps in the relevant legal system. In this regard, the Commission observed that it is assisting Member States to effectively implement the FD through exchange of best practices at the level of both the Commission-led Expert Group on the FD and the EU Agency for Fundamental Rights-led Working Party on Improving Reporting of Hate Crimes.[32]

December 2014. The UK government gave assurances, however, that it does not intend to depart from the established EU minimum standards, regardless of its participation in the FD. *See House of Commons – European Scrutiny Committee*, 'Documents considered by the Committee on 26 February 2014', paras 24.10–24.13. On the UK's block opt-out, see generally *House of Commons – European Scrutiny Committee*, 'The UK's Block Opt-out of Pre-Lisbon Criminal Law and Policing', Twenty-first Report of Session 2013–14.

28 Commission Report on Implementation, 3–4, 6–7.

29 Commission Report on Implementation, 4–6.

30 See e.g. Parliamentary Questions by Péter Niedermüller (11 November 2015, E-014632-15), by Soraya Post et al. (9 April 2015, E-005599-15), by Beatriz Becerra Basterrechea (2 October 2015, E-013439-15), by Marina Albiol Guzmán and Ernest Urtasun (29 June 2015, E-010445-15), by Hugues Bayet (16 June 2015, E-009812-15), by Kristina Winberg (23 March 2015, E-004591-15), by Ramon Tremosa i Balcells (10 October 2014, E-007830-14), by Marc Tarabella (19 January 2015, E-000631-15); see also Parliamentary Questions by Benedek Jávor et al. (17 July 2015, E-011498-15). It is worth noticing that a review of the totality of questions concerning the implementation of the FD reveals that the absolute majority of them is raised in connection with incidents that allegedly occurred in Spain.

31 Answer given by Ms Jourová on behalf of the Commission (1 July 2015, E-005599/2015).

32 Answer given by Ms Jourová on behalf of the Commission (17 September 2015, E-010144/2015).

The Commission further indicated that it has identified three *priority areas* on which its efforts in ensuring full implementation have concentrated, namely: (i) denial of 'Nazi-Axis crimes' (read: Holocaust denial), (ii) racist and xenophobic motivation as aggravating circumstance, and (iii) jurisdiction for online hate speech.[33]

While the Commission has not yet initiated any infringement proceedings based on the FD, it declared that it will not shy away from doing so when needed.[34] It also stressed that the FD is a 'key priority' in the EU Agenda for Security. Conversely, when parliamentarians sought to prompt the Commission to make an assessment as to whether a particular situation that they referred to fell within the scope of the FD, the European body refrained from doing so, deferring the issue to domestic authorities, the only ones that are competent to prosecute specific cases and determine whether they constitute incitement to racial hatred or violence.[35]

4.2 Some issues to be addressed in assessing proper implementation

Aside from the Commission's proclaimed intentions, several questions need to be addressed to appraise the real latitude that EU Member States are afforded in the transposition process. For example, to what extent are Member States allowed, under EU law, to rely on pre-existing domestic legislation to claim that the FD does not need any additional measure of implementation? In the same vein, one may wonder to what extent Member States are bound by the specific language that the FD employs to define the prohibited conduct: does a broad-range provision targeting incitement to hatred suffice to meet the FD-imposed requirement that denial of the Holocaust (and of other serious crimes) be punished? All these questions will become crucial when the Commission first brings infringement proceedings before the Court of Justice against Member States that are considered non-compliant with the requirements of the FD.

In seeking to provide a tentative answer, one should begin by recalling that, as with EU directives, framework decisions are binding as to the *goals* that they set, while leaving broad discretion to the Member States in the selection of the preferred *means* to fulfil them. Under the present circumstances, therefore, it seems reasonable to assume that in the transposition process national legislatures may frame a criminal offence as they see fit, so long as the scope of applicability of the

---

33 Answer given by Ms Jourová on behalf of the Commission (17 September 2015, E-010144/2015).

34 Answer given by Ms Jourová on behalf of the Commission (1 July 2015, E-005599/2015); id. (22 May 2015, E-002258/2015).

35 See e.g. Answer given by Ms Jourová on behalf of the Commission (4 January 2016, E-013682/2015); id. (29 July 2015, E-008258/2015); id. (3 December 2015, E-009812/2015); id. (26 June 2015, E-002792/2015); id. (9 April 2015, E-009214/2014); id. (21 January 2015, E-007829/14, E-007882/14 and E-007830/14); id. (13 January 2015, E-008778/2014).

newly introduced provision encompasses the conduct identified by the FD. In other words, what matters is that the entire spectrum of behaviour that would be punishable pursuant to the FD be equally punishable under domestic legislation, without gaps of impunity.

This interpretation is supported by the language of the FD, which requires Member States to 'take the measures necessary' to ensure that a range of conduct be punishable.[36] On the face of it, the obligation is not so much for Member States to adopt an identical definition of the offences, but to ensure, by whatever means they consider to be appropriate, that the final result is accomplished, that is, that the acts laid down by the FD are penalised.

A more specific question may now be addressed, namely whether a pre-existing offence against incitement to hatred or violence may qualify as adequate transposition of the anti-denialism provisions contained in the FD. Of course, in approaching the issue, one needs to caution that, as set out in the Commission Report on Implementation,[37] domestic systems vary widely in respect of the precise definition of incitement to hatred or violence; accordingly, any general point ought to be taken with a grain of salt. That being said, the question turns to whether the conduct described under Article 1(1)(d) – that is, 'condoning, denying or grossly trivialising' the Nazi crimes – may be subsumed under that envisaged under Article 1(1)(a) – that is, 'incitement to violence or hatred'.

The answer would appear to be in the affirmative, as envisioned above, given that the denial of the Nazi crimes need only be punished where it is carried out in a manner 'likely to' incite to violence or hatred. The difference between an act 'inciting' to hatred (Article 1(1)(a)) and one 'likely to incite' to hatred (Article 1(1)(d)) should not be overemphasised. Indeed, it is commonly accepted that for an expression to make out the crime of incitement to hatred, it merely needs to be deemed 'likely to incite', given that certainty is often not attainable when it comes to evaluate the effects of a statement on the recipients' state of mind. Requiring a higher standard of proof would render the burden on the prosecution unworkable for most cases.

Finally, it should be recalled that judges are under an obligation to construe domestic criminal law in accordance with the 'wording and purpose' of any EU framework decision – the so-called 'principle of conforming interpretation'.[38] In systems where incitement to hatred is punishable and yet denialism is not specifically criminalised, such a rule of interpretation may offer support to a court's finding that hate speech may also encompass statements denying, condoning or trivialising the Holocaust or other international crimes. In any event, this interpretative operation can never result in the scope of the offence, as laid down in national law, being extended, lest the principle of *nullum crimen sine lege* be

---

36 FD, Article 1(1).
37 Commission Report on Implementation, 3–4.
38 Court of Justice of the European Union, Case C-105/03 *Maria Pupino*, 16 June 2005, para. 43.

infringed.[39] This is clearly borne out by the well-settled case law of the Court of Justice, according to which, as with EU directives, framework decisions cannot have the effect of determining or aggravating criminal liability, unless that effect derives from national legislation adopted for their implementation.[40]

5 Any harmonising effects?

One may conclude that the FD brought about relatively minor changes in domestic legislation because it falls short of imposing stringent obligations on the Member States. First of all the *express* criminalisation of negationism – although stimulated – is not required; as mentioned, it suffices for the States to punish it if and when conduct qualifies as incitement to hatred or violence. Furthermore, when it comes to the definition of the crime of negationism, there is a conspicuous variety of optional elements from which domestic legislatures may choose in the implementation stage.

States are not therefore legally bound to adapt their existing regimes to an externally imposed model of incrimination, since the FD leaves room for both implicit and explicit prohibition, and allows for several optional elements of crime to be introduced. That said, the fact remains that a tendency either to introduce or expand the scope of the crime of denialism has gained momentum in conjunction with the adoption of the FD, revealing its *persuasive character*. The harmonisation of the definition of the crime appears to be encouraged, in particular, with respect to three elements

First, the FD standardises the definition of negationism around the three acts of condoning, denial and gross trivialisation. States should thus amend their legislation to reflect this description of the unlawful conduct. In reality, however, notwith-standing the divergent kinds of conduct adopted in different systems, the crime of denialism proved to be quite uniformly applied in the countries where it is expressly banned, due to their courts' flexible interpretation. In France, for instance, even though only the conduct of '*contestation*' of the Holocaust is punishable by law, convictions have also been handed down for expressions relating more closely to the concepts of trivialisation or condoning, as long as the defendant's 'bad faith' was demonstrated.[41] Therefore, in spite of the potential discrepancy between the definitions in national laws and the FD, the FD may help achieve the object of harmonisation by legitimising existing broad judicial interpretation.

---

39 Court of Justice of the European Union, Joined Cases C-387/02, C-391/02 and C-403/02 *Berlusconi and Others*, 3 May 2005, para. 74.

40 Court of Justice of the European Union, Case C-105/03 *Maria Pupino*, 16 June 2005, paras 44–5.

41 See e.g. Cour de cassation, Chambre criminelle ('Cass. crim.') (Criminal Chamber of the Court of Cassation of France), No. 98-88.204, 12 September 2000, Garaudy; Cass. crim., No. 94-85126, 17 June 1997, in *Recueil Dalloz* (1998), Jur., 40; Tribunal correctionnel of Paris (First-instance criminal tribunal), 8 February 2008, Jean-Marie Le Pen (upheld on appeal on 21 January 2009).

Such judicial practice – which is in danger of violating the principle of *nullum crimen sine lege* – is fostered by the factual overlap that often exists between the theoretically distinct acts of condoning, denial and gross trivialisation.

The second element harmonised by the FD is the definition of the international crimes whose denial is to be banned. In this respect, States are required to make reference to the definitions set out in the Statute of the International Criminal Court and the Charter of the Nuremberg Tribunal. Since the constituent elements of these crimes are sometimes defined differently under domestic law,[42] the reference to uniform internationally established provisions is likely to advance legislative approximation among Member States. Nevertheless, in view of the non-fundamental character of such discrepancies in the domestic definitions of the crimes, the harmonisation of this aspect is probably going to have a limited impact on the whole.

The third element can be considered vital to the understanding of current developments in the crime of denialism. The FD urges Member States to expand the application of the crime beyond the denial of the Holocaust, punishing also the denial of an array of other serious crimes. Deriving from the *slippery slope* effect,[43] this expansive tendency is criticised below as the major drawback of anti-denialism legislation in general.

6 Expansive trends towards a wider criminalisation of denialism

Criminal provisions against denialism, limited to the Holocaust, arose in countries upon which history placed a special 'moral responsibility'[44] to tackle an alarming increase in anti-Semitic acts towards the late 1980s.[45] Arguably, the object to be

---

42 See e.g. with reference to genocide, Estonian Criminal Code, Section 90 and Latvian Criminal Code, Section 71 (extending the definition to include acts committed against social groups); French Criminal Code, Article 211-1 (protecting also any groups that can be defined on the basis of other arbitrary criteria).

43 See *R v. Keegstra* [1990] 3 SCR 697, at 73 ('[C]ondoning a democracy's collective decision to protect itself from certain types of expression may lead to a slippery slope on which encroachments on expression central to [free speech's] values are permitted').

44 D.P. Kommers, *The Constitutional Jurisprudence of the Federal Republic of Germany* (Durham: Duke University Press, 2nd edn, 1997), at 386 (referring to the celebrated *Auschwitzlüge* case of 13 April 1994).

45 Academic literature on the crime of denialism is vast. Listed here are some of the main monographic works: T. Hochmann, *Le négationnisme face aux limites de la liberté d'expression* (Paris: Pedone, 2013); E. Fronza, *Il negazionismo come reato* (Milan: Giuffrè, 2012); R. Kahn, *Holocaust Denial and the Law. A Comparative Study* (New York: Palgrave-Macmillan, 2004); T. Wandres, *Die Strafbarkeit des Auschwitz-Leugnens* (Berlin: Duncker und Humblot, 2000); G. Werle and T. Wandres, *Auschwitz vor Gericht* (Munich: Beck, 1995). Notable articles on the matter include: those collected in L. Hennebel and T. Hochmann (eds), *Genocide Denials and the Law* (Oxford: Oxford University Press, 2011); W. Brugger, 'Ban on or Protection of Hate Speech? Some Observations Based on German and American Law', *Tulane European & Civil Law Forum* 17 (2002), 1; P. Wachsmann, 'Liberté d'expression et négationnisme', *Revue trimestrielle des droits de*

safeguarded is not only the security of a certain ethnic or religious group, but also the 'ethical pact' underlying the foundation of many post-World War II democratic political systems in continental Europe.[46]

In any event, the protection of a legally established historical truth cannot *per se* amount to a legitimate aim pursued by the crime of denialism, since it is not for democratic regimes to authoritatively rule on historical truth, by forbidding the maintenance of a given historiographical position – however abhorrent it might be.[47]

The question, therefore, is what is the legitimate interest protected by the crime of Holocaust denial, especially where its definition does not require the conduct to qualify as incitement to racial or religious hatred. In this case, the punishment of denial as such, without the need to prove any present threat or harm, is grounded in a conclusive presumption. Since it is assumed that the mere negation or trivialisation of the Holocaust *invariably* implies a Jewish-concocted fabrication of the commonly accepted narrative of Nazi extermination of the Jews, this conduct is deemed harmful in and of itself. Anti-Semitism is therefore *iuris et de iure* presumed to underlie all expressions denying the Holocaust. It follows that criminal punishment is warranted at any such instance in an effort to safeguard the human dignity of victims. Holocaust denial is regarded – and accordingly punished – as a subtle form of anti-Semitism, and hence racism.

However, as the FD demonstrates, the scope of the criminal prohibition has gradually extended its reach beyond the Holocaust, thereby calling into question this initial rationale. There are a number of reasons for this expansion.

First, the development of communication technology has prompted States in which denialism is punishable to put pressure on other countries to follow suit, given the inefficacy of national-based solutions *vis-à-vis* the global circulation of data through the internet and other transnational networks of information.

Second, there are the demands of victims of crimes other than the Holocaust that their own past suffering be afforded equal treatment with that of the Jews. Confronted with these requests, States that have already adopted the crime of Holocaust denial find themselves in a weak position, due to accusations of applying a double standard. This might be different in Germany, where a special regard paid to the Holocaust is incontestably accepted, if not obliged. However,

---

l'homme 46 (2001), 585; D. Beisel, 'Die Strafbarkeit der Auschwitzlüge', *Neue Juristische Wochenschrift* 48 (1995), 997; G. Werle, 'Der Holocaust als Gegenstand der bundes-deutschen Strafjustiz', *Neue Juristische Wochenschrift* 45 (1992), 2529.

46 E. Fronza, 'The Criminal Protection of Memory. Some Observations About the Offence of Holocaust Denial' in L. Hennebel and T. Hochmann (eds), note 18 above, 155–80, at 179.

47 Human Rights Committee, General Comment No. 34, CCPR/C/GC/34, 12 September 2011, para. 49 ('Laws that penalize the expression of opinions about historical facts are incompatible with [...] freedom of opinion and expression. The Covenant does not permit general prohibition of expressions of an erroneous opinion or an incorrect interpretation of past events').

other countries might consider unpersuasive the argument that the Holocaust is unique when it comes to face other victim-groups' claims to be accorded equal treatment for their own past agony. In these countries, the potential political gain from expanding the scope of banned denial may easily outweigh any loss caused by the opposition, including campaigns of historians.[48] So States usually lack strong interests to oppose the extension of the crime's scope to an increasing number of historical events.

7 On a slippery slope: recent cases of denialism beyond Holocaust denial

The foregoing reasons paved the way for the progressive extension of the contours of the crime of denialism. In doing so, the legislatures have travelled down a slippery slope which it is difficult to remount. From the protection of the Holocaust only, the crime is being progressively extended, first to cover all genocides, then all crimes against humanity, and finally nearly all core international crimes, as confirmed by the FD. Even this trend does not seem to entirely satisfy the victims' demands, as reflected in the insistence by a number of Eastern European countries to include in the FD crimes committed by the 'communist totalitarian regimes'.[49]

Several recent examples demonstrate the fate, and the dangers, of requests for protection put forward by different victim groups.

French Armenians have long attempted to have the massacres carried out by the Ottoman Empire officially recognised as genocide and the denial thereof criminally sanctioned. Whereas the first goal was achieved in 2001 when the French parliament passed a law publicly recognising the events as genocide,[50] the latter followed a much more turbulent path. A bill to make the denial of the Armenian genocide an offence was presented and approved in the lower House, but stalled for years and was eventually rejected by the Senate on the ground that it is not for the law to establish the legal classification of past events.[51] With a *coup*

---

48 See e.g. the strong opposition of French historians against the so-called *lois mémorielles* (statement by French Association 'Liberté pour l'histoire', in *Liberation*, 13 December 2005) and the protest of Italian historians concerning the then Ministry of Justice's proposal to introduce the crime of denialism ('Manifesto di critica', in *L'Unità*, 23 January 2007).

49 See § 2.2 above.

50 Law No. 2001-70, 29 January 2001.

51 Commission des lois, 'Répression de la contestation de l'existence du génocide arménien – Examen du rapport de M. Jean-Jacques Hyest sur la proposition de loi n° 607 (2009–2010), présentée par M. Serge Lagauche et plusieurs de ses collègues', 13 April 2011. See also, as part of the broader debate on the *lois mémorielles* in France, 'Rapport d'information', No. 1262, presented on 18 November 2008 by the President of the *Assemblée nationale* M. Bernard Accoyer, at 181 ('Considère que le rôle du Parlement n'est pas d'adopter des lois qualifiant ou portant une appréciation sur des faits historiques, a fortiori lorsque celles-ci s'accompagnent de sanctions pénales').

de théâtre, however, French President Nicolas Sarkozy moved his party to make a U-turn and vote in favour of criminalising the denial of the Armenian genocide, presumably in advance of the incumbent election.[52] Nonetheless, the bill never entered into force, owing to a *Décision* of the *Conseil constitutionnel* which struck it down as unconstitutional.[53]

In the Ukraine, the debate is ongoing as to whether the famine of 1932–33 (called *Holodomor*) qualifies as a genocide perpetrated by the Soviet regime. In 2006 the Ukrainian parliament, led by Viktor Yushchenko's party, declared it a genocide and outlawed its public denial.[54] President Viktor Yanukovych, who succeeded Yushchenko, was indeed sued – but in the end acquitted – of genocide denial on the basis of the law that had been passed under Yushchenko. In particular, Yanukovych maintained that the events referred to as the Great Famine do not fulfil the requirements of the crime of genocide, since they involved the whole geographic region of Volga, not only the Ukraine, and derived from a disastrous policy of the Soviet regime, not from Stalin's specific intent to torment Ukrainians.[55] Avoiding taking a position on the contentious qualification of the *Holodomor* as genocide, the European Parliament and the Council of Europe Parliamentary Assembly recognised its status of a crime against humanity.[56]

In Rwanda, the prohibition of denialism has similarly been used as a legal weapon against political opponents. Victoire Ingabire, the opposition leader, is still detained on charges partially based on minimisation of the genocide suffered by the Tutsi in 1994.[57] She is accused of having argued that war crimes were committed also by the Tutsi and that those responsible should face justice. Still in Rwanda, an American professor and former defence counsel before the International Criminal Tribunal for Rwanda, Peter Erlinder, was arrested in 2010 on charges of minimisation of the Rwandan genocide.[58]

---

52 Proposition de loi No. 52 'visant à réprimer la contestation de l'existence des génocides reconnus par la loi', adopted by the French *Sénat* on 23 January 2012.
53 Décision No. 2012–647, 28 February 2012. See L. Pech, 'Lois mémorielles et liberté d'expression: De la controverse à l'ambiguïté. Note sous la décision du Conseil constitutionnel n° 2012–647 DC du 28 février 2012', *Revue française de droit constitutionnel* 91.3 (2012), 563–614.
54 See, for a detailed account, L. Cajani, note 16 above, at 20–2.
55 Yanukovyck's reply to Mr. Laasko's (Finland) question, Report (Second part) of the twelfth sitting of the Parliamentary Assembly of the Council of Europe, 27 April 2010.
56 European Parliament, resolution No. P6_TA(2008)0523, 23 October 2008, on the 'Commemoration of the Holodomor, the artificial famine in Ukraine (1932–1933)', para. 1(a); Parliamentary Assembly of the Council of Europe, resolution No. 1723 (2010), 28 April 2010, para. 11.
57 www.france24.com/en/20100421-rwanda-opposition-leader-arrested-genocide-denial-charges-victoire-ingabire. See also *The Guardian*, 'Rwanda Journalists Jailed for Genocide Denial Launch Supreme Court Appeal', by Owen Bowcott, 29 January 2012.
58 abovethelaw.com/2010/06/genocide-denying-law-professor-peter-erlinder-imprisoned-in-rwanda; ICTR, 98-41-A, Bagosora et al., 'Decision on A. Ntabakuze's Motion for

In Switzerland, a broad prohibition against denialism has been in effect since 1995. Article 261*bis*(4) of the Criminal Code sanctions the crime of denial, gross minimisation and justification of genocide or other crimes against humanity. Pursuant to this provision, in 2007 the Swiss Federal Tribunal upheld the first criminal conviction – and, to our knowledge, one of the very few convictions[59] – handed down in Europe for denial or justification of the Armenian massacre.[60] In this case, the accused did not dispute the existence of the massacres and deportations endured by the Armenians; rather, he contended that they were justified by the ongoing war in which atrocities were being committed by both sides, concluding that considering these events a genocide is a 'mensonge international'.[61] To be punished, therefore, are not only denials of factual events *per se*, but also personal views on their legal classification where, like in the present case, the court finds that a racist motive characterises the conduct.

Encouraged by the outcome of this seminal case, two organisations sought to mark another step forward in the progressive extension of the crime of denialism. In 2010 these organisations filed a complaint with the office of the investigating judge of Vaud (Switzerland), requesting the criminal prosecution of two authors of the right-wing-leaning newspaper *La Nation* for the denial of the Serb genocide of Srebrenica.[62] It was submitted that, by describing the Srebrenica genocide as a 'pseudo-massacre', these two authors denied the genocide and other crimes against humanity established *inter alia* by the International Criminal Tribunal for the former Yugoslavia. Since the investigating judge of Vaud dropped the case only on the ground of lack of racist motive,[63] similar cases involving recent

Injunctions Against the Government of Rwanda Regarding the Arrest and Investigation of Lead Counsel Peter Erlinder', Appeals Chamber, 6 October 2010.

59 According to our research, after the *Perinçek* case only three other people have been convicted in Switzerland for denial of the Armenian genocide: see *Tribunal fédéral*, ATF 6B_297/2010, 16 September 2010 (so-called *Ali Mercan* case).

60 Doğu Perinçek was convicted by the District Court of Lausanne on 9 March 2007; decision upheld on appeal by the Vaud Tribunal cantonal on 19 June 2007 and, finally, by the Swiss Federal Tribunal on 12 December 2007, judgment No. 6B_398/ 2007. Both a Chamber and the Grand Chamber of the European Court of Human Rights found this conviction to violate freedom of expression: European Court of Human Rights ('ECtHR'), *Perinçek v. Switzerland*, 17 December 2013 and 15 October 2015, 27510/08. For a comment on these two landmark judgments, see P. Lobba, 'Testing the "Uniqueness": Denial of the Holocaust vs Denial of Other Crimes before the European Court of Human Rights', in U. Belavusau and A. Gliszczyńska-Grabias (eds), *Law and Memory: Addressing Historical Injustice through Law* (Cambridge University Press, 2017); Id., 'A European Halt to Laws Against Genocide Denial?', *European Criminal Law Review* 4.1 (2014), 59–77.

61 Swiss Federal Tribunal, 6B_398/2007, note 60 above, section A.

62 Joint Press Release of the Société pour les peuples menacés (SPM) and of Track Impunity Always (TRIAL), 'Des Suisses nient le génocide de Srebrenica', Lausanne, 19 April 2010.

63 Procureur général adjoint Jean Treccani, 'Ordonnance de classement', PE10.009990-JTR, 8 March 2011, at 5 ('Les prévenus ne paraissent pas avoir été animés par la volonté de porter atteinte aux victimes des exactions serbes [...] [I]ls paraissent bien

historical events are likely to be brought before Swiss judicial authorities in the near future.

8 Overall remarks on the crime of denialism

The cases described above highlight some issues relating to the criminalisation of denialism in general, and to its current expanding trend in particular. To begin with, complex problems are raised where the crime targets not only the denial of material facts, but extends also to disputes concerning the facts' legal characterisation.[64] The questions then would focus on which entity is in charge of such characterisation and on the criteria for its decisions given that, for instance, the understanding of genocide accepted by historians does not coincide with the legal definition of the crime.[65] Entrusting the resolution of the matter to judicial organs, whether domestic or international, is an unsatisfactory answer. In this way, the decisive word on the nature of past events would be stripped away from historians and the public debate at large and assigned to tribunals whose judgments are – unlike history's – final and thus irreconcilable with timeless review and progressive refinement.[66] Moreover it should be borne in mind that tribunals are not called upon to assess the entire context and circumstances of the event before them, but to adjudicate on the facts submitted in the indictment, as presented by the parties during the trial.[67] Their task is to determine the guilt or innocence of the accused, rather than establish an accurate and complete historical record[68] – at most,

plutôt avoir voulu dénoncer principalement les médias [...] Ils ont focalisé leur attention sur les Serbes et non pas sur leurs victimes').

64 See UN Assembly General resolution A/RES/61/255, 26 January 2007 (urging all states to reject the denial of the 'Holocaust as a historical event', not in its legal qualification as genocide).

65 See S. Straus, 'Contested Meanings and Conflicting Imperatives: A Conceptual Analysis of Genocide', *Journal of Genocide Research* 3.3 (2001), 349–75, at 349, 359, 370; T. Barta, N. Finzsch and D. Stannard, 'Three Responses to "Can There Be Genocide Without the Intent to Commit Genocide?"', *Journal of Genocide Research* 10.1 (2008), 111–33; see also P. Boghossian, 'The Concept of Genocide', *Journal of Genocide Research* 12.1–2 (2010), 69–80.

66 M. Damaska, 'What is the Point of International Criminal Justice?', *Chicago-Kent Law Review* 83.1 (2008), 329–65, at 335–8 (adducing several reasons for the courts' incapacity to contribute genuinely to historical research); C. Ginzburg, *The Judge and the Historian* (London: Verso, 1999), at 117 (arguing that judges and historians have two completely different tasks); Y. Thomas, 'La vérité, le temps, le juge et l'historien', *Le Débat* 102 (1998), 17–36.

67 See e.g. F. Gaynor, 'Uneasy Partners – Evidence, Truth and History in International Trials', *Journal of International Criminal Justice* 10.5 (2012), 1257–75, and the precursory work of Italian distinguished scholar P. Calamandrei, 'Il giudice e lo storico', *Rivista di diritto e procedura civile* (1939), 105.

68 International Criminal Tribunal for the former Yugoslavia ('ICTY'), *Stanišić and Simatović*, IT-03-69-PT, 'Decision Pursuant to Rule 73bis(D)', Trial Chamber, 4 February 2008, para. 21 (responding to the prosecutor's submission that restricting the indictment after the death of Slobodan Milošević would risk the creation of an

they may facilitate the quest for historical truth by providing documentary support for it.[69]

The major downside of the prohibition of Holocaust denial lies, however, as foreshadowed above, in the *slippery slope* effect, which leads to the extension of the scope of the crime to include the denial of a potentially infinite set of other past atrocities.

The intricacy of the matter is illustrated by a fluctuating jurisprudence of the European Court of Human Rights. During an initial phase, the Court held that the denial of '*clearly established historical facts*, such as the Holocaust', falls outside the protective umbrella of the European Convention, and cannot therefore claim protection under its free speech clause.[70] The category of facts excluded from the scope of freedom of expression was then expanded, at least in terms of abstract declaration, to cover the denial or justification of most *core international crimes*.[71]

The danger underlying this position is that, in relation to this category of unprotected expression, the Court would not need to assess whether the restriction on free speech is necessary and proportionate, but could reject the application summarily, solely on the basis of its content.[72] The problem arises inasmuch as the nature of the newly forbidden expression is not such as to justify the irrebuttable presumption on which the crime of Holocaust denial generally rests. While sanctioning Holocaust denial by itself might be reasonable in view of the arguably invariable anti-Semitic motives behind it which renders unnecessary an inquiry into the specific circumstances of the case, the same cannot be said of other acts of denial, which remain context-dependent. It is doubtful, for example, whether racist or other pernicious intentions *necessarily* underlie or result from opinions disputing the nature of the Armenian or Srebrenica genocides, no matter the manner and the context in which the utterances were made. Where

inaccurate historical record, the Chamber emphasised that 'the Tribunal was establish to administer justice, and not to create a historical record').

69 Extraordinary Chambers in the Courts of Cambodia, *Kaing Guek Eav alias Duch*, Case 001, 'Appeal Judgement', Supreme Court Chamber, 3 February 2012, para. 708 (affirming that part of the Court's mandate is 'providing documentary support to the progressive quest for historical truth [... so] promoting a public and genuine discussion on the past grounded upon a firm basis, thereby minimising denial, distortion of facts, and partial truths'). See also L. Douglas, *The Memory of Judgment. Making Law and History in the Trials of the Holocaust* (New Haven-London: Yale University Press, 2001).

70 ECtHR, *Lehideux and Isorni v. France*, 23 September 1998, 24662/94, para. 47 (emphasis added).

71 ECtHR, *Janowiec and Others v. Russia*, 55508/07 & 29520/09, 16 April 2012, para. 165. See also ECtHR, *Fáber v. Hungary*, 24 July 2012, 40721/08, para. 58 (referring to the 'glorification of war crimes, crimes against humanity or genocide').

72 On the shortcomings deriving from this content-based approach, see H. Cannie and D. Voorhoof, 'The Abuse Clause and Freedom of Expression in the European Human Rights Convention: An Added Value for Democracy and Human Rights Protection?', *Netherlands Quarterly of Human Rights* 29.1 (2011), 54–83.

such an irrebuttable presumption is untenable, restrictions on freedom of expression should be justified only by compelling circumstances that mark the conduct as harmful, to be assessed on a case-by-case basis. Instead, the unqualified incrimination of denialism at large ought to be ruled out due to its excessive curtailment of the fundamental right to free speech.

The latter approach seems to have obtained an authoritative endorsement in the Court's most recent jurisprudence, originating from the aforementioned case of *Perinçek*. For the first time, the Grand Chamber clearly confined the automatic presumption of harm to the Holocaust. In doing so, it implicitly acknowledged that whereas Holocaust denial, due to historical and contextual reasons, is inherently associated with racist and totalitarian ideologies, the same cannot be predicated of other types of denialism.[73] Punishment of the latter requires specific evidence to attest the pernicious nature of the expression and is bound to undergo a close examination into its necessity and proportionality.

This is not to say that the Court barred States from making denialism a crime. Restrictions of the kind, however, have to be grounded on some *tangible symptoms of harm*, such as accusations that victims falsified history, justifications of crimes, or particularly virulent statements that are disseminated in a form that is impossible to ignore. In sum, States cannot impose a blanket ban on denialism as such, but are required to strike a reasonable balance between the protection of the victims' dignity and free speech. In this way, the Court intended to guard against unwarranted restrictions on freedom of expression, preventing the irrebuttable presumption that has been applied to Holocaust denial from spilling over into other forms of denialism.

9 The crime of 'racist denialism': the lesser evil?

A possible option to target denialism only when it is harmful is to restrict punishment to conduct qualified by racist or discriminatory intent. In Europe, this model of incrimination has been adopted by only two countries: Portugal[74] and (apparently) Switzerland,[75] contrary to the majority of systems which expressly criminalise denialism. The reason for the limited use of a racist/discriminatory intent requirement is simple: to subject the punishment of denialism to this kind of *mens rea* is unattractive since a crime so designed would have little to no impact. In countries – like all European ones – where expression of racial hatred, incitement and discrimination are already outlawed, an explicit prohibition of 'racist denialism' would merely describe conduct that falls already within the scope of

---

73 ECtHR, *Perinçek v. Switzerland*, 15 October 2015, 27510/08, para. 234.
74 Penal Code of Portugal, Article 240(2)(b) (in which denialism is embedded in the general provision against hate speech).
75 Penal Code of Switzerland, Article 261*bis*(4), as interpreted in the decisions mentioned at notes 59, 60 and 61 above.

general provisions against hate speech. An offence of this kind would therefore be devoid of any legal influence,[76] even though it could stimulate greater degrees of repression than implicit prohibition.

Aside from the actual impact of an express ban on racist denialism, the punishment of denialism only to the extent it amounts to incitement to racial hatred or discrimination appears to be the lesser evil.[77] The danger of unequal treatment of victim groups would be avoided and, most importantly, freedom of speech would probably escape undue restriction.

On the other hand, it should be recalled that criminal prohibitions focused on the perpetrator's intent always entail a degree of judicial discretion and subjective perception that may lead to abuse. The Swiss cases described above are illustrative of this risk. In both *Perinçek* and *La Nation*, the defendants appeared inspired by the desire to rehabilitate the image of their respective country by minimising or denying the crimes suffered by its victims. However, the journalists of *La Nation* were not prosecuted on the ground that they aimed principally at denouncing the bias of media against Serbs and did not focus their attention on the victims.[78] On the contrary, Perinçek's racist motive was mainly deduced from his reference to the laws of war and the fact that crimes were committed by both sides, to justify the massacres.[79] The point is not to criticise these outcomes, but to show that the frontier between legitimate and banned historical revisionism can be a very fine line.

It has been shown that a model of incrimination based on the racist intent is not incompatible with the FD, which leaves it chiefly for the States to choose how to shape the prohibition of denialism. However, this narrowly tailored approach seems unlikely to gain popularity with European States, given the risk of conveying the undesirable message that States are lowering their guard against racism and anti-Semitism.

Therefore, the present-day trend of restricting free speech for the alleged greater good seems likely to continue. The immediate consequence is that States

76 However, see Law No. 115, 16 June 2016 (introducing in the Italian system the denial of the Holocaust and other international crimes as an aggravating circumstance within the pre-existing crime of incitement to racial and religious hatred; in this case, even though the provision does not affect the scope of the offence, it does have legal influence, namely increasing the statutory range of sentence).

77 See Report of the Special Rapporteur on the promotion and protection of the right to freedom of opinion and expression, 7 September 2012, A/67/357, paras 32–3, 43–50 (putting forward strict requirements that must be complied with by laws criminalising hate speech and noting that, while criminal law should focus only on most serious and extreme instances, there is a need to go beyond legal measures to address expression of hatred and intolerance).

78 'Ordonnance de classement', PE10.009990-JTR, note 63 above, at 5.

79 Tribunal d'arrondissement de Lausanne, 'Jugement', PE05.025301, 9 March 2007, at 9, 13–4.

may take advantage of these legal developments as a cheap pretext by which to justify new legislation targeting government-critical expression.[80] The long-term risk consists, as Ronald Dworkin pointed out, in eroding the overall capacity of free speech to withstand future attempts of interference.[81]

80 See e.g. D.F. Orentlicher, 'Criminalizing Hate Speech in the Crucible of Trial: Pro-secutor v. Nahimana', *American University International Law Review* 21.4 (2006), 557–96, at 592–3 (quoting J. Simon, 'Of Hate and Genocide: In Africa, Exploiting the Past', *Columbia Journalism Review*, Jan/Feb 2006, now available at cpj.org/2006/01/of-hate-and-genocide.php).
81 R. Dworkin, 'Foreword', in I. Hare-J. Weinstein (eds), *Extreme Speech and Democracy* (Oxford: Oxford University Press, 2009), vi, ix. See also I. Hare, 'Crosses, Crescents and Sacred Cows: Criminalising Incitement to Religious Hatred', *Public Law* (2006), 521–38, at 533–4.

Chapter 14

Combating genocide denial via law

État des lieux of anti-denial legislation

Caroline Fournet and Clotilde Pégorier[1]

I Introduction

Though long-since the object of rigorous academic attention and scrutiny,[2] the issue of genocide denial continues to generate a substantial amount of controversy and dispute. Unlike the crime of genocide itself, which benefits from an accepted and authoritative definition under international law,[3] genocide denial remains undefined and continues to exist as a hybrid concept within the legal landscape. The question of how or whether criminal sanctions might be imposed for acts of genocide denial, which stands at the centre of the present chapter, is, as a consequence, much contested. At root, the issue raises two sets of essentially conflicting values and standards. On the one hand, there is the critical perspective that regards penalisation of denial as constituting not only an inapt intrusion upon the terrain of history but also a violation of the right to freedom of expression and, as such, a threat to fundamental democratic principles. On the other hand, there lies the viewpoint that attaches foremost importance to the memorialisation of violent events and the securing of justice and recognition for the victims – a perspective underpinned by an understanding of the seriousness of the act of denial and its effects upon the identity and, indeed, the very existence of the targeted group.

---

1 The authors would like to thank Professor Geoff Gilbert for his helpful comments on an earlier draft of this chapter.
2 See generally Hennebel, Ludovic and Hochmann, Thomas (eds), *Genocide Denials and the Law* (Oxford: Oxford University Press, 2011).
3 See Art. II, Convention for the Prevention and Punishment of the Crime of Genocide, United Nations, 1948. Approved and proposed for signature, ratification or accession by the General Assembly of the United Nations, Resolution 260 A (III) of 9 December 1948 (entry into force: 12 January 1951) [hereafter referred to as the Genocide Convention]. See also Art. 2 of the Statute of the International Criminal Tribunal for Rwanda (ICTR), Art. 4 of the Statute of the International Criminal Tribunal for the Former Yugoslavia (ICTY) and Art. 6 of the Statute of the International Criminal Court (ICC) which all reproduce *verbatim* the Genocide Convention's definition.

These opposing sets of standards mark out the area of tension within which the discussion on the criminalisation of genocide denial necessarily takes place. That the subject raises a whole range of complex and sensitive issues is clear, as is the fact that not all can be addressed within the framework of the present contribution. Instead, the aim here is to take a narrower focus on a selection of core concerns. We will first consider how genocide denial, in its perverse distortion of the truth, bears resemblance to hate speech, and address the question of whether genocide denial can, under certain circumstances, constitute a form of hate speech. Following this initial line of enquiry, focus will then be turned to the fundamental issue of the balance between genocide denial and freedom of expression, whereby particular emphasis will be placed on four primary concerns. First, we will reflect upon the core question of whether genocide denial represents an exception to freedom of expression legislation. Subsequently, we will direct attention towards what we regard to be two especially problematic developments observable in both national legislation and recent cases before the European Court of Human Rights – namely, the implicit hierarchisation of genocidal instances on the one hand and, on the other, the tendency to impose a set of unwarranted geographical limitations to anti-denial legislation. We will then consider the extent to which such issues contradict more standardised guidelines developed in European Union (EU) law. The final section of the chapter will address the overarching issue of the legality of the criminalisation of genocide denial in light of recent developments.

2 Genocide denial and hate speech: two sides of the same coin?

First, let us consider the extent of the similarities, if any, between genocide denial and hate speech. A useful point of departure might be supplied here by Charny's reflection that the attempt to impose denial on the world can amount to both an incitement to mass murder and a celebration of the crimes perpetrated against victims.[4] Michel has observed in a similar vein that denying the existence of genocide 'is precisely [...] to approve and recommend it'.[5]

Where denial is used not only to reduce survivors, witnesses and/or researchers to liars but also to rehabilitate and support former genocidal regimes, there appears to be reasonable ground to consider it as possibly falling within the category of hate speech, here understood as 'incitement to hatred or discrimination against persons because they belong to a certain group'.[6] At the international

---

4 Charny, Israel W. (ed.), *Genocide, A Critical Bibliographic Review, Volume Two* (London: Mansell, 1991), p. 22.
5 Michel, Natacha (ed.), *Paroles à la bouche du présent – Le négationnisme: histoire ou politique?* (Marseille: Editions Al Dante, Collection Axolotl, 1997), p. 14. Translation by the authors. The original version reads: 'nier l'existence du crime est précisément [...] en faire la louange et la préconisation.'
6 Van Noorloos, Marloes, *Hate Speech Revisited – A Comparative and Historical Perspective on Hate Speech Law in the Netherlands and England & Wales* (Antwerp: Intersentia, 2012), p. 4.

level, hate speech is addressed most directly by Article 20(2) of the International Covenant on Civil and Political Rights, which expressly requires State parties to prohibit '[a]ny advocacy of national, racial or religious hatred that constitutes incitement to discrimination, hostility or violence'.[7] In a similar vein, Article 4(a) of the International Convention on the Elimination of all Forms of Racial Discrimination requires that State parties proscribe 'all dissemination of ideas based on racial superiority or hatred, incitement to racial discrimination, as well as all acts of violence or incitement to such acts against any race or group of persons of another colour or ethnic origin'.[8] Yet, neither of these two instruments – nor, indeed, any of the other provisions prohibiting hate speech, hate propaganda and incitement to racial hatred – mention genocide denial. If, in spite of the absence of direct reference, these provisions were to be interpreted as including genocide denial, the act of denial would thus 'only' amount to a prohibited conduct under human rights law, which could *potentially* be criminalised under domestic law. The above-mentioned provisions merely require State parties to prohibit the wrongful conduct, and States remain free to decide whether or not they qualify it as a crime.

Yet, past case law could be hinting at future developments in this area, even if a certain degree of caution ought to be exercised. On the one hand, cases such as *J.R.T. and the W.G. Party* v. *Canada* (1981)[9] and *Faurisson* v. *France* (1993)[10] provide examples of how courts have ratified restrictions on freedom of expression in

---

7   Art. 20(2) of the International Covenant on Civil and Political Rights, adopted and opened for signature, ratification and accession by General Assembly Resolution 2200A(XXI) of 16 December 1966 (entry into force: 23 May 1976).

8   Art. 4(a) of the International Convention on the Elimination of all Forms of Racial Discrimination adopted and opened for signature and ratification by General Assembly resolution 2106 (XX) of 21 December 1965 (entry into force: 4 January 1969).

9   See *J.R.T. and the W.G. Party* v. *Canada (104/81)*, Admissibility, UN Doc. CCPR/C/ 18/D/104/1981, Communication no. 104/1981, IHRL 2545 (UNHRC 1983), 6 April 1983, Human Rights Committee [UNHRC], para. 8. The applicant complained that a Canadian court order forbidding him from operating an anti-Semitic telephone service violated his right to freedom of expression. The United Nations Human Rights Committee found the application inadmissible, principally because 'the opinions which [the applicant] seeks to disseminate through the telephone system clearly constitute the advocacy of racial or religious hatred which Canada has an obligation under Article 20(2) of the Covenant to prohibit'.

10   See *Robert Faurisson* v. *France*, Communication No. 550/1993, UN Doc. CCPR/C/ 58/D/550/1993 (1996). The details of the Faurisson case are well known and do not need rehearsing in detail here. The applicant's infamous claim saw him convicted under France's *loi Gayssot*; the conviction was subsequently upheld by the UN Human Rights Committee, noting that although the application of this law 'may lead [...] to decisions or measures incompatible with the Covenant', it is 'not called upon to criticize the abstract laws enacted by States parties', but rather tasked with 'ascertain [ing] whether the conditions of the restrictions imposed on the right to freedom of expression are met in the communications which are brought before it' (para 9.3).

connection with hate speech, particularly as they relate to anti-Semitic incitement. On the other hand, it is, at least since Julius Streicher's condemnation by the Nuremberg Tribunal for his writings in *Der Stürmer*,[11] generally accepted that the dissemination of hate messages may be instrumental in fuelling conflicts and triggering the perpetration of mass atrocities. This can probably explain why hate speech – which is outlawed under human rights law – has not remained completely absent from the international criminal justice arena. Interestingly, though erroneously, international criminal justice has turned to human rights law on a number of occasions to criminalise hate speech, thereby attempting to bridge the gap between the two legal corpuses. Such was notably the path followed by the ICTR in the *Media* case: when considering the role played by the media in the 1994 genocide, the Trial Chamber stressed that if the attack on Rwandese President Habyarimana and the downing of his plane on 6 April 1994 'served as a trigger for the events that followed', then '*RTLM, Kangura and CDR were the bullets in the gun*'.[12] For:

> [t]he trigger had such a deadly impact because the gun was loaded. The Chamber therefore considers the killing of Tutsi civilians can be said to have resulted, at least in part, from the message of ethnic targeting for death that was clearly and effectively disseminated through RTLM, *Kangura* and CDR, before and after 6 April 1994.[13]

This finding of the ICTR is, on the one hand, problematic in that it breeds confusion between international criminal norms and human rights norms, and merges direct and public incitement to commit genocide and hate speech. On the other hand, it also casts into sharp relief the need to punish hate speech. The latter point notwithstanding, there can be no doubt that the ICTR's interpretation was in this instance misguided. Hate speech and direct and public incitement to commit genocide currently pertain to different categories of legal norms. Hate speech can only be a proscribed conduct under domestic law and has yet to be characterised as an international crime. By contrast, direct and public incitement to commit genocide has been recognised as an international crime regardless of whether it is proscribed under domestic law.[14] As the law stands today, hate speech is not an international crime over which international courts

---

11 *Trial of the Major War Criminals Before the International Military Tribunal*, Volume XXII, Nuremberg 1948, pp. 547–9.
12 ICTR, Judgment and Sentence, *Prosecutor* v. *Nahimana, Barayagwiza and Ngeze*, Case No. ICTR-99-52-T, T. Ch. I, 3 December 2003, para. 953 (emphasis added). The defendants were convicted of direct and public incitement to commit genocide as well as of genocide. The Trial Chamber thus considered the media not only as the instigators of genocide but also as direct perpetrators of genocide itself. See id. paras 973–7A.
13 Ibid., para. 953.
14 See *supra* note 3.

and tribunals have, or can claim to have, jurisdiction. As Trial Chamber III of the ICTY unequivocally stated: '[t]he sharp split over treaty law in this area is indicative that such speech may not be regarded as a crime under customary international law'.[15] As Orentlicher has likewise stressed, 'if hate speech "is not protected under international law", it has never been established as a *crime* under international law'.[16]

In other words, by interpreting the definition of an international crime by reference to a could-be domestic crime, the ICTR clearly erred in law. At the same time, it arguably hinted at a significant flaw in the existing legal provisions – one which has, in turn, generated confusion in practice and yielded inconsistency within the case law, as illustrated by the two following contrasting standpoints. In the *Ruggiu* case, the ICTR had explicitly qualified as acts of persecution 'direct and public radio broadcasts all aimed at singling out and attacking the Tutsi ethnic group and Belgians on discriminatory grounds', and had established a clear causal link with the genocide that ensued.[17] Taking an opposite stand, the ICTY, in the *Kordić and Čerkez* case, refused to qualify hate speech as persecution and thus as a crime against humanity falling under its jurisdiction.[18]

It is arguable that the non-recognition of hate speech as an international crime can be detrimental to implementing sanctions against discourses, which, by fuelling conflicts and promoting the escalation of violence, engage in what ultimately amounts to criminal conduct. Further reflection on the possibility of qualifying hate speech as an international crime, accompanied by further consideration of a possible inclusion of genocide denial within the realm of hate speech, might help towards putting a halt to existing judicial divergences. This is, however, pure speculation and, as of now, genocide denial is absent from both hate speech and hate propaganda legislation at the international level. In terms of finding a practicable resolution in the present, our attentions must be turned elsewhere.

3 Genocide denial and the limits of freedom of expression

An alternative to the solution mooted above is to consider whether genocide denial might be regarded as an exception to freedom of expression. This issue takes us to the core of those primary concerns noted in the introduction – concerns that Schabas aptly described:

---

15 ICTY, Judgment, *Prosecutor* v. *Kordić and Čerkez*, Case No. IT-95-14/2-T, T. Ch. III, 26 February 2001, footnote 272.
16 Orentlicher, Diane, 'Criminalizing Hate Speech in the Crucible of Trial: *Prosecutor v. Nahimana*', (2006) 21 *American University International Law Review*, 557–96 at 587 (emphasis in the original).
17 ICTR, Judgment and Sentence, *Prosecutor* v. *Ruggiu*, Case No. ICTR-97-32-I, T. Ch. I, 1 June 2000, para. 22.
18 ICTY, Judgment, *Prosecutor* v. *Kordić and Čerkez*, Case No. IT-95-14/2-T, T. Ch. III, 26 February 2001, para. 209.

My own views on this complex issue have evolved over the years. They may change in the future, too. Sometimes, I find myself sharing the opinion of the last persuasive person with whom I have spoken, my perspective tilting in one direction or another. I find myself torn between the militant anti-racism of punishing denial and a latent libertarianism that bristles at any attempt to muzzle expression. I think that at various times in my life, I have argued for both extremes on these issues. Now, I find myself somewhere in the middle. My preferable compass, international human rights law, seems to have two needles that point in opposite directions.[19]

Anyone who has closely examined and engaged with such issues – particularly from a legal angle – will most probably relate to these words. That the right to freedom of expression is a fundamental pillar of democratic societies needs no stressing. Yet, the gravity of denial is such that it could be seen as amounting to direct and public incitement to commit genocide, as prohibited by Article 3(c) of the Genocide Convention.[20] It could even be argued that it is nothing short of a genocidal act in and of itself. Stanton has systematised this 'routine' practice[21] as the 'eighth stage of genocide' – i.e. as a direct continuation of the initial act, whereby the perpetrators 'deny that they committed any crimes, and often blame what happened on the victims'.[22] Piralian further remarked: 'how could we remember individuals who have never existed, and how, in turn, could one deprived of ancestors ever exist? Where would he come from? ... In that sense, *the denial of the number of deaths is part of the genocidal project* as this backwards interpretation of time is nothing but an attempt to erase the origins';[23] an attempt famously qualified by Vidal-Naquet as one of 'extermination on paper'.[24]

19 Schabas, William, 'Preface', in Hennebel, Ludovic and Hochmann, Thomas (eds), *supra* note 2, pp. xiii–xvi at xiii.
20 See Art. III (c) Genocide Convention; Art. 2 (3) (c) ICTR Statute; Art. 4 (3) (c) ICTY Statute. In contrast, Article 25 (3) (e) of the ICC Statute considers direct and public incitement to commit genocide not as a crime per se but as a mode of incurring criminal responsibility for genocide.
21 See Smith, Roger W., 'Denial of the Armenian Genocide', in Charny, Israel W. (ed.), *supra* note 4, pp. 63–75 at 63.
22 Stanton, Gregory H., *The 8 Stages of Genocide*, Genocide watch. Available at: www.genocidewatch.org/genocide/8stagesofgenocide.html (accessed 17 February 2016).
23 Piralian, Hélène, *Génocide et Transmission* (Paris: Editions L'Harmattan, 1994), p. 52. Translation by the authors (emphasis added). The original version reads: 'Car comment pourrait-on se souvenir de personnes n'ayant jamais existé et comment celui qui n'a pas d'antécédent pourrait-il exister à son tour? D'où viendrait-il? ... En ce sens, le déni du nombre des morts fait bien partie du projet génocidaire, puisqu'en prenant ainsi le temps à rebours, c'est bien d'une tentative d'effacement des origines mêmes dont il s'agit.'
24 Vidal-Naquet, Pierre, *Les Assassins de la Mémoire – 'Un Eichmann de Papier' et Autres Essais sur le Révisionnisme* (Paris: La Découverte, 1987), p. 40. Translation by the authors. The original version reads: 'tentative d'extermination sur le papier'.

Lemkin had also explained how genocide denial aims precisely at killing the victims a second time by 'destroying the world's memory of them'[25] – an idea subsequently reiterated by Wiesel for whom denial constitutes a 'double killing',[26] that is to say, a re-enactment of the death of the victims by a destruction of any memory of them and an attempt at annihilating the dignity of the survivors.[27] In the words of Arendt:

> The murderer leaves a corpse behind and does not pretend that his victim has never existed; if he wipes out any traces, they are those of his own identity, and not the memory and grief of the persons who loved his victim; he destroys a life, but he does not destroy the fact of existence itself.[28]

The common premise across such viewpoints is that the denial of the victims' very existence negates the existence of the group as such, and thus the destruction of the group – or, in other words, the genocide – proceeds unabated. It is for such reasons that the dialectic between denial and free speech marks one of the most complex conundrums facing human rights law, raising crucial – and extremely contemporary – questions regarding the compatibility of limitations to freedom of speech with human rights standards.

Both the French *Conseil constitutionnel*, in its decision of 28 February 2012 on the proposed bill criminalising the denial of the Armenian genocide,[29] and the European Court of Human Rights, in the *Perinçek* case,[30] have latterly made rulings that suggest that the right to freedom of expression trumps the prohibition of denial. These decisions may be – and have been – seen as signalling the death knell for anti-denial legislation. Such a conclusion may, however, be somewhat too hasty, and a closer reflection on the limitations that attend to freedom of expression in general might provide space for a more differentiated response that continues to hold open the possibility for criminal sanctions.

At the regional and international levels, the protection of freedom of expression is enshrined in a number of instruments including the 1948 Universal Declaration

25 Lemkin, Raphaël, *Axis Rule in Occupied Europe – Laws of Occupation, Analysis of Government, Proposals for Redress* (Washington: Carnegie Endowment for International Peace, Division of International Law, 1944), p. xvii.
26 Elie Wiesel, quoted in 'Statement by Concerned Scholars and Writers', *The New York Times*, 24 April 1998.
27 See also Stanton, *supra* note 22.
28 Arendt, Hannah, *The Origins of Totalitarianism* (New York: A Harvest Book, Harcourt Inc., 1994 [first edn: 1966]), p. 442.
29 *Conseil constitutionnel*, decision no. 2012-647-DC, 28 February 2012, para. 6. Available at: www.conseil-constitutionnel.fr/conseil-constitutionnel/english/case-law/decision/decision-no-2012-647-dc-of-28-february-2012.114637.html (accessed 17 February 2016).
30 ECtHR, Judgment, *Perinçek* v. *Switzerland*, Application No. 27510/08, Grand Chamber, 15 October 2015.

of Human Rights,[31] the 1950 European Convention for the Protection of Human Rights and Fundamental Freedoms,[32] the 1966 International Covenant on Civil and Political Rights,[33] and the 1969 American Convention on Human Rights.[34] In its 1976 *Handyside* judgment, the European Court of Human Rights stated that freedom of expression applies not only to ideas and thoughts that are 'favourably received or regarded as inoffensive or as a matter of indifference', but also to those that 'offend, shock or disturb the State or any sector of the population' – all in the name of the values of pluralism, tolerance and broadmindedness which constitute a 'democratic society'.[35] The principle expressed here provides the basis for the protection of freedom of expression in human rights law. To consider this to provide blanket coverage for all ideas and thoughts is, however, misguided: the right to freedom of expression is not absolute and can be restricted by States under certain circumstances, as a means of weighing this liberty against those of others. In line with this, Article 10(2) of the ECHR explicitly allows for restrictions to this right and the Strasbourg Court has expressly included within the scope of admissible restrictions the criminalisation of Holocaust denial:

> There can be no doubt that denying the reality of clearly established historical facts, such as the Holocaust, as the applicant does in his book, does not constitute historical research akin to a quest for the truth. The aim and the result of that approach are completely different, the real purpose being to rehabilitate the National-Socialist regime and, as a consequence, accuse the victims themselves of falsifying history. Denying crimes against humanity is therefore one of the most serious forms of racial defamation of Jews and of incitement to hatred of them [...] The Court [...] considers that the applicant attempts to deflect Article 10 of the Convention from its real purpose by using his right to freedom of expression for ends which are contrary to the text and spirit of the Convention. Such ends, if admitted, would contribute to the destruction of the rights and freedoms guaranteed by the Convention.[36]

31 Art. 19 of the Universal Declaration of Human Rights, UN GA, Paris, 10 December 1948, GA Resolution 217 A (III), *International Bill of Human Rights*, 183rd plenary meeting, 10 December 1948.

32 Art. 10 of the European Convention for the Protection of Human Rights and Fundamental Freedoms adopted by the Council of Europe in Rome on 4 November 1950 (entry into force: 3 September 1953) [hereafter referred to as the European Convention or ECHR].

33 Art. 19 of the International Covenant on Civil and Political Rights, *supra* note 7.

34 Art. 13 of the American Convention on Human Rights ('Pact of San José'), adopted by the Organization of American States on 22 November 1969, San José, Costa Rica (entry into force: 18 July 1978).

35 ECtHR, Judgment, *Handyside* v. *UK*, Application No. 5493/72, 7 December 1976, para. 49.

36 ECtHR, Judgment, *Garaudy* v. *France*, Application No. 65831/01, 24 June 2003.

The logic underlying this verdict relates to the philosophical groundings of the protection of freedom of expression in the European context, namely, the preservation of democracy and democratic values. Modes of expression that are anti-democratic, or considered dangerous or harmful to the defence of democracy, thus do not enjoy immediate protection. It stems from this precedent that it is, above all, the public dissemination of such ideas and thoughts that is condemned, not the opinion in itself – the focus is not only on *what* is said, but also on *how* it is said, *where* and *to whom*.

Detractors of anti-denial legislation generally put forward the risks contained in the intrusion of the law into the domain of history and the dangers of a possible judicially made truth. If this argument ought to be taken into account, a close look at the relevant case law nonetheless indicates that the dangers of a sacralised version of history by judges are fairly minimal. Reflecting on the French anti-denial legislation, Salas observed that rather than trying to impose a particular historical truth, French courts have taken sanctions against messianic and propagandist discourses,[37] merely imposing on historians 'obligations of prudence, objective caution and intellectual neutrality'[38] – and this even before the adoption of the *loi Gayssot*. Already in 1981, in the *Faurisson* case, the *Tribunal de Grande Instance* of Paris had condemned '[t]he historian who concludes that the genocide of the Jews, as well as the existence of the gas chambers, constitute one whole lie which has allowed for a gigantic political and financial swindle [has breached] the obligations of prudence, objective caution and intellectual neutrality which must be respected by the academic researcher'.[39] As Salas noted, if such obligations are not respected, the role of the court will be to demonstrate 'the bad faith, the systematic lies and the perversity of the intentions', through the means of a contradictory debate. As he further observed, the judge has not been turned into the guardian of historical truth, and judicial control in cases of denial is in fact minimal. In his words, '[w]e are therefore far from a historical truth for which the judge would be the standard-bearer. We seem closer to a control of the manifest errors of appreciation. What matters is to unveil, behind the masks of historians, a manifestation of anti-Semitic propaganda',[40] or, in other words, a manifestation of hate propaganda.

37 Salas, Denis, 'Le droit peut-il contribuer au travail de mémoire?', in Association française pour l'histoire de la Justice, Commission nationale consultative des droits de l'homme, Ecole nationale de la magistrature, *La lutte contre le négationnisme* (Paris: La documentation Française, 2003), pp. 36–45 at 41.

38 See Tribunal de Grande Instance de Paris, Jugement, *Affaire Faurisson, Ligue internationale contre le racisme et l'antisémitisme et autres c. R. Faurisson*, 8 July 1981.

39 Translated by the authors. The original version reads: 'L'historien qui conclut que le génocide des juifs, tout comme l'existence affirmée des chambres à gaz, ne forment qu'un seul et même mensonge historique ayant permis une gigantesque escroquerie politico-financière [manque] aux obligations de prudence, de circonspection objective et de neutralité intellectuelle qui s'imposent au chercheur'. *Affaire Faurisson, supra* note 38.

40 Salas, Denis, *supra* note 37 at 41–2. Translation by the authors. The original version reads: 'On est donc loin d'une vérité historique dont le juge serait le porte-drapeau. On semble plus proche d'un contrôle des erreurs manifestes d'appréciation. Ce qui

In light of this, and in view of the gravity of the act of denial and the threat it potentially poses to democracy, two conclusions might be drawn; first, that instances of denial ought to be adjudged on a case-by-case basis, whereby all the above factors are granted due attention, so as to assess whether criminal sanctions would contravene democratic standards; and second, that legislative measures that outlaw denial, and the support they have found in Strasbourg, are well founded in law. Altogether more troubling, however, is a noticeable difference in the treatment of denial in relation to particular genocides – a development that seems, in recent times, to be perverting the legal and judicial landscapes, and which will, for this reason, be considered here in some detail.

4 Holocaust denial v. genocide denial: double standard in Strasbourg?

To exemplify this tendency, we will initially remain with the French context. For though the *loi Gayssot* does, as noted, famously penalise Holocaust denial, it stops short of criminalising the denial of other genocides. The obvious point of comparison here are the attempts to introduce legislation penalising the denial of the Armenian genocide. In October 2006, the French *Assemblée nationale* adopted, on first reading, a text proposing criminal sanctions against 'those who contest, by any of the means listed under Article 23 of the above-mentioned law, the existence of the 1915 Armenian genocide'.[41] In May 2011, the *Sénat* rejected the bill.[42] Later in the same year, a revised bill was put forward by the *Assemblée nationale*, now targeting 'those who contest or minimise in an excessive manner, by any means listed under Article 23 of the above-mentioned law, the existence of one or more crimes of genocide as defined under Article 211–1 of the Criminal Code and which are recognised as such under French law'.[43] This new bill was subsequently approved by both the *Assemblée nationale*[44] and the

compte est de dévoiler, derrière les masques de l'historien, une manifestation de propagande antisémite.'

41 Translation by the authors. The original version reads: 'ceux qui auront contesté, par un des moyens énoncés à l'article 23 de ladite loi, l'existence du génocide arménien de 1915.' See Assemblée nationale, Proposition de loi no. 3030 tendant à réprimer la contestation du génocide arménien (12 October 2006). Available at: www.senat.fr/leg/ppl06-020.html (accessed 17 February 2016). The text was submitted to the *Sénat* on 12 October 2006 but not put on the agenda.

42 The text was rejected by the *Sénat* on 4 May 2011. Available at: www.senat.fr/amendements/2009-2010/607/Amdt_1.html (accessed 17 February 2016).

43 Translation by the authors. The original version reads: 'ceux qui ont contesté ou minimisé de façon outrancière, par un des moyens énoncés à l'article 23, l'existence d'un ou plusieurs crimes de génocide défini à l'article 211–1 du code pénal et reconnus comme tels par la loi française.' See *Assemblée nationale*, Proposition de loi visant à réprimer la contestation de l'existence des génocides reconnus par la loi, texte adopté n° 813 (22 December 2011). Available at: www.assemblee-nationale.fr/13/ta/ta0813.asp (accessed 17 February 2016).

44 Ibid.

Sénat.[45] In February 2012, however, the *Conseil constitutionnel* deemed the law to be unconstitutional on the grounds that it would limit the fundamental right to freedom of expression and communication. In its decision, it held specifically:

> that a legislative provision having the objective of 'recognising' a crime of genocide would not itself have the normative scope which is characteristic of the law; that nonetheless, Article 1 of the law referred punishes the denial or minimisation of the existence of one or more crimes of genocide 'recognised as such under French law'; that in thereby punishing the denial of the existence and the legal classification of crimes which Parliament itself has recognised and classified as such, Parliament has imposed an unconstitutional limitation on the exercise of freedom of expression and communication.[46]

Bearing in mind that the Armenian genocide has, since 2001, already been recognised as such under French law,[47] and that this law had, at the time, not been considered unconstitutional for having 'a normative scope uncharacteristic of the law', this decision of the *Conseil constitutionnel* would appear to do little else than impede the criminalisation of the denial of this particular genocide while, under the *loi Gayssot*, denial of the Holocaust remains a punishable offence.[48] On several occasions since, President Hollande has reiterated his support for a law criminalising the denial of the Armenian genocide,[49] and he recently formally

45 *Sénat*, texte adopté n° 52 (23 January 2012).
46 *Conseil constitutionnel*, decision no. 2012-647-DC, 28 February 2012, para. 6. Available at: www.conseil-constitutionnel.fr/conseil-constitutionnel/english/case-law/decision/decision-no-2012-647-dc-of-28-february-2012.114637.html (accessed 17 February 2016).
47 Loi n° 2001-70 relative à la reconnaissance du génocide arménien de 1915 (29 January 2001). This law, which contains only one single article, is straightforwardly phrased in the following terms: 'la France reconnaît publiquement le génocide arménien de 1915' ['France publicly recognises the 1915 Armenian genocide']. This law had been interpreted by the *Tribunal de grande instance de Paris* as prohibiting the denial of the Armenian genocide. See Tribunal de Grande Instance de Paris, Judgment, *CDCA et autres* v. *Editions Robert Laffont, Encyclopédies Quid*, 17e chambre civile, 6 July 2005.
48 The *Conseil constitutionnel* very recently confirmed the constitutionality of the *loi Gayssot*. See *Conseil constitutionnel*, decision no. 2015-512 QPC, 8 January 2016. Available at: www.conseil-constitutionnel.fr/conseil-constitutionnel/francais/les-decisions/acces-par-date/decisions-depuis-1959/2016/2015-512-qpc/decision-n-2015-512-qpc-du-8-janvier-2016.146840.html (accessed 17 February 2016).
49 During his visit to Turkey in January 2014, President Hollande asked Turkey to perform its 'duty of remembrance'. He reaffirmed the importance of an anti-denial law in January 2015 before the *Conseil de coordination des organisations arméniennes de France*. In his speech delivered on 24 April 2015 to mark the centenary of the Armenian genocide he insisted on the importance of commemorating all instances of genocide, including explicitly the one against the Armenians. Available at: www.elysee.fr/declarations/article/discours-lors-des-commemorations-du-centenaire-du-genocide-armenien-2 (accessed 17 February 2016).

asked Jean-Paul Costa, former president of the European Court of Human Rights, to find the best legal way to ensure the protection of the memory of the Armenian genocide through a law that would – this time – give rise to no contestation.[50] As the legislation currently stands, however, there remains a clear discrepancy relating to particular instances of genocide.

The evident incoherence in the French legislation is problematic to say the least. Again recently, there has been a clear illustration of the apparent difference in terms of the willingness to criminalise the denial of particular genocides. While attempts to push through legislation on the Armenian genocide are marked by reticence and resistance, French courts had no hesitation in condemning Dieudonné M'Bala M'Bala for public insults characterised by Holocaust denial and anti-Semitic discourse during one of his performances.[51] What is questionable here is not the condemnation of M'Bala M'Bala for Holocaust denial but rather the fact that by protecting some genocides from denial and not others, the French legislator has created a discrepancy – if not a hierarchy in crimes – that is hardly justifiable.

Broadening our gaze, it is apparent that this is not a French trait; similar discrepancies also seem to have infiltrated the case law of the European Court of Human Rights. Following his condemnation by French courts, M'Bala M'Bala lodged an application with the Strasbourg Court for breach of Article 10 – an application that was declared inadmissible[52] on the grounds that:

> since [M'Bala M'Bala's] acts were unmistakeably negationist and anti-Semitic in nature … [he] had sought to deflect Article 10 from its real purpose by using his right to freedom of expression for ends which were incompatible with the letter and spirit of the Convention and which, if admitted, would contribute to the destruction of Convention rights and freedoms.[53]

Yet, less than a month before, the Grand Chamber had reached an opposite decision in the case opposing Dogu Perinçek to Switzerland.[54] While on a lecture tour in Switzerland in 2005, the applicant, leader of the Turkish Workers' Party, had made several public declarations that the Armenian genocide was no more than an 'international lie'.[55] Following a criminal complaint filed by the

50 François Hollande, Speech before the *Conseil de coordination des organisations arméniennes de France*, 28 January 2016. Available at: www.elysee.fr/declarations/article/discours-au-conseil-de-coordination-des-organisations-armeniennes-de-france-3/ (accessed 17 February 2016).

51 See Cour d'appel de Paris, Judgment, 17 March 2011 and Cour de cassation, ch. crim., N° de pourvoi: 11-82866, 16 October 2012, *Bulletin criminel* 2012, n° 217.

52 ECtHR, Decision, *M'Bala M'Bala* v. *France*, Application No. 25239/13, 10 November 2015.

53 Ibid.

54 *Perinçek* v. *Switzerland*, *supra* note 30.

55 ECtHR, Judgment, *Perinçek* v. *Switzerland*, Application No. 27510/08, 17 December 2013, paras 7, 13, 51, 63 and 71.

association *Suisse-Arménie*, the *tribunal de police* in Lausanne convicted him of racial discrimination according to Article 261*bis* of the Swiss Criminal Code, finding that his motives had been of a fundamentally racist character rather than the expression of a wish to contribute to an elevated historical or public debate.[56] Perinçek's subsequent appeal against the finding of the police court was dismissed by the *Cour de cassation pénale du Tribunal cantonal du canton de Vaud* on the grounds that the Armenian genocide is, just like the Holocaust, an incontestable historical truth, recognised as such by the Swiss legislature.[57] Following the dismissal of his appeal to the Swiss Federal Court,[58] Perinçek brought his case to Strasbourg, claiming a breach of his freedom of expression as protected by Article 10 of the ECHR. In December 2013, five out of the seven judges hearing the case ruled in favour of Perinçek, stating that the grounds given by the national authorities to validate the conviction were insufficient.[59] In a judgment of 15 October 2015, the Grand Chamber confirmed, by a small majority of ten votes to seven, the finding of violation of Article 10.[60]

How, then, might this discrepancy in Strasbourg be justified? To assess this, a closer look at the *Perinçek* decision is needed. A first point to note is that the Grand Chamber initially distanced itself from determining whether laws criminalising genocide denial are justified, thereby seemingly deferring to national courts. Nonetheless, it granted, much as the Chamber had done in 2013,[61] quite some weight to the political aspect of the applicant's speech, unconvincingly drawing from it the fact that his comments related to a topic of legitimate public interest and did not amount to a call for intolerance and hatred.[62] The Chamber

56 See *Tribunal de police de l'arrondissement de Lausanne*, Judgment, 9 March 2007. Article 261*bis* § 4 of the Criminal Code states that 'any person who publicly denigrates or discriminates against another or a group of persons on the grounds of their race, ethnic origin or religion in a manner that violates human dignity, whether verbally, in writing or pictorially, by using gestures, through acts of aggression or by other means, or any person who on any of these grounds denies, trivialises or seeks justification for genocide or other crimes against humanity'. Official translation from the Swiss Federal Council. Available at: www.admin.ch/opc/en/classified-compilation/19370083/index.html (accessed 17 February 2016).

57 *Cour de cassation pénale du Tribunal cantonal du canton de Vaud*, Judgment, 13 June 2007.

58 *Tribunal fédéral, Cour de droit pénal*, Judgment, 12 December 2007.

59 *Perinçek* v. *Switzerland, supra* note 55, para. 129.

60 *Perinçek* v. *Switzerland, supra* note 30. See Garibian, Sévane, 'ECHR Ruling Doesn't Mean an "End" to Genocide Denial Criminalization', *Panorama*, 26 October 2015. Available at: www.panorama.am/en/news/2015/10/26/sevan-gharibyan/1468914 (accessed 17 February 2016). See also Garibian, Sévane, 'The Polarization in Grand Chamber is Important', AGOS, 27 October 2015. Available at: www.agos.com.tr/en/article/13158/svane-garibian-the-polarization-in-grand-chamber-is-important (accessed 17 February 2016).

61 See *Perinçek* v. *Switzerland, supra* note 55, para. 231: 'Even though the applicant's statements touched upon historical and legal issues, the context in which they were made – at public events where the applicant was speaking to like-minded supporters – shows that he spoke as a politician, not as a historical or legal scholar.'

62 Ibid., paras 239–41.

also noted that the context in which the statements were made was not characterised by heightened tensions or specific historical circumstances that might give them greater inflammatory potential.[63] Neither consideration is particularly compelling in terms of justifying the difference in the decisions – like Perinçek, M'Bala M'Bala is engaged in a form of political discourse, yet the Strasbourg Court ignored the alleged political aspects of his speech. Likewise, it did not consider whether the applicant's show took place in a context of tensions. How, precisely, Perinçek's discourse differs from that of M'Bala M'Bala, and how or why it should be deemed more worthy of protection, thus remains obscure. Is the Court establishing a hierarchy of genocides, with the memories of some of them worthy of protection against denial and others not?[64]

The Court's justification for the decision in *Perinçek* may be seen to grant additional weight to this view. Two key considerations might be highlighted in this regard. First, the Court found the Swiss provision to be too broad and general in comparison with the legislation in force in other high contracting parties and to '[stand] out at one end of the comparative spectrum'.[65] In its written memorandum, the Swiss government had outlined how its provision on genocide denial was adopted in line with the work and recommendations of the Committee on the Elimination of Racial Discrimination (CERD). The Grand Chamber questioned, however, whether the CERD obliged the Swiss government to criminalise denial, averring that the Committee held that '"the expression of opinions about historical facts" should not be prohibited or punished'.[66] In doing so, the Grand Chamber conveniently left out the CERD's recommendation to criminalise negationist discourse – a key point picked up on in the dissenting opinion of Judges Spielmann, Casadevall, Berro, De Gaetano, Sicilianos, Silvis and Kūris.[67] In its annual report in 1997, the Committee had praised the legislation on denial introduced by Germany and Belgium while, however, considering their exclusive focus on the genocide perpetrated by Nazi Germany too restrictive.[68] Taking here an opposite stand, the Grand Chamber adjudged the Swiss law to be too general. That the Grand Chamber does not feel bound by the CERD is, in itself, not especially problematic; that it selectively picks and chooses among the CERD's findings is, however, questionable.

---

63 Ibid., para. 153.
64 See Garibian, Sévane, 'Liberté d'expression à Strasbourg: deux poids, deux mesures?', *Le Temps*, 30 November 2015. Available at: www.letemps.ch/opinions/ 2015/11/30/liberte-expression-strasbourg-deux-poids-deux-mesures (accessed 17 February 2016).
65 *Perinçek v. Switzerland, supra* note 30, para. 256.
66 Ibid., para. 261.
67 ECtHR, Joint dissenting opinion of judges Spielmann, Casadevall, Berro, De Gaetano, Sicilianos, Silvis and Kūris, *Perinçek v. Switzerland, supra* note 30, para. 10.
68 Annual Report of the Committee for the Elimination of Racial Discrimination, 26 September 1997, UN Doc. A/52/18, pp. 32 and 33.

Second, and although it specified that national authorities were in a better position to decide on the necessity to criminalise genocide denial, the Grand Chamber nonetheless felt fit to decide that Perinçek's comments could not be considered as violating the dignity of members of the Armenian community to such an extent as to warrant a criminal law response in Switzerland.[69] Part of the rationale here was that the links between Switzerland and the Armenian people were not particularly strong and that, as such, it was 'not necessary, in a democratic society, to subject the applicant to a criminal penalty in order to protect the rights of the Armenian community [...]'.[70] This statement appears somewhat troubling, as it seems to convey that a State might only, in theory at least, denounce and criminalise denial of a particular genocide if it has – or had – its own close links to the victim group. As Judges Spielmann, Casadevall, Berro, De Gaetano, Sicilianos, Silvis and Kūris noted in their joint dissenting opinion:

> Drawing all the logical inferences from the geographically restricted approach apparently adopted by the majority, one might come to the view that denial in Europe of genocides perpetrated in other continents, such as the Rwandan genocide or the genocide carried out by the Khmer Rouge regime in Cambodia, would be protected by freedom of expression without any limits, or with scarcely any. We do not believe that such a vision reflects the universal values enshrined in the Convention.[71]

Further still, the geographical limitations drawn by the Grand Chamber could lead one to the view that, other than in the country where the genocide was perpetrated, genocide denial simply cannot be criminalised. After all, which other State might claim to have close enough links with the victim group? In this view, Rwanda would probably qualify as the only State entitled to criminalise the denial of the 1994 genocide. Similarly, Bosnia would be the only legitimate State able to penalise the denial of the Srebrenica genocide. To date, the Holocaust is the sole genocide to have transcended frontiers and to have spread throughout Europe – is it therefore the only genocide worthy of protection against denial in Europe, based on geographical considerations? The findings of the Grand Chamber would appear to answer this question in the affirmative:

> This is particularly relevant with regard to the Holocaust. For the Court, the justification for making its denial a criminal offence lies not so much in that it is a clearly established historical fact but in that, in view of the historical context in the States concerned – the cases examined by the former Commission and the Court have thus far concerned Austria, Belgium, Germany

69 *Perinçek* v. *Switzerland, supra* note 30, para. 280.
70 Ibid.
71 Joint dissenting opinion of judges Spielmann, Casadevall, Berro, De Gaetano, Sicilianos, Silvis and Kūris, *Perinçek* v. *Switzerland, supra* note 30, para. 7.

and France … – its denial, even if dressed up as impartial historical research, must invariably be seen as connoting an antidemocratic ideology and anti-Semitism. Holocaust denial is thus doubly dangerous, especially in States which have experienced the Nazi horrors, and which may be regarded as having a special moral responsibility to distance themselves from the mass atrocities that they have perpetrated or abetted by, among other things, outlawing their denial.

By contrast, it has not been argued that there was a direct link between Switzerland and the events that took place in the Ottoman Empire in 1915 and the following years. *The only such link may come from the presence of an Armenian community on Swiss soil, but it is a tenuous one.*[72]

In the eyes of the Court, this 'tenuous link' also explains that 'statements that contest, even in virulent terms, the significance of historical events that carry a special sensitivity for a country and touch on its national identity cannot in themselves be regarded as seriously affecting their addressees'.[73] Not content with imposing geographical limitations, the Grand Chamber also seemingly created a timeframe and, in view of 'the amount of time that had elapsed since the events to which the applicant was referring', concluded 'that his statements cannot be seen as having the significantly upsetting effect sought to be attributed to them'.[74] The Grand Chamber here seems to be suggesting that the passage of time heals the sufferings generated by genocide and its denial – a suggestion that seems at odds with the international non-applicability of statutory limitations to genocide[75] and which prompts the question of the future of anti-Holocaust denial legislation in 30 years.

For now, however, the Holocaust seems to be exempt from any such condition, for, as stated by the Court, 'Holocaust denial, even if dressed up as impartial historical research, must invariably be seen as connoting an antidemocratic ideology and anti-Semitism … and must thus, at this stage, be regarded as particularly upsetting for the persons concerned'.[76] This presumption of anti-democratic and anti-Semitic (or in other words racist) character that attaches exclusively to Holocaust denial[77] is hardly justifiable. That genocide denial can be deprived of hate and/or racist motives is already difficult to imagine concretely but can be, theoretically at least, accepted. What seems unsustainable, however, is the exclusivity and automaticity of this presumption to Holocaust denial; an exclusivity which also appears, as shall be briefly discussed here prior to concluding, to sit uncomfortably with other European endeavours aimed at punishing genocide denial.

---

72   *Perinçek* v. *Switzerland*, *supra* note 30, paras 243–4 (emphasis added).
73   Ibid., para. 253.
74   Ibid., para. 252.
75   See Art. 29, ICC Statute.
76   *Perinçek* v. *Switzerland*, *supra* note 30, para. 253.
77   See also ibid. para. 234. See Garibian, Sévane, 'Liberté d'expression à Strasbourg: deux poids, deux mesures?', *supra* note 64.

5 The criminalisation of genocide denial: equality of treatment in Brussels?

In 1995, the European Parliament's Kahn Commission made a proposal that all Member States should establish specific laws on Holocaust denial and the trivialisation of other crimes against humanity. Within the framework of the EU, attempts continue to be made to reach a common basis of rules for confronting denial that can be readily applied across national borders – a task made all the more difficult by the fundamental differences in national attitudes toward freedom of expression and the possibility of its proscription in law. An initial move in the direction of establishing common rules was marked by the adoption of the Joint Action 96/443/JHA of 15 July 1996 regarding actions to combat racism and xenophobia.[78] States were urged to take steps to ensure that the public denial of the crimes listed under Article 6 of the Charter of the International Military Tribunal (IMT) – and thus linked to the Second World War – is a punishable offence insofar as it involves conduct that is contemptuous of, or degrading to, a group defined via reference to colour, race, religion, or national or ethnic origin. This led to the adoption of the EU Framework Decision on combating certain forms and expressions of racism and xenophobia by means of criminal law[79] – a move which, while leaving some room for States to limit the scope of national provisions criminalising genocide denial, nonetheless harmonises a European-wide approach by compelling States to penalise denial when performed in a manner likely either to incite to violence or hatred or to disturb public order. Interestingly, the Framework Decision emancipated the prohibition of denial from the Second World War by including within its scope not only the denial of those crimes that fell under the jurisdiction of the IMT but also of those crimes that trigger the jurisdiction of the ICC. It could also be seen as heralding far-reaching changes, requesting that each Member State 'take the measures necessary to ensure' that '*publicly condoning, denying or grossly trivialising crimes of genocide, crimes against humanity and war crimes* as defined in Articles 6, 7 and 8 of the Statute of the International Criminal Court' and '*publicly condoning, denying or grossly trivialising the crimes defined in Article 6 of the Charter of the International Military Tribunal* appended to the London Agreement of 8 August 1945' are 'punishable by criminal penalties'.[80]

For this Framework Decision to be a European initiative holds a remarkable symbolic value. Europe, theatre of violence for much of the twentieth century and

---

78 Joint Action 96/443/JHA of 15 July 1996 adopted by the Council on the basis of Article K.3 of the Treaty on European Union, concerning action to combat racism and xenophobia.

79 Council framework decision 2008/913/JHA on combating certain forms and expressions of racism and xenophobia by means of criminal law, 28 November 2008, OJ L 328/55, 6 December 2008.

80 Ibid. (emphasis added). See Lobba, Paolo, 'Punishing Denialism beyond Holocaust Denial: EU Framework Decision 2008/913/JHA and Other Expansive Trends', (2014) 5 *New Journal of European Criminal Law*, 58–77.

arena of some of the most heinous deeds perpetrated in the name of racist and totalitarian ideologies, is now taking a clear stand against racism and xenophobia as well as against the denial of genocides, crimes against humanity and war crimes. Yet, this legislative step may well remain purely symbolic. The deadline for the transposition of the Decision in the domestic systems of the Member States, 28 November 2010, is now long gone and the majority of the Western European legal systems have failed to comply with their obligations in this context, demonstrating once again that the adoption of anti-denial legislation is a complex undertaking.

6 Conclusion

The aim of this contribution has not been to advocate in favour of or against the criminalisation of genocide denial but rather, and as indicated in its very title, to offer an *état des lieux* of the current legal situation. Its purpose has essentially been threefold. First, it has attempted to demonstrate the ongoing uncertainty that continues to attach to the legal qualification of genocide denial, and which stems from the possible variety of legal sources in both human rights law and international criminal law. Second, it has exposed the limits of freedom of expression, which cannot simply be a catch-all defence for legitimising all speech and expression. Third, it has highlighted two troubling developments in recent legislation and case law – namely the construction of an apparent hierarchy of genocides and the imposition of geographical limitations – that obstruct rather than aid a consistent response to instances of denial.

The enquiry on the balance between genocide denial and freedom of expression, as an overarching concern, is related first and foremost to human rights standards and legal norms. That there remains here some uncertainty is clear, founded on the fact that denial has not, as yet, been legally qualified as a form of hate speech. This lack of qualification still carries some potential to undermine, or at the very least problematise, the prohibition of denial. The limitations on freedom of expression, together with the character of denial as a clear infringement upon, and threat to, democratic principles, opens the way for an understanding of anti-denial legislation as compatible with human rights standards. Were denial to be recognised as incitement to genocide – that is to say, as a violation of international criminal law – the grounds for prohibition would undeniably be stronger. In view of the grave nature of the act, and its potential to form part of the pattern of genocidal occurrence, an additional provision in the Genocide Convention to cover such acts may also constitute a positive development. Such a revision remains, however, highly unlikely: not only has the Convention never been revised since its adoption, but current ongoing uncertainties and controversies surrounding the issue of genocide denial are bound to put a halt to any attempt to amend it.

In view of such difficulties in enacting legislation, a concluding remark might be made on the viability of legal measures as a means of combating genocide denial. Perhaps it is the case that the legal reflection on the adequacy of anti-denial legislation needs to adopt a more purpose-based approach and consider the goal of such legislation. For advocating the adoption of a legislation that is never likely to materialise or which is going to be so controversial that it will never be implemented in practice might well be defeating the ultimate aim of effectively discrediting deniers' claims. Deniers 'misstate, misquote, falsify statistics, and falsely attribute conclusions to reliable sources';[81] they falsify history and distort the truth to trigger debates on an issue where there is, precisely, no debate or, in the words of Lipstadt, no 'other side'.[82] Denying genocide is thus not an opinion, it is a lie. Which poses the question: can a lie be effectively countered via legal prohibition?

81 Lipstadt, Deborah, *Denying the Holocaust – The Growing Assault on Truth and Memory* (Harlow: Penguin Books, 1994), p. 111.
82 Ibid.

Chapter 15

Why not the law?

Options for dealing with genocide and Holocaust denial

Paul Behrens

1 Introduction

The disturbing effect of denialism manifests itself in various forms. One of its most troubling aspects must be seen in the implied message that it typically carries: that the survivors of grave atrocities are dishonest about their own experiences.[1] Where such statements are made publicly or are directly addressed at victims, their consequences can be devastating: they impose new suffering on those who already have to deal with the traumatic consequences of the inhumane treatment to which they had been subjected in the past.

Denialism leads to marginalisation. Where it is carried out with the relevant intention, it represents an attempt to attack the dignity of those who deserve the greatest degree of solidarity by the society in which they live. It thus challenges the State as well: if left unchecked, denialist activities can foster grave divisions and may even prepare the ground for the commission of new crimes against groups who had already been victims to atrocities.[2]

On that basis, it is understandable that recourse to the criminal justice system has become a tool of choice for some societies in their search for methods to counter denialism. Today, several States prohibit denial of the Holocaust; others have enshrined laws dealing with denial of genocide more generally.[3] Yet criminalisation also broaches issues that require further analysis: it raises, in particular, questions about the co-existence of criminalisation with specific human rights whose guarantee may be incumbent upon the relevant State, and it also invites

---

1 See on this Human Rights Committee, *Robert Faurisson v. France*, Communication No. 550/1993, UN Doc. CCPR/C/58/D/550/1993 (1996), Individual opinion by Elizabeth Evatt and David Kretzmer, co-signed by Eckart Klein, para. 6; and Aleksandra Gliszczyńska-Grabiasa, 'Memory Laws or Memory Loss? Europe in Search of its Historical Identity through the National and International Law', 3 *Polish Yearbook of International Law* (2014), 172.

2 On the facilitation of renewed oppression through negationism, see Gliszczyńska-Grabiasa, n 1 above. See also ECtHR Grand Chamber, *Perinçek v. Switzerland* (Application no. 27510/08), (2016) 63 EHRR 6, Judgment, 15 October 2015, 243.

3 See above, Chapter 11, at nn 30–3.

doubts about the efficiency of sanctions of the criminal justice system where denialist activities are concerned.

This chapter explores these points by providing, in its first part, a critique of the reasons and the consequences of criminalisation in this context. In a second part, it explores several alternatives to laws on denial in its 'basic' form, including modifications of the legal approach, but also the possibility of truth and reconciliation commissions and direct confrontation with the deniers. The last part offers concluding thoughts on the risks that attach to criminalisation and on the efficiency of alternative options.

The concept of 'genocide' in this chapter (unless otherwise indicated) is the social, rather than the legal, understanding of the term:[4] it is thus primarily understood as the broader historical macro phenomenon rather than individual conduct that attracted criminal liability. The conflation of the two concepts is, however, at the root of some of the difficulties that have arisen in the application of genocide denial laws – a point to which this study will return.[5]

2 A critical review of criminalisation and its consequences

For States seeking to counter denialist activities, the sanctions of criminal law appear to offer appropriate tools on the basis of two main perspectives: they respond to the harm that denialism may carry, but they also convey a moral message to perpetrators and society alike.

However, the very nature of the relevant activities and the character of legal sanctions mean that doubts about the suitability of this path cannot be dismissed. Criminalisation also raises questions with regard to its impact on human rights obligations of the State resorting to sanctions of this kind, and lastly, the question arises whether legal sanctions are indeed efficient measures in the fight against denialism, or if they might, in fact, have counter-productive effects.

These are considerations which invite a more detailed analysis of criminalisation. The following sub-sections thus engage in a critical examination of the relevant aspects: sub-section 2.1 deals with the rationale underlying criminalisation, sub-section 2.2 with its impact on human rights, and sub-section 2.3 with the efficiency of the relevant measures.

2.1 The rationale underlying criminalisation: questions of harm and morals

The very concept of law signifies more than an accumulation of rules: if that were not the case, it would not be much different from the rules of hierarchy governing

---

4 See on this distinction Stefan Kirsch, 'The Social and the Legal Concept of Genocide', in Paul Behrens and Ralph Henham, *Elements of Genocide* (Routledge, 2012), 7 et seq.; and Larissa van den Herik, 'The Schism between the Legal and the Social Concept of Genocide in Light of the Responsibility to Protect', in Ralph Henham and Paul Behrens, *The Criminal Law of Genocide* (Ashgate, 2007), 75 et seq.
5 See below after n 51.

a criminal organisation. Nor could a State ever be said to possess an effective legal system if obedience to the law relied on it being enforced every step of the way: no State has sufficient resources for that kind of enforcement system. The reason why law tends to 'work' is that the population on the whole is willing to accept it, and the reason it accepts it is because it is understood as embodying, at least on a most basic level, a moral mandate.[6]

That is particularly true where criminal law is concerned: legal moralism represents one of the principal ways of justifying its existence.[7] A system that allows for significant intrusions into the lives of individuals calls for a particularly strong moral mandate as its basis.

The sharp sanctions that the State feels entitled to adopt receive their justification through the fact that the perpetrator's conduct deviated manifestly from fundamental values of society. Legal moralism has attracted criticism in the past,[8] but it is at the very least difficult to deny that it is one of the functions of the criminal law to reassert the value system which the State has established for itself.

For States seeking to counter denialism, the seductive appeal of legal moralism is apparent. The rules and sanctions of the law appear as bearers of a specific message: if a society has chosen this route, it has elevated truth and the memory of the events to the level of values worthy of the protection of the criminal justice system. In States in which the perpetrators of these crimes first came to power, laws of this kind may be intended to carry a message of special meaning: not only that of a renunciation of the policies of the past, but one also of solidarity with the victims.

It is a different question whether these aspirations are achieved and whether criminal law is the best tool to achieve them. For one, it is not always clear whether the law does indeed convey a message of solidarity. Its message may go in the opposite direction: i.e. that society would not be inclined to show solidarity were it not for the cudgel of the law. The value system which is thus promoted may look quite different to an impartial observer than to the drafters of such legislation.

Furthermore, criminalisation of denial is, by necessity, exclusive: even if the message of solidarity were adequately conveyed, it would be solidarity only with victims of particular crimes. The divisive effect of such laws carries the danger of blurring the moral message that the legislators intended to send out.

One example is the European Framework Decision, which addresses denialism in the context of crimes against humanity, genocide and war crimes, but only when those crimes were directed 'against a group of persons or a member of such a group defined by reference to race, colour, religion, descent or national or

---

6 For a different view on the underlying intentions of the law, cf Richard Quinney, *The Social Reality of Crime* (1970).
7 See on this Chris Clarkson, Heather Keating, Sally Cunningham, *Criminal Law* (Sweet & Maxwell, 2007), 5.
8 Often with good reason, cf Tony Honoré, 'The Dependence of Morality on Law', 13 *Oxford Journal of Legal Studies* (1993), 1, in particular at 4 and 9.

ethnic origin'.[9] The fact that victims defined, for example, by their political belief are not covered by the Decision, led to the somewhat embarrassing situation that the Council of the European Union (EU), in a press release, had to assure observers that it still 'deplore[d] all of these crimes'.[10]

There is another aspect which raises questions about legal moralism as the rationale underlying criminalisation. The invocation of this basis carries the danger that the prevailing moral framework of a particular society appears as an independent justification, separate from the value system of the international community, in which the State is embedded. But a State's incorporation in that system presupposes acceptance of its fundamental values which thus are capable of giving shape to the moral message behind the relevant legal provision and may lead to a restriction or expansion of its scope. Chief among these values are the human rights whose protection the State owes to individuals under its jurisdiction. As these are questions that come into play not only where legal moralism is concerned, it appears appropriate to allow them consideration in a separate section.[11]

Where the criminal justice system is concerned, legal moralism as a rationale for the existence of norms of criminal law is often joined by another consideration: the understanding that criminal law finds its justification in the need to punish perpetrators of harm.[12] It is a perspective whose force derives from the very foundations of civil society: the assumption of society's right to exist implies a right of protection against those engaged in harming it.

On the face of it, the harm principle appears well suited as a basis for the outlawing of denial and revisionism. Its significance is manifested in several ways. For one, denialist activities have a direct impact on the survivors of the under-lying atrocities. The nature of that impact may vary and will in some cases include both psychological and physical damage. In any event, however, denial-ism objectively carries a message that targets the dignity of the survivors, and it appears appropriate in this context to consider such conduct akin to criminal insult.[13]

But the fact has also been emphasised that consequences of the conduct can extend beyond their impact on survivors. Given the often racist agenda that

---

9 Council Framework Decision 2008/913/JHA of 28 November 2008 on Combating Certain Forms and Expressions of Racism and Xenophobia by Means of Criminal Law, *Official Journal* L 328, 06/12/2008 P.0055–0058 (hereinafter Framework Decision), Art.1(1)(c).

10 Council of the European Union, 'I' Item Note, 11523/07, 19 July 2007, at register. consilium.europa.eu/pdf/en/07/st11/st11523.en07.pdf. For similarly restrictive norms, see s. 130(3) of the German Criminal Code and the French Loi Gayssot, cf Jacqueline Lechtholz-Zey, 'The Laws Banning Genocide Denial', 9 *Genocide Prevention Now* (2012) at note 22.

11 See below, text at note 24.

12 See Clarkson et al., n 7 above.

13 On the concept of insults in international and domestic law, see Paul Behrens, *Diplomatic Interference and the Law* (Oxford and Oregon: Hart Publishing, 2016), 220–1.

underlies genocide denial,[14] such activities typically carry a discriminatory message to the target audience – and this, indeed, may often lie at the heart of the conduct.

This was a point that the Spanish government outlined in the case of Pedro Varela Geiss – a bookseller who was charged with the distribution of material that 'denied, trivialized or justified' the Holocaust.[15] Counsel for the government pointed out that 'professing [...] doctrines' of genocide denial might create an environment that fosters certain forms of legal discrimination, followed by encouragement of the emigration of parts of the population, then spreading to 'all fields of human coexistence until [it reaches] the extremes of extermination and annihilation well documented by History'.[16]

Denialism, if this view were followed, carries the seed for the commission of further international crimes. It is not an entirely theoretical argument: the fact may be recalled that the Iranian President Ahmadinejad, at the 2006 'Holocaust Review Conference', to which he had invited some of the world's most prominent deniers,[17] made use of this platform to repeat his verbal aggression against Israel, stating that 'the Zionist regime [will] soon be wiped out'.[18]

From this perspective, the harm principle appears to offer a sound basis for an endeavour to outlaw denialist activities.

At the same time, the exceptionally intrusive nature of criminal law also demands that a particularly high threshold has to be imposed on conduct that is to fall within its framework. The mere possibility of certain harm cannot suffice; what is required is that such harm is the product of conduct of this kind and that such conduct indeed calls for criminalisation on this basis.

This raises questions about the behaviour at the root of the harm that the legislation seeks to avoid. Both in the cases of Varela Geiss and of Ahmadinejad, the argument can be advanced that that conduct was not formed solely by the activity of denial as such (which shall here be termed 'basic denial'). The reason why the relevant harm could have materialised was the fact that the statements of denial were accessible to a wider audience.

If 'basic denial' as such were criminalised, it would suffice that the relevant words were spoken in the privacy of the perpetrator's living room (perchance overheard by a neighbour), or to a very limited audience which may even be opposed to the perpetrator's views. The consequences of conduct of this kind might be significantly limited.

---

14 Cf Russell L. Weaver, Nicolas Delpierre and Laurence Boissier, 'Holocaust Denial and Governmentally Declared "Truth": French and American Perspectives', 41 *Tex. Tech L. Rev.* (2009), 512.
15 Pablo Salvador Coderch and Antoni Rubí Puig, 'Genocide Denial and Freedom of Speech', *In Dret. Revista Para el Análisis del Derecho* (2008), 13.
16 Ibid., at 16.
17 *US Fed News*, 'Top Academics, Political Leaders Seek "Incitement to Genocide" Charges Against Iran, President Ahmadinejad', 12 December 2006.
18 Ibid. See Chapter 11 above.

Even then, however, harm exists, if it is accepted that the dignity of a relevant group (such as the surviving victims) has come under attack. But the assumption that the law might be the appropriate means to regulate dignity, has faced criticism in the past.

Knechtle, when discussing the EU Framework Decision on racism and xenophobia and its provisions on denialism,[19] expresses the view that dignity 'comes from within – well beyond the reach of the law', and suggests that human dignity is best recognised by the State if it 'respect[s] the individual's right to speak'.[20]

In this generalised form, this statement is open to criticism: just as a State granting unbridled liberty ends up promoting not its weakest citizens, but its greatest bullies, so a State granting unbridled freedom of speech may end up supporting not those who speak the truth but those who shout the loudest. Yet it is true that laws outlawing denial may generate a counter-productive impact: instead of accepting as self-evident that victims of international crimes exist and are deserving of dignity, the message is now advanced that these facts live in such an imperilled state that they require the crutch of the law. Whether this enhances the dignity of the survivors is at best questionable.

If on the other hand the offensive conduct were understood in a more restrictive sense – encompassing not every form of basic denial, but at least the dissemination of this message to an audience – it would be possible to capture additional harmful consequences through the law.[21] Even if the immediate audience did not show any direct reaction to the message, it is possible that the message has a persuasive effect upon them, and that they in turn would be encouraged to engage in denialism. In that sense, denial is capable of creating secondary harm,[22] for the spreading of the word can be seen as giving rise to a wide range of consequences, from the establishment of a racist climate to the effects to which the Spanish government referred in Varela Geiss.[23]

But the acceptance of secondary harm carries its own difficulties. It presupposes, in particular, a chain of causation between the conduct of the perpetrator and the end result. The existence of such a chain is not always inevitable: intervening steps are often required to achieve the result that the law seeks to prevent. Criminal law which relies on secondary harm as its rationale, is a dangerous beast: once it has been accepted as justification in one case, it may easily be employed in other contexts in which the motivation behind a particular law may be based on partisan political views rather than the genuine need to prevent specified damage.

---

19 Cf Article 1(1)(c) Framework Decision, n 9 above.
20 John C. Knechtle, 'Holocaust Denial and the Concept of Dignity in the European Union', 36 *Fla. St. U. L. Rev.* (2008), 41, 43.
21 See on this aspect below, text at n 73 et seq.
22 See on secondary harms in particular Anthony Dillof, 'Modal Retributivism: A Theory of Sanctions for Attempts and Other Criminal Wrongs', 45 *U. Rich. L. Rev.* (2011), 647, 662.
23 See above, text at n 16.

2.2 Criminalisation in the context of human rights

The possibility that laws on genocide and Holocaust denial may have a restrictive impact on human rights is one of the key issues in the contemporary debate on criminalisation.

Freedom of expression, as enshrined in the leading human rights treaties,[24] occupies a prominent place in that discussion. It is a right that finds defenders even among fierce antagonists of Holocaust deniers: Deborah Lipstadt for one, whom David Irving had sued for libel following his portrayal as a denier in her 1994 book,[25] stated in 2006 that she did not 'think Holocaust denial should be a crime [...] I am a free speech person, I am against censorship'.[26] Simone Veil, a politician and survivor of Auschwitz, similarly noted her concerns about the French Loi Gayssot.[27]

At the same time, the question has arisen of whether the denial of certain facts comes within the reach of the right to begin with. The European Court of Human Rights (ECtHR) found in *Lingens* in 1986 that 'a careful distinction needs to be made between facts and value-judgments. The existence of facts can be demonstrated, whereas the truth of value-judgments is not susceptible of proof'.[28]

That, however, appears to be a somewhat simplified understanding – in light in particular of the difficulties that the 'demonstration of facts' can occasionally encounter.

One may consider a situation in which bones are unearthed amid allegations that international crimes have taken place. The need for interpretative assessment begins with the very question of whether the remains are human in nature. If uniforms are found, can they be positively said to belong to one particular party to a conflict? Can a positive assessment be made that death was caused in a violent way? If that is done, can a positive assessment be made as to the authors of the killings?

If these questions are seen as 'mere' questions of factual assessment, then a State could regulate statements made on any of these points.[29] But the truth is

---

24 International Covenant on Civil and Political Rights (ICCPR), 16 December 1966, 999 UNTS 171, Art.19(2); American Convention on Human Rights (ACHR), 21 November 1969, 1144 UNTS 123, Art.13(1); European Convention for the Protection of Human Rights and Fundamental Freedoms (ECHR), 4 April 1950, 213 UNTS 221, Art.10(1).
25 Deborah Lipstadt, *Denying the Holocaust* (Plume, 1994); *Irving v. Penguin Books Ltd, Deborah E. Lipstadt*, 2000 WL 362478.
26 Brendan O'Neill, '"Irving? Let the Guy Go Home"', 4 January 2006, *BBC Online*, at news.bbc.co.uk/1/hi/uk/4578534.stm.
27 Ludovic Hennebel and Thomas Hochmann, *Genocide Denials and the Law* (Oxford University Press, 2011), 203.
28 *Lingens v. Austria* (Application no. 9815/82), Judgment 8 July 1986, para. 46.
29 An obvious example is the question of the authorship of the Katyn massacres. *Agence France Presse*, 'Memorial to Polish Victims of Stalin Unveiled in Kiev', 21 September 2012. For a more recent situation, see Oliver Holmes and Mariam Karouny, 'Dozens of Syrian Civilians Killed in Homs', *The Independent*, 12 March 2012.

that even statements of fact require assessment, beginning with the allocation of conceptual categories to objects and reaching an inevitable stage where the need for more complex layers of conclusions is involved.

There is evidence that some courts consider problematic the differentiation which the ECtHR had adopted. In *Zundel*, the Canadian Supreme Court found that the distinction between claims of fact and expressions of opinion was 'a question of great difficulty and the question of falsity of a statement is often a matter of debate'.[30] And when the US Supreme Court in *Alvarez* had to deal with the 'Stolen Valor Act' of 2005 – a statute making it an offence for anyone to pretend to have received a 'decoration or medal authorized by Congress for the Armed Forces of the United States' – ,[31] it confirmed that the Act violated the First Amendment to the US Constitution (protecting, *inter alia*, freedom of speech).[32] In his concurring opinion, Justice Breyer took exception to the argument that false factual statements should enjoy no protection, finding that they might, under certain circumstances, even 'serve useful human objectives' – for instance, if they were used to protect privacy, to provide ill people with comfort, and in contexts in which false statements were made to allow their examination and 'to promote a form of thought that ultimately helps realize the truth'.[33]

In the context of human rights law, this appears a preferable approach. It is, furthermore, an interpretation that carries a greater degree of compatibility with a literal understanding of the leading instruments, whose protection clearly extends beyond the freedom of expression of 'opinions'.[34]

That does not mean that the emerging freedom is unbridled. The European Convention on Human Rights (ECHR) does allow for limitations, which the relevant State can adopt for a number of reasons, including 'the protection of morals' and the 'protection of the reputation or rights of others'.[35] The same exceptions are envisaged in the ICCPR[36] and in the American Convention on Human Rights (ACHR).[37]

In principle, therefore, criminalisation on these grounds is an option. But it has to comply with the specific conditions that attach to limitations of this kind. Restrictions, in particular, will not be justified if they were not necessary to safeguard the relevant interest.[38] That introduces a consideration of

---

30 *R v. Zundel* [1992] 2 S.C.R. 731, 732, 734, at www.iidh.ed.cr/comunidades/libertad expresion/docs/le_otroscanada/r.%20v.%20zundel.htm.
31 18 U.S.C. § 704(b).
32 *United States v. Alvarez*, 567 U.S. – 132 S. Ct. 2537, 2564 (2012).
33 Ibid., at 2541 (Breyer, J., concurring).
34 Art.10(1) ECHR protects 'freedom of expression'. See also Art. 19 ICCPR; Art. 13(1) ACHR.
35 Art.10(2) ECHR.
36 Art.19(3) ICCPR.
37 Art.13(2) ACHR.
38 Art.10(2) ECHR; Art.19 ICCPR; Art.13 ACHR.

proportionality,[39] and laws on denialism therefore have to take the barriers which that principle imposes.[40] A law cannot thus be said to be 'necessary' if it is not a suitable means to achieve this purpose in the first place or if there were alternatives that would have been equally effective, but would have imposed less of a restriction on the affected human right.

Criminalisation of denialism raises questions in both regards, and the criticism which it encounters becomes clearer when these aspects are discussed in more detail. The question of efficiency will be addressed in the next sub-section; alternatives to criminalisation will be examined in section 3.

Freedom of expression is not the only human right which criminalisation may affect. Depending on the context, other rights may feel its impact: if, for instance, the relevant law bans denial even in cases where the statements were uttered in the perpetrator's own rooms, its consequences on the right to privacy will have to be considered.[41]

A case arising in Rwanda in 2010 demonstrates that the rights of defendants in criminal trials may also be affected. The case concerned the American academic and lawyer Peter Erlinder, who was defence counsel for Ntabakuze before the International Criminal Tribunal for Rwanda (ICTR).[42] He had also intended to work on the defence team of a Rwandan opposition leader, who had been arrested on the charge of promoting genocide ideology.[43] When Erlinder arrived in Rwanda to take up his work, he himself was arrested on charges of genocide denial.[44]

Rwanda had, in 2008, adopted Law No. 18/2008 on the punishment of genocide ideology,[45] which had come under considerable criticism for the vague language it employed and the consequences of its application,[46] including its perceived use to muzzle legitimate political opposition.[47]

In the case of Erlinder, the Rwandan prosecution authorities specifically referred to his work at the ICTR and reportedly said that he had 'denied and

---

39 Cf ECtHR, *Soltysyak v. Russia*, Application no. 4663/05, Judgment, 10 February 2011, para. 48

40 On aspects of the principle of proportionality under international law, see Paul Behrens, 'Diplomatic Interference and Competing Interests in International Law', 82 *BYIL* (2012), 226 et seq.

41 Cf Art.8 ECHR; Art.17 ICCPR; Art.11(2) ACHR.

42 Edmund Kagire/Patrick Condon, 'Rwandan Police Arrest US Lawyer', *Associated Press Worldstream*, 29 May 2010.

43 BBC Online, 'Rwanda Arrests US Lawyer Erlinder for Genocide Denial', 28 May 2010, at www.bbc.co.uk/news/10187580.

44 Ibid.

45 The law according to Amnesty International, *Safer to Stay Silent* (2010), 13, 14.

46 For details of this law, see Chapter 9 above. Criticism was voiced, *inter alia*, by Amnesty International, n 45 above; and Human Rights Watch, *Law and Reality. Progress of Judicial Reform in Rwanda* (2008).

47 See on this Amnesty International, n 45 above, 20–2.

minimized the genocide by stating that the soldiers he was defending neither planned nor carried out the genocide'.[48]

Erlinder's arrest evoked strong criticism – the ICTR requested his immediate release,[49] and the American Bar Association called on Rwanda to observe the United Nations (UN) Basic Principles on the Role of Lawyers,[50] which impose on governments the obligation to ensure that lawyers are able to perform the functions of their profession without improper interference.[51]

The position adopted by the Rwandan prosecution was indeed problematic. At its root was the inappropriate application of statements on the liability of individual perpetrators to genocide as a macro phenomenon, and thus the conflation of two different concepts. This raises concerns in relation to human rights: not only those of Erlinder,[52] but also those of his clients at the ICTR.

If genocide denial laws could be applied in ongoing criminal trials to the effect that defendants charged with genocide could no longer claim that they were innocent, the consequences would be staggering: laws of this kind would make a mockery of the presumption of innocence guaranteed under all leading human rights instruments.[53] The possibility that criminalisation of denial can result in trials in which the only option is a plea of guilty, conjures up an image of Kafkaesque (or Cardassian[54]) justice that must, at the very least, be considered deeply troubling.

2.3 The efficiency of laws against genocide and Holocaust denial

A particular criticism with regard to criminalisation is founded on doubts relating to its efficiency, if measured by the aim underlying its adoption. The effect may indeed be the opposite of its purpose: in the case of the Canadian Holocaust denier Keegstra, the dissenting justices pointed out that the criminal process will not only 'attract extensive media coverage and confer on the accused publicity for his dubious causes, it may even bring him sympathy'.[55]

---

48 Office of the Registrar of the ICTR, *Note Verbale to the Ministry of Foreign Affairs and Cooperation of the Government of Rwanda*, ICTR/RO/06/10/175, 15 June 2010.
49 Ibid.
50 William Mitchell College of Law, *Statements of Support of Prof. Erlinder*, 3 June 2010, at web.wmitchell.edu/news/2010/06/statements-of-support-for-prof-erlinder/.
51 UN Basic Principles on the Role of Lawyers, UN Doc. A/CONF.144/28/Rev.1 at 118 (1990), 16(a).
52 See ibid., at 23.
53 See on this Art.6(2) ECHR; Art.14(2) ICCPR; Art.8(2) ACHR. See also, on the right to effective legal assistance, Art.6(3)(c) ECHR; Art.14(3)(d) ICCPR; Art.8(2)(d) ACHR.
54 A fictitious world in whose justice system the defendants are presumed guilty from the outset and in which the purpose of a trial is 'to demonstrate the futility of behaviour contrary to good order', *Star Trek: Deep Space Nine: Tribunal (2:25)*, Paramount Television 1994.
55 *R. v. Keegstra* [1990] 3 S.C.R. 697.

Where the leading figures in the denialist movement are concerned, the assessment of the efficiency of criminalisation certainly fails to provide encouraging results. David Irving was arrested in 2005 and released a year later, but his stay in prison seems not to have led to a significant change of his views. Upon returning from Austria he reportedly stated that he had been 'obliged to show remorse' during his trial, but had now decided he had 'no need any longer to show remorse'.[56] Nor did the case of Faurisson in France show a different development: receiving a criminal conviction and a suspended prison sentence in October 2006[57] did little to deter him from attending, two months later, the Iranian conference on 'Review of the Holocaust'.[58]

The view that criminal sanctions are capable of changing the opinions of those who must be held responsible for the creation of denialism, is indeed difficult to justify. The fact that the State has resorted to the criminal justice system as a response to statements of denial rather plays into their belief system, in which they stand at the receiving end of a conspiracy to suppress their version about the underlying international crimes.[59]

Even where the followers of the movement are concerned, supporters of criminalisation have yet to demonstrate the efficiency of sanctions of this kind. At least where prison sentences are concerned, the existing evidence suggests that the consequences of the judicial decision may go in the opposite direction. In some prisons, deniers have a good chance of being exposed to propaganda from the extreme right, even if they had not previously been members of these movements or not part of their 'hard core'. In 2012 it was reported that in the German state of Brandenburg, some 25–30% of prisoners in young offender institutions veered towards the mindset of the extreme right.[60]

And extremist organisations are keen to stay in touch with their imprisoned members, thus strengthening their ideological commitment and ensuring their continued integration in that scene.[61] It has also been suggested that to those

56 Mark Oliver and agencies, 'Irving Shows Little Remorse on Return to UK', *The Guardian*, 22 December 2006.
57 *Le Monde*, 'Le négationniste Robert Faurisson a été condamné à trois mois de prison avec sursis', 3 October 2006.
58 See Chapter 11 above.
59 See Lechtholz-Zey, n 10 above at nn 44, 45.
60 Deutscher Bundestag: Drucksachen und Protokolle 17/8983 (14 March 2012), 2. In the young offender institution in Halle (in the German state of Saxony-Anhalt), some 20% of inmates were estimated to fall in this category. Ibid. See also Werner Nickolai, 'Bericht über eine Fahrt nach Auschwitz mit rechtsradikalen jugendlichen Strafgefangenen', in Hajo Funke and Dietrich Neuhaus (eds), *Auf dem Weg zur Nation? Über deutsche Identität nach Auschwitz* (Frankfurt am Main, 1989), 123.
61 BT-Drucksache, n 60 above, 7. See, for instance, for the activities of the 'Hilfsorganisation für nationale politische Gefangene und deren Angehörige' in Germany, ibid., 4; and for those of the 'White Prisoner and Supporter Day', Kathrin Haimerl, 'Wolle, Halt Durch!', *Süddeutsche Zeitung Online*, 14 January 2012; at www.sueddeutsche.de/politik/braune-solidaritaet-mit-nsu-verdaechtigen-wolle-halt-durch-1.1256785.

already in the extremist camp, imprisonment may appear not so much as a deterring experience, but as a further step on the 'career ladder' of their peer group.[62]

Some observers are aware of the questions attaching to the intended effect of criminalisation. In the case of the Loi Gayssot, Weaver, Delpierre and Boissier concede that the law is unlikely to change the mindset of the deniers, but voice the hope that the law might affect others who would otherwise be tempted to join the movement.[63] Laws on denialism might thus be directed at general, rather than specific, deterrence.

But there is reason to meet hopes of this kind with a degree of caution: they constitute expectations which criminal law, on its own, may struggle to fulfil.

For one, the ideas to which deniers subscribe do not disappear merely because their expression has been made punishable. Lechtholz-Zey is right when she points out that, in the age of the internet, the relevant ideas remain merely a mouse click away,[64] and with that, the recruitment of new followers remains a reality.

But even in societies in which denialism has no strong basis in the population, the link between the weakness of the movement and the threat of legal sanction is not a foregone conclusion. The fact that an average member of society might not fall prey to the efforts of deniers, may indeed have more to do with the educational efforts of the State (and the overwhelming force of the facts) than with the adoption of criminalisation. Crediting the criminal justice system with successes of this kind, means putting confidence in the law which the law may not deserve.

What is more: some of the difficulties that attach to specific deterrence, apply to general deterrence as well. The thought, in particular, cannot be dismissed that laws of this kind may have the very effect that criminalisation seeks to prevent. In 2006, Lipstadt put her objection to the legislative response thus: 'I don't find these laws efficacious. I think they turn Holocaust denial into forbidden fruit, and make it more attractive to people who want to toy with the system or challenge the system.'[65] But it is the very characteristic of forbidden fruit that it tempts not only those who want to challenge the system anyway but even those who would be perfectly content to refrain from such experiments, were it not for the lure of the taboo.

3 Options for dealing with genocide and Holocaust denial

If the criminalisation of basic denial has shortcomings, questions must be raised about alternatives in the field. An obvious solution would be the adoption of laws that impose additional conditions on criminalisation, but there are also methods

---

62 See on this Werner Nickolai, 'Warum den Rechtsextremisten mit Strafvollzug nicht zu begegnen ist', in Werner Nickolai and Richard Reindl (eds), *Sozialer Ausschluss durch Einschluss* (Freiburg im Breisgau: Lambertus Verlag, 2001), 183.

63 Weaver et al., n 14 above, 495.

64 Lechtholz-Zey, n 10 above, at 46.

65 O'Neill, n 26 above.

outside legal sanctions, including measures at a political and an educational level, which may promise a certain degree of efficiency.

3.1 A modified legal approach

The extensive nature of some laws on revision and denial[66] suggests that a modification of the legal approach might offer a way of addressing the problem while retaining the advantages of the legal sanction that have been outlined above.[67] And modifications have been suggested in the past.

John Knechtle, for one, proposes a limitation in the applicability of criminalising laws by restricting them to societies for which they can be expected to have particular relevance ('subject societies').[68] A law on Holocaust denial would thus be suitable for Germany, but inappropriate for Indonesia; and a law on the denial of the crimes committed during the occupation of East Timor would be 'appropriate for Indonesia and/or East Timor, but not Germany'.[69]

At first blush, it seems a persuasive view. The underlying atrocities will usually have affected not all States to the same degree, and not all societies will feel that they have the same relationship to them. However, a critical evaluation reveals certain weaknesses.

For one, it is not always easy to determine what exactly a 'subject society' is. In the case of international crimes, the State of the perpetrator and that of the victims may not be the same. The place of the commission of the crime will often be the latter, but it may be a strange (and insulting) suggestion that that state has need for a law against denial.

But the other State might be a questionable starting point, too. Given the increased significance of international mercenaries and soldiers of fortune, the 'State of the perpetrator' may well be one whose population has no real link with the crimes and was in fact fundamentally opposed to them.[70]

Second, the fact that certain atrocities may be of particular relevance to certain societies does not yet answer the question whether criminalisation is appropriate or necessary. Much depends on the way in which the relevant society has dealt with the memory of such crimes – with the recognition given to the suffering of the victims and the basis which the denialist movement enjoys. The temporal

---

66 See e.g. the Rwandan example, text at n 45 et seq.
67 See above, text after n 8 and after n 18.
68 Knechtle, n 20 above, 52.
69 Ibid., 52 and 53.
70 The Ruggiu case may be recalled in this context. Ruggiu was a Belgian journalist, who worked for Radio-Télévision Libre de Milles Collines in Rwanda in 1994 – a broadcasting station which exhorted the Hutus to actions against the Tutsi population. Ruggiu himself was found guilty of direct and public incitement to genocide. ICTR (Trial Chamber), *The Prosecutor v. Georges Ruggiu*, Case no. ICTR-97-32-I, Judgment 1 June 2000, VI. Verdict.

distance to the crime[71] can only be one aspect – and not necessarily the conclusive one – in the assessment of the need for criminalisation. Some societies may
have believably demonstrated their acknowledgment of crimes that are still within
living memory and have engaged in efforts towards reconciliation. Others may
yet be in denial over crimes committed half a millennium ago.

Third, why should denial of the suffering of the East Timorese not be a crime
in Germany? Why should Holocaust denial not be a crime in Indonesia? It was
one of the ground-breaking aspects of the main Nuremberg Trial that it identified
the international character of certain crimes; and the understanding that some
forms of conduct are of concern to the entire international community has since
constituted a cornerstone of international criminal law. The suggestion that the
protection of the dignity and memory of the survivors should be a matter of
relevance only to specific societies is not a solution: it is an unjustifiably retrograde
development.[72]

If this approach thus remains open to criticism, the question can be asked
whether restrictions to the substance of the law offer a better option.

This indeed is a path that has been chosen in the past. The Council Framework Decision, for instance, addresses denialism as a criminal offence only where
it is done 'publicly', and only when carried out 'in a manner likely to incite to
violence or hatred' against a protected group or one of its members.[73] Laws of
this kind therefore envisage the probability of additional harm – frequently
defined as the generation of a certain danger to public peace.

It is an option that appears more feasible than the prohibition of basic denial
per se. In *Alvarez*, Justice Breyer accepted that certain laws prohibiting false statements did exist in the United States, but added that their scope tended to be
limited by a requirement of the existence or the likelihood of certain forms of
harm.[74] Examples he cited were statutes on defamation, fraud and perjury.[75]

If this approach were followed, the incorporation of specified harm in the
codification of the crime, in particular through the introduction of the element of
disturbance to the peace, would certainly clarify the justification of criminalisation
on the basis of an existing social need. It would not relieve the lawmaker from
the obligation to comply with the conditions of human rights law, of which the
specificity of the law curtailing freedom of speech is one,[76] and it would still be

---

71 See Knechtle, n 20 above, 43. See also Berel Lang, 'Six Questions On (Or About)
    Holocaust Denial', 49 *History and Theory* (2010), 167.
72 See also *Perinçek*, n 2 above, Joint Dissenting Opinion of Judges Spielmann et al.,
    para. 7.
73 Framework Decision, n 9 above, Article 1(1)(c) and (d). See also German Criminal
    Code, s 130(3), at www.gesetze-im-internet.de/englisch_stgb/englisch_stgb.html#
    p1200 (translation by M. Bohlander).
74 *Alvarez*, n 32 above (Breyer, J., concurring), at 2541.
75 Ibid.
76 See for instance, in the context of freedom of speech, ECtHR *Grigoriades v. Greece*, 27
    Eur. Ct. H.R. 1 (1997), para. 37.

necessary to examine the impact that such laws may have on other rights that may be affected. Subject to these caveats, however, laws that extend the *actus reus* to cover additional harm have a greater capacity of avoiding the concerns that were outlined in the previous section.

But in adopting this approach, lawmakers have to be aware that the core character of the legislation has changed. Its focus is no longer genocide denial as such; the protection of respect for the dignity of the victims becomes a secondary aspect. The measures that have been discussed in this context are, in essence, laws on public order offences.

3.2 Truth and reconciliation

The experience of a situation in which international crimes were committed has led in some societies to the setting up of institutions whose task it was (in part) to work towards the establishment and preservation of truth in the aftermath of these events. As this frequently concerned communities that had only relatively recently emerged from situations of this kind (South Africa being the most prominent example),[77] truth and reconciliation commissions are often considered in the context of transitional justice.

However, given the particular focus on the finding of 'truth', it is also possible to understand such mechanisms as alternatives to the criminalisation of denialism. In this context, they have advantages which, to that degree, are absent in the legal option.

For one, they represent a community effort at establishing the historical record. As institutions which involve both victims and perpetrators and which often operate on a large scale,[78] they stand a good chance of exercising an impact on large sections of society. These initiatives thus offer a sound basis for the internalisation of the memory of these events by society as a whole, and may enable the community to reach consensus on the record of the relevant situation.[79]

They also carry the advantage that they provide the opportunity of obtaining a first-hand account of the events from the perpetrators themselves. The weakness of the denialist cause is particularly apparent when its supporters have to deal with statements made by the authors of the underlying crimes. At the same time, this aspect of truth and reconciliation is not without difficulties. The fact that, in the South African case, for instance, amnesty was available to some of those who made 'full disclosure' of their deeds,[80] raises the question whether statements of

77 See on this Olivia Lin, 'Demythologizing Restorative Justice: South Africa's Truth and Reconciliation Commission and Rwanda's Gacaca Courts in Context', 12 *ILSA Journal of International and Comparative Law* (2005), 42.
78 Ibid., 61.
79 See on this John Shamsey, '80 Years Too Late: The International Criminal Court and the 20th Century's First Genocide', 11 *Journal of Transnational Law and Policy* (2002), 378.
80 Lin, n 77 above, 60.

this kind were in the end motivated by a genuine desire to tell the truth and to make amends, or whether they were deliberately phrased in a way which their authors considered to comply with the expectations of the commission.[81]

The communal effort underlining truth and reconciliation faces further challenges. The participation of victims in the relevant sessions was certainly a defining feature in the South African model.[82] But it presupposes an initiative which cannot always be expected. In situations of past genocides, it would be quite understandable that victims would refuse to participate in the same institution as the perpetrators. One of the identified purposes of denial laws – the expression of solidarity with the victims – may then appear to be relegated to second place: it is the attempt to effect the reconstruction and healing of society which takes centre stage.

A further problem arises from the fact that not all States emerging from international crimes allow for a clear distinction between 'victim societies' and 'perpetrator societies'. In the modern age, the underlying crimes are often the last stage in a long-standing situation of civil war, in which the allocation of the roles of victim and perpetrator might depend on little more than military fortune. Where that is the case, the determination of the 'accurate' historical record can be a difficult task. The intention of the perpetrators might no longer be the rendering of a contribution to the establishment of truth, but the telling of their understanding of 'truth',[83] and the proceedings risk becoming a political battle-ground, leaving dispassionate observers with little more than the question of Pilate.[84]

Yet for all its difficulties, institutions of this kind must be credited with the fact that they appreciate the significance of truth not only for individual victims, but for society as a whole. It is a direct approach which, by confronting perpetrators with the accounts of victims, does not offer them an easy flight into the realm of denial.

Seen from that perspective, truth and reconciliation touches upon a point which, in debates on alternatives to criminalisation, is something of an elephant in the room. Is direct confrontation ever a possibility and one that promises efficiency? It is a question which is of relevance to those in particular who can speak with authority or expertise on the underlying crimes – survivors and historians among them – and it has not lent itself to a simple answer.

---

81 Ibid., 66.
82 Ibid., 60.
83 See Manouri Muttetuwegama, in Harvard Law School Human Rights Program, *Truth Commissions: A Comparative Assessment. An Interdisciplinary Discussion Held at Harvard Law School in May 1996* (Cambridge, USA, 1997), 16 (with regard to the Sinhalese factions in Sri Lanka).
84 'What is truth?' John 18:38. The South African Truth and Reconciliation Commission, however, showed awareness of the existence of different meanings of truth: see Richard Wilson, *The Politics of Truth and Reconciliation in South Africa* (Cambridge University Press, 2001), 36.

3.3 Confronting the deniers

The 'direct approach' has certainly been adopted in the past: academics have on occasion engaged with members of the movement,[85] and survivors have likewise confronted deniers with evidence of the events.[86]

But not everybody accepts the usefulness of this approach. Lipstadt's statement in this regard has become famous: debating deniers, she wrote, 'would be like trying to nail a glob of jelly to the wall'.[87] The apparent problem lies in the fact that if a partner in conversation refuses to acknowledge logical reasoning, the very foundations of meaningful discourse are missing.

To Lipstadt, it is a more promising option to address the general public and to engage in educational efforts about the underlying crimes.[88] That, certainly, has to be an indispensable aspect of any concerted effort to deal with denialism. Yet one method need not exclude the other. Some initiatives adopt a combined approach: Project Nizkor, for instance, offers a huge online archive on documents on the Holocaust and on the activities of deniers themselves, and thus represents an important educational effort.[89] But it also engages directly with the deniers: it provides a point-by-point response to questions raised by the Institute for Historical Review,[90] and members of the Nizkor team have directly corresponded with deniers and challenged their views.[91]

Whether such approaches are efficient is a different matter. Doubts about the chances of changing the views of deniers have their justification. But it is in this context that the distinction between leaders and followers plays a decisive role: direct confrontation may yield fundamentally different results depending on the motivation and the position of those who engage in denialism.

With regard to more prominent figures in the movement, the confrontational approach might not be expected to achieve efficient results. Even there, exceptions exist. When Rabbi Jack Bemporad and the American law professor Breger in 2010 organised a visit of several imams and Muslim scholars to the Auschwitz concentration camp, the participation of Yasir Qadhi, dean of academics at the

85 In 2008, for instance, the historian Robert Gerwarth debated David Irving on Irish television, John Lawrence, 'Irving Speech to College Society Cancelled', *The Irish Times*, 8 March 2008; *RTÉ*, 'The Late Late Show Response to Viewers' Comments on Irving Interview', at web.archive.org/web/20080315163604/www.rte.ie/tv/latelate/irvingresponse.html.

86 See in particular, on the case of Mel Mermelstein in the 1980s, Lipstadt, n 25 above, 138–41.

87 Ibid., 221.

88 Ibid. and at 222.

89 The project's website is available at www.nizkor.org. On Project Nizkor, see also John Schwartz, 'With Innovative Use, the Web Empowers the First Amendment', *The Washington Post*, 15 July 1996.

90 Project Nizkor, 'The IHR's Questions and Answers, and Nizkor's Reponses. A Reply to the IHR/Zündel's "66 Q&A"', at www.nizkor.org/features/qar/qar00.html.

91 Cf Project Nizkor, 'David Irving. Correspondence', at www.nizkor.org/hweb/people/i/irving-david/correspondence/.

Al Maghrib Institute in New Haven, triggered criticism:[92] Qadhi had told an audience in 2001 that Hitler 'never intended to mass-destroy the Jews' and encouraged them to read a book about the 'hoax' of the Holocaust.[93]

Yet following the journey, Qadhi referred to the 'sheer inhumanity' of the Holocaust and declared, in response to the criticism, that '[i]t was even more necessary for me to go and see how wrong I was'.[94] The participating Muslim leaders (including Qadhi) issued a statement condemning attempts to deny the Holocaust and declared 'such denials or any justification of this tragedy as against the Islamic code of ethics'.[95]

But such cases are rare. Those who have a more influential role in the movement often act from motives that do not easily allow them to change their position. A denier with political reasons stands to gain little by accepting the truth, and a denier who seeks publicity, stands to lose everything.

However, the same assessment might not be valid where followers of the movement are concerned. Motivation is again of importance: a follower who repeats phrases of denial under the influence of a group of like-minded people, might act differently if removed from that group and in the context of a serious conversation. A follower who accepts statements of denial because he believes them to be true, shows that, at least on a basic level, truth still has value to him; and a confrontation with evidence of the events might not be an entirely fruitless undertaking.

Initiatives have come into existence whose work carries an impact in this context. Some of them are dedicated to offering affected persons a way out of adherence to groups on the extreme right (where Holocaust denial has traditionally found a strong base). In Sweden and Germany, for instance, the 'Exit' programme helps members of such groups to leave their communities.[96] It has had some success: five years after the establishment of the German version, its director stated that the project had helped 225 persons to leave such environments.[97] But these projects typically rely on voluntary participation, and they are not

92 Hilary Krieger, 'US Anti-Semitism Czar Hopes Imams' Trip to Auschwitz Resonates Widely', *The Jerusalem Post*, 22 August 2010; Laura Rozen, 'Imams Join U.S. Officials at Nazi Sites', *Politico.com*, 18 August 2010.
93 Andrea Elliott, 'A Marked Man in America', *The New York Times*, 20 March 2011.
94 Krieger, n 92 above.
95 *The Virginian Pilot*, 'Understanding on a Trip of Horrors', 25 August 2010.
96 See *Stockholm News*, 'Former Extremists Will Get Help to Quit', *Stockholm News*, 11 April 2011, at www.stockholmnews.com/more.aspx?NID=7038; Anne Märtens, 'Bye-bye Kameraden!', *taz*, 1 December 2005. See also, for the programme, 'Taking Responsibility – Breaking Away from Hate and Violence', BT-Drucksache, n 60 above, 6; for a Danish project, Danish Ministry for Social Affairs, 'Deradicalisation. Targeted Intervention. Introduction to a Pilot Project', at www.sm.dk/data/Lists/Publikationer/Attachments/554/Folder%20Deradicalisation%20Targeted%20Intervention.pdf; and for an overview of EU programmes, Danish Ministry for Refugee, Immigration and Integration Affairs, *The Challenge of Extremism. Examples of Deradicalisation and Disengagement Programmes in the EU*, October 2010.
97 Märtens, n 96 above.

specifically designed as options for dealing with denialism, although debating the 'ideology' of these groups is often part of the initiative.[98]

A more direct approach is taken by the society 'Für die Zukunft lernen' (Learning for the Future), whose seat is the German town of Breisach-Oberrimsingen.[99] For the past 20 years, its president, Werner Nickolai, has been involved in a project which seeks to inform young people about the Holocaust. Every year, Nickolai, a professor at the Catholic University of Applied Sciences in Freiburg, embarks on a ten-day journey to the Auschwitz concentration camp, together with young people from the extreme right, including juvenile prisoners.[100] They are accompanied by their care workers and some of Nickolai's students.[101] During their stay at Auschwitz, they engage in maintenance work at the remains of the camp, but also meet survivors of the Holocaust.[102] As in most of the other projects, participation is a voluntary commitment.[103]

Nickolai himself, prior to his academic career, had been employed as a social worker in a juvenile prison for 15 years[104] – an experience which may have helped him keep expectations on a realistic plane. He has remarked that the purpose of the journeys was not to shock young people, but to convey political information in such a way that it 'reaches them'.[105] He is aware of the limitations and points out that the young people with whom he travels do not necessarily understand the link between the crimes committed against the Jews at Auschwitz and the mistreatment of members of minorities today.[106]

But there is one tangible result that the travels do achieve: in 2000, Nickolai noted that there had not been a single case in which persons accompanying him still stuck to Holocaust denial after former concentration camp prisoners had personally told them about the gas chambers.[107]

---

98 Cf *The Challenge of Extremism*, n 96 above, 12, with reference to the programme 'Taking Responsibility – Breaking Away from Hate and Violence', and at 18 with reference to the British 'Prevent' project, and at 26 with reference to the Danish project 'Deradicalisation – Targeted Intervention'.
99 See Werner Nickolai et al., *Für die Zukunft lernen*, at www.fuer-die-zukunft-lernen.de.
100 Bettina Schaefer, 'Lass uns über Auschwitz sprechen', at www.lass-uns-ueber-ausch witz-sprechen.eu/multiplikatoren.html; A. Spalinger, 'Was hat Auschwitz jungen Skinheads zu sagen?; Ein deutscher Verein versucht "rechter" Gewalt zu begegnen', *Neue Zürcher Zeitung*, 9 June 2000; Michael Werner, '"Zum Glück war ich in der Zeit nicht dort". Verein aus dem badischen Breisach fährt mit rechts orientierten Jugendlichen nach Auschwitz', *Südwestdeutsche Zeitung*, 15 January 2000, at www.fuer-die-zukunft-lernen.de/swbericht.html; Werner Nickolai, 'Die inneren Wunden werden nie ganz heilen', *Neue Caritas* 9/2010, at www.caritas.de/neue-caritas/heftarchiv/jahrga ng2010/artikel/dieinnerenwundenwerdennieganzheilen.
101 Werner, n 100 above.
102 Ibid.
103 Ibid.
104 Nickolai, n 100 above.
105 Werner, n 100 above.
106 Ibid.
107 Spalinger, n 100 above.

Personal confrontation with the facts of the Holocaust appears to play a significant role in this development – as, arguably, does the encounter with inescapable visual evidence. To Nickolai, it is of importance that 'all senses' of the young people are addressed.[108] Yasir Qadhi's experience underlines this aspect of the confrontational approach: after his journey, Qadhi stated that any 'Holocaust denier should deserve a free ticket to see Auschwitz and Birkenau [...] because seeing is just not the same as reading about it'.[109]

The confrontational approach, then, is not necessarily devoid of merit. But it requires accurate distinctions if it is to lead to convincing results. Confronting those who promote denial to generate publicity for themselves, may often result in little more than an enhancement of their public profile. Even with regard to followers who are still embedded in their peer groups and who in general accept its influence, the efficiency of the approach may be questioned.

A direct encounter with visual evidence of the events and a meeting with survivors may be a more persuasive option. Taking young extremists out of their comfort zone – which was, after all, defined by parameters set by their particular background – may well have been a significant contributory factor in the success of the Nickolai project – in spite of its avowed intention to inform, rather than to shock.

4 Concluding considerations

That criminalisation has become a popular choice for policy makers seeking to counter denialism is not difficult to understand. But the use of legal sanctions has shortcomings which cannot easily be ignored. The potential of a clash between laws prohibiting certain statements and human rights is one consideration in that regard. It is joined by the segregating effect of legislation of this kind: by criminalising statements about certain international crimes at the expense of others, they engage in the problematic business of constructing a hierarchy of suffering.[110]

Furthermore, in some situations, the danger of the use of legislation of this kind for political ends has emerged – the Rwandan law on the punishment of genocide ideology highlights the difficulties in that regard. Most of all, however, the effects of criminalisation are open to critique. There is little evidence that such sanctions are instrumental in changing the mind of deniers, and their exclusionary effects further play into the perception of the perpetrators: it underlines their ideological position that they are outsiders to 'ordinary' society anyway. It is in fact one of the cornerstones of the denialist movement that it often sees itself as resisting the 'conformist conspiracy' of mainstream history and is prepared to accept the consequences that arise from this.

---

108   Werner, n 100 above.
109   A. Goldmann, 'At the Death Camps, Muslim Leaders Grapple with Jews' Pain', *The Forward*, 20 August 2010.
110   Cf Gliszczyńska-Grabiasa, n 1 above, 183.

But if the law is not the solution, alternatives must be offered that may achieve more efficient results. Various options have been explored in this chapter, but the most convincing approach might require a combination of several methods. It is suggested that the following aspects have an impact on this consideration.

First, genocide and Holocaust denial takes place in different societies and in different contexts. The identification of the most appropriate ratio of methods to counter denialism is therefore dependent on situational parameters. In some societies, the widespread nature of denial may require more of a communal effort, including a heightened emphasis on public education and the establishment of institutions capable of reaching out to society as a whole. Where denialism is promoted merely by a small minority within a society, the focus might shift to options for dealing with the leaders and followers of that movement.

Second, not all deniers are cut from the same cloth. The political leader who built a following on denialism, the author whose prominence relies on denialist ideology, act from motivations which differ from those at the bottom of the movement, who may often not have given much thought to the evidence of the atrocities or indeed to the consequences of denialist activities. Genuine curiosity may occasionally be encountered in the latter group, but cannot be expected in the former, and the appropriate methods of dealing with the conduct of deniers will therefore have to vary accordingly.

Third, even within a particular target group, a detailed assessment of the available methods is indispensable. The impact of an academic article on a juvenile delinquent may be doubted; the showing of a film on the atrocities that he denied might be more effective; the confrontation with actual physical remnants of international crimes and meetings with survivors have carried some success in the past. Fine-tuning these approaches is key to the development of a persuasive response mechanism; and that in turn requires a certain insight into the psychological conditioning of the followers of denialism. Since the disassociation from 'mainstream society' is often at the core of their ideology, the success of any option to counter denialism might well be measured not by the degree to which their exclusion from the community has been achieved, but by the degree to which society has managed to effect their reintegration.

Applying these considerations may seem a fair amount of effort, and the question may arise of whether members of the denialist movement 'deserve' this amount of consideration.

That, however, would be an understanding which fails to appreciate the wider context of the measures. Their primary objective is still the countering of denial, and it is the protection of truth, of the memory and the dignity of the survivors which count among their primary beneficiaries.

Among the beneficiaries is society itself – a society which is too easily tempted by the toolbox of the criminal justice system and too willing to forget the question at the core of the issue: how to deal with false and hurtful statements, and how to live with those who fall prey to their lure.

Concluding thoughts

Paul Behrens, Nicholas Terry and Olaf Jensen

In March 2016, Microsoft introduced a new project to the world: a chatbot named 'Tay' – a computer program designed to engage with young Americans on Twitter. Tay was not only able to hold brief conversations, but was capable of learning: '[t]he more you chat with Tay', said Microsoft, 'the smarter she gets'.[1] Yet it did not take Tay long to discover the mischievous side of the internet. Twitter users soon taught Tay to make racist comments, to declare her support for genocide and to engage in Holocaust denial.[2] The chatbot was turned off within 24 hours.[3]

The story of Tay marks an interesting development in the field of artificial intelligence, but to those dealing with Holocaust and genocide denial, it carries a more ominous and almost symbolic note: it is the reflection of a problem with which they are well acquainted. Denialism is all too often accepted, without any effort at critical reflection, by those who have fewer excuses than Tay: by students who feel entitled to rely on the writings of deniers for no better reason than that they were published in a journal of pseudoscholarly appearance, or on a website that appeared professionally designed.

Conduct of that kind certainly raises questions about the handling of information and highlights the ever increasing need to develop skills relating not only to the collection but also the critical assessment of information.

Criticism, however, requires criteria: if the basic set of parameters against which the messages of the denialist movement can be measured, is missing, critical assessment cannot be expected. That causes problems where events are concerned to which a younger generation feels no immediate connection. That is true even in relation to the Holocaust: at a time when the numbers of survivors are dwindling and first-hand memories are fading, the potential especially of

---

1 Elle Hunt, 'Tay, Microsoft's AI Chatbot, Gets a Crash Course in Racism from Twitter', *The Guardian*, 24 March 2016.
2 Jane Wakefield, 'Microsoft Chatbot is Taught to Swear on Twitter', *BBC Online*, 24 March 2016, at www.bbc.co.uk/news/technology-35890188; Dave Lee, 'Tay: Microsoft Issues Apology Over Racist Chatbot Fiasco', *BBC Online*, 25 March 2016, at www.bbc.co.uk/news/technology-35902104.
3 Lee, ibid.

younger people to resist the messages of denialism can be considerably reduced. The degree to which subsequent generations retain awareness of the historical events is notoriously difficult to measure,[4] but some surveys indicate that such knowledge is indeed diminishing: a 2007 poll conducted in the United Kingdom among 18–29 year olds, for instance, found that 28% of that age group 'did not know if the Holocaust happened'.[5] The situation is not helped by a worrying trivialisation of the Holocaust and the crimes of the Nazi regime in general, in which even leaders of State and government have, at times, engaged.[6]

And yet, it would be wrong to say that the temporal divide is the only factor that can lead to an environment of that kind. Ignorance of the relevant atrocities is not a new phenomenon, nor is it a new development that the governments of States, for various reasons, seek to reduce the level of attention accorded to these events. What the current study has shown is that the interplay between denial on the one side and ignorance on the other is a phenomenon whose roots, in the case of the Holocaust, can be traced to the days when the atrocities were committed. The fact, however, that the two aspects are mutually supportive, that denial not only detracts from the factual record but in turn thrives on a culture of ignorance, is one of the key findings of this book and forms the backdrop to several of its chapters.

In this study, denialism has been explored in a great range of contexts which show variations both regarding their geographical distribution and regarding the events whose memory deniers target. Denial – and the reactions by individual States and the international community – has thus been discussed in relation to the Holocaust and the atrocities committed against the Armenians, the Soviet Gulag system, and genocide in Bosnia and in Rwanda. That an analysis of this kind would highlight differences with regard to the deniers and the approaches that they pursue cannot surprise. Yet such variations emerge even where the same context is concerned. Denial of the Holocaust, for instance, has been found to

---

4 One may in this context recall the 1993 Roper poll which found that 22% of American adults seriously doubted, or did not know, whether the Holocaust had happened; see Jonathan Petropoulos, 'Confronting the "Holocaust as Hoax" Phenomenon as Teachers', 28 *The History Teacher* (1995), 523 (referring to it as an 'undeniably problematic' poll). A new Roper poll in 1994 which 'corrected a flawed question in an earlier survey' found that there were 2% of 'committed or consistent deniers of the Holocaust' in America, Michael R. Kagay, 'Poll On Doubt of Holocaust is Corrected', *The New York Times*, 8 July 1994. It bears observing that ignorance and denial are not necessarily the same thing, and there are also gradations in levels of knowledge (e.g. awareness of the Holocaust in its wider outline may differ from knowledge about particular death camps – see on this Jerry Amernic, 'Why We're Forgetting the Holocaust', *National Post*, 28 November 2011).
5 Amernic, ibid.
6 A recent example is that of the President of the Philippines, Rodrigo Duterte, who in September 2016 compared himself to Hitler and the fight against drugs to the Holocaust. Oliver Holmes, 'Rodrigo Duterte Vows to Kill 3 million Drug Addicts and Likens himself to Hitler', *The Guardian*, 1 October 2016.

stem from a variety of roots: denial by the authors of the atrocities themselves, in an attempt to conceal the nature and extent of their crimes, was followed by denialist activities on the part of those who acted from political motivations, who sought publicity or who simply followed the messages issued by the leaders of their movement.

The existing differences, but also the cohesion of the movement itself, can provide valuable lessons for the understanding of the relevant conduct; but they also offer important insights for the adoption of options to deal with denialist activities. The fact, for instance, that splits in the movement have at times occurred and that some members of the extreme right have decided no longer to follow the denialist line, may well indicate the efficiency of certain methods of countering denial by comparison to others.

At the same time, the divergence of the existing situations also highlights the fact that denial, under certain circumstances, can have consequences that reach far beyond the direct discriminatory effects of hate speech. That is a point of particular significance where activities of that kind make their appearance in situations already marked by volatile relations between States. The roles that denial played in relations between Iran and Israel, and between Turkey and Armenia, offer examples in this field.

Yet even within the context of the same country, the consequences of denial can be significant. By its adoption of a pseudoscholarly appearance, the conduct of deniers frequently challenges the position of historians and scholars of social sciences and thus raises questions about the parameters of quality that apply to the carrying out of professional research in these fields. But this study has found that there are also situations in which the results of these activities can exceed effects of this kind. The fact must not be forgotten that denial of international crimes is, at times, adopted as a State policy, and the counterfactual version of events might then be enforced through numerous sanctions at the disposal of the relevant government and may seriously impede scholarly work.

Considerations of this kind raise questions about the appropriate reaction to denialism and the type of actor that should be expected to adopt the relevant measures. The discussions of this book have shown that it may be appropriate – perhaps even indispensable – to think of the formulation of responses as a community effort. Denialism concerns society as a whole and challenges its values, and it is thus society which is called upon to provide ways not only to deal with the relevant activities, but also to send out a message of solidarity to victim groups. Some societies have indeed deliberately adopted response mechanisms through the establishment of institutions of transitional justice, including truth and reconciliation commissions. But responding to denialism may also involve institutions whose primary purpose lies in a different, albeit related field: courts, for instance, which are tasked with the adjudication of the relevant international crimes themselves may also face obligations that involve them in the fight against denial.

Among options at the disposal of societies in this context, criminalisation occupies a central role, both in academic discourse and in the policies of an increasing number of States. It is for that reason that a significant part of this study has been dedicated to the legislative response, to the circumstances leading to its adoption, but also to the difficulties it encounters.

And these difficulties begin with the very question of whether laws against denialism are a suitable option for all countries and in all situations. In Rwanda, it was the very fact that genocide had been committed in 1994 and that its legacy was still felt in the country which served as a justification to the Kagame government for the adoption of legislation against denial: the purported aim was to overcome the divisions and to prevent a return to the dark days of the atrocities. In Europe, on the other hand, the European Court of Human Rights appeared to cast doubt on the need for the criminalisation of the denial of events that occurred a hundred years in the past.[7] But it is a view that invites criticism, not least because it may well engage its supporters in the questionable business of constructing a hierarchy of genocides.

Further challenges arise from the impact that legislation on denial may exercise on freedom of speech and other rights guaranteed under international law. It is, in fact, this particular consideration which must be held responsible for the prevailing lack of consensus among the international community on the adoption of criminalising measures – a disagreement which is not confined to positions taken by individual States but apparent from the views expressed by international institutions as well. Nor could it be said that the relevant concerns are invariably without basis: the study of the situation in Rwanda in particular, whose government has been accused of the adoption of overbroad laws against denialism and excessively severe sanctions, has led to the question whether such measures may, in the wrong hands, be subject to abuse and may, instead of aiding the preservation of memory and dignity, serve to muzzle the political opposition.

Yet even outside these contexts and even in situations in which criminalisation complies with the mandates of human rights law, the efficiency of measures of this kind is far from clear. It is in particular with regard to deniers whose purpose is founded on political motivations or on the ambition to gain publicity for themselves that the legal sanction may fail to have the expected positive consequences and can indeed generate counterproductive results.

But if criminalisation is subject to doubts, the availability of other measures at the disposal of societies affected by denialism and the international community as a whole has to be explored. It is at that stage that the consideration introduced above is of some significance: if notable differences can be made between persons engaging in denial – according to their motivations and their positions within the movement – the appropriate method of countering denial must be shaped accordingly. The same option is not necessarily suitable for all situations: educational approaches may be a hopeless endeavour from the outset where the leaders of the movement are concerned, but may play an important role with regard to

---

7 ECtHR Grand Chamber, *Perinçek v. Switzerland* (Application no. 27510/08), (2016) 63 EHRR 6, Judgment, 15 October 2015, para. 252.

those who unthinkingly parrot phrases of denial. Direct confrontation with evidence and witness statements may well have a chance of success in the latter case while being of limited effect in the former. *Il n'est pire sourd que celui ne veut pas entendre*, as the French saying has it – no one is quite as deaf as those who do not want to hear.

But this study has also shown that it is not enough to aim educational efforts at confirmed members of the denialist movement only. Even a fairly small denialist movement can work with significant and damaging results if the level of knowledge among the general population on the underlying international crimes is low. Addressing this difficulty, increasing the understanding and awareness of the relevant atrocities among society, imposes particular obligations on historians, international lawyers, anthropologists and scholars of other sciences. It is a long-term effort whose results cannot be expected to be immediately apparent, and it may involve intensive engagement at schools and universities, in print and visual media and on the internet.

But only an educated society has the tools to withstand the onslaught of misinformation at the hands of the denialist movement; and only a society that is prepared for the ongoing attacks on truth is able to accord denial and negationism the place it should have occupied from the outset: a position which, in the eyes of every rational person, is firmly located at the outer fringes of absurdity.

Index

academic responses to effects of denialism 4
Adelaide Institute 42, 44
Adenauer, Konrad 72
Ahmadinejad, Mahmoud 2, 5, 47, 158, 159, 160, 162, 168, 234
Akayesu, Jean-Paul 139
Akçam, Taner 181, 183
Althans, Bela Ewald 79, 80
Amnesty International 100, 124, 125, 129, 130, 137, 184
Andrews, Kay 24
anti-denial legislation: approach by current study 212, 228; and Austria 162, 191, 192; and Belgium 162, 192; and Czech Republic 162, 192; and European Union 161, 189–210, 227–228; and France 162, 191, 192, 219–222; and Germany 70–93, 162, 192; and Hungary 162, 192; and Israel 161, 162; and Liechtenstein 192; and Lithuania 192; and Luxembourg 162, 192; and Poland 162, 192; and Romania 162, 192; and Rwanda 94–144, 161; and Slovakia 192; and Slovenia 192; and Spain 192; and Switzerland 164, 192, 205–206, 222–226; and Ukraine 161; background to 211; equal approach to Holocaust denial and genocide denial 220, 227; and European Court of Human Rights 220; and European Court of Justice 227; genocide denial and hate speech in relation 212; limits of freedom of expression 215
anti-Semitism: conspiracy theories 10, 34; denialism and 143; distancing by right-wing political parties 44; Germany 72, 75, 77, 81; and hate speech 163, 214; and Holocaust denial 202, 207, 219, 222, 226; increase in Europe 201; United Kingdom 9, 15, 46; United States 45; websites 51, 52
anti-Zionism 35, 40, 46, 52
Arendt, Hannah 217
Armenian genocide: centenary commemoration 170; and freedom of expression in Turkey 180, 197; Turkish denial 170; and Turkish foreign policy 176; and Turkish national identity 171, 197
Atzmon, Gilad 47
Aynat, Enrique 39

Barkun, Michael 53
Beara, Ljubiša 147
Bemporad, Jack 246
Birdwood, Lady Jane 18
Boisdefeu, Jean-Marie 39
Boissier, Laurence 241
Breyer, J. 237, 243
British National Party 2, 45, 46
Browning, Christopher 28
Budde, Enno 72, 73
Butz, Arthur 12, 14, 39, 41

Caplan, Gerald 134
CARE International 129
Carto, Willis 36, 37, 38, 44, 53
Castillejo Cuellar, Alejandro 65
Central Intelligence Agency (CIA) 23, 29
Charny, L.W. 172, 212
'cheerleader' deniers 43
Christian traditionalism and fundamentalism 46
Christophersen, Thies 74, 75
Clark, Janine Natalya 149, 150

Lightning Source UK Ltd.
Milton Keynes UK
UKHW022237140421
382015UK00005B/49

9 780367 024253